KILLER STUFF
and TONS OF MONEY

KILLER STUFF
and TONS OF MONEY

SEEKING HISTORY AND HIDDEN GEMS
IN FLEA-MARKET AMERICA

Maureen Stanton

THE PENGUIN PRESS
New York
2011

THE PENGUIN PRESS
Published by the Penguin Group
Penguin Group (USA) Inc., 375 Hudson Street, New York, New York 10014,
U.S.A. • Penguin Group (Canada), 90 Eglinton Avenue East, Suite 700, Toronto, Ontario,
Canada M4P 2Y3 (a division of Pearson Penguin Canada Inc.) • Penguin Books Ltd,
80 Strand, London WC2R 0RL, England • Penguin Ireland, 25 St. Stephen's Green,
Dublin 2, Ireland (a division of Penguin Books Ltd) • Penguin Books Australia Ltd,
250 Camberwell Road, Camberwell, Victoria 3124, Australia (a division of Pearson Australia
Group Pty Ltd) • Penguin Books India Pvt Ltd, 11 Community Centre, Panchsheel Park,
New Delhi – 110 017, India • Penguin Group (NZ), 67 Apollo Drive, Rosedale,
Auckland 0632, New Zealand (a division of Pearson New Zealand Ltd) •
Penguin Books (South Africa) (Pty) Ltd, 24 Sturdee Avenue, Rosebank,
Johannesburg 2196, South Africa

Penguin Books Ltd, Registered Offices: 80 Strand, London WC2R 0RL, England

First published in 2011 by The Penguin Press, a member of Penguin Group (USA) Inc.

A portion of this book appeared in different form as "Roadshow Rage" in *The Florida Review*.

LIBRARY OF CONGRESS CATALOGING IN PUBLICATION DATA
Stanton, Maureen.
Killer stuff and tons of money : seeking history and hidden gems in flea-market America /
Maureen Stanton.
p.   cm.
Includes bibliographical references and index.
ISBN 978-1-59420-293-3
1. Antiques business—United States.   2. Flea markets—United States.   I. Title.   II. Title:
Seeking history and hidden gems in flea-market America.
NK1133.28.S73   2011   2010053099
381'.1920973—dc22

Printed in the United States of America

1   3   5   7   9   10   8   6   4   2

DESIGNED BY NICOLE LA ROCHE

For my parents, Clarissa Starr

and Patrick Stanton

CONTENTS

A NOTE TO THE READER

My journey into the flea market and antiques subculture began in 2000, when Curt Avery, whom I met in college in the 1980s, flew from Massachusetts for an auction in Ohio, where I was in graduate school. I was immediately intrigued by the story—that with $4,000 in his pocket he traveled a thousand miles after a couple of old bottles, that he stared at a single bottle for a half hour during the preview, turning it this way and that, holding it up to the light, running his fingers over its lip. How he hid behind a pole at the rear of the room to bid, using me as a decoy to fool his competitor. Four years passed, and I had a chance to work a flea market with him. Over the course of the next six years, when I could get away from my job, I entered this strange "flea" realm as a participant observer. Curt Avery gave me access into this world, tutored me, and spoke to me for hours and hours about the antiques business, partly as a favor, but mostly I believe because he wants people to understand and appreciate antiques.

From the beginning, Curt Avery asked to remain anonymous, which allowed him to speak candidly, and to remain the private, modest person he is ("Why should there be a book about me?"). In our Facebooked, YouTubed, celebrity-idolizing culture, it's rare that someone does *not* want attention. To honor my agreement with him, and to protect his privacy and the privacy of others, I have changed his name and the names of some dealers, collectors, and customers, and I have made slight moderations to other identifying characteristics. I used real names for public

figures, *Antiques Roadshow* personnel, celebrity collectors, museum curators, top dealers, auctioneers (except "Walt Johnson"), show promoters,
store and/or Web site owners, and others whose names have previously
been made public in articles. This is a work of nonfiction; there are no
composite characters, no fabricated scenes or dialogue. Most of the material I observed myself, though a few stories were related to me. As a
work of synthesis, this book owes a great debt to dozens of historians,
journalists, cultural critics, anthropologists, collectors, and scholars, on
whom I relied for documentary research. I am not an antiques dealer,
collector, or historian; I sought only to convey a subculture that fasci-
nates me. Any misrepresentations or mistakes about the field of antiques
and collecting are fully my own.

Treasure Hunters:
The Reality

Curt Avery has an idea for a reality show: Give ten antiques dealers a thousand bucks each and turn them loose on the carnival fields of Brimfield, the country's largest outdoor flea market and antiques show. "You continually buy up, trading for more money, more valuable objects," he says. "You take a piece of shit and you turn it into a Chippendale chair."

For Avery, this is not a reality show, but reality. The stakes are higher than a brief moment of fame. Avery must do this every day to put food on the table, pay bills, for his son's braces, his daughter's dance lessons, for the college fund, his own retirement. Every week he plays to win, searching through piles of junk at flea markets or through fancy antiques stores, avoiding the glut of reproductions, the clever fakes ("land mines," he calls them), outmaneuvering his competitors at auctions, applying twenty years of hard-won knowledge, wisdom that he gained the long way—awake at dawn for flea markets, up till midnight hitting the books—and the expensive way, the most painful lessons of all: buying "mistakes." Another antiques dealer I met, Wesley Swanson, learned about antiques by "losing thousands of dollars," he says, "just not all at once."

It's not an easy life. There are no paid sick days or vacation time, no pension fund or retirement plan, no corporate ladder where hard work gets you recognized, no year-end bonus or profit sharing. No safety net. In this endeavor, you survive by your wits alone. Or not. In his early days when the learning curve was ahead of him and profits meager, Curt's wife, Linda, out of work with their second child, would beseech him to sell a bottle from his collection, trade a nineteenth-century bitters bottle, perhaps, for a plastic one filled with juice. "How many guys my age are in this business?" Avery says. "It's like giving up on normal life and running away with the circus."

But how many people have a job where every day is a hunt for treasure, every day infused with the hope and possibility of finding a pot of gold, something to love and keep, something unique. "Gold is where you find it," Avery says, meaning that a great antique can show up anywhere—junk stores, yard sales, flea markets, auctions, high-end antique shows. "The beauty of this business," he says, "is that you can do it anywhere. You just need a checkbook, a pen, and a pair of eyes." True, but the checkbook needs a healthy balance, and the eyes must be knowing. "It's all about recognition," he says. He tells me about a period card table that sat in a Gloucester, Massachusetts, consignment shop for "months and months" priced at $600, until one day a savvy antiques dealer recognized the table's value, bought it, and sold it at auction for some $14,000. Each day in the life of an antiques dealer challenges his or her knowledge and instincts, an aesthetic IQ test. Recognizing the prize is no easy feat. A seven-by-ten-foot painting hung in an elementary school auditorium in North Attleboro, Massachusetts, for forty-eight years—its value unknown—until one day a man recognized the painting as *Afghans*, an important work by Alexandre Iacovleff. The painting was appraised at over $800,000.

Even with knowledge, it takes a workaholic compulsion to unearth treasures—rising before dawn for flea markets, knocking on doors, taking one last tour around the antiques shows after everyone else has left, outfoxing other dealers, doing time in the attics and basements of homeowners looking to divest. Like a rock star on tour, Avery is on the road peddling his wares nearly every weekend: New York, Pennsylvania, Rhode Island, New Hampshire, Vermont, Maine, Massachusetts, Connecticut, a grueling circuit of thirty to forty shows each year.

There are dealers who take the easy way out by selling reproductions, or passing off fakes and forgeries to unwitting collectors, "crossing over to the dark side," Avery says—the greatest peril to the pleasure and business of antiques. Like gold prospectors in the Wild West, the antiques and flea market world can attract "colorful" characters, sometimes unsavory or unscrupulous, sometimes canny and diligent. The competition is fierce, the rules few, and the true treasures are rare or well hidden except to the sharp eye of the autodidact.

Like all dealers, Curt Avery awaits the "perfect storm" of antiques, the day when all the factors converge in a cosmic alignment—a bit of arcane knowledge from two decades of self-study that signals this object is the one, the opportunity created through hard work, being out early and up late, and the most elusive factor, luck, the antiques gods smiling on him, his competition asleep or absent, and he's got a pocket full of cash—a brilliant shimmering instant on a dusty flea-market field or in a posh antiques shop, when there before him that object sits on a table or shelf—the lottery ticket, the "retirement piece," the "super-best," the Holy Grail—and he knows it.

CHAPTER I

Opium Bottles and Knuckleheads

It's 5:00 A.M. on a May Sunday in Massachusetts, and still dark outside. Curt Avery sits in front of me in his fully loaded pickup truck, part of a mile-long line of dealers waiting to get into the Rotary Club flea market. We inch along for an hour, as the rising sun evaporates dew from my windshield. Inside a chain-link fence, flagmen wave dealers into allotted spaces. Avery is peeved because the setup is disorganized and he must wait in line instead of being able to quickly park and then "pick" the show, antique-world parlance for plucking hidden gems off other dealers' tables. Ahead of me, I see him brake, jump out of his idling truck and sprint down a lane where dealers who arrived earlier are setting up. Half a minute later, he jogs back and tosses what looks like a small footstool into the front seat. He moves his truck another thirty feet, spies something down another aisle and leaps out to buy it. Drive-by antiquing.

He finally pulls into his spot and immediately a man materializes, nosing around the back of the truck, but Avery has come mainly to buy, so once he unloads sawhorses and plywood, he locks his truck and we cruise the aisles. The gates don't open for another three hours, but the "show" starts the minute Avery passes through the chain-link fence. By the time the unwitting public arrives, it will be over, the good stuff gone. There will likely be no great finds left. This is the show before the show, when dealers trade with one another out of their still unemptied trucks. Coffee cup in hand, Avery hunkers down the lanes. I follow. "Fresh blood," he says, spotting a Ryder truck. A rental truck can mean that somebody has inherited an estate, or some other one-time circumstance. Amateurs. People who don't do this for a living, who haven't taken the time to research their stuff, who want to turn a quick buck. The objects are new to the market; they haven't been floating around from show to show, the ink on the price tags faded or blurred illegible by rain. "Fresh tags can be good," Avery says. "Or a guy just trying to dump something by lowering the price with a big fat fresh tag."

As we approach the Ryder truck, Avery scans the objects, like the Six Million Dollar Man with telescopic vision. Twenty feet away from the table, he sings a ditty into my ear: "I just made a hundred *doll*-ars." He picks up a butter churn, a small glass canister with a wooden paddle wheel inside, pays the asking price of $40. "They made very few one-quart butter churns," he says out of the dealer's earshot, "because for all the work you did, you only got a little butter. You do the same amount of work in a two-quart churn and double the butter. Once they figured that out, they didn't make too many of the one-quarts. They're rare." This bit of esoterica—and Avery has hundreds of such factoids—will earn him a clean C-note when he resells the one-quart churn for close to $200. This is my first five minutes in Avery's world, and he makes finding treasure look easy. But the easy money is deceptive. Avery's apparently effortless profit is the result of years of being on the scene, gleaning tips from other dealers, working at an auction house for minimum wage, studying obscure reference books. "It's a long education," he says. "You really don't start until you spend $100. I can remember the first time I broke the $100 mark. It was traumatizing."

Now the Ryder truck woman is unloading a variety of two-inch-tall, delicately shaped perfume bottles. Avery picks one up, asks how much. "Five bucks," she says. It's an anomaly to see Avery gingerly handling the fragile bottle. He was a wrestler in high school, and still has the wrestler's form, a low center of gravity, with beefy arms and legs and a barrel chest. He has tattooed biceps, a wild mop of carbon-black curls, and a five o'clock shadow by noon. With his dark, deep-set eyes and heavy eye-lashes, he's handsome in a rugged, Bruce Springsteen way.

As the woman unloads more bottles, Avery picks up each one, asks the price. Same as before, five bucks. Finally he says, "How much for all of them?" He walks away with a shoe box of thirty antique perfume bottles for $100. Probably some woman who collected perfumes died and her collection, her lifelong passion, ended up in the hands of these people, who didn't know its value, and—it would appear—didn't care. Avery will later sell the bottles on eBay, most for $20 to $50 each, and one for $150. This is capitalism down and dirty, no guarantees, no regrets. There is a rebellious, outré air to the flea market, "suburban subversive," one researcher called it, "libidinous," said another.

"Flea markets," Avery says, "are the carnal part of this business."

THE TERM "FLEA MARKET" is from the French *marche aux puces*. In mid-to-late nineteenth-century Paris, *biffins* (rag-and-bone men), *chiffonniers* (ragmen), and *pêcheurs de lune* ("moon fishermen") sifted through trash in search of resellable items—glass, nails, animal carcasses, human hair, rags, cans. Hair was used to make wigs, carcasses rendered into candles, animal bones used for buttons or glue. Metal and glass were melted and recast. Sardine cans were fashioned into cheap toys, like tiny tin soldiers. An estimated thirty thousand ragmen hooked scraps of cloth out of the trash to sell to paper producers. Stories of the flea market's origin vary. One account claims it arose when the municipality of Paris organized trash collection to prevent outbreaks of infectious diseases, like cholera. In 1884, the government of Paris passed an ordinance that required every building to be equipped with a lidded garbage can, an effort spearheaded by a city official named Monsieur Poubelle. His name is fixed in history—*poubelle* is French for garbage can.

Another theory says that city rents were rising and scrap dealers, who bought the scavenged goods from the rag-and-bone men, moved to cheaper locales on the outskirts of Paris. Emperor Napoleon III charged a civil servant named Baron Haussmann with rebuilding Paris. Under Haussmann's vision, crooked streets were straightened and whole neighborhoods razed, including run-down buildings that housed salvage dealers. The poor were divided from the well-to-do. Haussmann's boulevards were designed to inspire commerce, though mainly for the bourgeoisie. Trades involving "an oven or a hammer" were banished from certain areas. Another story suggests that rag pickers and other secondhand merchants could sell goods outside the jurisdiction of Paris without paying city taxes, so they congregated beyond the city gates at Saint-Ouen near Porte de Clignancourt. Since the rags and other merchandise were likely infested with fleas and lice, the market earned the nickname *marche aux puces*.

Probably all of these forces contributed to the development of the flea market, but by 1890, the town managers of Saint-Ouen built roads and walkways, and merchants erected stalls. Vendors at Saint-Ouen paid a fee to exhibit their goods, as dealers do today. The original *marche aux puces* at Saint-Ouen, which bills itself as the world's largest antique market with 2,500 vendors across seventeen acres, is now a protected architectural heritage site that attracts up to 150,000 visitors each weekend, more than the Eiffel Tower.

AVERY AND I wander up and down the aisles, stopping to chat with other dealers—what shows they'll work this summer, rumors of a real Louis Vuitton suitcase discovered here earlier this morning for $50, worth thousands. We wend our way down the field, skipping some booths, veering toward others. Avery buys a set of Quimper plates for $10. Quimper (pronounced kem-pair) is a town in the Brittany region of France where faience pottery, a type of glazed earthenware, has been made since 1690. The Quimper plates that Avery buys feature small, Dutch-looking figures, bonneted women with aprons, and men with tall hats and yellow or blue pantaloons. In an antique shop, a set like this might cost twenty times the ten bucks Avery paid.

At the next booth, he buys a glass paperweight for $3, a rather ugly translucent blob that he says is from the early nineteenth century, and worth about $150. This seems like finding nuggets of gold in a shallow stream. It's exciting and addicting, but it's clear that the breadth and depth of knowledge needed to get to this point is daunting. Knowledge is what makes this robbery okay. Robbery is not the right word, though, because the information is available to anyone willing to study, to do the homework. "If you buy something off someone's table, you don't owe them anything," Avery says. The dealer is responsible for setting the asking price. *Caveat venditor.* He tells me about a woman who bought an eighteenth-century tapestry "for nothing" and resold it for six figures. The first dealer learned of the six-figure sale, which left her with a sour taste, especially as the buyer had "beat her up" on the price. "That first dealer fucked up," Avery says. "It's different when you see a great thing and you *still* haggle down the price. My philosophy is, just give them the money. I don't bargain then. I just buy it. I never want that person coming back to me and saying, 'You knocked me down $10, you cheap motherfucker.'"

Avery has even double-checked a price to give the seller a second chance. One year at the Brimfield flea market, in the "Pennsylvania Triangle," where three top Pennsylvania dealers set up, he saw a piece of redware. "I asked the price and the kid said $25," Avery says. He didn't think that could be right given the dealer's reputation, so he asked the kid to check again. "The kid yells over to his father, 'How much for this?' The father said $25." As to the value of the redware piece, "Add two zeros," Avery says. I ask him how this happens with knowledgeable dealers. "They just missed," he says.

Avery and I shop for a couple hours, and when the show opens to the general public at 9:00 A.M., we return to unload his truck. Avery isn't selling much here. This is not the crowd for pricey antiques. This is a flea-market crowd, people who want a bargain, people who lack knowledge yet still want to find something valuable for cheap, people—I shamefully realize—just like me. I am Avery's nightmare customer. "At this flea market, ten thousand people show up, but only nine people know anything," he says. "I saw a little girl about Kristina's age pick up something from my booth." Kristina is Avery's eight-year-old daughter. "I said to her, 'I bet you can't tell me what that's for.' And she said, 'Oh, I think it's a bed warmer.' The mother said, 'I thought it was a popcorn popper.' The kid learned it on a field trip to Plimoth Plantation or something."

A woman picks up a small, delicate bottle from Avery's table, asks how much.

"Twenty," he says.

"Cents?" she asks.

"Dollars," he says.

She quickly sets it back on the table. The bottle is four inches tall, about the circumference of a nickel, with a brownish tarry residue inside and a crusty cork jammed in the top, circa 1890. Raised lettering on the glass reads *Dr. McMunn's Elixir of Opium*. A fragment of the label signed by the apothecary attests that the opium is "genuine." I recall from my "History of Lizzie Borden" class in college that Borden took opium and morphine (its derivative) regularly, indeed on the day she axed to death her father and stepmother (allegedly: she was acquitted). Avery has a few opium bottles—he gives me one as a gift—but they are fairly hard to find, which seems odd since opium was so widely used. In a single year, 1859, just one glass factory in France produced eighty million bottles for opium. Until it was banned in 1905, opium was cheaper than beer or gin, and easily purchased in grocery stores, by mail, and over the counter at pharmacies. Parents even gave opium to fussy babies, a product like Street's Infants' Quietness, which "quieted" many infants through death by overdose. In *Confessions of an English Opium-Eater*, Thomas de Quincey called opium a "panacea for all human woes" and "the secret of happiness." Opium addiction was so widespread that an English pharmacist, C. R. Alder Wright, formulated a derivative called diacetylmorphine, which he hoped would be less addicting. The new drug, sold by the German company Bayer, was called Heroin for its heroic ability to cure. Heroin was the best-selling drug brand of its time.

After I learn about the opium bottles, later at a small one-day antique show with Avery, a girl about eleven years old picks up the bottle and reads the lettering. "What's opium?" she asks, pronouncing it "opp-ee-um." I tell her a little bit about the bottles. "Awesome," she says. "So much history in a little bottle."

A WOMAN PICKS UP a $90 Japanese Imari porcelain plate from Avery's table, says to a friend, "Oh, I saw one just like that at Job Lot," a warehouse filled with liquidation items. I grimace as the woman wanders away. Avery disparages the shopping strategies of this class of buyers. "They are *aiming* for cracked things," he says. "I can have the perfect plate in my hand and it's $12, but they'll be like, 'Oh no, I'm fine with these. Do you have any more like this?' I couldn't sell a good thing to these knuckleheads." I cringe, as this has been my strategy—buy the slightly "off" thing for cheaper. I, too, am a "knucklehead."

Earlier that day, Avery bought an antique chest of drawers for $20, a lovely smallish piece of solid oak. No fiberboard or cheesy plywood backing or fake wood-grain veneer. He put a tag of $80 on the dresser, about half its retail value at a better show. Dozens of people admire it. It's such a bargain that I'm tempted to buy it even though I have no place for it. I am amazed that Avery can't sell this solid oak dresser for less than anyone would pay for a factory-assembled, particleboard imitation from Walmart. He drops the price to $50, and now this becomes a sociological experiment—a test of what, I'm not sure, perhaps a theory about American culture, that we are easily satisfied with simulacra, the surface of things over substance and quality. The dresser still doesn't sell.

At the flea market, Avery sells objects far below their value. He's willing to be flexible and take a hit on his prices here, but he has his bottom line. "I had this really, really good lampshade in cranberry glass with an oval cut to clear," he says. "They dip the blowpipe in clear glass, then in cranberry glass, and then blow it into form." After the piece is shaped, a pattern is cut into it. "This lampshade was rare, from the 1850s," he says. "It was beautiful. It had a couple of chips, but it was just a rare, rare thing." Avery glances occasionally at the people wandering through his booth. He continues. "I started at $200, but I had trouble selling the lampshade because it was a single, so I marked it at $129. This woman says, 'Would you take $80?' I looked at her and I go, 'NO.' I mean, I'll smash it before I'll sell it for $80. The lady was like, 'Would you take $85?' I said, 'Do you even know what you are buying?' The lady looked at me. 'Oh, yes, yes.' I go, 'It's $100.'" For that price, the woman couldn't refuse.

"This isn't about the money," Avery says. "It's about appreciation." We joke that he should make customers pass a quiz before they're allowed to buy something, to prove they *deserve* the piece. For Avery, this is about a love of objects, a keen understanding of the skill invested in creating a lampshade without the benefit of technology. In the nineteenth century, a glassblower's apprenticeship was seven years. For Avery, an antique has value beyond utility. He and other dealers and collectors are lay historians, approaching their subject through the back door. Avery is a teacher at heart. When I arrived at his house before the show, he brought me into his living room and pointed to a framed sampler on the wall. "What do you notice about this?" he asked.

I looked at the eighteen-inch-square sampler, frayed at the edges with spots of dry rot, the alphabet embroidered across the top and the bottom by some young girl, lessons in feminine crafts. If I saw this at a flea market, I might pay $10. It's pretty, but worn and faded. I studied the sampler and found nothing odd or amiss. I didn't notice that one of the alphabets omits the letter *J*. "The letter *J*," Avery said, "was not in usage until 1780 to 1790. Prior to that, the letters *I* and *J* were written as *I*. You had to discern which letter was in use by the context. Obviously 'is' was meant to be 'is' and not 'js.'" On Avery's sampler, the upper alphabet includes the letters *I* and *J* while the bottom alphabet omits the *J*. The sampler is transitional, Avery hypothesizes; the girl who sewed it had forgotten in one instance to include the new letter *J*. He dates the sampler to the late eighteenth century and values it at $600. The sampler tells a story of a girl's life, what girls were taught, but it also tells a story of the English language. The sampler is literally a stitch in time.

AFTER THE ROTARY SHOW, on my drive home to Maine, I stop at an indoor flea market just before it closes. I spot a perfume bottle that is *exactly like one Avery bought*, with a hand-painted gold stripe around its belly, in delicate purple glass, for $20. At home, I'm still patting myself on the back for negotiating $4 off the asking price when I discover through a quick Internet search hundreds, if not thousands, of identical bottles for sale, blown a week or a month ago in Turkey, asking price: a buck. I recall some of the things I'd learned from Avery that I'd failed to apply: wrong color, no discernible wear, and too easy a find, especially at the *end* of the day. That twenty bucks was my first installment on a home-school education in antiques. The real proving ground is the Brimfield flea market and antiques show, reportedly the largest in the country. For dealers, Avery says, "Brimfield is boot camp."

CHAPTER 2

One Man's Trash

In John Cheever's 1941 story "Publick House," a young man comes home to find "an unnatural profusion of antiques in the hallway" of the eighteenth-century summer home his widowed mother has transformed into a tea room. She's pawning the family heirlooms for funds to run the restaurant. "Yes, the rugs are for sale—real Maine hooked rugs. The small one is $15," his mother tells a guest. The woman's elderly father is sick of the "god-damned tearoom people." He says to her, "You've sold all my things. You sold my mother's china. You sold the rugs. You sold the portraits. You've made a business out of it—selling the past. What kind of business is that—selling the past?"

In spite of his love for old things, Curt Avery never set out to "sell the past," but perhaps antiquities were in his destiny. Avery grew up surrounded by the ghosts of history. His hometown in Massachusetts was one of the earliest European settlements, established around 1627 when pilgrims left the sandy shores of Plymouth in search of fertile soil. "Where I grew up it was a time capsule," Avery says. His home, built in 1861, had nine small, oddly shaped rooms, one of which was connected by a small door to the upstairs loft of a cavernous barn, with three carriage stalls in berms below ground. The yard, ringed by a small stream, abutted a field where his sister kept a pony. Beyond the tiny brook was a stand of old-growth pine. One day when he was about ten, he saw some trash sticking out of the ground just beyond the stream. He poked at the dirt and uncovered a bottle.

Before the advent of incinerators, and then trash collection and land-fills, people dumped their trash on the streets. In most American cities, pigs ran loose eating garbage (and were, in turn, sometimes eaten by the poor). Small towns built "piggeries," where swine were fed garbage, and people buried trash at the edge of their property or tossed it down the outhouse or "privy." When Avery, as a boy, stumbled upon the century-old dump in his backyard, his hobby of "bottle digging" was born.

He and his childhood friend, Dennis, spent many days digging the old dump. "It was like that whole treasure thing," Avery says. "'Look at what we found! This has got to be worth $1 million!' Dennis found a pair of spectacles one day. I was so jealous," he recalls, "but I found something that he wanted, so we traded." He laughs. "It goes back that far." Avery tells me about the bottle digging "rage" in the sixties and seventies. "You didn't have to go far to find somebody who dug." The first bottle digger Avery met was a friend of his mother's, who helped him identify his bottles, and offered to take him digging. When Avery was in high school, Ken Hartwell moved into town, and he and Avery dug together. They would locate older houses and dig the embankments behind them. "Ken and I got really good at digging holes in people's backyards without their knowing," he says. Bottle digging is a quasi-archaeological endeavor, sans the tiny brushes and sieves and advanced degrees, and it often involves a petty crime: trespassing. "To some people," Avery says, "bottle digging is rape-and-pillage archaeology."

With their loot from digging, they set up at bottle shows on the East Coast in summers during high school and college, meandering along back roads in Avery's Volkswagen, sleeping under the stars. "Ken and I would get in the car and aim toward a bottle show, finding dumps to dig along the way. We never once paid for a campsite. We'd sleep in the bushes." He continues, "One time we were going to Saratoga for a bottle show and along the way we found a Ballston Spa bottle. We felt like such hot shits." In the nineteenth century, wealthy Americans traveled to Ballston Spa near Saratoga, New York, to partake of the natural mineral springs, literally, a "watering hole." The spring water, which contained salt, calcium, and magnesium, was bottled and sold as a cure. "We dug a Franklin Spring water bottle and sold it for $350 the next day at the show. It was a rare bottle. It's still a rare bottle. I've never had another one," he says. "I'm sure we went out and bought beer and got drunk as hell."

Avery's wife Linda, tall, dark-haired, with big brown eyes, recalls two things about their first date in college: the Rolling Stones and bottles. Early in their relationship, Avery took Linda bottle digging in the woods in a suburb of Boston. They were caught by local cops and questioned about trespassing. Linda saved the town paper's police blotter as a souvenir of their courtship, a report of "suspicious characters."

GROWING UP, dump picking was a ritual in my family. On Saturdays, my mother took me and my siblings to the town dump, where we rescued old chaise longues, furniture in need of minor repair, and phones. My mother had an odd predilection for reassembling rotary phones. I vividly recall her amid tiny phone parts, working with a long thin screwdriver. Her penchant for dump picking was about recovering something valuable discarded by someone less thrifty, less resourceful. She grew up poor, the daughter of a widowed housekeeper; scavenging was the economic imprint of her childhood. For me, dump picking was a treasure hunt.

Scavenging is a habit that dies hard, or maybe never dies. In college, the lessons of my childhood meshed with my desire to be unconventional. I wore thrift store couture, and haunted junk stores. When I met Avery in college and learned of his bottle digging hobby, I asked if I could go with him, so one Saturday we drove to an old church in Massachusetts that he dated by the architecture as 1700s. The parking lot was empty, so we trespassed into the woods behind the church, stepping over a mossy stone wall. He walked around like a surveyor, scanning the leaf clutter. "We'll dig here," he said, pointing to a spot that looked random to me. To his trained eye, a slight rise of the earth bespoke the century-old dumping ground. We shoveled off the duff and the top layers of dirt. Twenty minutes later I stood knee-high in a hole. Avery said, "Why don't you dig here?" After I traded spots with him, my shovel instantly clinked against glass, and I realized he'd positioned me to find the treasure. On our hands and knees, we clawed the dirt, unearthing cracked china, bottles, and jars. I found a whole "Sawyer's Crystal Blueing," an aqua-tinted, mold-cast bottle that once contained bluing, used when washing clothes, to make the whites look whiter. The first colonists washed their clothes on Mondays, so laundry day became "blue Monday."

I dug up a "Dr. Cumming's Vegetine," a "Marvelous Cold Cream— Richard Hudnut, New York," and a brown bottle with embossed lettering: "Liquozone, Manufactured Only By The Liquid Ozone Co., Chicago, USA." Liquozone was a "snake oil" potion sold in the late 1800s as a cure for everything—from dandruff to cancer, its ads boasted—including diarrhea, eczema, goiter, malaria, piles, and scrofula, a disease of the lymph nodes that caused growths around the neck. Liquozone was purported to be liquid oxygen, which if true would have killed you. It was later debunked as 99 percent water with some sulphuric acid, and banned.

The bottles are puzzle pieces offering a brief glimpse into life one hundred years ago. I was amazed that such old artifacts fetch only a dollar or two at a flea market. My favorite find was a ceramic doll just two inches high, unsmiling and armless. "That's turn-of-the-century," Avery said. "You can see the seams from the mold. Worth about ten bucks." I fell in love with the doll. There was something transformative about the primacy of that experience, which affected me like no history book ever had. The doll made history *real*, the way I suppose the Shroud of Turin proves Jesus real for some people.

FOR AVERY, bottle digging was the genesis of his life as an antiques dealer. The first antique he bought specifically to resell was something he recognized from his digging days. "I was on a job in Wolfeboro, New Hampshire, on Lake Winnipesaukee, the oldest vacation community in the United States," he says. Avery worked as a delivery driver in high school and college. "During our lunch break, I went into an antique shop and I found a stack of five redware cups from the nineteenth century. I knew what redware was because I'd dug it up." He paid $15 for the redware pieces, and later took them to a flea market. "I put them in a knapsack and walked around looking at dealers' stuff, talking to them. I peddled them all for $15 to $25 each."

Avery started with five pieces of redware in a knapsack. Fifteen years later, when he sets out for the Brimfield Flea Market in July, his pickup truck fully loaded, he'll be hauling $30,000 worth of antiques.

CHAPTER 3

Boot Camp

The alarm startles me awake at 3:00 A.M. on a Tuesday morning in July. Heart pounding, nauseated from lack of sleep, for a moment I am lost in the blackness until I remember where I am: transposed to the life of an itinerant antiques dealer. It's too early for birds, for food, even for coffee, as I pull on clothes and head downstairs to meet Avery. I'd arrived at his house the night before to accommodate our early departure for Brimfield, the Mother of All Flea Markets. For six days in May and again in July and September, the sleepy burg of Brimfield becomes a tent city, with up to 5,000 dealers, like temporary squatters, and as many as 250,000 visitors. The dealers' booths spread across twenty different fields along a mile of Route 20, Brimfield's main drag, forming a patchwork quilt of smaller "shows" with staggered opening times. "There's so much to see you can go blind," Avery says. "Brimfield is half antiques, half collectibles, and half flea-market junk." His fuzzy math speaks to the sheer superfluity of Brimfield.

The Brimfield Flea Market began in 1959 in Brimfield, Massachusetts, a village settled in the early 1700s, now with 3,700 citizens. Brimfield's organizers boast that it's the largest outdoor flea market and antiques show in the United States, though two other markets claim this distinction as well. The manager of the Rose Bowl flea market in Pasadena, California, which started in 1968 and attracts 3,000 vendors, said, "It's understood that this is the world's largest flea market." First Monday Trade Days in Canton, Texas, its manager claimed, is "the world's oldest and largest flea market," with 3,000 vendors occupying 400 acres. First Monday Trade Days began in 1850, when a U.S. circuit judge held court on the first Monday of the month. People gathered from near and far to follow the action, perhaps witness a hanging, and the crowd attracted hawkers.

As an unregulated industry, there are no reliable figures for the number of flea markets. One source, *The Official Directory to U.S. Flea Markets*, reported that there were 4,000 flea markets located between Kansas and Texas alone. A mid-1990s study estimated that more than 3,500 flea markets produced $10 billion in gross sales annually. As of 2004, according to the National Flea Market Association, there were about two and a half million flea-market vendors, with annual sales exceeding $30 billion.

Brimfield has the ambience of a protest march or an outdoor concert. One year, the Rolling Stones showed up in a limousine. At Brimfield, babies are born, people die, romances blossom. In 2002, a couple got married at 6:00 A.M. while they stood in line waiting for the J&J antique show to begin. When the gates opened, the newlyweds, the groom in shorts and a tux, the bride in a dress, ran around shopping. One presumes they were searching for "something old" to go along with the new, the borrowed, and the blue. Brimfield, with its mile-long stretch of booths on both sides of the road, hundreds of feet deep, is like a reverse parade, where people stroll along looking at fixed displays. It's an enormous outdoor museum, the Smithsonian on the fly and up for sale. In fact, in 1983 the Smithsonian sponsored a research expedition to Brimfield, headed by anthropologist Dr. Charlene James-Duguid, who dispelled the myth that flea markets were "filled with vagrants and gypsies."

I SLIDE INTO the passenger seat of Avery's pickup, odometer reading: 234,621. He bought the truck when he set up at his first Brimfield fifteen years ago. He squeezes in behind the steering wheel, downs three aspirin with a slug of Pepto-Bismol. "The antique dealer's cocktail," he says, then stuffs the bottle in his mobile pharmacy, the pocket compartment of the driver's-side door, which contains the necessary remedies for the modern-day peddler: bug spray, deodorant, toothpaste, Balmex (for thigh chafing from hours of walking on sweltering days, or in wet clothes during rainouts), a small bottle of shampoo. His style is minimalist, baggy shorts, a worn T-shirt, two pairs of athletic socks (to alleviate painful flare-ups of plantar fasciitis from hours on his feet), and sneakers. His luggage is a plastic supermarket bag with an extra shirt and changes of underwear and socks, which he squashes behind the headrest.

Every other possible space is filled with objects. Nineteenth-century oil portraits are wedged behind the seat. A turn-of-the-century cane with a fourteen-karat gold knob, and another cane with a carved ivory handle poke out from under the seat, each dangling a price tag of $250. A few marbles rest on the truck floor, along with a hammer. It's a trade-off: he could carry more clothes, a chair, a cooler, but that means he'd forfeit precious square footage, space for one or two more antiques, which could translate into thousands of dollars.

I'm still waking up, but Avery's on his second cup of black coffee, which he drinks cold. Like an avid fisherman, he's got a thousand stories, deals he's made, the ones that got away. "Last year I bought this pitcher from a dealer named Chet. It was this big fancy teapot thing. I looked at it and I said, 'My God, that's yellowware squared.'" Yellowware is thick, sturdy pottery fired from the ochre clay found in the Northeast and the Ohio River valley in the early nineteenth through mid-twentieth centuries. Avery had bought the pitcher for $500. "Turns out that between the time I bought it and now," he says, "the papers showed one of these pitchers with the lid missing selling for $3,000. Well, this guy Chet saw the article, too, and he says, 'You know that pitcher I sold you? One of those just sold for a lot of money.'" Avery bought the piece on instinct. He wasn't sure of its value, but even if he had been, I ask, how could he be blamed for his knowledge? "And this guy completely understands that," Avery says, "but unfortunately, he's also human. He didn't really grumble, but because of that, I'll spend five hundred bucks at his booth whether I need the stuff or not. It's a reciprocal thing." I ask Avery if he'd sold the pitcher yet. "I'll give it to this midwestern auction house to sell, Ohio or somewhere. They specialize in pottery." Antique dealing is all about taking an item out of the wrong setting and placing it in its rightful frame of reference. As Avery says, "Context is everything."

Off the highway, we pass through Sturbridge, then Brimfield. These towns are picture-postcard scenes with steepled white churches overlooking trimmed lawns of the commons, graced by huge oaks and maples, and usually a cast-iron cannon, or statuary of some forgotten local hero on a horse or shouldering a musket. These towns look like movie sets, almost caricatures, but in the layout of the roads and in the architecture you can glimpse life in a previous century—the narrow roads once paths for horses and buggies, the triangles of grass that denote the "common," where villagers gathered to trade, hold militia training, or graze cattle. The setting is apposite to the occasion—peddling centuries-old stuff.

We pass a church that rents its lawn for parking, ten bucks per spot. "Fifteen years ago there would have been a hundred cars in this lot already," Avery says. "Brimfield and antiques in general aren't as popular as they used to be. What a shame." This is a lament I will hear from many dealers, though Avery is an optimist. "It's purely a lack of knowledge that separates consumers from antiques," he says. "No one would think of buying a new piece of furniture, outside of a couch, if they knew about antiques." I admire his faith in the latent tastes of the American populace. It's more aesthetic credit than I would give us. Down the main strip you see tents and booths and stuff for sale on the sidewalks, and food vendors, Ben & Jerry's, Dollar Burgers, fresh-squeezed lemonade, fried dough. Young, robust cops in Bermuda-shorts uniforms patrol the streets from mountain bikes. Teenage boys wheel dollies, yelling, "Porter for hi-yah," the same scrawled in Magic Marker on their T-shirts.

At the farthest end of the main thoroughfare is Acres North, a four-hour-long, gated show with two hundred dealers, the first of two shows this week at which Avery will sell. Entrance to Acres North is carefully guarded. Giant signs warn, "NO SELLING UNTIL 1:00 P.M.," when the show officially opens. The shows are a battle between the promoters, who want to assure their gate audience—for a $5 fee—gets quality "fresh" merchandise, and dealers, who want to "pick" the field before the show opens. Antiques dealers have a constant need for fresh things to mark up and resell. An ad for one Brimfield show says, "Expect to find hundreds of exhibitor displays of *fresh merchandise*." Some pickers offer Avery $50 to $100 to "assist" him, getting into the show early under this pretense, but today I am his assistant. (Pickers have been known to hop the fence in back, taking their chances with cow pies or a grazing bull.)

The sponsors at the gate direct traffic, make announcements over the PA system: "Elgin Crittendon, you are in the wrong space," they announce twice, punitively. Avery and I pass through the chain-link fence onto a bucolic, tree-rimmed pasture with cows in the lower acres, the smoky foothills of the Berkshires as backdrop. Avery erects his tent first, a routine he could perform blindfolded, and then sets up five tables. I help him unwrap hundreds of items, anxious about making a $1,000 slip of the hand. The day quickly grows stiflingly hot and sticky. After just two hours my breathing is labored and my fingers have swollen into sausages. We have until 1:00 P.M. to set up, and so in the 90-degree swelter, we unwrap "smalls" and place them on tables. Avery's marketing strategy is to overload his booth. His theory seems sound; you can never predict what will sell. In a quick census, I estimate that he's brought over three hundred objects. He spent two days carefully selecting merchandise and loading his truck. But in spite of the preparation, what might sell is still a guessing game. Most of the objects range from $100 to $1,000, with a couple dozen higher-ticket items, like a rare inkwell for which he paid $1,500 and hopes to sell for double.

WE ARE JUST ABOUT finished setting up when 1:00 P.M. hits and the gates open. From our vantage point halfway down the field, we can see them coming, the buyers, making steady, hurried progress, not running, which would seem undignified, more like race-walking, that odd sport. They approach in a way that reminds me of *Dawn of the Dead* zombies: at first they appear distant and untroubling and then suddenly they're upon you in a devouring swarm, with their straw hats and fanny packs and walkie-talkies and cell phones and thick wads of cash and two-wheeled carts for hauling loot.

"Got any violins?"

"Fountain pens?"

"Do you have any scouting stuff?"

A one-legged man crutches by and shouts, "Cast iron cookware? Pots? Pans? Waffle irons?" What is it about cast iron cookware that strikes him? Why does he want, love, *need* an old waffle iron? (Investment perhaps: a "Favorite Piqua Ware" double-loaf cast iron cornbread pan sold for a record $21,000 in 2006.) I will see Joel, the cast-iron guy, every day this week, handsome, ponytailed, muscled arms and chest, and at other New England antiques shows calling out his familiar plea, "Cast iron cookware?" Indeed, he is a legend, appearing in the novel *Brimfield* by Michael Fortuna, and in *Brimfield Rush* by Bob Wyss. Trying to be helpful, I ask Avery if he has any cast iron cookware. He replies, "This guy, Joel, works incredibly hard. At every Brimfield he asks every dealer for thirty years if he has cast iron cookware. What are the odds of me finding something he doesn't already have?"

People walk around wearing headsets, looking deranged, muttering to themselves. Husband-and-wife teams split up to maximize efficiency. "Honey, I'm in row C, near the concession. I've spotted a topsy-turvy doll." Avery has a topsy-turvy doll for $200, perched in a wooden bowl, a strange hybrid cloth figure with two heads at opposite ends, one black and one white. A skirt covers one of the doll's heads and torso when upright. "Turn me up and turn me back, first I'm white and then I'm black" reads a nineteenth-century ad for the dolls. Stitched together at the torso, the doll defies the notion of segregation.

MINUTES BEFORE THE SHOW opened, Avery walked toward the men's room, but never made it there. On the way, he bought two stoneware jugs for $400 from a dealer a few booths down, took the price tag off and placed them on his table. Now he's just sold them—his first sale of the day—for $550. "A hundred and fifty–dollar profit in three minutes," he says. "A new world's record." A girl in her twenties breathlessly asks, "Musical instruments?" as she moves quickly from table to table. I hear her voice like a lyric, "Sir, do you have any musical instruments?" A polite, almost plaintive call that fades as she hurries along the rows. "Anything on fireworks at all?" a man shouts into the booth, and then vanishes. There's a dozen people in Avery's booth inspecting objects.

"How much?" A woman holds up a pink "lusterware" dog figurine.

"Ninety-five," Avery shouts. She sets it down.

Ten minutes into the show, Avery sells a set of 1800s andirons in the shape of hound dogs for $800. A soft-spoken man asks the price of a nineteenth-century carved fisherman nutcracker. Even the lowly nut-cracker has an illustrious history. Archaeologists found stone nut-cracking tools buried near the Dead Sea dating 780,000 years ago. The Leaven-worth Nutcracker Museum in Germany owns a nutcracker forged near the time of Christ. There is even a "father of nutcrackers," Wilhelm Füchtner, who commercialized the production of nutcrackers in 1872. His great-great-great grandson still designs nutcrackers. The fisherman nutcracker is $150, Avery tells the man, who peels off bills and walks away happily with his nutcracker wrapped in newspaper.

Since I know nothing about antiques, I am of little help, but Avery asks me to keep my eye out for theft. He displays small, expensive items, "pocket pals," in glass cases. There are no store detectives, two-way mir-rors, hidden cameras, security guards. Only our consciences regulate the exchanges here. "Or lack thereof," Avery says. Later, we learn that a dealer down the row not only failed to sell a single thing, but had some-thing stolen.

A fortyish man with long hair on a kid's banana bike rides past: "Got any marbles?" At first I think he is an obsessed weirdo, but in fact he is a savvy shopper. His tiny bike is easily packed in his car, and allows him rapid transit to hundreds of booths. The marble collector is the epitome of efficiency, not deficiency. Marbles are one of the oldest toys known. Retired toy manufacturer Bert Cohen owns two 2,300-year-old Roman marbles (among 300,000, which fill two floors of his house). In the

United States in the 1920s, the game of marbles was so popular that Charles "Buster" Rech, the first champion "mibster" of the national marbles tournament in 1922, was fêted with a fifty-piece brass band before ten thousand fans.

Marbles have marvelous names: cat's eye, clam broth, end-of-day cloud, Popeye corkscrews. An Indian is a marble hand-cut from a cane of glass. A single, late-1800s, German-made Indian sold for $4,082 in 2001. Marrididdles are homemade clay marbles you hardened in your own oven, and sulphides are clear marbles with a figure inside, like a bust of Theodore Roosevelt. In the 1880s, Samuel Dyke of Akron, Ohio, patented a machine to mass-produce clay marbles. At its peak, his factory produced a million marbles a day, which filled five railroad boxcars. For a penny, a kid could buy a fistful. Today, these clay marbles are still cheap. In a shoe box on Avery's table, the earthen-colored, slightly misshapen orbs cost a quarter a piece.

In the banana-bike-riding marble collector, I recognize an enviable trait: *passion*. A dealer who bought a c. 1760 fan-crested, banister-back armchair with Spanish feet said in the *Maine Antique Digest*, "It crushed my heart it is so good." Avery's been smitten, too. Speaking of a Prior-Hamblin School portrait, he said, "I fell in love with that thing." He won the painting at an auction. "It was such a star, such a queen," he said. I've never collected anything beyond childhood, and though I can't imagine what objects might attract me now, I long to feel this passion collectors feel, to fall in love with *something*.

Assembling a collection suggests a deep engagement with living; objects link people to the continuous chain of life. In his eloquent memoir, *Collections of Nothing*, William Davies King writes, "Collecting is a way of linking past, present, and future. Objects from the past get collected in the present to preserve them for the future." Collecting is about *time* itself—that thing none of us has enough of, all of us will run out of, and nobody can ever contain, stop, control, or change. Objects reflect identity—the sense of *self*. Jean-Paul Sartre wrote, "Possession is a magical relation; I *am* these objects which I possess." We are what we own.

Andy Warhol, who claimed to have visited a flea market, auction, or antique store every day, and whose possessions filled all but two rooms of his five-story Manhattan townhouse, wrote, "Buying is much more American than thinking," which evokes a different philosophy: I buy, therefore I am.

WITHIN FIFTEEN MINUTES of opening Avery has pocketed hundreds of dollars. This is a "slow" show, he says, almost apologetically. The hot weather in July keeps shoppers away. Still, for an hour business is steady, with a half dozen serious buyers in the booth at any given time. The negotiation between dealer and buyer is like the mating dance of the blue-footed booby, choreographed and ritualized. The buyer picks up the object, fondles it, puts it down, looks at something else. Avery steps over, offers some information. "I just got that out of a house yesterday. It's fresh as can be." "Fresh" means the buyer has first pick, the item has not been dragged from show to show, unwanted, unloved. "Fresh" means the buyer gets the item at the bottom rung of the resale ladder.

The buyer hesitates, says, "What's the best you can do?" Avery offers a price lower than his sticker, there's some haggling, and the item is sold. Or not. Avery has his bottom line, and he'll carry an object around to a few shows rather than dip below the price he wants. I saw him load and unload and load and unload and load again an eight-foot-tall corner cabinet, a real back-breaker, that he started at $1,300, and dropped to $900. He got an offer of $800 at the second show, but said, "Fuck it, I'll wrap it up and take it home before I sell this for $800." And home it went.

Negotiation is an obligatory pas de deux, though sometimes the haggling more closely resembles sumo wrestling. One woman returns to Avery's booth three times over the afternoon, wheedling, hoping he'll come down on a framed tapestry "Welcome" sign that he says is "way under the money" at $135. But she won't budge, and he won't budge, and the sign remains unsold. The next day in another booth, we see the same sign in worse condition than Avery's, priced at $185.

THE AVERAGE AGE of the buyers seems to be over forty, with an oc-
casional twenty-something among the crowd—like the earnest, handsome
man who is caressing Avery's butter churn. "Do you have a one-quart?"
he asks. Avery says he's not sure that he packed it, he might have left it
at home. "Does it have a wooden paddle? Do you think it is in one of
your boxes?" Avery checks, but he didn't bring the churn. The young
man seems chagrined, as if his mission will not be complete without a
one-quart butter churn. (Or, if he's like most collectors, *another* one.)
Some collectors advertise for items, turn their bodies into strolling mar-
quees. It is not enough to ferret out the object; they must attract objects
to themselves. A tall stick-figure man wears a straw hat that reads: I BUY
POLITICAL ITEMS. I see him the next day at the next show, and the day after
that. There are many people wearing T-shirts emblazoned front and back
with their personal advertisements. I BUY USED POST OFFICE ITEMS. Another man printed on his shirt WANTED: OLD POLICE BADGES. These people are ambulatory advertisements for their obsessions—like the woman
wearing a heart-shaped sandwich board. Her homemade sign reads front
and back: I BUY VALENTINES. She wears her heart not on her sleeve, but
on her whole body.

For a solid hour, objects leap off the tables in Avery's booth as if each
piece were claiming its rightful buyer. There is something satisfying
about this, as if a balance is being restored, something made right. Objects rescued from obscurity in attics, cellars, or landfills are matched with
owners who will appreciate them, "understand them," Avery says. There
is resurrection in these acts. How much? How old? What is this thing?
What was it used for? Avery is a roving history teacher, a price guide, a
salesman, a purveyor of esoterica. Cash flies out of customers' wallets into
Avery's. On this "slow" day, Avery takes in $1,500 that first hour. The
atmosphere is carnivalesque—people speaking into cell phones, trailing
two-wheeled carts, an air of frantic pursuit. The competition is fierce,
and time is of the essence. Fresh merchandise sells quickly. Avery whole-
sales much of his merchandise to other dealers who run fancy shops on

Martha's Vineyard, or in Connecticut and New York City, or dealers looking for items whose values can be doubled, the object "flipped" quickly for "short money." Avery's friends are also his competitors. Dealers on the hunt circle the field like wild dogs—we see the same faces pass by three and four times, as if they are on a merry-go-round.

FOR THE TWENTY HOURS of packing, travel time, setup, and tear-down, the show will be all but over in the first hour, like a Thanksgiving dinner you prepare for two days and consume in ten minutes. During the doldrums, when dealers are required to stay four hours until the show ends, Avery gives me lessons. In his glass case, there are two martini-like glasses. I say, "Why are these $150 each? They look like something from Pier 1, like a Mexican import." Avery steps out from under his tent and holds the glasses at arm's length against the sky. "See these lines?" Crizzling. The fine circular age lines are so abundant that it's a wonder the glass hasn't shattered in 250 years. He shows me a "rush light" for $495, which looks like pliers glued to a wooden base, with one handle bent into a candle holder. "They took a piece of rush from the swamp and dipped it in wax or animal fat and lit it and it burned your fucking house down," he says. Rush lights were the poor man's illumination in the eighteenth century, for people who couldn't afford oil lamps or tallow candles. A rush light burned for about an hour, which was perhaps just as well. "That thing burned down a lot of houses in colonial times," Avery says.

After the initial blitz, dealers shop or chat, play "show and tell." Avery's friend Tucker Small visits from his booth down the row. Tucker is a short, square-shaped man who appears younger than his fifty-six years. He has a puppy dog appeal, with soupy brown eyes. Tucker shows Avery a stoneware jug. "I paid three beans for this. Am I safe?" Avery assures Tucker that his jug is real, and he can ask $450 or $500. A social worker by day, Tucker is a "weekend warrior," accumulating merchandise throughout the year to sell at three or four shows. Tucker studied history in college and collected bottles. At an auction once, the bottle he wanted was in a mixed lot, so he bought the lot to get the one bottle, and decided to sell the rest. "I said to my wife, 'This might be a way to make money,'" he says. He invested $800 from his savings on antiques, and set up at a local show. "I sold $400 worth of stuff, and then $400 at another show. I had my money back and I still had a bunch of stuff. That was twenty years ago."

Avery's friend Sam, an electrician during the week, stops by with a large wooden bowl hand-carved from the burl of an oak tree. The burl bowl has thin spots of wear and a beautiful swirling grain. "This piece has soul," Sam says. The bowl does seem like a living, breathing thing, with its sensual organic shape, the wood smoothed over centuries by human hands. Sam leaves the bowl in Avery's booth to sell; he'll give Avery a small kickback for the favor.

Ken Hartwell stops by, Avery's friend from bottle digging days. Ken is a waifish figure, delicately handsome with fine features, though he carries an air of *tristesse*, like Montgomery Clift. I ask Ken about his best find ever. He mentions a sugar bowl he bought for $25 at a yard sale and sold for $10,000. I ask Tucker. He bought a lily pad pitcher for $450 and sold it for $5,000. Next it's Avery's turn. He says he bought a glass boot for $1 and sold it for $1,000. I know Avery has better stories, more glamorous finds, but he plays his cards close to his chest, does not want to engender ill will. His knowledge is deeper because he is a professional and not a dilettante. He quadruples or sextuples his investment regularly. He must. As he often says, "I have a family to feed." But knowledge can be a liability; some dealers will raise the price on something if Avery shows interest—or else they suddenly change their minds about selling it, then jack up the price and redisplay the item later.

The storytelling shows how much of one's success in antiques—in spite of deep knowledge—can be dumb luck. For some people, it's nothing but dumb luck. In 1991, a retired truck driver in California bought a splatter painting at a junk shop for $5. She and a friend were going to drink beer and throw darts at the canvas, but they "never got around to it." Now some experts claim the painting is by Jackson Pollock, though the fingerprint on the canvas, thought to be Pollock's, and other evidence, is in dispute. The painting, as of this writing, is on sale in a Toronto gallery for $50 million. Knowledge is the key to success in this business, the bread and butter of the trade. Charlene James-Duguid, who led Smithsonian's expedition to Brimfield, concluded, "Without knowledge you cannot make a living or enjoy the passion of collecting." But luck is an enormous factor, too. Luck is what makes this life exciting. Avery hasn't had his big hit yet, not in fifteen years and 234,621 miles. But the possibility is always there. Could be next week. Could be never. Could be today.

When I ask all three dealers to name their biggest loss, their biggest "gaffe," silence falls for a few seconds. "We don't talk about that," Avery says, and they laugh. Later, Avery tells me about a syrup jug, "an extremely rare thing," that he bought for a dollar. "I thought it was a $3,500 object. I thought it was the Holy Grail. It was so worn out. It was hard to believe it wasn't real." I ask him how he learned it was fake. He says he looked online and saw some guy was manufacturing the jugs. "Even Sotheby's gets fooled," he says.

STANDING IN the North Field after the rush, waiting for five o'clock when dealers can tear down their booths, is like sailing through dead water. This is when the "housewives" show up, people looking for something to fill a corner, to match a sofa, or something they've seen in *Martha Stewart Living*, a curio shelf, a wooden tool box. An authentic tool box from the nineteenth century would cost a couple hundred dollars. Cheap reproductions can be had for twenty. Sometimes the "housewives" are willing to pay for real antiques. Avery always takes time to educate, to cultivate someone's interest. It's a gift he offers, this bit of history. By telling its story, he infuses a "thing" with meaning. What meaning can be attached to objects from Walmart, manufactured by sweat shop workers? Two writers, Joshua Glenn and Rob Walker, hired people to write backstories for "junk" they bought from thrift stores. Once these trinkets had a history and a story, albeit fictitious, they sold on eBay for many times the original price. A Russian doll they bought for $3 sold for $193 with a story attached. "We sold $128.74 worth of insignificant doodads for $3,612.51," Glenn said. "There really is something hardwired in us to want things to be meaningful."

An old wooden "trencher" like the one in Avery's booth, which looks like a miniature dugout canoe, becomes almost magical when you know that it was hand-carved, that it graced the table of a farmer two hundred years ago, that the paint leached into the wood was cow or goat milk tinted with dyes from crushed insects or plants, purchased from a dye peddler. If we know how to interpret objects, to hear the stories they tell, we become connected to them, affected by them. As Avery says of a two-hundred-year-old corner cupboard in his house, "I get a warm feeling every time I walk by it."

But most of these late afternoon shoppers only want "the look," as Avery says. Pier 1 or IKEA will do for them, or here at Brimfield, the reproductions in the booths outside these gated shows. These fringe booths are filled with old-looking brand-new objects, distressed tables and benches. In these booths, antiques are manufactured on the spot. Spice cabinets with "Olde English" stenciling, imported from China, left out in the rain to age. Reproductions, or "repros." It's a dirty word among antiques dealers, for good reason. Repros can kill a category as quick as a blight. Serious buyers get nervous if they can't discern the real from the ersatz. "The South American and African imports have killed the market for Native American and tribal stuff," Avery says. "Guys like me are afraid to get involved. Every time I see a beaded thing it could be Mexican or Brazilian." Reproductions transform "rare" and "unique" into common and cheap.

FIVE O'CLOCK FINALLY ARRIVES with an announcement that the show is over. If the weather doesn't do you in, then the packing and un-packing will kill you. It's like moving the contents of a small apartment over and over, wrapping and unwrapping the same objects as if you were stuck in that movie *Groundhog Day*, emptying boxes out of the back of the truck in the morning, packing it up at night, unpacking the next morning.

If the packing doesn't kill you, the sleeping arrangements might. Some dealers have comfy-looking trailers, with tiny kitchens and cushiony fold-out beds. (Many appear to be retirees, for whom flea marketing is a hobby to earn extra cash.) Avery, like many dealers, sleeps in his truck to save expenses, but more important, to guard his precious cargo. Except tonight his truck is packed full. So when we finish loading his truck at 10:00 P.M., the last ones on the field, we erect tents along the fence. The night is sultry, and after tossing and turning in the stale air inside my tent, I decide to spread my sleeping bag on the ground. Outside, the cool air is wonderful, but the mosquitoes are swarming like the people at Avery's table today. I coat myself with Cutter, using it like hairspray, or perfume, and collapse into a fitful sleep just as I hear birds singing. I doze for an hour before Avery wakes me at 6:00 A.M. on Wednesday. It's time to shop.

CHAPTER 4

An Antiques Dealer Is Made

Growing up, Curt Avery had a paper route, played Little League, and in high school was on the wrestling team. But like many 1970s teens, myself included, he strayed from the straight path. "Here's a quote from my geometry teacher," he says. "'Curt, fat, dumb, and lazy is no way to go through life.'"

"You weren't fat," I say. Avery's high school photo shows a skinny boy with a nimbus of curly black hair.

"The teacher was trying to illustrate a point," he says, "like, I need to try harder. It was a zinger, though. I still wonder, was I that bad?"

Avery has a zest for adventure, and a kinetic energy now channeled into his vocation, but as a teenager, he expended it on reckless high jinks. One night he came home after partying, hopped bareback on his sister's pony, and raced around the yard. The confused creature made a mad dash for the shed, Avery clinging to its mane. The horse balked and threw him "ass over teakettle" into the side of the barn. Fed up with his wildness, his parents locked him out of the house. "I was doing all this bad stuff every night of the week," he recalls. "My parents didn't want anything to do with me. I was a hellion. I didn't listen to them. I was belligerent." He doesn't blame his parents. "I deserved it," he says. He stayed at Ken Hartwell's house for a while, then with another friend, then ended up in a local dive, renting a room for forty bucks a week. "It was a dump, this big yellow building with all these tiny rooms the size of bathrooms," he says. "I could almost reach out and touch the walls. It had a bed, a shitty chair. It was bad, real bad." Avery was nineteen and living in a flophouse. "It was a low point of my life, but there were a few points like that back then. It was like, 'What am I doing with my life?'"

Avery worked for a local moving company, hitchhiking into Boston to attend college. In the winter, work slowed. "I was getting like fifteen hours a week, just enough to pay the rent, eat peanut butter and jelly sandwiches. Buy beer, first and foremost. I was a mess." One day, his childhood friend, Dennis, said he could get Avery a job with a moving company out in California, so Avery packed up and left. He didn't even tell his parents. "We weren't really speaking. I was a fuckup," he says. He'd intended to stay in California for a couple weeks, but six months passed. "I was living with four guys in Hermosa Beach. It's near Rancho Palos Verdes, which is where Farrah Fawcett lived." He laughs. "I was always hoping to get *that* moving job." In California, Avery says, "There was drugs and booze and rock and roll. You could get just about anything out there in 1980. You ever see that movie, *Blow*, with Johnny Depp? It's a little along the lines of my life."

Avery returned to Massachusetts for his girlfriend's father's funeral. "If her father had not died, I don't know what would have happened," he says. "I might have stayed in California forever, just lollygagged along." Back east, he "somehow" reenrolled in college at the University of Massachusetts in Amherst, two hours from his hometown. His story has that hazy quality, connections missing. One November weekend home from college, Avery and his friend stole his sister's license plates and attached them to Avery's unregistered car. "First we went swimming in the ocean," he remembers. "I put my wet underwear on the antenna." Under the banner of the frozen boxers, they drove crazily down narrow country roads until, inevitably, Avery lost control and plowed through a stand of trees, dead-stopping at a stone wall, one of those ubiquitous property boundaries in Massachusetts' woods. The impact knocked two of Avery's teeth through his lip. He remembers trying to reverse the car but going nowhere, not realizing that the car was hung up on the wall. The crash happened on a town line, so cops from both towns responded, arguing over who would arrest them. Then an ambulance came and took Avery to a nearby hospital in a third town, Hull, where they patched him up. Avery thought he'd escaped arrest, and would tiptoe out of the hospital scot-free, but upon his release, he was greeted by Hull cops. There was a warrant out for his arrest for a bar fight in that town. "I spent the night shivering in a jail cell," he says. When his parents arrived at five in the morning to pick him up, he said to them, "I can't believe you drove all the way to Amherst." Avery had forgotten he'd left Amherst, two hours away, and was now in Hull. "They just shook their heads," he says.

In spite of his recklessness, Avery earned a bachelor's degree in bio-chemistry with grades good enough to be accepted into Yale Medical School's physician's assistant program. He declined to attend, more out of an inability to decide than any strong conviction, but he found a job as a chemist with an environmental cleanup outfit. "A company would send in a drum of sulfuric acid, used to polish metal, for example," he says. "I would do a pH test and make sure the drum wasn't labeled wrong. It was kind of a simple label, but you couldn't afford to make a mistake." It's hard to envision Avery in white hazmat gear. His antiques-dealer couture of baggy shorts and T-shirt better fits his personality. "They'd stick this vacuum hose into the bunghole of the drum, but there was a lot of spill-age," he says. "There was all this chemicular shit in the pumping station. I used to look at this toxic cloud and say, 'What the fuck am I doing here?'"

After a year, Avery lost the job. "They promoted this less qualified person because he played golf with the boss, and then they tried to move me to the night shift. I was fucking up a lot after work, and they'd heard about it. One day they fired me." After his stint with toxic chemicals, he defaulted to moving furniture, and then he tried to start his own com-pany. He would land a job, rent a U-Haul truck, and tell the customer that his company truck was in the shop. He placed an ad in the newspa-per for "Affordable Moving," but didn't get any calls. Weeks later, when his phone rang and someone asked for Affordable Moving, he said, "Sorry, you have the wrong number." After he'd hung up, he suddenly remembered his ad. Even when he found clients, it was hard to find reliable help. "Once I had to do a three-room moving job by myself," he says. In the end, the venture just didn't work. He was still a decade away from entering the world of antiques.

AS A DEALER, Curt Avery came up from the bottom, literally, from a hole in the ground, bottle digging. "Nobody ever sat me down and taught me," he says. "In ten minutes, someone could have explained to me how to change my life, but nobody did." In contrast, Leigh and Leslie Keno, *Antiques Roadshow* appraisers and the rock stars of the antiques world, seem born to the trade. The Kenos' grandparents were collectors, their parents antiques dealers. As children, the twins camped at Brimfield, shopping by flashlight. "Leigh and I had been selling items on our own from about the age of ten," Leslie wrote. By fourteen, the Kenos set a world auction record for American stoneware (their "first love") when they bought a salt-glazed jug for $3,500. As a student in art history at Hamilton College, Leigh produced a catalogue of the college's Americana collection. Leslie, studying American art at Williams College, catalogued that institution's formerly unresearched collection of antique furniture. The Kenos' book, *Hidden Treasures*, is part memoir—photos of the towheaded six-year-olds at a flea market inspecting a weathervane, as bespectacled adolescents displaying stoneware, and as long-haired teens with yet more jugs and crocks—and part thrill-of-the-hunt stories, at Sotheby's, for example, chasing an eighteenth-century Cadwalader hairy-paw-foot armchair for a world record price of $2.75 million. Leigh came up through the best auction houses, Doyle Galleries and Christie's, and is now president of Keno Auctions. Leslie is vice president of American furniture and decorative arts for Sotheby's in New York, a position he earned at age twenty-six. "Our love of objects is so much a part of our makeup—" Leslie wrote, "our very souls."

But perhaps Avery had the soul of an antiques dealer long before he knew it. "The first antique I ever sold I bought when I was a kid, probably ten or twelve, but I didn't buy it to sell it," he says. "I went to a yard sale at this really old house with my grandpa, and I bought an 1890s bottle for a dime. I sold it for $10 way later in life."

Along with the various jobs he held in his twenties—delivery truck driver, furniture mover—Avery set up once or twice a year at bottle shows. "In the winter, when work was slow, I sold bottles on the side, but I found it hard to make money. Bottles didn't show up enough." One day Ken Hartwell told Avery about Brimfield. "It sounded so strange," Avery says. Hartwell's friend got a job cleaning out an old pharmacy in Boston. "The place was a time capsule," Avery says. "They crammed all this old stuff in the basement. There was a Melvin & Badger bottle, a hex-shaped poison bottle, blue, nice looking. Poison bottles always have ribbing or some texture. In the days before electricity, you didn't want to wake up in the middle of the night, grab the wrong bottle and drink bedbug killer." Hartwell and Avery helped Hartwell's friend sell the booty at Brimfield, where he earned a small fortune.

"So one day I decided to pack up my truck and go to Brimfield myself," Avery says. "Back then, I had extra room in my truck, and it took me fifteen minutes to unload!" He shakes his head. In his twenty-by-twenty plot, he set up a couple of rickety card tables and sold discarded furniture from moving jobs, and bottles and other artifacts he'd dug up, like doll heads. "I sold them by *size*," he says, $5 for the small ones, $15 for the large, unaware that he should have priced them by age, condition, maker, rarity, other qualities. "An open mouth is better than closed in dolls."

"I had a vision of putting stuff on tables and then slowly pricing each item, but as soon as I opened my truck, a small crowd gathered," he says. "At Brimfield, people can smell a fool." The competition grew ugly. A woman asked how much for a lamp font and he quoted her $25. A man behind her—the crowd was three deep by then—shouted, "I'll give you twenty-five!" Since Avery had promised the font to the woman, he honored his price, a principle he abides by still. He learned later that the font—the part of the lamp that holds oil—was Sandwich glass, worth hundreds. "They came and whored me out," he says. "At the end of the day, I made $500. It felt like a fucking million."

AFTER HIS FIRST STINT at Brimfield, Avery took a hiatus for almost ten years. "I didn't see that as a viable way to make a living." Years passed, the decade of his twenties. Avery and Linda married, driving off for their honeymoon in a rented antique car, a classic, cream-colored 1954 Bentley, perhaps a harbinger of Avery's life on the road selling antiques. He became a father to Dylan, then Kristina. On a moving job one day, he met a woman who asked him to help at her auction. "Word got around that I knew how to move furniture without damaging it," he says. He was hired as a runner at other auction houses. "That was a real 'in.' I learned by osmosis, from being around the stuff." Right away, his job as a runner paid off. "The first auction I actually sat in on, there was a Sandwich glass trumpet vase listed as Pairpoint," he says. The auctioneer had described a rare, older Sandwich glass piece as a contemporary piece by the Pairpoint Glass Works. Avery bought the vase for $25 and sold it two weeks later for $1,500. "So then I started going every week, but of course that's the last time *that* ever happened!"

For two years he floated between different auction houses, working a couple nights a week, moving furniture during the day. "The more I was immersed in the antiques world, the more I learned," he says. Being a runner had other benefits. One night when he was working a Rhode Island auction, a tough old guy, Vinnie, whose sidekick "carries a .38 and a big wad of cash," asked him for a favor. "Vinnie approaches me and says"—Avery makes his voice gravelly, like Brando in *The Godfather*— "'Hey kid, put up the sticks.'" Vinnie wanted to bid on a pair of candlesticks, so Avery bumped them to the front of the list. Then Avery tipped Vinnie off to replaced feet on a tiger maple chest. Vinnie remembered the favor. Later, "at a little dirt hole auction house in Rhode Island," Avery bought a nest of three baskets for $65. "When I was walking out, some guy says to me, 'Hey, you know Vinnie here wanted to hit them baskets,' but then Vinnie said, 'No. Let the kid have them.'"

Avery's pay as a runner was a paltry $85 a night, but the real payoff was knowledge. "It was invaluable to see and handle the objects," he says. When he wasn't working auctions, he sat in the audience like it was a classroom. "I spent a year or more sitting through Gustave White Auctions, just learning." Since 1925, Gustave J.S. White Auctioneers have sold the estates of Rhode Island's wealthy blue-blood families. "They always had great stuff, and the customers killed each other," Avery says. "I never bought, but I learned." He quit working as a runner at auctions when he realized he could make more money "sitting in the audience." In the winters, Avery studied auction catalogues, museum publications, books like Wallace Nutting's *Furniture Treasury.* "That's an eye trainer," he says, as is the McKearins' "bible of glass," *Two Hundred Years of American Blown Glass.* "You can make a lot of money once you understand what's going on in that book." And he gleaned tips from established dealers, like Edward, a forty-year veteran in the antiques trade. "He has such esoteric information, it's unbelievable," Avery says. "I learned about sewing balls. Women used to hang them from their aprons, and they'd stick pins and needles in them. Some of them were elaborate, silver, with names engraved." Over time, Avery started to buy and sell things outside the bottle and glass category. Then there was a shift. "One year I made the same money selling antiques as I did moving furniture, and then the next year I made more than twice what I'd made moving furniture. It was like, 'Wow, this is more viable than what I was doing before.' Next thing I knew . . . you realize all of a sudden . . . you're an antique dealer."

IN ANTIQUES, the road from apprentice to journeyman to master is long and expensive. Avery seems to recall every mistake he ever made, perhaps because mistakes cost money. "I sold Edward a yarn-sewn stool," he says. "I completely fucked up on that thing. I sold it to him for $250, and it was worth like $2,000. It's funny I can laugh at that, but that's how you learn." Cost of the lesson: $1,750. Another lesson: "I bought an inkwell for $600, and sold it for $900 to Jimmy," one of Avery's dealer friends. "I proceeded to watch him sell it for $1,700 a few days later, and then that

guy was asking $3,800. I learned what that thing was worth in the end."
Cost of the lesson: $3,500.

Avery has progressed from being the guy sitting at the auction watching the players to one of the players whom others watch. "I used to be
amazed at how people did things, like, 'How do you know that?' Now
I've been transformed into one of those people, where other people are
asking, 'How does he know that?'"And now the math is reversed. Instead
of calculating the cost to gain knowledge, he's calculating the profit from
his knowledge, like the "cracked cup" he spotted in an antiques store for
$35. "Dotware. It's early, like 1690 to 1710. It looks like a tiny drinking
cup, maybe the size of a shot glass. You can barely get your finger in
there, but it's not a child's cup," he says. "A lot of times I'll just flip something like this for $2,000, but this piece was a milestone, a benchmark
piece for me. I wanted to *be somebody* on that piece." He showed the
dotware to Edward, his mentor, the man who bought the yarn-sewn stool
that Avery "fucked up" on. "I just wanted to impress him, to say, 'See?
I've come a long way.'" Edward "flipped out" over the cup. "In all his
years of collecting, he'd never owned a piece of dotware." Edward connected Avery to a collector, who bought the cup for $2,500. Avery was
grateful to Edward for making the connection, but in one sense, he says,
"I lost something in the fact that I didn't sell it myself." In the antiques
world, objects reflect on the dealer. When a high-end dealer or collector
sees that Avery has a rare ceramic piece, it adds to his reputation. But
then there's reality. "First things first. If I get a chance to sell it, I'm going
to sell it."

I ask Avery what categories he's studying lately. "Decoys," he says.
"Decoys are wicked hard." Decoys, "vernacular sculpture" or folk art, can
fetch huge sums. Elmer Crowell, who lived on Cape Cod in the first part
of the twentieth century, was called "the greatest decoy maker of all time."
In 2007, two Elmer Crowell decoys, a pintail drake and a sleeping Canada
goose, sold for $1.1 million each. Avery recently bought a decoy at an
antiques show for a couple hundred dollars. "I don't know what it is
but . . ." he pauses, "it's definitely something." In antiques, there's always
more to learn. Even Leslie Keno, at the top of his game as a vice president

at Sotheby's, admits he's still learning every day. "When I first started, I was naive," Avery says. "I was convinced that the more I educated myself, it would return to me. Now, more and more I can see that categories fall by the wayside, or people only want 'super-best' stuff that's incredibly hard to find," he says. "Maybe someday I'll find the 'super-best.'"

CHAPTER 5

That Good, Good Thing

If the Brimfield flea market were a neighborhood, you'd have mansions next door to single-wide trailers, a mixed demographic. This makes Brimfield an ideal place for a dealer to sell *and* buy, and that's half Avery's mission here, the quest for the "super-best." After waking up damp and musty on the Acres North field Wednesday morning at six, I brush my teeth and splash water on my face, stuff my backpack with notepads, tape recorder, sunscreen, water, my inhaler, sunglasses, everything I need to survive Brimfield's fields of glory. Avery and I grab coffee and walk past a huge barn called the Post Card Ephemera Center, which I think is strange. Ephemera is something that doesn't last, isn't meant for durability, paper goods, yet these collectors are engaged in an effort to oppose time itself, to *keep* a thing designed to discard. Collecting anything, one scholar wrote, is "an effort to transcend the ephemerality of experience." Collecting ephemera is perhaps a redoubled effort to prolong time.

Avery usually shops alone, but when he pairs up with another dealer, they split the aisles—one takes the left side, the other takes the right—to avoid hassles over who spotted what first. He tells me about shopping with his friend Jerry. "I told Jerry that I'd meet him back at the car at noon. Jerry said, 'Aren't we going together?' He thought this was going to be a fun adventure. I go, 'Jerry, I'm here on business.' He didn't understand. I'm on a mission. I got my khakis on, I got my saw-tooth knife,

I'm ready for action. It's like Vietnam. I work alone." Today, I'll try not to get in Avery's way. Since I'm just an observer, a know-nothing, I'm not competing with him.

There are several shows we'll try to cover. We'll kill some time at the New England Motel show, which opens at 6:00 A.M. Then the Heart of the Mart show opens at 9:00 A.M. with over 500 dealers. At noon we'll shop the Hertan's show, a short, intense, five-hour show with 150 dealers. The next day, Thursday, we'll shop the May's field with over 600 dealers, before setting up Thursday night to sell at the weekend J&J show. "It takes years to figure out Brimfield," Avery says. "You have to know where to be on what day."

The New England Motel show is named for a small motel in the center of the field that still operates. "This field has never been kind to me," Avery says. Since people line up at 5:00 A.M. to shop the 300 dealers, our hour-late arrival means the field will probably be "picked like a Christmas chicken." But the lack of urgency means that Avery has time to teach me about objects. "Buy any Boston crock with a fish incision," he says. "If you see Paul Cushman on any ovoid crock, buy it." We move to another table. "This is a trade axe," he says. "When settlers first came over, the Indians had these shaped rocks and they weren't efficient, so we traded iron tomahawks to the Indians. We brought iron from England, and then there was an iron works at Saugus." The Hammersmith Iron Works in Saugus, Massachusetts, began smelting around 1646, using bog iron from nearby wetlands. The owner, John Winthrop, Jr., son of Massachusetts Bay Colony's governor, paid fifty pounds each to ship skilled workers from England. Avery picks up the axe from a table. "Here's an interesting fact about trade axes," he says. "They're 'haft.' The earliest ones were round, and then they figured out to make it flat in the back. If you ever get one with a round 'haft' they are very early, like 1600s." I ask Avery how he could tell the axe blade was not forged in China.

"It's hard to explain," he says. "The metal is pitted. It just looks like this." The fact is that you can't tell unless you've seen many real ones, put in foot-time, conducted your own "field" research. As Avery talks, I worry that I'm cramping his style, cutting into the profitability of his shopping time. We move to the next dealer. "This is a tinderbox," he says. "Inside is a small slate you bang to make a spark. The cover is a little piece of horn or bone. Those are worth like $150 or $250." Avery sets the tinderbox back on the table. "I like metal stuff," he says. "It's so misunderstood. You could put that out for five bucks and it will sit there all day."

What I'm learning from Avery is how much I *don't* know. I have an unrefined eye, and a poor knowledge of history. I seem to lack the necessary intuition for this trade. The objects I pick up are usually fake, worthless, overpriced, or reproductions. I want so badly to *know something*, a piece of arcana. This is the information age, after all. As we walk along, I overhear a man say about a bottle, "I got weak in the knees over that." The weak-kneed guy turns out to be Avery's friend Dave. "Dave is a dealer's dealer," Avery says by way of introduction. "He lets people make some money. Sells it for a profit, but leaves some profit in it for others. There are not too many of those around anymore."

"I'm an anachronism," Dave says. *So's everything here*, I want to add. All of these objects, these tons of things, are out of time. Who needs ember tongs anymore, or sugar snips or bone marrow tools? Avery greets another dealer, a young woman who is looking to buy thirty nineteenth-century portraits for an upscale restaurant. She'll pay between $400 and $800 each; Avery says he'll keep it in mind. He's a regular at Brimfield, and so he greets friends every few minutes, sometimes stopping to chat, which slows down his shopping. "Good luck out there," he says to his dealer friends. He gives me abbreviated bios, the man rumored to be a mobster ("Don't name him or I'll be sleeping with the fishes"), the dealer who socked away a table with wrong legs and brought it out as "right" a year later, dealers who are fair, knowledgeable, auctioneers both crooked and honest, the big players and the up and coming.

At quarter to nine, Avery and I line up for the opening of the Heart of the Mart field, which slopes toward an algae-filmed duck pond, edged with weeping willows. At the less-known back entrance, the line is shorter. As the clock strikes nine, we pay $5, get our hands stamped, and now we're the ones doing that odd race-walk. We look in booth after booth, on table after table. "This booth is a clusterfuck of bad things," Avery says passing by one dealer. "It's almost sinful." About another booth: "This guy right here is an abomination, but you gotta look." Avery is looking for "things that catch the eye." "Picking" the field is an art. You have to take advantage of another dealer's lack of knowledge. Nobody can be an expert in every category.

Avery scans a table, assessing maybe two hundred bottles in less than thirty seconds. I pick up a bottle that looks interesting. "Chinese, repro, total gaffe," he mutters after glancing at it for a tenth of a second. He teaches me his code language for critiquing items when shopping in pairs, developed with his friend Alex, who would pick up an item and ask loudly, "Hey Curt, what do you think of this?" Avery doesn't want to insult a dealer by saying, "It's a fake piece of shit." Instead, if Alex, or now I, ask Avery about something that is worthless or fake, he responds, "Dude, that *rocks*!" At the next table, I pick up a rectangular, loden green ceramic planter marked "Hagar." I purchased similar planters at yard sales, thinking that a maker's mark generally signified a good thing. "Hägar the Horrible," Avery says, invoking the cartoon Viking. "Remember that." It's an effective mnemonic that forever imprints in my mind an important tidbit about anything "Hagar": it *rocks*.

I FOLLOW AVERY for another hour before I'm ready to collapse. Thank God it's overcast and cooler. At 10:00 A.M. we've been at this for four hours, and I'm operating on two hours of sleep. I wait at the picnic tables while Avery continues shopping, sleeping on the pillow of my forearm. I awake not knowing where I am for a moment. Avery and another dealer, Betsy, a short, stout woman in her sixties, join me. Betsy, a thirty-year veteran of the antiques world, is lugging a two-wheeled grocery cart; in any other context she'd look like a bag lady. Betsy tells us she sold a firkin in jade-green milk paint the day before. (A firkin is a wooden tub used for apple butter or cheese. Firkins, pipkins, piggins—containers for grain or butter or pickles, the nineteenth-century equivalent of Tupperware.) Hours later, at the end of the day, Betsy's friend approached her excitedly.

"Look what I found!" he said, and pulled out the very same firkin. "I sold that this morning," Betsy told him. Her friend groaned, knowing he could have had it cheaper.

Avery tells me a similar story. "Years ago I saw an oval bandbox, in early wallpaper with big patterns. It was nice looking, 1840s, with a scene called 'Peep at the Moon.' It showed someone looking through a telescope at the moon. Of course, back then nobody knew what was on the moon, and what this box showed through the telescope, it was funny—the moon almost looked like Florida— palm trees and stuff. I thought it was a really good box, handsome." Avery bought the bandbox for $50. "Edward knows much more about those than I do, but he said, 'It's not for me. They replaced the band.' But I was all excited. I didn't really know the potential. I thought that since Edward didn't want the box, it must not be that good." At the next show, Avery put the box out for $250. "This major buyer came along," he says. "This guy spends hundreds of thousands of dollars a year on antiques. I could tell right away by his interest that the box was much better than what I'd put on it. But you know, I'll sell it to him and that's the end of it. Good luck with it. Well, he sold it to someone else within five minutes, and then I saw it on another table, and then another table, and by the end of that day it had traded hands at least three times."

Later, scanning *Antiques & Fine Art* magazine, I see a photo of the exact "Peep at the Moon" box Avery once owned. These paper-covered boxes were originally used to contain lace collar bands. Avery's box was inspired by a newspaper story, later known as the "great moon hoax of 1835." In order to boost sales, the New York *Sun* fabricated articles about life on the moon, claiming the information was excerpted from a paper by British astronomer Sir John Herschel, who observed through a powerful telescope a "lush jungle inhabited by fantastical creatures and a race of batmen"—furry, winged humanoids ("Verspertilio-homo"). Kory Rogers, a curator at the Shelburne Museum in Vermont, which owns a collection of bandboxes, said, "Evangelical Christians were all excited about proselytizing to the bat-men, but they couldn't figure out how to get to the moon." Besides the Shelburne, bandboxes are housed in the Cooper-

Hewitt National Design Museum in New York City and the Farmers' Museum in Cooperstown, New York. Rogers said he plays a game with his colleagues, naming the one thing they would take from the museum's entire holdings. For him, it's "Peep at the Moon." These boxes—including the one Avery held in his hands and sold for $250—can fetch huge sums. In 2006, an auction record was set for a bandbox: $26,680.

JUST BEFORE NOON, we head over to Hertan's field, the third antique show we'll shop today. Hertan's is a small lot shaded by tall pines, the ground a russet carpet, like a forest in a fairy tale. At Hertan's, dealers are forbidden to unpack until a gong sounds at exactly noon and the crowd rushes in, hundreds of people chaotically circling. We pass the same people four and five times as round and round we go, literally bumping into them. Antiquing as contact sport, almost. At times, I feel as if I should be tethered to Avery like a kindergartener so as not to get swept away in the madding crowd. "You can tell the dealers from the retail crowd," Avery says. "The dealer has that thousand-yard stare."

Avery misses out on a set of Staffordshire cups and saucers in mint condition, only $125. He hovers as another dealer handles them, hoping the man will pass, but his competition knows what he's got and won't let go. Avery hasn't found too much worth buying today. I ask him how often he finds good antiques, how many "hits" per shopping foray. "You just see a pattern," he says. "I might find three things in one week, and nothing for the next three weeks. It's like fishing. The antique gods, they might be smiling on you that day."

At a table we've perused twice already, Avery spots a mochaware mug as it's being lifted out of the box, and buys it for $75. He's seen a similar one sell for $4,000. The lid on this one is cracked, but he thinks he can still get $1,000 for it. Mochaware—a distinct swirly brown-blue-white glazed pottery—is increasingly difficult to find. "Mochaware is highly desirable now," Avery says. "You put a piece out, and it's like putting bait in a fish pond. I did not see a good piece of mocha out here all week." Mochaware is "rare stuff," he says, so rare "you can be mean. If it's worth

$350, put $550. Someone will buy it. They'll get mad, but they'll buy it because nobody else is offering it." One collector even cashed in his retirement funds to buy a piece of mochaware. A representative from the auction house told a reporter that the man "expects a better return on the ceramics."

Avery scans tables as dealers empty boxes, moves on, then circles back to the same table to see what new thing has been brought out, and repeats this circling for hours until all the dealers have finished setting up and there is nothing new, you've seen it all and the field has been churned into butter by all the frenetic chasing, in which case you might quit for the day, except if you are Curt Avery, then you circle one or two more times after all your friends have gone and the dealers are packing up. Avery applies his training as a wrestler to antiquing. He paraphrases the philosophy of his hero, Dan Gable, a 1972 Olympic gold medalist and NCAA wrestling coach, whose University of Iowa team won fifteen titles. "There is no secret, there are no shortcuts," Avery says. "Outlast your opponent. Just do more work than your opponent." He adds, "Wrestling is not for everyone, but maybe it should be. That's the way I feel about antiques."

In this last hour of the Hertan show, after we've circled the field a dozen times, Avery stops to chat with a redheaded man from New York City, who has a stoneware crock on his table priced at $11,000, which seems odd; an object costing the same as a new Toyota Corolla I've been looking at is being sold on a collapsible table in a field as if the man were selling lemonade or fried dough. After shopping for hours, I begin to recognize which antiques are common and which are rare, like mochaware. Everybody has tin candle molds. Everybody has some yellowware or ironstone plates or dough scrapers. "This level stuff is everywhere," Avery says. "You could choke yourself on it." Some items are rare, some are very old, but not all antiques are easy to unload. Trends and desirability are key factors. Something seen in *Martha Stewart Living* can affect the market. Martha Stewart, the arbiter of taste, was the keynote speaker at the Merchandise Mart International Antiques Fair in Chicago in 2009, a top show that boasts one hundred of the world's top dealers.

"Martha Stewart drives a lot of sales," Avery says. "She was really big on yellowware bowls." He mimics Stewart's voice—*"Don't be afraid to use them."*

"Did she say that?" I ask.

"No, I totally made that up."

Avery and I come across a Chippendale dresser. "If they are maple, they can be worth lots of money," he says. "If they are pine, they're not worth much." In colonial America, the pine used for furniture was old growth. In the shade of presettlement forests, a first-growth pine tree formed tight rings, and so the wood was dense. Centuries-old pine can feel as heavy as oak. "There aren't any more pines like that used in furniture," Avery says. "They don't exist." The dresser we see is maple, chin-high, with five drawers, nothing fancy, on sale for $2,500 because it's missing knobs and needs repair. "It's been skinned," Avery says, the paint removed. "Some person will come along and make it right and resell it for $10,000." We move along, leaving behind a potential $7,500 profit.

AFTER ELEVEN HOURS of shopping on Wednesday, we drive two hours to Avery's house for a bed and shower, and so he can see his family. But we're up at dawn on Thursday for the drive back to Brimfield, and the opening day of the May's Field show, with over six hundred dealers. (Hertan's is open on Thursday, too, but after the first mad day there's nothing left but "smoke and bones," Avery says.) Avery's strategy for May's is to stand across the street from the gate rather than tack on to the queue snaking down the sidewalk. When the gate opens at 9:00 A.M., we'll rush across the street and be ahead of that long line. A small crowd shares this strategy. Cops brush people back off the street. Avery and I make a plan in case we are separated. I don't want to slow him down. Speed makes the difference between finding the gems or losing them to other pickers. In the next ten minutes, I'll witness Avery arrive at a booth five seconds too late and miss a potential $1,000 profit on a pewter charger priced at $75.

A bell sounds and the crowd rushes across the street. Quickly we are stuck in a protoplasm of humans. All parts of me are being touched by bodies. Things are tight but orderly, until two men exchange harsh words about pushing. They settle down, thankfully—one has the sense that a brawl could erupt with slight provocation—and we are carried by the forward motion of the mob through a Z-shaped entrance and spit onto the field. Avery walks quickly toward the back, moving like a humming-bird from flower to flower, zipping, hovering, zipping to the next table. As we pass by a huge booth that seems promising for its sheer size, Avery says, "That guy hasn't had anything interesting in twenty years." Still, he *must* look. Nothing. (Even with this poor track record, the next year Avery finds a bottle there for $40 that he sells for $1,500. Persistence pays.)

The dealers are forbidden to unload until the bell rings, when the buyers are let loose in the field like the running of the bulls at Pamplona. As he had done at Hertan's the day before, Avery used the same strategy: circle and circle, stopping to check items as they are unloaded, moving along, circling back to the same tables, around and around and around. Avery spots a redware pipkin as the dealer pulls it out of a box and buys it for $250 before the piece hits the table. He'll "double up" on that. Next he finds a wooden desktop box from 1929, with an applied star design, a piece of folk art for which he pays $300. "There's a fine line between junk and really good folk art," he says. He'll try $800, but will settle for $600.

As we make rounds, I recognize tramp art, geometrically carved boxes and mirror frames from the mid-nineteenth century, whittled out of dis-carded cigar boxes by hobos. It was illegal for merchants to use a cigar box more than once, so this wood was plentiful. In one booth are two taxidermied passenger pigeons, beautiful, scarlet-eyed birds under a glass dome, on sale for $6,000. I wish I could rescue them, but it's far too late. Once numbering up to five billion birds, the last passenger pigeon in the world, "Martha," died in the Cincinnati Zoo in 1914.

As we shop, Avery passes lesser objects. "I'm not here for that," he tells himself. If he spends his time on a jug or bottle on which he can make $50, then he's not dedicating his time to items on which he earns $200 or $500 or $1,000 or more. In this business, time *is* money. At Brimfield,

Curt says, "The high-end dealers don't come up here. They send their boys with cell phones." Avery continually strives to improve his merchandise and his clientele. He sells directly to collectors, but also to dealers who run boutique shops where you dare not sneeze. "My job is to find the stuff for 50 percent of what it's worth, sell it to them for 70 percent," he says. "If it's a real good thing, they'll give me 85 percent because it makes them look good and they have a new fresh good thing. The trick is now to find that good, good thing."

As he points to underpriced, low-ticket objects, he repeats, "That's not what I'm here for." It must be hard for Avery to walk by hundred-dollar bills in the form of crocks or plates or toothpick holders. "Sometimes I feel like a cheesy little dealer buying stupid steins," he says. "I should be above that. It's hard to break old habits." In *Objects of Desire*, Thatcher Freund's tale of top-tier antiques dealers in the 1980s, he writes of the self-discipline needed. "When a man bought and sold things worth tens of thousands of dollars, he had to discipline himself *not* to buy a candle stand for $350, even when he knew he could sell it at $1500. If he wanted to be a great dealer, he had to have great things."

As Avery points out the lesser things, I purchase a few, courageously willing to part with $5 for something worth $50. Avery and I come upon a booth at which a lady has just started to unload merchandise from her minivan. It's not a "booth" per se, just a blanket on the ground on which she's strewn objects. The woman is an anomaly, arriving hours after the gate opens. Her prices are low for the field—she's tagged everything between $1 and $5. As the woman empties her van, we hang around like hyenas creeping closer to the downed zebra. I see an interesting reticulated bowl, with decorative bumps that are beautiful and ugly—if they were on a body they'd be boils; they look like tiny volcanoes. I buy it for $2. "Good eye," Avery says. (Later, I research the maker's mark, a crown and "mark of Pompeyi." I find a similar bowl on eBay for $75 and feel triumphant!) Avery buys a cruddy tin thing for $1 that I'd picked up and put back down, a nineteenth-century match strike worth about $100. He points to an old advertising crock, says to me, "Buy this." I buy it for $5, no questions asked. (The next day at his booth at the J&J show, the crock sells for $30. Avery hands me the money, and like a junkie, I'm hooked on my first taste of profit—even though I did nothing to earn it.)

After we've circled the field, we circle again. Dealers are still unpacking. Avery finds a heavy, wide-rimmed pewter plate for $150 that the dealer just pulled from a box. He likes what he hears from the seller. "I just got it at auction yesterday, haven't had time to research it. Could be a sleeper." A rim as wide as this on a pewter plate could mean "very early." Americans ate off pewter plates, and wooden trenchers or "treen" (wooden dinnerware), before the heyday of cheap, imported china in the late eighteenth century. Next, Avery patiently stands behind a woman picking through a display of blue glass. She buys two or three pieces and walks off. Avery steps up to look. He scratches the handle of a creamer, holds it up to the sun, pings the glass, runs his fingertip over the lip. He stares and stares at the creamer, and finally buys it for $475. As we walk away he says, "The lady in front of me bought all the wrong things." The English glass, not the more desirable American pieces. "Thank God for lack of knowledge," he says.

After shopping until 3:30 P.M., we rest at a picnic table. Avery takes the creamer out of his backpack. It's Stiegel type, from the eighteenth century. In the mid-1700s, he explains, Baron von Stiegel ran an iron furnace in Pennsylvania, and then started a glass factory. "In the 1930s, these were rare museum pieces and very desirable. Collectors were begging for these," he says. High demand always leads to a proliferation of fakes. Avery shows me how to discern a fake. He mimes the slight kiss of the creamer against a tea cup when you pour cream. "There is a gentle wear pattern on the spout, but not on the other parts of the rim. On fakes, the wear pattern is too even," he says. He turns his creamer over and inspects the bottom. "In fakes, they put too deep scratches in them, and the scratches go all in one direction." He imitates some guy rubbing a creamer on a surface while watching television. "On the bottom, there should be wear at places the bowl hits the table, not in the middle or all over." To test the wear pattern, you sprinkle powder on a table and place the vase on it. The powder shows the spots where the creamer naturally touches the table. "There's stuff in the pontil that takes time to get there," hundreds of years. The pontil is the scab where the blower broke off the piece from the blowpipe. He holds the creamer up to the light. "Striations in the glass are normally bad, but could be good in this case. It may make the glass attributable," he says. Striations generally indicate Mexican, but not always.

He tucks the creamer into his backpack, and we walk to his truck. It's time to join the line of cars waiting to set up on the J&J field for tomorrow's show. After scouring four antiques shows for seventeen hours over two days, after checking out hundreds of booths and seeing ten thousand things, Avery has bought a handful of objects to resell. I'm beginning to see how hard it is, even with years of knowledge and near-masochistic effort, to find that "good, good thing."

CHAPTER 6

Everything Rich and Strange

If half the challenge is finding that good thing, the other half is selling it. Antiques dealers depend on collectors and vice versa, at best a happy symbiotic relationship. Luckily, there are a lot of people who collect. Fully one third of North Americans define themselves as "collectors." In one study, over 60 percent of American households reported having at least one collection. As soon as humans had a relationship with objects, it seems, we began to gather and organize—to collect. Anthropologists trace the earliest evidence of collecting to an eighty-thousand-year-old cave in France, where they found a cache of "interesting" pebbles. Archaeologists have found collections of objects in ancient burial mounds dating back five thousand years, and throughout the ages: stone axes, amber pieces, copper and bronze tools, weapons, iron implements, gold, coins, and jewelry. In just one auxiliary room in King Tut's fourteenth-century B.C.E. tomb, archaeologists found four bedsteads, a papyrus rush-work garden chair, footstools, a cabinet with gilt knobs, a faience decorated hatbox that still contained a linen hat sewn with lapis lazuli, carnelian, and feldspar beads, and the toy box of the boy king filled with ivory game boards, mechanical toys, slings, archery gear. "The young Tut ankh Amen must have been an amateur collector of walking-sticks and staves," wrote Howard Carter, who uncovered the tomb in 1922, "for here . . . we found a great number."

Collections have been found in Persian tombs from the fifth century B.C.E., and ancient Greeks housed collections of art and treasures in temples. Individuals, families, and town councils collected during the Roman empire. Caius Verres, governor of Sicily in 73 B.C.E., committed murder to acquire statues and precious metals for his enormous collection. (The philosopher and politician Cicero, himself a collector, called Verres's appetite for collecting "maniacal and violent.") During the Middle Ages, ordinary Europeans owned the bare necessities—clothes, rudimentary furniture, cookware. Collecting treasures was the domain of the Church, particularly the acquisition of relics, pieces of saints, and holy objects thought to have the power to perform miracles: splinters from Christ's cross, milk from the Virgin Mary, pieces of Moses's staff.

In the early fifteenth century, the Medici dynasty heralded a shift in collecting from church reliquaries to "studiolos"—private studies designed for retreat, filled with books, art, and precious objects. Cosimo de' Medici used his banking fortune to build a vast collection of art, books, musical instruments, silver and gold objects, tapestries, leather goods. His son Piero the Gouty (he was crippled by arthritis), continued the collecting tradition. Servants carried Piero into his galleries, where, according to Florentine architect Antonio Filarete, he relished discussing the "powers and excellencies" of his objects—his favorite was, allegedly, a unicorn horn (in fact a narwhal tusk). Piero's son Lorenzo the Magnificent inherited and expanded the family collection with paintings, sculptures, and oddities like bezoars, "stones" found in the digestive tracts of goats and other ruminants (generally hardened hairballs), thought to have magical and healing properties.

Throughout the Age of Discovery, from the 1500s to the 1700s, collectors sought to capture the riches of the unfurling world. With advances in science—like the microscope in 1590 and the telescope in 1608—the human vista extended inward and outward. Innovations in engineering and navigation spurred travel, which inspired collecting, as did improvements in printing; published travel stories excited readers with tales of exotic lands. The various bits and oddments assembled in a collection presented a mosaic image: the strange new world could be seen, or at least imagined. As Philipp Blom wrote in *To Have and to Hold*, "dragons and mermaids, armadillos and blowfish, Indian headgear and Eskimo shoes all pointed to a world bigger than had been known." The rise of capitalism spread wealth, which fueled the collecting phenomenon; eventually ordinary people could display the magnificence of the world at home in a *Wunderkammer*, a cabinet for things of wonder.

IN THE SIXTEENTH CENTURY, King Philip II of Spain collected over 7,000 objects, including 144 human heads, 306 arms and legs, thousands of bones and body parts, along with original works of art by Titian and Hieronymus Bosch, among others. His nephew Prince Rudolf, who in 1575 became the Holy Roman Emperor, bested his uncle's collection by inviting artists, craftsmen, and alchemists to his castle to create things, a sort of preemptive collecting. Rudolf hired agents to collect exotica from around the world and ship the objects to his castle in Prague. He built a separate *Kunstkammer* (chamber for art objects), with thirty-seven cabinets to house some of his collection, categorized into works of man—Islamic art, Chinese porcelain, books, musical instruments, clocks, telescopes, compasses, arms and armor, astrolabes (an early sextant-like instrument)—and works of nature—unicorn horns, mandrakes (etymologically *man* and *dragon*, the root was thought to resemble a human), and the supposed jaw of a siren from Odysseus's journey.

In the early 1600s, the duke of Buckingham hired John Tradescant the Elder, a horticulturist, to hunt for treasures. Tradescant issued to various captains and seamen a shopping list of things the duke "desyred," including, "River horsses head of the Bigest kind that can be gotten" and "All sorts of Shining Stones or of Any Strang Shapes." The last item on the duke's list: "Anything that Is Strang." (This criterion hasn't changed. In Curt Avery's words, "Weird is good.") In his travels, Tradescant amassed his own collection, and he and his son created an "Ark" that housed, among other objects, a stone chip from John the Baptist's tomb, a bracelet made of thighs of Indian flies, blood that rained on the Isle of Wight, a hat band fashioned from snake bones, a coat made of fish guts. He collected the hands of a mermaid and a mummy, a splinter of wood from Christ's cross, two ribs of a whale, an ape's head, cheese, a circumcision tool used by Jews, girdles worn by Turks, and a robe worn by the "King of Virginia." After John the Younger's death in 1662, the objects formed the collection of the Ashmolean Museum at Oxford, thought to be the first museum.

In the early 1700s, Dr. Frederik Ruysch, a Dutch anatomist who invented an embalming technique, built one of the oddest collections in Europe—a panoply of human bodies and organs. Ruysch conducted dissections on dead criminals, or drowning victims (the streets were dark and it was easy to fall into a canal) in a *theatrum anatomicum*, where the wealthy paid for stage-side seats. Dr. Ruysch also secured from midwives the dead bodies of infants, which he preserved in jars. Tsar Peter the Great of Russia purchased Ruysch's entire collection, relocated it to St. Petersburg, and one-upped it by collecting a live body, Foma the Dwarf, born with two digits on each of his hands and feet. Peter also "collected" teeth, sometimes yanking them from the mouths of his visitors, and "not always because they needed to come out." Remnants of Peter's collection—"two headed mutant foetuses and odd body parts"—survive today in St. Petersburg's Museum of Anthropology and Ethnography.

Humans make order out of chaos. Beyond collecting the riches and exotica of the world, one then had to organize the bounty. The habits of collectors shifted from amassing beautiful and strange things to taxonomizing. Charles Willson Peale, an artist and inventor from Philadelphia, collected plant and animal specimens, but just one of each, no duplicates. He turned his home into a museum in 1784 to exhibit his 4,000 insects, 1,600 taxidermied birds, 90 species of mammals, and a complete mastodon skeleton he helped uncover from a site in Newburgh, New York.

In America, founders like Thomas Jefferson collected, but collecting didn't take hold among the general population until the mid-to-late nineteenth century. During the Civil War, the Sanitary Commission held "sanitary fairs" as fund-raisers for the wounded, with displays of antiques from America's colonial period—spinning wheels and teapots and pewter plates. Celebrations of the country's centennial in 1876 featured old-time artifacts and antiques. The centennial was a "turning point in America's appreciation of the past," wrote historian Briann Greenfield in *Out of the Attic*.

After the industrial revolution, when goods were cranked out on assembly lines and machine-made, people became nostalgic for old-fashioned craftsmanship. Victorian arbiters of taste condemned the flood of shoddy, factory-made products. Art critic Charles Locke Eastlake's book *Hints on Household Taste in Furniture, Upholstery, and Other Details* was reprinted eight times, and published in America in 1874. "[D]istinguishing good from bad design in familiar objects of domestic life is a faculty which most educated people—and women especially—conceive that they possess," Eastlake wrote, but, he lamented, "this very quality is commonly deficient" among the "generally ignorant" as well as the "most educated." The cause was taken up in 1878 by Clarence Cook in *The House Beautiful: Essays on Beds and Tables, Stools and Candlesticks*.

The first half of the twentieth century "saw the invention of antiques as aesthetic objects," writes Greenfield. During the antiques "craze" in the 1920s, average people with a passion for "antiqueering" sought American arts, crafts, furniture, and artifacts. Museum exhibits fostered collectors' interests, like the Metropolitan Museum of Art's exhibit of American decorative arts in 1909, and the opening of its American Wing in 1924. Upscale department stores like Jordan Marsh, Wanamaker's, and Lord & Taylor had "antique departments." *The Magazine Antiques*, still in print today, was founded in January 1922, the same year that the Association of Antique Dealers was formed in Boston. The magazine's editor, Homer Eaton Keyes, in his inaugural letter to readers, wrote of the "courage" and "foolhardiness" of launching a magazine on antiques "into a super-modern world." One of the first antique shops known was opened in 1890 by Fred Bishop Tuck in Exeter, New Hampshire. In Boston in 1904, there were three antique shops listed in a business directory, but by 1924, there were forty-seven.

In this heyday of collecting, wealthy American robber barons—like the Medicis and the royalty of Europe before them—collected to demonstrate their vast fortunes. J. Pierpont Morgan, who collected stamps, coins, and autographs as a boy, used his inheritance from his banker father, and his own fortune from investments, to buy entire collections, acquiring European art and artifacts—Leonardo da Vinci's notebooks, Catherine the Great's snuff box, Shakespeare's first folios, Napoleon's watch. At his death in 1913, Morgan's collection was valued at sixty million. William Randolph Hearst, who also collected stamps and coins in childhood, spent $50 million on art for his mansion in California, employing a staff of thirty to steward his collection. He, too, raided the palaces and monasteries of Europe, a practice which troubled some Europeans. "Fleets of ships weekly cross the Atlantic to the states laden with our old-time treasures," worried British social critic Charles Edward Jerningham in his 1911 book on collecting, *The Bargain Book*. "[O]ur finest estates are one by one falling into the hands of American owners." To the new millionaires of America, Jerningham worried, "everything is for sale." These "moguls"—Morgan, Hearst, Mellon, Rockefeller, and their ilk, Philipp Blom wrote, "seemed set on denuding Europe of its treasures."

Collecting antiques has been cyclical in twentieth-century America, dropping off during the Depression, and booming in the 1960s and 1970s, when another wave of wealthy Americans loaded their mansions with antiques. At Princeton in the late 1930s, Malcolm Forbes spent "most of my monthly college allowance for eighteen months" on a card written by Lincoln to Edwin Stanton, secretary of war, requesting flags for Lincoln's son, Tad, to wave from the White House at a parade celebrating the South's surrender at Appomattox. Over the next five decades, Forbes and his children built a massive collection, overseen by five full-time curators. "Each collection is alive," Forbes wrote in 1989. Just the letters, manuscripts, and documents from the Forbes collection sold in 2002 for $20,069,990. The 1970s and "shows like Brimfield" were "the golden age of antiquing," Leigh Keno wrote in his memoir. "[I]t felt like a new frontier." Curt Avery recalls this revival. "There was a time, like in the seventies, when antiques were hugely popular," he says. "Brimfield was rockin'— even into the eighties."

The 1990s was called "the decade of collecting" by a former director of collectibles at Christie's, and Harry Rinker, who hosted the cable show *Collector Inspector*, noted that prior to eBay in 1995, there were fewer than 1,500 categories of collectibles. Post-eBay, Rinker wrote, "that number exceeds 30,000 and continues to grow." Even so, the interest in collecting antiques has waned. Wesley Swanson, a dealer for thirty years, said, "The antiques trade was really hot twenty years ago. It's to the point now where everything—unless they are spectacular items—is fifty cents on the dollar compared to five years ago." Swanson continued, "There was a day in the trade where you could go to an auction and fill your van and within two weeks have everything sold." *Back in the day*—a refrain I heard from many veteran dealers.

Still, when Avery sets up to sell at the J&J Antique show, the premier show of Brimfield, his booth will be filled with a few hundred good antiques, and his heart filled with hope that the collectors will come out to buy. A salesman "is got to dream," as Arthur Miller poignantly wrote, especially a traveling one like Avery. It comes with the territory.

CHAPTER 7

Ovoid Nuts and Southern Belles

On Thursday, after shopping all day, at 4:00 P.M. Avery and I join the caravan of some six hundred trucks and vans and campers waiting to set up for the J&J show, the "original and largest" show of Brimfield, a "premier" antique show. In 2010, Brimfield topped *Country Living* magazine's list of "America's Best Antique Shows"—and J&J is the best of the best. The dealers' contracts state, "No reproductions on the field." The J&J show, which runs all day Friday and Saturday, began in 1959 when auctioneer Gordon Reid, "the father of all Brimfield antique shows," organized a show in his backyard. Now his two daughters, Judy and Jill, run the show. The original house is on site, cordoned off and posted "NO TRESPASSING." The field doesn't open for setup until 7:00 P.M., but if you don't get in line early, by the time you get onto the field, you'll be unloading till dawn, which is when the show opens, 6:00 A.M.

So for two hours, Avery and I have a tailgate picnic with fried chicken and potato salad. At 7:00 P.M., the line of cars crawls toward the gate. Inside, we drive over to the back left corner, Avery's spot for over a decade, between Joan Christianson, a dealer in her late fifties, and Tucker Small. It's useful to have friends nearby to spell you for bathroom runs. We set up the tent methodically, attach poles, fasten the tarpaulin roof with bungee cords. We move silently, efficiently, purposefully; we have but an hour or two of light. We erect Avery's plywood and sawhorse tables, his shelves and glass cases, and load them with "merch."

As the sky darkens, shoppers occasionally shine flashlights on Avery's wares. "In the old days, there were a wicked lot of night shoppers," he says. "I used to make six or eight sales while I was setting up. When that happens, you're off to a wicked start. Now, it's sad." In recent years, show organizers have cracked down on night shopping. To enforce the no-preshow-buying policy, a man patrols in a golf cart. There's a rumor tonight that someone was thrown off the field for early buying. Around 11:00 P.M., we tuck the tables inside, roll down the tent flaps, and secure them with crime-deterrent bungee cords. On this field surrounded by a chain link fence, patrolled by an old guy in a golf cart, millions of dollars' worth of antiques are secured by large rubber bands and plastic sheeting.

Wired from the work, Avery and I stroll the aisles, surreptitiously flashlight-shop, say hello to his friends. By 1:00 A.M., I beg off and return to my tent at the back of the field along the chain link fence, as far as I can get from the booths and the sodium lights. I toss and turn on the hard ground. My neighbors in their Winnebego run their generator for air conditioning on this humid July night, their exhaust vents six feet from my tent. In the near distance the *clink clink clink* of hammers on tent stakes echoes throughout the night.

AT 5:00 A.M., my alarm goes off and I dress, use the running water in the dealers' changing area, and the freshly cleaned Porta-Potties. Sipping scalding, watery coffee from the concession stand, we unfasten bungee cords and roll up the dew-covered tent walls, wipe moisture off glass cases, price items. Charcoal underbellies of clouds threaten rain. A sticky heat rises already. "The weatherman is the natural enemy of the antique dealer," Avery says. Weather can "crush" a show, "too wet or too hot," he says. "When you hear cicadas at six A.M., it's a wicked bad sign. You know it's going to be ninety-eight degrees." Heat stress, which Avery has never suffered, "took out" two of his workers, me and his son, Dylan, in different years, but at the same one-day July show on Cape Cod. (On the way home that day, Avery had to stop the truck periodically so I could vomit, which did not stop him from enjoying Chinese takeout, duck sauce set in the ashtray.) Wind is a danger, too. At Brimfield one year, the dealer next to Avery neglected to stake his tent. "He had fifty-five chandeliers hanging from the ceiling," Avery recalls. "When the wind knocked the tent over, it sounded like a plane crash."

At 6:00 A.M., the crowd rolls in thickly. Avery makes a sale within ten minutes, $2,500 for an eighteenth-century, clipper-ship-decorated tin snuff box. Then it pours and all movement, all commerce stops as two inches of rain fall in half an hour; we can judge by the water accumulated in the Pairpoint vases on Avery's tables. We are standing in puddles. The cardboard boxes stored under the tables are soaked. Our fingers are pruned. The rain stops as suddenly as it started, and people come out from under the tents and squish through puddles. I see Joel, the cast-iron collector. A woman from New York picks up a few things for her cottage, a brass pitcher and wash basin, two majolica plates, candlesticks. She writes a check for $600. A pair of six-inch-tall Staffordshire dog figurines sell for $225. Avery found them in a consignment shop for $35. "They were in there for a month," he says. "A group shop where the inside people buy everything." For every deal like the Staffordshire dogs, Avery has twenty objects he cannot sell or hasn't sold yet that he must lug to five more shows before they sell, if they ever do, or before he relegates them to a box in his basement or garage or other room in his house, which have been slowly filling up, like his truck, beyond capacity.

The day before, Avery bought a couple dozen blue poison bottles for $450 from Tucker, who is going through a divorce and is selling his collection. Tucker says he's getting out of the sideline of antiques. (When I see him a year later at a show, I say to Avery, "I thought Tucker was quitting the antiques business." Avery says, "It's like the mafia. You can't get out. We're all lifers.") Avery is helping Tucker by purchasing the poisons, which he'll piece out, but he's inadvertently taking advantage of Tucker's misfortune. That's the nature of this business. People sell heirlooms or collections or valuable objects in times of divorce, death, financial woe, illness. Tragedy or bad luck or mishaps can be the catalysts for a flood of merchandise into the market. The chairman of "one of the world's largest auction houses" allegedly perused the London *Times* obituaries for leads to estates.

Two men examine Avery's matte green Weller umbrella stand in mint condition. "Look at the form," one says. "The form is fabulous." Avery's asking $1,995. They admire, but they don't buy. A beefy, older man with a thick, vaguely Mediterranean accent sidles up to Avery. "Want to buy an eight-thousand-year-old statue? I brought it from Italy." This looks shady, the sotto voce offer, the rough-looking man. Avery shakes his head politely. "I wouldn't know anything about it. Try something from two hundred years ago." Two curators from a small museum in Connecticut are searching for late-nineteenth-century objects to complete a display. Most of Avery's merchandise is too early, but he takes their business cards just in case.

A pair of caricature blond-and-pretty southern belles are browsing in the booth. They stand out, dressed to the nines, mascaraed for a posh party. They are buyers for the catalog arm of *Southern Living* magazine, a direct-sales network called Southern Living at Home. The founder, Dianne Mooney, invites potential home party hosts to "rejuvenate your spirit" by becoming a "consultant," which can "broaden your perspective and take you to places you may never have imagined possible." The *Southern Living* outfit is unabashed about being reproductionists. The catalog copy reads, "On a trip to the prestigious auction houses of New York City, we came across a set of antique English serving pieces that were the essence of style and sophistication—we knew we had to bring the look to you." *The look.* The dreaded "look." Mooney writes, "We've taken great care to re-create that classic style . . . using modern materials to offer you the look and feel of treasured antiques at a fraction of the cost." I've heard dealers lament "the look" repeatedly. People who might have purchased antiques are now satisfied with reproductions. They don't want the substantive object, the unique, the real, but are happy with something that on the surface looks like an antique. Cubic zirconium instead of diamonds. Urns and vases in the *Southern Living* catalog are "antique inspired" or "modeled after an eighteenth-century French urn." Their rooster candelabra is "skillfully crafted after a French antique." An "Americana Wall Bucket" has a "distress, antique style." The catalog is targeted at specific strata of middle- to upper-middle-class women who desire "sassy" wall sconces and artist-designed Bunko sets to "wow your Bunko buddies."

The *Southern Living* buyers spend a good half hour in Avery's booth, looking for "the look." He seems to enjoy tutoring them—it doesn't hurt that they add a sheen of glamour to this rustic setting. His attention pays off. They buy a lemonade server and a pewter coffee urn, both from the 1800s, which they will use as prototypes for reproduction in some Chinese factory, they tell me, which will then be sold through the catalog. When they leave, I ask Avery if he feels bad selling to these buyers and thereby contributing to the flood of reproductions, the demise of the antiques trade, for what amounts to about a $300 profit. He shrugs. He can't stop the process. They'll just buy something from the next guy. "I've got a family to feed," he says. Months later, unbeknownst to Avery, his wife, Linda, will be invited to a *Southern Living* home party, where out of pathological politeness (and the unspoken requirement to buy something at these "parties") she feels obligated to purchase some over-priced cheaply made faux antique, not appreciating the irony until she mentions to Avery that her purchase has completed the very cycle of ersatz mass-produced reproductions that is killing his livelihood.

On Friday, the show runs until 5:00 P.M., an eleven-hour shift, which seems inhumane, especially when the dealers were setting up their booths into the wee hours that morning. At dinner, Curt and Tucker give me a lesson in surfaces, the difference between a "crusty" surface and an "attic" surface. Tucker, newly single, flirts aggressively, the sort of old-fashioned male chauvinism that might otherwise annoy me, but he applies it so democratically I can't help but feel a weird admiration for his effort. He flirts with the sixty-five-year-old waitress as energetically as the twenty-year-old. "Tucker is a lover, not a fighter," Avery says.

SATURDAY IS RETAIL DAY. Nobody expects much in the way of sales, but dealers are obligated to stay until the end. The show opens a bit later, 9:00 A.M. We can sleep in and still have time to shop another show in a building on the Acres North field. On the top shelf of a glass case in one booth, Avery spots a small scrimshaw or ivory cup, incised with a flag and eagle decoration, a tortoise shell bottom. "That's fucking great," he says. "A killer small." The piece is from the 1700s. The dealer, a short, bald man, perhaps seventy-five, tells Avery it's been in his collection for years. He just decided to bring it out for this show. Avery asks if he can carry the cup outside to inspect it in the sunlight. He studies the cup with a magnifying glass for twenty minutes. "I thought it may be bone, but I don't see any veins," he says. "It's a lot of money, but it's a lot of piece." Back inside, he hands the dealer $1,000 just as another man shows up and asks for the cup. This is the third time the other man has been by to see the cup, but now he's too late. He congratulates Avery on his purchase, which for now Avery will tuck in his collection, part of his retirement plan.

Back at the J&J show, the action is slow but steady until noon, when we hit dead water. "Once the seriousness stops, it's marble time," Avery says. "It's half-past marble time." Big fat old clay marbles, an inch in diameter, a whole box of them he hadn't bothered to put out. He decides to conduct an experiment and price them at $1 each. Many people run their fingers through the marbles, pick them up, admire the colors. They are an attention getter, a lure for customers to check out the booth. But nobody buys a single marble for a buck.

In the afternoon, dealers are cranky from lack of sleep, and from the "retail" crowd. I feel a bit sheepish because the Saturday crowds are filled with people like me, those who can't really afford antiques, but are here just to look. Two women come into Avery's booth and pick up a pair of clear-glass lamps. They talk about how lovely the lamps will look, and they hold them this way and that. Avery explains that they are a rare form of eighteenth-century whale oil lamps. There is a trace of congealed grease in the fonts, perhaps spermaceti, the waxy substance from the heads of sperm whales, the most expensive and cleanest burning oil. In the late 1700s, hoping to increase imports of spermaceti to England for street lamps, John Adams claimed that the oil would "burn bright till nine o'clock of the morning, and chase away, before the watchman, all the villains." The whale oil lamps are one of the most romantic objects I've seen in Avery's booth, evoking our prepetroleum, pre-Edison history, the thrill and devastation of the whale hunt, *Moby-Dick* and Captain Ahab. Whales and oil and light: the inspiration for literature, the simple human need to lengthen the darkening day. The shimmering glow from whale oil street lamps may have banished London's criminals two hundred years ago, but it's the price of the lamps today that chases these women away. When Avery quotes $695, they audibly gasp, and hasten out of the booth.

I overhear people on the J&J field talking into cell phones: "I'm on the expensive field," and another person, "Everything here is outrageously overpriced." The flea-market setup juxtaposed with pricey antiques confuses some people. Avery has a huge, mint-condition spongeware pitcher, valued at about $750, but priced to sell at $350. A woman picks up the pitcher, asks, "Can you do any better?" Avery responds, "It doesn't *get* any better." He drops his price, but not enough. Avery reminisces about Brimfield in the good old days, a habitual conversation among veteran dealers. "There was a guy who walked through the booth today, he's an ovoid nut," he says. "He'll buy any pear-shaped jug with a name on it that he doesn't already have. He's a really nice guy. Here's the problem—at Brimfield years ago, you'd have twenty fucking guys like that."

Sydney, a diminutive man in his late fifties, talks shop with Avery. He was a teacher who spent summers selling antiques. "I've been interested in antiques since I was twelve," he says, "but seriously into it as a sideline for thirty years." Sydney taught a course on antiques to prisoners, how to run a small business. Teaching the antiques trade to people who might have questionable ethics could be risky. In 1981, pottery pieces supposedly made by renowned British potter Bernard Leach were sold in London for thousands through Christie's, Sotheby's, Phillips, Bonhams. The bowls and dishes were made by prisoners in a ceramics class, who used Leach's primer, *A Potter's Book*, to mimic form, glaze, and Leach's signature. Like Leach, they even left thumbprints on the pots. In his book, Leach wrote, "I have tried to formulate a criterion by which good pots may be judged." It appears he succeeded. A spokesperson for Bonhams admitted the fake Leach pieces were "excellent." A Christie's expert called them "marvelous." Prison authorities were "delighted" that the inmates were so enthusiastic about their new hobby.

An attractive forty-something redheaded woman asks Avery about his antique coffee grinders. He spends twenty minutes talking to her. In the end, she doesn't buy a coffee grinder, but now she knows. A man named Jeff Bell, who's writing a book on bells, looks at Avery's two old bells. He explains that the ringing of bells signaled a death, nine rings for a man, six for a woman, three for a child—and every ring after indicated the age of the deceased. One of Avery's bells is pre-1880. "The top has been replaced," Bell says. "It's a Chatham bell"—he can tell by the bands carved into the wood.

Two women, both dealers, talk to Avery about marbles as they pick through a box of small ones, more valuable than the dollar clunkers. They buy a few good examples. A minute after they leave, Avery remembers another box of marbles in his truck. He grabs the box and jogs down the aisle shouting, "Marble girls! Marble girls!" Despite his effort, no sale.

Saturday afternoon is 90 degrees, a misery of heat and humidity. One dealer is stretched out in a rectangle of shade underneath his table, dozing like a dog. I drive to the store and buy five bags of ice. Later, we dump the melting ice on the grass and walk barefoot over it, the opposite of walking on hot coals. Avery takes a half-melted bag of ice and hangs it from a tarp he's rigged from his truck to the booth, a shade canopy for sitting. He stabs the bag with his pocket knife, and sticks his head under the icy flow. "A Brimfield shower," he says.

In the last slow half hour before we pack up and roll out of town, Avery with $13,000 in his pocket from two shows, we cruise around the field. We stop to say hello to a dealer who shows Avery a pie cabinet he bought for $250 that morning and just sold for $750. "It was right there all week," the guy says. Avery looks over the cabinet, makes some small talk. After we leave, he says, "It's a fake." He can tell by the process they used to stain the wood. But neither the dealer nor the buyer discerned this. "The biggest hint is that it was still there after five days on the field. With so many knowing eyes passing over it, if it was real it would have been gone." Honest ignorance, he calls this phenomenon, unavoidable in the antiques trade as dealers are at different stages of learning. What's more insidious, more perilous—perhaps the single greatest threat to the antiques trade—is the opposite of "honest ignorance": dishonest knowledge.

All Sad Things Are Just Like This

Dylan and Scotty were just going over their cruet collection when they decided to climb some trees . . . Dylan bumped into a chihuahua named Tiny who was running to tell the police that there was an evil antique dealer who stole other people's antiques. The boys told Tiny that they would capture the evil antique dealer . . . They were going to put a granite-ware milk jug on top of a fishing net. Then they would hide behind the trees. . . . They saw the thief walking down the road. He saw the jug and went to grab it. They pulled up the net and caught the thief. Then they took him to the police, and he was never heard from again.

The Evil Antique Dealer by Dylan Avery

Avery's son wrote this undoubtedly one-of-a-kind story in fourth grade. In spite of the satisfying ending, it's not so easy to catch an antiques thief. In 2007, in broad daylight, a "middle-aged couple, he of stocky build" stole an original 1638 Rembrandt etching from a Chicago art gallery. As of this writing, the culprits were "never heard from again." Neither were the thieves who during daytime hours walked off with $100,000 worth of Chinese jade from the Victoria and Albert Museum in London in

2004. A month later, thieves boldly grabbed fifteen pieces of important Meissen porcelain, worth $4,000 each, from the same museum. Across town that year, crooks brazenly helped themselves to priceless Chinese jewelry from the British Museum. Mostly, though, antiques are "stolen" through forgery. By one account, forgeries and thefts of art and antiques ranks fourth in worldwide criminal activities, behind drugs, guns, and money laundering. The FBI tracks major art theft and forgery, but in the vast middle range of the antiques world, there's little policing.

After reproductions, fakes are the greatest threat to the viability of the antiques trade. Fakers, Curt Avery says, "have fucked up the antique world almost permanently." Fakes bother him, a lot. "Everyone is crossing over to the dark side," he says. "I don't know what to do about it." In *The Inferno*, Dante reserved a "dark side" in his schematic of hell—the tenth chasm of the eighth ring, close to Satan himself—for "falsifiers of all sorts," including forgers, alchemists, and counterfeiters.

As long as there has been art, antiques, and valuable objects, it seems, there have been fakers. In 670 B.C.E., forgers molded coins from base metals and gilded them to look like solid gold. At the height of the Roman empire, when collecting—and thus forgery—flourished, silver cups carried a provenance as belonging to Achilles, clothing to Odysseus. Even Michelangelo, as a young apprentice, painted a Ghirlandaio, smoked the canvas to add age, and passed it off as authentic. Fakes were so prominent in seventeenth-century Chinese markets that the poet Shao Changheng was inspired to write a verse called "Bogus Antiques." He wrote of "Sutra papers" aged by "smoking," and "patination" created with "chemicals." His final stanza:

> How many authentic antiques can there be?
> No wonder the market is filled with forgeries.
> Trust your ears and ignore what you see—
> All sad things in the world are just like this.

Religious relics were widely faked for centuries. One dupe was the Roman Catholic Diocese of Montreal, which in 1885 owned the largest cathedral in North America, but did not own a single relic. "There was not a saint's bone of any kind in the whole diocese and not even the smallest splinter of the True Cross," reported *The New York Times*. To remedy this, the bishop purchased the bones of St. Claudius and St. Juliana, "second-class saints," but still able to perform "easy" miracles. "The authenticity of these relics," the *Times* reported, was "attested" by "a certificate purporting to be signed by the Pope." But after four years and no miracles, the bishop ordered an investigation, which revealed that the pope's certificate had been forged.

Around 1710, the Royal Porcelain Manufactory in Meissen, Germany, near Dresden, cracked the secret to making fine porcelain, or "china," long held by Chinese and Japanese potters. Soon after, forgers began to make copies, so by 1723 all Meissen wares bore a mark to distinguish the real from the fakes. In 1896, goldsmith Israel Rouchomovski from Odessa, Russia, crafted a solid gold tiara from an ancient design found in a textbook, and sold the tiara as a replica to an antiques dealer for $1,000. The dealer concocted a story that the tiara was a gift to the Scythian king Saitaphernes, who lived in 200 B.C.E., and sold it to the Louvre for $50,000. (Louvre officials reportedly ignored critics' suspicions that the tiara was too well preserved.)

Even Israel Sack, the legendary top New York City antiques dealer during the antiques craze of the 1920s, who sold to the Fords and du Ponts, started out as a cabinet maker in a shop that faked antiques. Sack was the shop's "greatest concocter," he wrote, fabricating "monstrosities" that sold in high-end antique shops. In 1970, the Henry Ford Museum in Dearborn, Michigan, paid $9,000 for a Pilgrim-century "Brewster chair," an ornate, squarish, thronelike thing replete with spindles, said to be associated with William Brewster, a founder of Massachusetts Bay Colony. The creator of the chair, Armand LaMontagne, an ex–Rhode Island state cop and a sculptor whose works are in the Baseball and Basketball halls of fame, claimed to have made the fake chair to fool experts. After LaMontagne gave the chair away, an antiques dealer "stumbled" upon it in a house in Maine, bought it, sold it to another dealer, who sold it to the museum, where it resides today as an object lesson. The Winterthur Museum has 180 such object lessons, acquisitions discovered to be fake (among 85,000 artifacts in their collection), which they displayed in 1997 in their exhibit "Deceit, Deception, and Discovery." Dwight P. Lanmon, physicist turned art historian and curator at Winterthur in the 1970s, first questioned some of the museum's glass pieces, and analyzed them with a Kevex X-ray machine, developed for the aerospace program in the 1960s. He found that the glass lacked impurities typical of nineteenth-century glass.

British artist Eric Hebborn sold over one thousand "old master" drawings—Corot, Brueghel, Piranesi—to collectors and venerable institutions, like the National Gallery in Washington, D.C., and the British Library. After he was caught, Hebborn wrote *The Art Forger's Handbook*, in which he cheekily encouraged artists to "forge ahead." His primer is filled with recipes for concocting old paints and inks, instructions for aging surfaces ("stout, coffee, tea, chicory and liquorice" are useful for tinting paper), techniques for making feather quills and for creating "fox marks" (moisture damage). "In England in 1562," Hebborn wrote, "the forging of a signature was punishable by being pilloried, having one's ears cut off, one's nose slit up, one's land forfeited and life imprisonment." After 1634, forgers were sentenced to death. As recently as the late eighteenth century, counterfeiters in Massachusetts had their ears cut off, and forgers' ears were cropped; both were pilloried. Hebborn himself did not fare well in the end. His book was published posthumously in 1997, the year after his "mysterious death," the book jacket reads. Hebborn was found in a Rome square bludgeoned, his killers never caught. Like Dylan Avery's antique thief, Hebborn "was never heard from again."

Some fakers benefit from their crimes even after being caught. British artist John Myatt created over 240 fake paintings by Chagall, Braque, Giacometti, and other artists, which were sold through vaunted auction houses, high-end galleries, and reputable dealers. The scam succeeded not because of Myatt's technical expertise, but because the mastermind, a suave con man named John Drewe, was adept at faking provenance. Both went to prison, Drewe for four years, Myatt for four months. After prison, Myatt's career flourished. He painted imitations of famous works that sold for mid-five-figure prices, the canvases indelibly marked with his business name, "Genuine Fakes."

AT A SHOW ONCE, Avery said to a customer about a ceramic teapot, "It's very early, 1700s. It's an honest piece." Indeed objects can be "honest" or they can lie. "It's mind-blowing," Avery says about the proliferation of fakes. "I saw this guy—I have to leave him nameless—who found pieces of furniture with the wrong feet. He suppressed it for about six years, and now it has come back on the market as a 'new discovery' and now with unquestionably 'right' feet." Dealers have asked Avery to appraise a piece, but when the assessment was not happy news, they "mothballed" the object, and brought it out later for sale, "priced as real," Avery says, "as if the conversation never happened." A dealer showed Avery an early American jug that he thought lacked the proper wear. He said he wouldn't pay $750 for it. The next time he saw the jug it was at a "major auction house" and "suddenly had the proper wear." The jug sold for about $25,000, to "one of the finest collections in the country," he says.

In these times of Ponzi schemes, rigged profits, corporate greed, and in a largely unregulated realm like flea markets and antiques where compromise can be highly profitable, Avery's ethical stance is itself almost antique. Avery gives a wide berth to dealers he doesn't respect. "There's a handful of people I would stand behind in this business," he says. "I'd like to organize a show with ten handpicked dealers based on their credibility. Everybody would know the stuff was authentic." At the Winter Antiques Show at the Armory in New York, a top venue, some 140 experts vet the objects—many of which bear six- or seven-figure price tags—for "quality, authenticity, and condition." The object is removed if it doesn't meet the show's standards.

Fakes can kill a category—quickly. "The oriental rug market is dead right now," Avery says. He blames those dealers who misrepresent merchandise. Cheap cotton rugs can be chemically treated or ironed to look like highly prized silk. Machine-made rugs can be passed off as hand-loomed, or artificially distressed to look "antique." When this happens and buyers lose confidence, the market becomes a field of "land mines" and it "tanks," Avery says. "Everybody was buying 'country' for a while, paying a lot of money for it, and then they starting faking the paint. Then everybody was scared of paint, so natural surface stuff was all the rage. It's incredible. I used to hear, 'Yeah, it's all right, but it'd be nice if it had some paint on it.' Now everybody wants this natural stuff. The fakes have driven people to think this way." Fakes can drive down prices on real antiques. "It's amazing the difference in what people will pay for the same exact stuff once they see it has been put away in a museum since 1927," Avery says. "Northeast Auctions sold some early lighting—a chandelier with a replaced cup—that they'd gotten from the Currier Museum in New Hampshire, with a label showing the museum collection number. Normally I could buy that for $1,800, but it went for $9,000 because of the provenance. It shows how strong this early stuff would be if there weren't assholes out there making fakes. It ruins people's confidence."

Fakes can be premeditated acts of crime, or the result of a dealer's "honest ignorance." At a high-end antique show, Avery witnessed a wealthy collector buying a yarn winder. The only problem was that the collector thought he was buying an early lighting device, not a yarn winder. "It was a yarn winder that somebody made into early lighting," Avery says. "Old spinning wheels and yarn winders have early turnings. You can buy a yarn winder for $50, and you can buy a spinning wheel for $150, and you can make three $10,000 early lighting devices if you're willing to do that, and they do." He continues, "This dealer had this piece of shit—it was really obvious. You can tell it's a yarn winder because the pole comes up and then comes in and it's much skinnier. If you see that, you know it was a yarn winder, a *nothing* thing. I saw it preshow, and thought, *too bad this isn't real.*"

Like the thin blue line protecting crooked or feckless cops, there's a thin brown line in the antiques world, a code of silence. Buyers are on their own. "This dealer has been doing this for decades," Avery says. "Who else are you going to put your confidence in? Just because you have been doing this a long time doesn't mean you know what you are doing. Some of these guys never picked up a book in their life. And this dealer could talk the ears off a brass monkey. Everything in that booth looks old. It's a perfect recipe for disaster."

THE CATALOG for the British Museum's exhibit "Fake? The Art of Deception," which showcased more than six hundred fakes they acquired unknowingly, notes that as examples of the "wayward talents of . . . gifted rogues," fakes "claim our reluctant admiration." A statement from Artfake.net, a nonprofit educational site, reads: "Many of us share a secret admiration for the faker, despite the hurt and loss that their deceptions have caused. . . . Of the best remain the quiet ones, those fakers who succeed and will continue to do so, undiscovered and anonymous. . . . But surely we admire them most of all for their sheer genius."

One of the "quiet ones," a genius of his craft, is Wesley Swanson. As you might expect of an antique lover, Swanson lives in an old house with beamed ceilings, foot-wide floorboards that slope toward narrow doorways, gorgeous six-over-six wood frame windows. Swanson gestures for me to sit at the gate-leg table in his kitchen. I pull out a chair—an armless Windsor—that he says is worth $5,000. I silently pray the chair doesn't give out today after two hundred years, but then again, if it did, Swanson could fix it up in no time. "I am a restorer," he says, "one of the best around. I've been a restorer for thirty-six years."

Swanson has noble features, a fine straight nose, hazel eyes. His smooth skin belies his sixty-one years; he looks fifteen years younger. His complexion seems almost burnished, as if he'd used fine 220-grit sandpaper from his workshop on his face. He offers me a cup of tea, and sets the kettle boiling. Swanson started out teaching wood shop in high school, but then, he says, "Antique dealers found out I was a good cabinet maker. It's hard to find anybody who's good at fixing antiques." His voice is soft, and rarely fluctuates—the sort of steadiness you'd expect from his hand as well. When he first began restoring antiques, he charged three dollars an hour, the same amount he earned teaching. "It didn't take me long to figure out that I could buy the thing myself, fix it, get my labor and the profit. And that is why you are sitting on a chair that is worth $5,000 next to a 1680 to 1720 table." Restoring antiques is fine; not informing buyers about the restoration is crossing over to the dark side. Swanson repairs porcelain and ceramics ("redware is very hard—I have a special ingredient I add to the surface") and "any kind of furniture," like a candle stand he "did a finish job on," which sold at auction for $23,000. But mostly, he admits, "It's on the Windsor chairs that I make money."

MILLIONS OF PEOPLE BECAME acquainted with Windsor chairs in *The Patriot*, set in South Carolina in 1776, in which Mel Gibson's character, Benjamin Martin, puts the finishing touches on a Windsor rocking chair in his workshop. Martin sits in the chair for ten seconds and then it collapses beneath him. He hurls the broken chair into a messy pile of other fractured Windsors, meant to convey, it seems, how difficult it is to craft a Windsor chair. Windsors, it is believed, originated at Windsor Castle in England in the early 1700s. English aristocrats sat in Windsor chairs in gardens or set them in boats. A 1739 drawing by Jacques Rigaud, *View of the Queens Theatre from the Rotunda*, depicts a man and a woman at Stowe Gardens, Buckinghamshire, sitting in comb-back Windsors mounted on trolleys, pushed along by servants. The first recorded reference to a Windsor chair in the colonies was in the 1708 estate inventory of John Jones of Philadelphia, a center of Windsor chair making. (By 1790, Philadelphia craftsmen had exported over 6,000 Windsor chairs to other colonies and the West Indies.) At the Pennsylvania Historical Society, a painting of Congress voting for independence on July 4, 1776, shows Ben Franklin in a Windsor chair. And supposedly Jefferson penned parts of the Declaration of Independence from the oldest known example of a swivel Windsor chair.

The Philadelphia makers set the standard for quality in Windsors. An 1820s ad for a New Jersey maker claimed his Windsors were "equal to those made in Philadelphia." Philadelphia is where the "writing arm" Windsor was invented, a chair with a desk-arm, and sometimes a drawer under the seat to store paper, inks, quills, and sand shakers. Emerson wrote on a Windsor writing-arm chair at the Concord Antiquarian Society, where he went to write "without molestation," Wallace Nutting wrote in his 1917 book, *Windsor Chairs: An Illustrated Handbook*. History has proved the Windsor's "stick and socket" design durable. "A well-made Windsor, though light," Nutting wrote, "was far more rigid than the Jacobean chairs, which, however handsome, mostly have broken, and those that remain are treacherously weak." In America, chair makers used pine or poplar for the seats, hardwoods like maple or oak for stretchers and legs, and flexible woods like ash, hickory, beech, or birch for the swooping "continuous" arm backs. Paint concealed the mixed woods. Black paint was a "most excellent finish," Nutting wrote, as it covered "a multitude of sins."

LIKE ALL MASTER DECEIVERS, Wesley Swanson must want to be appreciated. It must be frustrating to be so good and yet unrecognized. But to stand in the spotlight of fame, and win begrudging admiration, fakers must be caught. Swanson's "restored" antiques are so good that in three decades they have never aroused suspicion. "There are only two people that I know of—there are probably more, but only two I know—who are that good," Swanson says. "Are you one?" I ask. He nods and smiles. "I'm the 'go to' man. When you think there is no way it can be done, and it's impossible, then I get the job." Like in the mafia, he's the fixer, the man who solves the problems. "I hose the thing," he says. "If there is a problem with a piece, I make it go away."

Swanson has a "don't ask, don't tell" policy on his bastardized antiques. He keeps his hands clean, in a manner, working behind the scenes, putting his restored pieces through auction houses. "I don't handle it directly," he says. "I have somebody else take it over for me, and they have enough clout so that they can get sweetheart deals. To be in that situation, you have to be quite well established. It has to be a high-end chair to bring it to me." His "associates" are fully aware of the restoration. "I had a guy come down to look at a chair. He offered $7,500. I said

to him, 'I cannot tell you that I did *not* make it.' He still wanted it,"
Swanson says, "even though that's like telling him I made it. I made the
whole thing."

Swanson has a code of honor, a set of ethics. "We don't ever take ad-
vantage of collectors. We only sell it through an auction where there is
no guarantee. My group of associates would never misrepresent a piece to
a retail person." Art forger Eric Hebborn, whose fakes fooled the National Gallery in Washington, D.C., and the British Museum, expressed
a similar ethic of selling his fakes only to "experts." Armand LaMontagne, whose Brewster chair fooled the Henry Ford Museum in Detroit,
created his 100 percent fake chair purposely to thumb his nose at experts
who "think they are infallible." The prisoners who sold fake Leach pottery told a reporter that they "could not stop laughing" at fooling the
experts. "My stuff goes through major galleries," Swanson says. "It's
buyer beware, no guarantee." Mark Jones, the curator at the British
Museum who organized their exhibit of fakes, wrote, "Fakes can teach
us many things, most obviously perhaps the fallibility of experts."

It may be less morally reprehensible to leave experts to their wits,
but experts are often buying for collectors. Many antiques dealers, like
Avery, guarantee their merchandise, but expertise is no protection with
Swanson's pieces. "I do things that people don't know can be done," he
says. He has sold "restored" antiques to museums; it's just that, as he says,
"they didn't know it."

"How well do the experts at auction houses inspect objects they accept
for sale?" I ask.

"A furniture expert looks it over," Swanson says. "My friend was all
torqued up because he brought a table that he knew was right, and he
brought a restored chair. They rejected the table and had no problem
with the chair."

Major auction houses have experts, but they also have qualifying statements that leave the burden of proof to the buyer. At many small-to-
midsize houses, goods are sold "as is" with "all sales final." Sotheby's has
an "authenticity guarantee," but the buyer bears the costs of finding mu-

tually acceptable "independent and recognized experts in the field" to prove something is not authentic. Most auction houses have "conditions of sale" stating that "estimates" or "appraisals" are not "facts" but "statements of opinion." As one gallery states, "It is the responsibility of the prospective bidders to examine lots." Curt Avery told me about a bottle that a Boston auction house had estimated at $2,000 to $4,000. He thought the bottle might be worth $10,000, but the lighting in the showroom was poor. ("You don't want to miss a star crack," he said.) He asked an auction employee about their policy guaranteeing the condition of the bottle. "It's a little squishy," the employee said.

TO CREATE FAKE MASTERPIECES, John Myatt learned how to "stand in someone else's shoes." He claimed that he entered into an "empathetic trance" while painting. Swanson's work takes the same intensity and focus. "You have to live with a piece for a while," he says. "You must bond with the piece and put your mind to where that other cabinet maker who has been dead for two hundred and fifty years, bond with his spirit," a reincarnation of both the maker and the object. "You look at the arms and the supports, notice the curves. You think, *how would this long-dead cabinet maker have made the legs?*"

I assumed that Swanson was using old parts to make repairs, hybrids that would be hard to detect, Frankenstein chairs, but he says, "I'm making the parts from brand-new wood." I ask if it takes a long time to age new wood, and his voice tenses. "Everything takes time," he says. I seem to have hit a nerve. "It's not the first ninety percent that makes the job, it's the last ten percent that separates the men from the boys," Swanson continues. "I'm anal retentive. I upset people with my obsession. They always say, 'You are putting in too much time!' I say, 'If you want to get the money, you put in the time.'" He tells me about an "associate" who complained about the time Swanson invests in each piece. "I said to him, 'In thirty years have you ever lost money on anything that I've ever worked on?' The answer is no."

Armand LaMontagne spent two months making his fake Brewster chair. He burned each piece of wood, then removed the char, then bleached it to remove carbon traces, then painted the chair, coated it with a water-glue mixture, covered it with dust, waxed it, smoked it, washed it with salt water and bleach to remove the smoke smell, repeated the entire sequence, created wear to mimic three hundred years of use, and finally dipped it in the ocean. Swanson puts in the time as well. "It takes me ten hours just to splice the legs out because of the way I do it." Because of his foolproof method, his legs are "undetectable," he says.

Swanson has a dozen Windsor chairs throughout his house, each one an object lesson. In a bedroom on the first floor, he points to "the grand-daddy of the fleet." I say, "The oldest?" Swanson looks disappointed. I cannot see subtleties; his exuberance is lost on me. That must be frustrat-ing, casting pearls before swine. I must remind him of his days teaching high school. But he soon recovers his élan. "It's just a more spectacular chair," he says. "See how bold the front posts are?" I point to a part that I realize a second too late is not a "post," but a crossbar. I've never actu-ally *looked* at a chair. Chairs are for sitting. I've never thought of them as works of art, things of beauty. "The front posts," he repeats, "the arm supports," his voice edgy. I nod, yes, bold posts. Swanson moves on. "The legs have really nice detail. I use this little lathe and green wood so it all shrinks, and it all heals right and fits right," he says. "Run your hand around in a circular motion." I dutifully feel the chair leg, not sure what I'm trying to detect. (Avery explains later: "An antique dealer's test is to see if the chair leg is round or oval. The leg will be somewhat green when it's put on and then it dries and shrinks, and then a hundred years goes by and the leg is 'out of round.' If you took a caliper, it would measure less in one direction.")

"Can you feel the oval shape to it?" Swanson asks. "Feel the bottom part. It's going to feel oval, just the way the rest of it is."

I've never been so intimate with furniture, and in Swanson's bedroom, bending down to caress the curvy, sensually smooth legs—of his chair— I'm a little embarrassed. "Now, this is the truth of the matter," he says.

"All four legs are new. The stretchers were from the same maker, but they came out of a different chair. The chair they came out of—I did a Frankenstein job on it—that went through Christie's a long time ago." Since the seat of a Windsor chair is carved from a single, two-inch-thick chunk of wood ("never glued up of two parts," Nutting wrote), I thought it might be difficult to replicate, but Swanson says, "I've made every single part of just about every single kind of chair there is. I've done an $8,000 chair that actually had a brand-new seat."

"Are there problems finding woods?" I ask.

"Chestnut is hard to come by," he says.

In 1904, an Asian fungus infected American chestnut trees. Within fifty years, the disease killed nine million acres of chestnuts from Maine to Georgia. Chestnut wood was lighter than oak, and rot-resistant like cedar. A chestnut tree could grow one hundred feet tall, with ten-foot-round trunks; the lumber from a single tree could fill a railroad car. I mention the blight to Swanson. "You're pretty smart, aren't you?" he says, a bit surprised. "So how the heck do you get antique chestnut? It's worth its weight in silver." He answers his own question. "You find it sometimes as planking from old barns. A guy gave me a piece a week ago."

The "stick and socket" construction of Windsors requires no hardware, but for other furniture, Swanson scavenges antique nails or screws, or artificially ages new hardware. "There's a trick that makes screws look like they've been in wood for a hundred and fifty years," he tells me. "You mix vinegar and salt and you drop it on the screw. In three days it will look like that screw has been in there for over a hundred years. Any place you made a scrape mark with your screwdriver will rust up, and it just looks absolutely, unquestionably right." He learned the vinegar trick from an "old-timer," but he knows someone who urinates on the hardware. "That rusts them pretty quickly."

THE FIRST PLACE to find a telltale sign of repair is the surface. Swanson has experimented with various pigments and processes to achieve undetectable verisimilitude in surfaces. "I'm a surface specialist, one of the best in the United States," he says. "Whether it's a color finish or a painted finish, I can match just about any finish." Swanson mixes his own paints and varnishes, with secret ingredients. "There's no book that tells you how to mix your own shellac-based black pigmented paint. Or what proportion to use," he says. Swanson studies the idiosyncrasies of each chair. "You have to match the color, the texture, and the sheen. The sheen varies on a Windsor because of the way people sit on them," he says. He shows me a "real dandy" of a chair, on which he replaced all four legs and the seat from new wood. "For that chair I had to actually match a Victorian pigmented shellac-based finish. My job was to match the paint on the legs to the rest of the chair. And the seat has been re-colored to match." He stares at the chair for a moment. "It sounds funny when you say the black has to be the same color, but black isn't black. It can be gray-black, black-black. It has to be shiny, but just a sheen more than a shine." ("A brightly shining Windsor is offensive," Nutting wrote.)

I ask if anyone would conduct a paint analysis. "The only thing they sometimes do if a piece is really expensive is they'll X-ray it, and look for splices or cracks." (LaMontagne's Brewster chair was revealed as fake when X-rays showed the pointed tip of a modern drill bit, rather than the spoon-shaped marks of an early brace and auger.) Swanson points to the chair I'm sitting in and says, "Sometimes the repair is so good that nobody would even question the splice on the leg. They wouldn't even bother to X-ray it because they'd think nobody is that good."

As I bend to inspect the chair, I ask which leg is spliced. "All four," he says. "You can study that till the cows come home. Believe me, you are not going to find where it's spliced. I do it in a way that nobody else does. I'm one of the best chair splicers, and you just can't tell." I suspect that the black paint hides the "sins," as Nutting wrote.

"Could you do this with an unpainted surface?" I ask.

"I've got them all over the place," he says, and points to one "in old finish" on which he'd spliced all four legs.

After matching the surface paint or varnish, Swanson must add "wear" to the chair. Especially on the seat, the wear must be perfect. "I know just how to do it," he says. "Use a penetrating dye and a heat gun, and drag it around on concrete. Drag it through the gravel a few times."

Swanson raises the question of guilt before I can ask it. "Someone said, 'Don't you feel guilty?' And I said, 'Well, seeing that no one is ever going to know, and seeing that every time anyone has ever bought anything I've worked on they have always made money, why should I feel guilty? I'm taking a piece that wouldn't have been properly done and bringing it back to a high level of authenticity as far as form.'" His next argument reminds me of the sort of thing my mother used to warn me against—if all the kids were jumping off a cliff, would you jump, too? "These people who walk around in suits with their noses in the air, they claim all their stuff is pure and wonderful," Swanson says. "They'll buy a piece that needs restoration, have somebody really good do the restoration, bury it for a year and then they'll pull it out"—he feigns a snooty air—"'Oh, it just came out of an estate. It's just the way I got it, and it's only $30,000.' It happens all the time, and it happens everywhere," Swanson says. "I can tell you stories about high-end dealers. Why do they need a full-time cabinet maker?"

WALLACE NUTTING WROTE his "little book" on Windsor chairs in 1917 to prevent a "bad revival" of Windsors, but also to help the reader avoid being an "easy mark for a faker." Nutting was a doctor of divinity and a photographer (he employed some two hundred colorists and sold millions of prints), but he loved early furniture. With his fortune from photography, he built a factory to make replicas of the antique furniture he loved. His aim was to "produce the best forms, put together in the finest manner." Unfortunately, unscrupulous dealers bought his reproductions, artificially aged them, and sold them as antiques. Nutting began to burn his name into his period reproductions. Later, he sold his shop, but the new owners grew lax in their standards, so Nutting sold his collection of antiques (to J. P. Morgan, Jr.) and used the proceeds to buy back his business. He lost $100,000, but he could not bear that the shabby work was marked with his name in script. In the new Nutting works, his name was printed "in plain capitals."

Nutting's book *Windsor Chairs* contains photos of over one hundred styles of Windsors: bow back, fan back, comb back, braced back, round back, duck-bill joint turned back, scroll back, and Sheraton square back. There are also Windsor high chairs, rockers, settees, barber's chairs, and "night" chairs—a commode with a cabinet to hide the chamber pot. Nutting rates each chair's "merit." The English double-back arm Windsor "lacks grace" and inspires Nutting's disdain: "Observe how stubby and shapeless the arms are." You get a sense that Nutting takes each chair personally. Of the bow-back, knuckle-arm Windsor, he writes, "The dainty little knuckles are wonderfully attractive." The "final merit" of Windsor chairs, he wrote, is beauty. With simple lines and "unpretentious charm," Windsor chairs, he said, are "dignified."

SWANSON HAS ACHIEVED a level of skill and artistry that very few people have. In one sense, it's a shame that he's not getting more attention for his craft. His dedication is impressive, his work beautiful, even in the service of deception. It's like a Zen koan: if the fake is so good that nobody notices, does it matter? John Myatt felt guilty about faking paintings at first, but later rationalized his acts. "If a collector believed one of his pieces was an authentic Braque," wrote Laney Salisbury and Aly Sujo in *Provenance*, the story of Myatt's fakes, "why spoil the thrill?"

"Sometimes you give them what they want," Swanson says. "They only want the look." He's had to remove *actual* kiln kisses—little flakes original to a ceramic bowl—because people thought it looked like damage. He's taken real, original parts off chairs and replaced them with fake parts because people don't know that sometimes the original design was a stylistic aberration. "This happened about a year ago," he says. "I took the original that was absolutely right, and I looked at it, and said, 'Oh my goodness. No one's going to believe this.' I actually had to doctor it up to make it look right even though it *was* right—you have to give everybody what they want."

Another time, Swanson explained to a dealer that there was no wedge originally in the chair's construction. "Pinning from the side is much stronger than wedging from the bottom. It's a superior way to hold in a front post," he says. "There was no wedge because it never was wedged. The dealer said, 'You know that, and I know that, but somebody is going to flip that chair over and look for that wedge.' So I had to go in there with a hammer and chisel and whack a couple of lines to make it look like it had a wedge." Occasionally, Swanson works his magic not just to restore, but to *improve*. He turned a flat-arm chair into a more valuable knuckle-grip. "The original side pieces fell off," he says. "So I thought, 'Well, if I'm going to have to glue on side pieces, why don't I just add a knuckle and make it into a rolled-grip?' I might as well make it a better chair," he says, "and that's what I did."

Swanson's office is the most modern room in the house with a computer, a stuffed couch, carpet. He points to a brace-back continuous arm Windsor. "See how the arm is shorter? That's so he could get up to the desk. And if you look at that angle"—he touches the back of the chair—"it's very straight. That one is basically honest and honorable."

"You mean one hundred percent real?" I ask.

Swanson is quiet for half a beat. "It had one break I had to repair, and I did some hokeypokey on the break repair." He must mean hocus-pocus, like magic, not hokeypokey, the silly dance, but who knows what he does in his shop, which he does not invite me into—an alchemist turning wood into gold. Swanson shows me another Windsor chair in his office. "Now this one over here will get by most of the world," he says. I envision a line of seven billion people inspecting the chair. "Look at the wear on the arms, the different paint layers. You can see this is an irregular shape instead of being perfectly round." I'm following as he points to various features, not quite grasping the significance. "Well, guess what?" he says. "I replaced the whole bow arm." He pauses for a dramatic beat as I absorb this feat. "And that front post," he says. "And all four legs."

THREE HOURS and a dozen Windsor chairs later, we're back in Swanson's kitchen. "I feel like I'm in the presence of a master craftsman," I say. "You are," he says. "I'm not a ringer. I'm the man." While we are talking, Swanson gently sands a piece of Imari china with 220-grit open-coat aluminum oxide sandpaper. "Now that it's smooth, I'll lay some finish over it. I'll lay it on with a brush. Lay it on heavy and then make it come out really smooth and then be done." I watch him as he quietly, patiently, almost reverently sands the edge of the ceramic vase. "I used to shoot rifles and pistols," he says. "To really be good you have to hold your breath. And when you are working with a very small artist's brush trying to put in little dabbles of color, I actually hold my breath." I ask Swanson if he's ever been found out. He shakes his head. "I bought a chair with another guy for like $400 and I put a new set of legs on it. He balked, and said, 'Everyone is going to know the legs are replaced.' I turned to him and said, 'I've been replacing legs for twenty years and I've never been caught on a set of legs.' We sold it for $2,500."

"You have a pretty good record," I say.

"One hundred percent," he says.

WALLACE NUTTING WAS PROFUSE in his love for Windsor chairs. A Windsor chair, he wrote, was "perhaps more suggestive of pleasant reflections than any other article of furniture." I can't help wondering what Nutting would make of Swanson's restored antiques, whether Nutting's reflections would be "pleasant." No doubt Nutting would admire the masterful craftsmanship, the authentic detail, the care—even love—that Swanson devotes to each piece. Perhaps he'd even forgive Swanson; after all, one of Nutting's own factory reproductions, a child's high chair "regarded for years as an extraordinarily fine Windsor," was displayed as real in the Winterthur Museum. Still, I'd guess that Nutting would cringe at passing off restored antiques as real. Another Nutting sentiment is apt:

"There is nothing more puzzling in human nature than its lapses from the good to the bad, in style as well as in morals."

In *Fake, Fraud, or Genuine?: Identifying Authentic American Antique Furniture*, former curator Myrna Kaye wrote, "You can't always be in the know, but you can always be suspicious," especially at auctions, which, unless you are an expert, are "treacherous territory." That treacherous territory is where I'm headed next.

CHAPTER 9

Hot Potato

On a drizzly, sleety morning, I fight commuter traffic into Boston—15 miles per hour on the four-lane interstate—and pull onto a side street in Cambridge. As I drive past the Hubley auction house, I see Curt Avery and Joan Christianson, who has carpooled with him, peering in the windows of the dark gallery. Typical for Avery, he's first to arrive. By the time I find a parking space on the crowded side streets, the door is open for preview at 8:00 A.M., two hours before the auction starts. Hubley Auctions, a small, family-run business, "is like something out of the 1940s," Avery says. Founded in 1935, F.B. Hubley called itself the "longest running auction gallery serving Greater Boston." Since 1943, it has been run by Robert Cann, ninety, who married Elinor Hubley, and their son, Robert Cann, Jr., who has thinning white hair and pale blue eyes, and a pale complexion, as if he does not get outside much or lacks iron in his blood. Both father and son are dapper with ties and dress shirts, tweed jackets, jutting aristocratic chins.

"Don't base your experience of auctions on this," Avery says. "These guys are old school." At Hubley's, bidders receive white index cards with magic-marker numbers. There's no online bidding, no phone bidding. They shut down the auction at 12:30 regardless of whether the lots have sold. This small, almost hidden auction house used to be Avery's secret. "Due to their connection with Harvard, they get estates," he says. "But they only put a little ad in the Boston paper on Wednesdays. I could buy country antiques for nothing all day long. I bought a Shaker rug for $5, and a set of flow-blue plates for very short money." Flow blue is from the 1830s to 1840s, he explains, "then there's the second generation, Victorian flow blue. This set was Victorian, but I didn't know the pattern. To me, flow blue is flow blue is flow blue." When the first part of the flow blue lot came up, a tureen and two "veggies," large serving dishes, Avery was going to bid up to $800, but won them for $350. "I was like, *wow, you gotta be shitting.*" When the platters came up for sale, he "smoked them," he says, winning them quickly. In the end, he walked away with an eighty-piece set for $1,700. "The first piece sold online for $1,900." He was "out of the lot" with the first sale. ("Out of the lot" is dealer idiom for earning back the money you paid for a box lot; every sale that follows is profit.) "Turned out it was one of the only American patterns," he says, "LaBelle, made in Wheeling, West Virginia."

That was Hubley's in the old days. Then the Canns hired an assistant who modernized the business, placing ads in trade papers, photographing items, and listing objects online. "The jig is up," Avery says. "Now the competition is showing up regularly." Avery goes to about a hundred auctions a year. "In five or ten of them," he says, "it's like shooting fish in a barrel. On that particular night, everything lines up. There are seventeen other auctions going on at the same time, nobody is at this one so there's no competition, and the auctioneer doesn't know his stuff or doesn't care. You can buy all night long."

Today's auction is Part Two of the estate of a rather eccentric man whose sole vocation was collecting. "He used to take taxis to auctions," Avery says. "He was the son of a wealthy Bostonian, kind of an oddball. A lot of trust-funders end up in this world." Now the collector has passed away and his collection is being dispersed. The first half of the auction featured the best items. "People came out of the woodwork," Avery says. "I spent $5,000 at the first auction." Avery is hoping there is something left to buy in the second half today, and that the heavy hitters won't bother showing. "There should be some sleepers among a lot of dirty, crappy shit."

AUCTIONS HAVE an ignominious origin. The first documented auctions, recorded by Herodotus, were conducted around 500 B.C.E. by Babylonians who sold off marriageable women, starting with the most beautiful. For "ugly" or disabled women, their fathers paid buyers to bid. The law even permitted the wife to be returned if the couple was "disagreeable," a money-back guarantee. The Roman emperor Caligula auctioned furniture and ornaments to pay off debt, as did Emperor Marcus Aurelius, who sold furniture in an auction that lasted two months. At the height of the Roman empire, auctions were held on the battlefield immediately after a victory. Auctioneers traveled along with troops, a handy arrangement to divvy the plunder. A soldier would drive his spear into the ground to begin the auction. If there was no auctioneer around, the victors took the spoils of war—including slaves—to an "auctionarium" for sale, where bidding was indicated by a "wink or a nod."

Amsterdam was the auction center of Europe until the early eighteenth century, when the Parisian houses began to dominate. Later, French economic conditions and the French Revolution caused the art-auction scene to shift to England with the opening of Sotheby's, Christie's, and Phillips. Sweden's Stockholms Auktionsverk, founded in 1674, is the oldest continually operating auction house, followed by Sotheby's, which opened its doors on March 11, 1744, with a sale of books. (Prior to this, British auctions were held in public houses, "pubs," and coffeehouses.) James Christie opened his auction house in 1766, and gained renown when he sold Sir Horace Walpole's art collection to Catherine the Great. In 1795, Christie's sold the jewels of Louis XV's mistress, Madame du Barry, after she was beheaded. By 1793, William Charles Bonham established a gallery. After two hundred years of mergers and acquisitions, in 2002, Bonham's purchased the venerable 145-year-old California auction house, Butterfields. As of this writing, Christie's, Sotheby's, and Bonhams & Butterfields are the largest auction houses in the world.

The most reprehensible history of the auction is the selling of human beings. Under Rome's first emperor, Augustus, buyers paid a 2 percent tax on the sale price of slaves, what is now called a "buyer's premium." In colonial America, before the creation of workhouses for the poor, town authorities auctioned male paupers as laborers for life, with proceeds filling the town coffers. The "worthy poor," those who were destitute through no fault of their own (the sick, elderly, or mentally incapacitated who had no family), were auctioned to the lowest bidder—the household that would charge the least amount to the town for their care.

Slavery was abolished in the eighteenth century in Britain and France, but the sale of African slaves continued to thrive in America and the Caribbean. Thomas Jefferson's "130 valuable negroes" were auctioned after his death in 1826. In America, there was a "preview" period, during which buyers could examine slaves for flaws. If the buyer later discovered a "defect," the auctioneer could be held liable for "breach of warranty." The horror and tragedy of human beings sold as chattel is plainly evident in the banality of a poster advertising an auction to be held "under the trees" on May 18, 1829, which lists "male and female slaves, including Robert Bagley, about 20 years old, a good House Servant," along with "fine rice, grain, paddy, books, muslins, needles, pins, ribbons . . . and at one o'clock, that celebrated English horse, Blucher."

In the United States in the first quarter of the 1800s, there was a campaign to abolish "the evils of auction," mainly to deter British merchant ships from dumping goods cheaply on the American market, but also to protest slave auctions. A pamphlet titled *Reasons Why the Present System of Auction Ought to Be Abolished* listed "sale of contraband goods," "gross fraud," "fictitious bidding," and "exaggerated descriptions" that "destroy a regard for the truth," all of which lead to a "deterioration of the morals of mercantile men." Auction supporters refuted these claims: "We contend that in this free and happy republic, every man has a right to be ruined in his own way." Here, here. A similar campaign was launched in England against corrupt auctioneers, "that irresponsible body of men . . . who know no laws or restrictions." Buyers were victims who purchased goods "upon the puffing recommendations" of the auctioneer, the "jug-

gler in chief." Auction houses, including Sotheby's and Christie's, encouraged a "grudging and groveling spirit," a protester wrote, in a class
of people who "ought to be above illiberality and meanness."

I hear the echo of these complaints a hundred years later. I ask Curt
Avery what laws apply to auction houses. "They operate by martial law,"
he says. "Auctioning can be a very dishonest business. That's why so
many auctioneers are rich. A smart dishonest person can make a shitload
of money being an auctioneer." I hear sentiments like this often, though
Avery and other dealers make a point of singling out particular auctioneers or houses for praise. Ken Van Blarcom is "a nice man and very honest," Avery says, as is "Ron Bourgeault of Northeast Auctions," and Carl
Nordblom. Skinner in Boston wins praise. But when not giving auctioneers their due, dealers tell me about "phantom bidders" on the phone, and
"house" numbers, "jumping bids"—calling out a figure higher than the
actual bid, slipping it by when the bidding is fast and furious. Auctioneers
will bid on their own merchandise to drive up the price, or "salt" the sale,
adding lesser items to a noteworthy collection. "Auctioneers are the
dirtiest people I've met in my life," Avery says. (To be fair, dealers have
for centuries formed auction "rings," colluding to illegally suppress or fix
prices, then divvying the goods among themselves later.)

Even Sotheby's and Christie's are not squeaky clean. In 2001, they
were found guilty of price fixing; they colluded to set nonnegotiable
commission rates for sellers, eliminating competition among the houses,
who at the time controlled over 90 percent of the art, jewelry, and furniture auction sales in the world. Each house was fined $256 million. And
Eldred's auction gallery in Massachusetts was sued by the Margaret
Woodbury Strong Museum in Rochester, New York, for the equivalent
of malpractice (in this case, misdiagnosis). In 2000, the museum gave Eldred's a Chinese vase to sell in its Asian arts auction. Eldred's listed the
piece as a "Famille Jaune Porcelain Palace Vase" from the nineteenth
century, which sold for $23,000 to a buyer from Taiwan. Four months
later, the buyer sold the vase through a Hong Kong auction for $1.55
million. Eldred's, the museum charged, failed to accurately appraise the
vase. The Hong Kong auction house described the vase as "A Spectacu-

lar and Very Rare Massive Famille Rose Yellow-Grown Vase," from the Quianong period in the *eighteenth* century. In 2004, the suit was settled out of court; neither side will disclose the details.

In spite of his complaints about auctioneers, Avery sees both sides in the Eldred's case. "Eldred's claims to be Orientalia experts, but the problem with Orientalia is—are you going to be an expert at stuff from seven different countries for a period of three thousand years and everything they made? You can't even do Americana and that's one country and two hundred years."

THE SHOWROOM AT HUBLEY'S has twenty-foot-high ceilings, uneven wood floors overlaid with oriental rugs, and tin ceiling panels. Burgundy velvet curtains close off a back room, as if the building were a theater in its previous life instead of a grocery store. There are shelves and shelves of objects, furniture throughout the showroom, architectural salvage set in the bay windows. A huge taxidermied swordfish mounted on one wall is part of the permanent decor. Hanging from the ceiling is a tin candle lantern, with six arms that spider out. "If that were real, it would be worth $10,000," Avery says.

Avery greets his friend Mitch, who works here as a runner. Mitch is the assistant who advertised the auctions and ruined Avery's well-kept secret. "We're not going to make it through everything, so we'll be taking requests," Mitch says. Buyers are allowed to gather smaller items that they want "put up" and bring them to the front of the room. Avery shows Mitch his hit list, five notepad pages scrawled with call numbers and the price he's willing to pay. His code system is partially designed to thwart people "plagiarizing" him, an age-old dilemma. A mid-nineteenth-century writer described auction bidders surreptitiously writing notes in their catalogs, "looking round to make sure that no one has noticed," and sending teenage "messenger boys" to bid for them. Sir Henry Wellcome, a wealthy pharmaceutical magnate in the early twentieth century, advised his collecting agents to use pseudonyms to "disguise their interests from auctioneers and dealers alike." Wellcome warned his agents "not to wear fine raiment . . . A top hat usually excites the cupidity of the dealer, and the higher the hat the higher the price."

Avery's knowledge can work against him. At auctions he is shadowed; less knowledgeable dealers "ride" him. "Tailgaters" look over his shoulder spying his notes, or chat him up at the coffee stand, sneakily glancing at his catalog to see what he's marked. The tailgaters drive up the price on objects they know little or nothing about except for the fact that Avery wants them, and if Avery is interested, the objects must be good. He tells me about an auction where he was bidding on a trencher. "It had real paint on the bottom," he says. "People thought it was fake, but I had a good feeling about it. I was standing in the back of the room, about to get it for *nothing*, then this woman craned her head around like an owl— she must have had fourteen bones in her neck—she saw I was bidding and she sort of smirked." The woman bid as the auction closed and won the trencher for $175, which Avery valued at $750. A short while later, Avery saw the very same trencher at Brimfield in another dealer's booth. "I bought it for $250," he says, "but that proves she had no idea of its worth because she sold it low enough that someone *else* was selling it for $250."

Once, Avery suspected that a dealer sitting next to him had cribbed off his notes. He'd left his catalog on a chair while helping someone move a piece of furniture. Later, when a box lot of ceramics came up for sale, he noticed the dealer preparing to bid, her "tell"—sitting up a little straighter, tucking her card under her leg. That dealer typically did not sell ceramics. Glancing at her catalog, Avery saw that she'd jotted figures in pencil next to the same lot numbers as his, in the right margin of her book. The rest of her marks from the preview period were in the left margin, in ink. Her penciled-in prices were an increment above Avery's, about $25 more. Avery accused her of plagiarizing. She denied the charge, so he put her to a test. "What is the best thing in this lot?" he asked her. "What's worth *this* amount?" He pointed to a figure she had written in pencil next to the lot number that contained a half dozen different items. She named something in the lot that was worthless. Busted.

One way to thwart competitors is to leave written bids, but this raises other issues. "If you leave a bid that is too high, the auctioneers think the piece is worth something and they may pull it and resell it later or put it in a specialty auction," Avery says. "At Skinner's you can leave a bid. I trust them." Some auction houses, like Hubley's, tag objects for which buyers have left bids, which is "just a red flag for the pirates," Avery says. "They can be blindfolded and stumble on the good stuff. They figure a dealer must have come through so it must be good."

I FOLLOW AVERY AROUND for an hour and a half during the preview. "You always hope for something esoteric that only you know about," he says. On one shelf is a "killer" sewing box, Japanese lacquered, filled with hand-carved ivory notions—spools, needle cases, thimbles. Next to that is a linsey-woolsey, a blanket hand-spun from linen and wool. "This thing looks like a moving blanket, but it's worth $1,000 *with problems*," Avery says. "It looks like *nothing*, like an itchy blanket used by hardened soldiers."

Avery places a stoneware jug on a tray to bring to the front for sale, and small plates I recognize as Sandwich glass, then looks at a green blown vase. "This is some Italian piece of shit." He picks up two copper candle lanterns, but sets them down. "I'm going to leave these here," he whispers. "You don't want to be exposed. Then you have the jerk-offs who go straight to the front of the room to see what everyone else has put up." The pirates. He points to another dealer, a tall man with curly gray hair. "See that guy? He'll be watching everything I do." (When the auction starts, the curly-haired man takes a seat right behind Avery.) Some people will hide objects during the preview, hoping their competition doesn't have a chance to inspect them, tucking paintings behind others, moving something to a low shelf where it's difficult to spot.

Avery unfolds a blue cloth that looks like a blanket. "Ingrain carpet," he says. Ingrain carpet, woven on the newly invented Jacquard loom (a one-person loom), used up to six different colors of wool, forming a pattern on each side, reversible. The wool was dyed before weaving, so "ingrain" is thought to refer to the color "in the grain" of the fabric. Avery picks up a copper teakettle from around 1750, bold and beautiful, with opalescent glass handles. "Nobody cares," he says. "In 1976, there'd be ten people vying for this. I don't even have anybody to sell it to." He places the kettle on the front table anyway. "I'll see if I can get it cheap." He points out a hetchel. "For carding wool," he says. The hetchel looks like an enormous, painful hairbrush, with nails instead of bristles—used to sort long fibers for linen, and short fibers for "tow," a coarser fabric. "Another forgotten item," Avery says. "That's one of the oldest things here. It's from the eighteenth century, but nobody gives a shit. It's one of those antiques of yesteryear, an *old* antique, but it's no good anymore."

We move on to a small, three-legged plant stand. "This would be great if it was old, but it's not," he says. Nearby is a group of four Hepplewhite chairs, circa 1800. "Oooh, these are going to bring money," he says. He flips one of the chairs and inspects the underside. "See if you can find anything wrong with this," he says. Oh no, a pop quiz. I never get the answers right. I tip over a second chair for comparison, amazed at the dozens of nail holes stippling the frame. "That's a good sign," Avery says. The upholstery has been changed many times in two hundred years. I fail to spot anything wrong. Avery points to a screw hole that's been filled, the lighter wood obvious now, a repair that compromises the chair's condition.

Next, he studies a red upholstered wing chair with rough, plain carving. "This could be the one thing in this auction worth a ton of money, but I just can't tell. I look at this thing and I'm confused," he says. The chair—if real—is circa 1760. Avery upends the chair, and on his hands and knees inspects the underside, the feet. "It's a perplexing thing," he says. "I'm not even sure what type of wood that is." He scratches the wood on the frame. "It's all hand-carved. This leg is rounded at the bottom, but this one isn't." He studies the chair for a good fifteen minutes, then sets it right. "The problem is that when you look at these chairs, all you can see are four feet. The fabric covers them." In high-end auctions, sellers will rip the upholstery to expose the chair's guts. "Someone might have paid $2,000 to reupholster a chair in silk, but a dealer will just slice through the back with a knife," Avery says. "You have to see if the parts inside are right. Otherwise, you have only the legs to study, and a few other things," he says. "If it wiggles it's good. If it's really heavy it's good. Wear on the feet, good."

Until the late sixteenth and early seventeenth centuries, commoners in Britain and America did not own chairs, or owned only one that was reserved for the head of the house, the "chairman." Others sat on stools, chests, benches, or the floor. In one seventeenth-century assessment of homes in the Chesapeake area, a third had either benches or chairs, but only one out of seven owned both a chair and a bench. Prosperity, or at least comfort, was not long in coming. By the early 1800s, using "power" tools like waterwheel lathes, chairs were assembled in large quantities. A Massachusetts inventory showed that the average number of chairs in a household doubled from about 1800 to the 1830s. In Europe, chairs were designed for the social activities of the day, like a spectator chair, called a *voyeuse* or *voyelle* (the armless version), designed to straddle and watch a card game or a cock fight. "Gossip chairs" could be moved to join different conversations in a room. The *fumeuse*, a smoker's chair, had a built-in compartment for pipes, matches, cigarettes, and a button-release drawer that served as a "spittoon." Wing chairs (called "easie chairs" in the seventeenth century), like the red one at Hubley's, were thought to shelter the sitter from cold drafts and were used by invalids or the elderly, but favored by the wealthy, too.

Avery doesn't mark down the chairs because they are a puzzle. Chairs are not his specialty, and he's not confident enough to bid. "Even Bill Gates needs assurance," he says. "He uses experts and advisers." A dealer Avery knows just sold a wing chair for $19,000. "I thought that was short money," he says, but an upholsterer used new wood and destroyed the value. "One like that in better condition sold for $140,000."

BY 9:00, THERE ARE only ten people in the room. Avery and Christianson trade notes so that they are not in competition. They've marked a number of the same items, so they dicker. She is interested in a piece of textile she calls a coverlet. "Let me take that one," Avery says. "You don't even know what it is." Avery tells her the fabric is not a coverlet, but "ingrain carpet." She gives him the ingrain, and he gives her some other textiles, and on some lots they go halves, a kind of peacekeeping settlement.

At 9:30, a half hour before the auction starts, two men arrive who, Avery says, "are going to make this miserable. They have deep pockets and they buy a ton of stuff. I can only hope they showed up too late to preview and they miss something." Now the runners are carrying furniture to the front of the room and setting up rows of chairs. The rostrum is rolled out, a massive stand that elevates the auctioneer six feet above the audience. He'll need that height to see the bidders' subtle movements. The runners then roll out a red velvet-covered pedestal to display small items.

I hit the ladies' room before the auction starts. Behind the velvet curtains, I pass through the cluttered back room, pick my way through towering stacks of stuff, gingerly step down a rickety staircase into a frightening cellar. A narrow trail cuts through piles of dress dummies, dozens of fireplace sets, furniture stacked on furniture, dusty heaps of old golf clubs and suitcases. This is a true Boston cellar, with low ceilings, water on the floor, hand-troweled horsehair plaster walls. At the back of this room is a nasty bathroom like in a grimy gas station.

Avery takes a seat in the front row. "I like to just sit in the front and not know what's going on behind me," he says. "Sometimes I have to take a break from auctions. I can't stand the tension, the competition. The comments—'Oh, are you going to buy everything?' I've got my four little lots." In the last fifteen minutes, all the seats fill, and a few people stand in back. The senior Cann, from the rostrum, says, "Welcome to our old-fashioned auction. Go ahead and have fun. I hope you get everything you want," a generous sentiment, but antithetical to the nature of an auction. If everyone got everything they wanted, there would be no competition and everything would sell for very, very cheap.

The auction opens with a lion-shaped yellowware mold, which has little action. The auctioneer says, "Sold for $45 to Number Eight up front." That's Avery. I didn't even know he was bidding. He keeps his card near his lap, and only flips it up a few inches to bid. I'm amazed the auctioneer can even see this small motion. Only by following Cann's eyes can I track the bidding as it bounces around the room. The auctioneer—perhaps to keep track—says things like, "I've got fifty in the first row," and points to Avery, which signals to Avery's competitors in the back that he's bidding. This irritates Avery. "I told him not to point me out." He gestures to Cann as a reminder. The old man does his best, but Avery is not entirely pleased when Cann says again, "I've got $225 down front."

"He's not pointing at me," Avery says, "but he's still gaffing me. As soon as he says he has a bid 'down front,' a hand goes up in the back." Avery keeps up a running commentary. "The green glass vase. That looks like something but it's not," he says. He loses a set of cranberry glass. "I was hoping to sneak that one out of here," he whispers, turning to see who won the lot. "Oh good, another auctioneer is here." Now there are three auctioneers in the audience, competitors with big money. Number 44 is Walt Johnson, who runs a midsize New England auction house. "He's made major hits," Avery says. "Everybody knows him." Johnson, in a gray jacket on his compact frame, has a hawk nose, glasses, and the glued hair of the Brylcreem era, a stern poker face, and a squarish head, though perhaps it's the stiff corners of his greased hair that lend his head a geometric shape. Johnson, standing in the rear of the hall, has a curious bidding style: he turns completely around as if he were interested in the weather outside, his back to the auctioneer, and flaps his card just over his shoulder.

A cake stand and eight small china cups are offered. "Start at fifty? Nobody. How about twenty-five? Twenty-five all over the house," says the auctioneer. Cann looks at a jumble of wooden things, and says, "Oh boy, what boxfuls of goodies we have here today." Avery wins the jumble for $150. "That's a lot of money for that," he says. The box contains a butter mold, a wooden noisemaker, something that looks like an enormous wooden pizza cutter, and a "bee box," which is shaped like an oval hand-mirror, with clear glass instead of a mirror. A small two-chambered box is mounted on the glass. You bait the box with honeycomb, which bees can smell from three miles away. A bee crawls inside the box and gorges on the bait. When the insect is released, it makes a "beeline" to the hive. The bee keeper follows, moving the trap incrementally closer. Eventually—up to a week later—the keeper locates the hive with its pay-load of honey.

Avery bids on every third lot, I estimate, but he loses more than he wins. "You can see I'm not doing that well," he says. But he adds, "There's nothing here I really need." He checks his notes on the grouping of Sandwich glass plates, but he loses them, and then loses another lot of goblets. Avery turns around. "Oh great. A new player," he mutters. John-son's partner. "Between the both of them, they're going to spend a lot of money," he says. "When auctioneers show up, it's a dealer's nightmare." As if to prove his point, Joan Christianson bids on a bird's-eye maple dresser box, but it goes to Johnson for $180.

HUBLEY'S IS AN ENGLISH-STYLE, or "ascending," auction—the bid-ding starts low and rises. In Dutch style or "descending" auctions, which are less common, the bidding starts high and drops. The players remain silent until someone yells out "Mine!" and wins. Dutch auctions, sales by "mineing," are like a game of chicken to see who flinches first. As far back as the fifteenth century, auctions were held by the "candle" method. The auctioneer lit one inch of candle, and bidders watched it burn. The win-ner was whoever made the final bid just as the flame guttered out. Sam-uel Pepys, secretary for the British Royal Navy, wrote in 1662 of a bidder at a candle auction who was "cunninger" than the rest: "just as the flame goes out, the smoke descends, which is a thing I never observed before, and by that he do know the instant when to bid last."

Regardless of the method of sale, auctions have prevailed across time because of one fundamental principle: buyers and sellers place faith in opposing premises. Buyers think they will get something cheap because prices are not fixed, while sellers think they'll earn a high price since there is competition. They are both right and both wrong.

A SET OF FIVE Meissen plates comes up and Avery steals them for $20. "They're probably all chipped," he says of the Meissen lot, which he hadn't previewed. Depending on age and other factors, a single Meissen piece can bring up to $5,000. For $150, Avery wins the pair of copper candle lanterns he'd left on the shelf during preview, but he loses a set of etched wineglasses. "If you want to buy something, I'll let you know what to pay for it," he offers. During the preview, I coveted an ochre velvet late-Victorian camelback love seat. I love the love seat, and even better, it's small enough to fit in the back of my car, but I'm too anxious to bid. The whole auction scene makes me tense, even though I have nothing at stake. When the couch comes up, my heart flutters and I'm too slow, frozen by nerves. The couch quickly closes at $70. Now, because I didn't win the couch, didn't even try, and because it sold for so little, I begin to obsess about it. I want the couch more than ever. Auction psychology is getting to me.

A lot of "salts" is offered, small individual salt bowls for Victorian table settings. Avery bids up to $110, but lets it go to someone else for $120. It seems such a slight difference, ten bucks more to own the salts, but then again, if he'd continued bidding, likely the other dealer would have continued, too. The "killer" Japanese sewing box comes up. The auctioneer starts at $200 and bidding rises quickly. "That's the best one of those I've seen," Avery says. The winning bid is $900. I ask Avery why he wouldn't vie for such a good object. "They are not easy to sell," he says. "It's a good thing for the New York market." Avery wins a cream-ware platter for $100. "It's got stains, but it's nice," he says. "I shouldn't be buying stuff like that. It's not moving well. It's a nice antique, but . . ." He's interrupted by the next item, which he wins—a pair of pressed glass Baccarat lamps for $70. "That was a smart buy," he says. "They're missing a $15 part. I'll have them fixed in no time and sell them for $250. I don't mind bastardizing those lamps." (He explains later: "Baccarat is overrated. I don't have a lot of respect for those lamps, and it's a minor bastardization.") Avery bids on two large white ironstone vessels, each painted with a nautical flag. He's got $150 on his notes, but he has no competition so gets them for $20. "One is probably a chamber pot," he says. "Someone might have used it on their sailboat."

"Here's a linsey-woolsey," the auctioneer says of a bluish cloth. Avery laughs under his breath. "It's not a linsey-woolsey." Joan wins the lot, and another textile lot comes up. The auctioneer calls them coverlets. "They're not coverlets," Avery says, loud enough for Cann to hear, but Cann does not correct himself. "The two pieces of fabric are halves of a rug that was ripped apart," Avery tells me. The problem is that bidders don't understand the value of the objects as *ingrain rugs*. Described as coverlets, people bid high. As the bidding increases, Avery says, "Oh, these idiots think they are coverlets." He loses the lot at $200. "If they said it was a rug, I could have had it for $40." At $40, he could sell the rugs for their higher value to someone who understands ingrain carpets. Others' ignorance works for and against him.

A period banjo clock is offered next. "This could bring plenty," Avery says. "I don't look at clocks. They are too confusing." The bidding goes up and up, six hundred, then seven, eight, nine, finally landing at $1,050. "Sold!" Halfway through the auction, Avery looks at the list of items he's won. "I've got stuff, but I'm not happy with it," he says. Now the auctioneer puts up a Spanish guitar. "That's not Spanish," says Avery. "It's a parlor guitar from around 1880." The musical instrument dealer is "cleaning up," he says. He's the only one here for that category, and after less than fifteen minutes, "Music Man" walks out carrying two guitars, a cello, and a violin, all for cheap.

After two hours, I start to squirm. It's painful sitting in the wooden chairs. "You get calluses on your ass," Avery says. "I call it auction ass. You get a big fat ass from sitting at auctions all day." Every now and then, the auctioneer scolds the audience, "Shhhhh!" The murmur dims, but slowly builds again. Avery wins the circa 1750 copper teakettle for $35. "Remember I predicted that?" he says. "It's outstanding, but nobody cares." Weeks later, I'll see the kettle in his booth, priced at $400. A wooden cane is offered with a solid 14-karat-gold handle. "It's a honey,"

Avery says. "People will just rip that top off and melt it. They don't care about its antique value. It's a shame." The cane sells for $275. With gold approaching $1,000 an ounce, somebody will make a sizable profit.

Once the "smalls" are auctioned off, the runners carry furniture to the front, or if the item is too big, they stand by the piece as the audience turns to look. Now there is a changing of the guard, as Mr. Cann, Jr., replaces his father at the rostrum, barely skipping a beat. A table comes up that he describes as "Pine secondary, probably New England."

"He should be able to see from twenty feet away that's a North Shore table," Avery says.

"With Flemish feet," the auctioneer continues.

"He is totally wrong," Avery says. "That's a Spanish foot."

Avery bids on a caned chair, but drops out before it peaks at $175 to Johnson. "He has more money than God," Avery says. A pair of tables is offered. "Trash. French provincial." I comment that the auctioneer does not "pass" on any item because a reserve has not been met. "This is one of the few places where everything is actually for sale," Avery says. "They don't play games." A dresser comes up with gorgeous translucent Sandwich glass knobs, which the auctioneer simply calls "beautiful knobs." Johnson walks up front to inspect the dresser while the bidding is under way, then jumps in and wins it. A "half-commode" comes up, a dresser with one drawer and cabinet, a marble top. "The front feet have been replaced, but this ought to bring three or four hundred," Avery says. "They are very desirable because everybody has a place for them." As predicted, the piece sells for $375. "The furniture guys will have parts in their shops and they'll fix the feet."

Now comes the clunky, red wing chair with big claw feet that Avery had carefully studied on his hands and knees. It sells to Johnson for $900, along with a yellow wing chair for $2,900. "I wasn't convinced that chair was old," Avery says. "I couldn't tell if it was old, or new and moldy."

There's a new guy here today, someone Avery has never seen before. "Retail guy," Avery calls him, since he is not acting like a dealer. "That guy's a dope," he says, looking across at the man, wiry, nervous-looking, in his late thirties. "He just bought a three-legged plant stand that's only a hundred years old, with terrible damage, for more than $300. In other words, that kid just paid $300 for a $75 table." (Avery calls men "kids" and women "girls." In this optimistic lexicon, nobody ages beyond teenhood.) He adds, "Retail people are a problem. These knucklehead retail idiots—they think they can do it better themselves. A guy puts himself in the stockbroker's hands. We should be able to be antique brokers."

A short while later, Avery bids on an eighteenth-century, three-legged candle stand, with a rough surface. The stand is circa 1740, "the dawn of the cabriole leg," he tells me. "This is the earliest candle stand I've seen with cabriole legs. It's almost transitional." Retail Guy keeps upping the ante, so Avery hesitates. "I have to play possum," he whispers. He pretends to waver, to *consider* before he takes the bid higher. His foe suspects that he's reaching the end, the maximum amount he is willing to pay. But playing possum only works if the other bidder doesn't know the value of the object. "I've hesitated at $350 on a $2,000 thing," Avery says. "You act like, 'Yeah, well, okay, I *guess* I'm in.'" The tailgater is only willing to take a chance because of the reputation of who's bidding against him. "I knew Retail Guy had no idea what he was doing when he paid $300 for that other candle stand, and I knew he'd be a problem," Avery says. The possum ploy works. Retail Guy lets go of the candle stand. "I could have had that for nothing," Avery says. "I was afraid of Retail Boy. If I'd stayed with it, he'd have been with me the whole way." If playing possum shakes a tracker, "hot potato" fixes them—rapid staccato bidding to inflate the price, and then suddenly dropping out. The other guy is stuck with an expensive lot, which may be worthless for all he knows.

IN 1996, WILLIAM VICKREY of Columbia University won the Nobel Prize in Economics for his work on auction theory. He formulated the concept of "asymmetrical information"—where one party knows more than another. Vickrey's work launched the field of auction theory and design. Huge financial stakes are involved in government auctions of timber and mining rights, offshore oil leases, treasury bonds, and band spectrum licenses. (The British government made $35.4 billion in 2004 from auctioning "third generation" bandwidth for mobile phone services.) The field of auction theory has grown rapidly in tandem with Internet auctions. It might surprise antiques dealers to learn that a recent study found that low starting bids yielded higher final prices, at least on the Internet. In 2006, researchers sought to discover the causes behind this "reversal of the anchoring effect," so they set up simultaneous auctions on eBay. Their study showed that when the starting bid is low, anyone can jump in ("reduced barriers to entry"). This increases activity, causing a "sheep effect" (my term—if everyone else wants something, then it must be valuable). Then the phenomenon of "sunk costs" kicks in—bidders want the time and energy they've invested to pay off—which leads to an "escalation of commitment."

In the split seconds of live auctions, I wonder if these subtle psychological influences work. So many factors vary between online and live auctions, and between regular commodities and antiques. It makes sense that if you start something at $25, you'll get bids "all over the room," and if the auctioneer starts something at $200, some bidders will never enter the game. "My friend Jimmy believes in just blasting the thing," Avery says. "He can't pay enough money fast enough. His theory is other bidders will get cold feet really fast. That fixes the tailgaters quickly. They chicken out." When Avery won the set of flow blue at Hubley's years ago, he psyched out the competition. After the first two lots, he established a precedent: "I'm taking *all* the flow blue." In each lot, he "dumped on everyone," and nobody bid against him. "They lose spirit," he says. "It's like going into a wrestling match and knowing you are going to lose." Sitting through auctions three times a week, as Avery does, takes physical and psychological stamina. "You have to have patience, and staying power," he says. "And you have to be a little brave. I'm just chickenshit sometimes."

THE FOUR HEPPLEWHITE CHAIRS are put up, the ones Avery had quizzed me on. He stays in to $165 before dropping out. Johnson wins them for $175 each. "Johnson is buying just about every piece of period furniture," Avery says. I ask him why Johnson would buy so much furniture. "He puts everything in his auction, and it will average out. If he pays too much on something, he'll make a sizeable profit on something else." Avery is still thinking about the candle stand, as he watches Retail Guy vying for another table. "Retail Guy is killing all the furniture," he says. "I could have had that candle stand for nothing. Nobody wanted it. It's too rough for them, but I like that."

Next, Cann offers a claw-foot chest. "Antique!" he says, without irony or humor, "Antique!" After that, a two-hundred-year-old ribbon-back Chippendale slip-seat chair sells for just $25—to Johnson. A dusty mirror with a marble inlay frame sells for $575. Johnson again. Another wall mirror appeals to Avery, so he's in up to $300, then drops out. Johnson wins again. "Johnson is cleaning up the room," Avery says. Now Avery battles for two oval, leaded-glass windows, architectural salvage, which he takes to $350, but loses to another dealer. The tension of bidding activates a muscle spasm in Avery's neck. Every so often his head jerks to one side, as if he were pointing you in a direction. *That way*, the yank of his head seems to suggest. The neck spasm confuses the auctioneer, who glances at Avery. *Was that a bid?* As the tension mounts, I can feel my own neck and shoulders tighten.

At noon it's clear they won't have time to sell everything before they close at 12:30, so Cann asks the audience to select things they want and bring them up front. After a hubbub, the action resumes with two cement lion fonts, which Avery loses to a bidder willing to pay $300. Two Chippendale mirrors with eagle appliqués, late nineteenth century, go to Johnson. Avery's neck spasms, but he wins a wrought iron plant stand, and then a Dresden tea set for $40. He's doing well on china, poorly on furniture.

A Chinese camphor wood chest comes up. Avery points to the rot on the bottom. "It's a $400 thing in terrible condition. What do you do? You leave it there," he says. But someone takes it for $200. Avery wins a tray of candlesticks for $10. "I only want one of them," he says. "You're going home with an antique candlestick." Seconds later, he wins an eighteenth-century or on-the-cusp Spode tea set for $25, worth a couple hundred on a bad day. "That was a ridiculous buy," he says. "Nobody was here for that." The senior Cann carries items out from the back room. He aims a piece of antique firefighting equipment at the audience and pretends to spray, a rare playful break in his stiff Cambridge demeanor. Next, the runners drag out three huge nine-by-twelve-foot oriental carpets. There is no interest in one of the rugs, but the other two inspire fierce fights. There are three rug buyers, and everyone in the room can feel the tension as they ratchet the bidding into the thousands. The audience claps at the end, saluting a high price, but also releasing built-up tension.

Then it's over. The clock strikes noon-thirty and Cann promptly ends the auction, as if he has someplace else to be. Everyone lines up with their checkbooks drawn. Avery pays $1,512.50, which includes the 10 percent premium to the auction house. He hands his slip to a runner, who gathers his stuff from the back room. He picks up the box lot of candlesticks, plucks out the Longwy stick. Longwy is a faience pottery factory begun in 1798 in France, known for exquisite pottery—Napoleon ordered Longwy dishes—but most renowned for cloisonné, glass fused onto metal or clay. Avery's single Longwy candlestick—$10 for the box lot—is worth several hundred dollars. There are a half dozen candlesticks left, and he tells me to choose one. I feel like a kid in a candy store. I select a six-inch-tall brass and faience candlestick. "Good choice," Avery says. "You have a hundred-year-old candlestick." Now I see how Avery's two-car garage, his basement, half his living room, and two storage units have filled over the course of nearly two decades in this business, buying lots with a dozen items in order to get one gem, the rest not valuable enough to deal with, but too valuable to jettison. Bit by bit, like the sands of an hourglass, his house filled to capacity.

Loading Avery's car, on the underside of a wrought iron plant stand I spy a Hubley's auction sticker dated forty years ago. The eccentric trust fund collector whose estate was auctioned must have taken a taxi to Hubley's around 1968, won the plant stand at an auction of someone else's collection, took it home, used it, loved it until his last day, and now here it is outliving its owner once again. There's something humbling about seeing the grimy sticker underneath the stand, one link in a continuous chain of ownership. Memento mori. Remember you must die. But the plant stand lives on, passed on to the next collector in an existential relay race. The next leg of the race is at a high-end show in Pennsylvania.

CHAPTER 10

Tea for Two

Avery and I are on the road at 5:00 A.M. in the pouring rain, heading to Pennsylvania for the York Country Classic, which is not a golf tournament, but a fancy antique show. Avery set up at York for the first time the year before and broke the $10,000 mark for an indoor show—a new benchmark—so it's worth the ten-hour drive, but this is the farthest he's ventured from New England. "Collectors and dealers used to find you," he says. "Now we have to drive to Pennsylvania to find these buyers for early American stuff."

The first time Avery did the York show, he spent the drive down worrying about his merchandise. "My stuff is going to pale compared to the stuff that will be down here, the quality," he'd said. After we'd arrived, one tour around the show relieved his merchandise inferiority complex. Plus, before the show he'd found a piece of stoneware that had been sitting for weeks in a large group shop in York—a jug with a bird sitting on a nest, which he thought was unusual—and sold it in the first five minutes of the show for $1,000 profit. He's hoping York will be as good this time.

The truck is packed to capacity. Behind the seat are two dress shirts on hangers, and some paintings. On the space between us, a twenty-four-slot candle mold rests on top of three small boxes, crowned with a mystery object wrapped in a towel. The atlas, from 1986 when Avery first set up at a bottle show, has torn pages, with roads that no longer exist. It's

November, but Avery wears Bermuda shorts and a T-shirt, as if he's been on the road so long that he hasn't noticed the change of season. He has a cold, though; his head is foggy and he's sniffing, but there are no "sick days" in this job. "I have so much invested in this show," he says, "I'd go to York if I had fucking pneumonia."

Avery has high hopes for his pièce de résistance, a painted rooster weathervane, or "weathercock." He is not out of his mind to be excited about a weathervane. A molded copper rooster weathervane—closed mouth, big flourishing tail—sold recently for $49,940 at a Boston auction. "Weathervanes are huge right now," he says, "especially with that Lauren guy paying five million." Weathervanes—"vernacular sculpture"—hit a peak in 2006 when the auction record for a single weathervane was set in January ($1,080,000), then broken in August ($1,216,000), then set again in October when Sotheby's sold a five-foot-tall copper Indian weathervane, circa 1900, to "that Lauren guy"—Polo Ralph Lauren executive Jerry Lauren (brother of Ralph), and his wife, Susan—for $5,840,000.

Some people thought the price was irrational exuberance. After all, the weathervane was a "machine-made, stamped-out thing," Avery says. There were seven bidders, which likely stoked the price, as well as the heated-up market for folk art. Lauren told *Antiques & Fine Art* magazine that "aside from marrying my wife, and the births of my children," buying the Indian weathervane was "one of the greatest thrills of my life." Every piece he and his wife collect, Lauren said, "is a love affair."

AVERY TALKS about his rooster weathervane for an hour. I enjoy this rumination, puzzling it out. I can see the level of thought he puts into his business. I understand his worries and hopes. "It's all about size and surface," he says. "This one is copper, and painted white. This is where it gets confusing. To me, it's a killer surface, maybe better than original." He continues, "I don't know how to price this thing. I bought it from another dealer for nothing—less than $200. I almost walked away from it." Avery's last weathervane, a small cow, was a hard sell. "It took me two years to sell it. Oh my God, it saw Brimfield, like, five times. Nobody would fucking buy it." The cow was "too simple" for big-time dealers, and there was no market among buyers who couldn't afford "a big fat weathervane."

"I finally sold it for $275," he says. "I just wanted to get rid of it." Object fatigue. Dealers get sick of a piece, discouraged. They lose confidence and dump it. I've seen Avery suffer object fatigue, but also take advantage of it. He bought a creamer from a friend who'd failed to sell it online for $400. The piece was "a bad example of a wicked hard to find thing." Avery relisted the creamer on eBay and it sold for $1,400. "Same thing," he says, "but better pictures, more confident description."

This rooster weathervane is different. "I've seen the pig, the cow, the horse"—other common forms—"and I was equating the rooster with those. This one is just a different animal—pardon the pun. It's not made by that factory." Avery found a similar rooster weathervane in an auction catalog, and called to see how much it brought, but the auctioneer left a muffled message on Avery's machine. Either the rooster sold "for a thousand" or "four thousand." Avery's friend Glen said the rooster "was in another league," maybe even $3,000 to $6,000. Glen arranged for a contact to look at the rooster weathervane in York. If Avery sells the piece to Glen's contact, he'll kick back a couple hundred to Glen, "but nothing is obligated," he says. "This guy will find us down here in York. I'm not allowed to contact him." It's like a spy novel, cloak and dagger—*the rooster has landed.* "Now you know everything I know," Avery says. "So what would you price it at?"

I've learned the considerations of valuing an antique: rarity (few were made or few remain, or the color, form, shape, or subject matter is uncommon); authenticity (the piece is "real" or "right," it's signed, or there's provenance); and condition ("mint" is untouched, "excellent" indicates minor flaws, "good" means possible repairs, some damage or breaks, and "poor" is, as Avery says, "a train wreck.") Then there are the more slippery factors, like desirability, what's in vogue, what the tastemakers are touting, Martha Stewart, *Country Living,* the slick home decorating magazines.

But knowing the potential value of an antique also takes instincts, a good eye. At an auction one day, Avery previewed a painting of a man fishing. "You can date it to the 1890s by the style of his fishing pole," he says. "It was a watercolor, well executed. Watercolors aren't as desirable, but this one was so well done." The catalog stated that the painting was signed by "T. Elliot." Avery checked his *Davenport's Art Reference*, but he didn't find an entry for T. Elliot. "I left a bid for $150 anyway. I just liked it." With art, Avery explains, there's a $300 rule. "You can get $300 for any old painting that looks good. Once you say $400, people start asking if it's done by a listed artist. Maybe the rule is up to $400 now." Avery won the painting for $110. At home, he discerned that the signature was not T. Elliot, but S. Gerry, for Samuel Lancaster Gerry, a mid-nineteenth-century landscape painter, leader of the White Mountain School, and founder of the Boston Art Club in 1858. A Samuel Lancaster Gerry oil sold in 2005 at Skinner's for over $5,000. Avery estimated the retail value of the watercolor to be $1,500. "If they had advertised that painting as a Samuel Lancaster Gerry, it would have brought at least eight or nine hundred. A comparable work went for that amount." He asks, "Do these painting dealers really know what they are doing? The auction house couldn't read the signature, so they blew it off. The art dealers should be willing to buy this even if they don't recognize the name because it's damn good looking, but they have no interest because it's not signed Aldro T. Hibbard and it's not a snow scene in Vermont." The moral of that story, he says, is that "the experts don't always know."

When Avery asks me for my opinion on pricing the weathervane, I have no idea, so I opt for safety. "Why not split the difference with Glen's price and the lower auction price?" Wrong answer, it appears from Avery's hesitation. The piece hasn't been tried yet. "The first time you want to try high," he says. "It's all in the surface. Is it better to have the original surface, or painted and pretty and nice and right? If that's the case, I can see some real high-end dealer asking $12,000." But he's not sure. "I'm still learning weathervanes," he says.

THE FIRST KNOWN WEATHERVANE adorned the forty-foot-tall Tower of Winds in Athens, built in 48 B.C.E. Each side of the octagonal tower bore a bas-relief of a wind god. Boreas, god of the north wind, was the "devouring one." Notus, god of southerly winds, stirred crop-destroying summer storms. Zephyrus of the west brought gentle breezes, but Kaikias, northeast wind god, whose name means "badness" or "evil," flung hailstones. Crowning the tower was Triton, an eight-foot-tall, bronze weathervane with the head and torso of a man and the tail of a fish—a sort of merman—holding a rod to indicate which way the wind blew.

The earliest American-made weathervane is thought to be a 1673 banner-shaped vane atop the Concord, Massachusetts, library. A coppersmith, Deacon Shem Drowne, famously crafted the thirty-eight-pound, four-foot-long gilded grasshopper with green glass eyes that has perched atop Boston's Faneuil Hall since 1742, surviving fires, earthquakes, and thefts. During the Revolutionary War, suspected British spies were tested to see if they could identify the form on top of Faneuil Hall. If they failed to answer correctly, they were thought guilty. When an earthquake in 1755 shook the grasshopper off the roof, a message from Drowne was found in its belly: "Again Like to have Met with my Utter Ruin by Fire but hopping Timely from my Publick Scituation Came of With Broken bones, & much Bruised." The grasshopper was "cured and fixed" and set back atop Faneuil Hall by Shem Drowne's son, Thomas.

In the mid-2000s, weathervanes were such a "hot" category that thieves were ripping them right off rooftops. There were more than twenty reports of stolen weathervanes in Maine, Massachusetts, Vermont, New Hampshire, and New York. In 2006, in a Pink Panther–like caper, thieves used climbing gear to scale a forty-foot barn in Waterville, Vermont, and steal "Black Hawk," a 150-year-old Morgan horse weathervane. They replaced the real weathervane with a cheap replica, hoping to buy time before the owners noticed. "Black Hawk" was particularly meaningful to its owners, the Thomas family, fifth-generation farmers who raise Morgan horses, a breed that originated in Vermont in 1791 with a two-year-old colt named "Figure," owned by Justin Morgan. Figure was the only horse in America to establish his own breed.

Avery jokes, "I should be able to get in on weathervanes when they cool down." Indeed the chill is in the air. In January of 2009, Sotheby's estimated that "Old Uncle Jake," a six-foot-one-inch fireman weather-vane, would bring $3 million to $5 million at their "Important Americana" auction. The weathervane was deemed so valuable it was transported by armed guards. Sotheby's folk art expert called it "one of the most important pieces of vernacular folk art sculpture" to come on the market "ever." "Old Uncle Jake" was made around 1850 for the Union Fire Hall in Winchester, Virginia (now the Charley Rouss Fire Company). The company replaced "Old Uncle Jake" with a replica, and the firemen had big plans for the millions they'd reap from the sale of the original: new equipment, a new firehouse. "Old Uncle Jake" is debonair in knee-high boots, an ascot knotted around his neck, lunging forward and pointing, as if he's spotted wisps of smoke in a distant forest, his bugle at the ready. But at Sotheby's, "Old Uncle Jake" didn't spark enough interest; the bids fell short of the low range of the estimate, and the weathervane failed to sell.

AVERY AND I ARRIVE in York at 1:00 P.M., drive through a dumpy section of town to a large fairgrounds with 4-H-like stables, a small convention center. The Convention and Visitor's Bureau has billed York as "The Factory Tour Capital of the World." We get out, stretch, and inspect Avery's booth across the aisle from Tucker Small's. For $1,000—three times the cost of a Brimfield plot—Avery gets walls and wallpaper, protection from the weather, flush toilets (no small luxury), a locking glass case, and electricity. In the generously wide aisles, there are tables with potted chrysanthemums. Most dealers install track lighting to spotlight objects. Avery has two big clip-on lamps that keep slipping. Most of the booths have indoor-outdoor carpet, or huge oriental rugs. Avery and Tucker have bare cement floors. The fanciest dealers' price tags are typed or written in calligraphy. Avery's price tags are Magic Marker on the back of advertising cards from a prior show. "It looks like a ten-year-old wrote it," he says. He assigns me the task of writing neater price tags, but my penmanship isn't much better.

We are allotted two folding plastic chairs, but in spite of Avery's foot pain from plantar fasciitis, he sacrifices one to display a tin bread box in mustard-yellow paint. We unpack box after box. I unwrap objects from newspaper, a Barney baby blanket, an early 1700s pewter whale oil plate warmer wrapped in an old, navy blue windbreaker. Avery just purchased a set of three geometric-design rugs for $350 at a Skinner's auction.

"They might be shirred rugs," he says. "They clip the tops after they are done hooking them, so it gets this pleated look." Early shirred rugs can be worth thousands. "These are supposed to be old," he says, "but they are just damn good looking, and that's what counts."

"How old are they?" I ask.

"They have wear on the edges," he says. "They almost seem too good to be true. Maybe they weren't a bargain. But I also think people missed them. They were in such a weird spot." He's trying to figure out how to price them. "I bought them right," he says, "and they are good looking." The rugs are mounted on foam board with a wire hanger in back. "I should have called Tildy," he says, his textile dealer friend, "but I just got them so I had to throw them in the truck."

As we move stuff into the hall, Avery mulls over the rugs. "These rugs are kind of bothering me." A moment later, he gets a flash. "You know what I'll do? I'll cut that back off. I won't be afraid to sell them if they are just hooked rugs." The undersides of the rugs are backed with fabric, so you can't tell for certain how they were made. Avery's guide, *American Hooked and Sewn Rugs*, has drawings of the backs of hooked, yarn-sewn, and shirred rugs. In the parking lot, Avery cuts one rug's backing with his pocket knife, but is not pleased; the rugs are not that old. He prices them at $1,495 for the trio, an experiment. "Rugs," he says. "I just don't know them that well."

Hooked, shirred, and rag rugs were utilitarian crafts—of necessity made from old clothes. Sal Paradise, Jack Kerouac's protagonist in *On the Road*, says his aunt made "a great rag rug woven of all the clothes in my family for years," a rug "as complex and as rich as the passage of time itself." To hook a rug, you pull a narrow loop of fabric—wool or cotton cut into spaghetti strips—one stitch at a time with a hooking tool (or a bent nail, if you were poor), through coarse backing, like a burlap grain sack. Until 1870, when women could buy burlap stamped with patterns, they designed their own rugs. Mrs. Eleanor Blackstone of Illinois hooked portraits of her six children into an eight-by-ten-foot rug. Blanche Blase, the eldest, born in 1861, sits in a rocker staring out the window at a crescent moon, while Roy Lot, born in 1871, pulls a sled named "Anne," his perky terrier, Pericles, tagging along. Nathaniel feeds an apple to a pony, while George paints a self-portrait. Anne picks flowers, and toddler Nellie holds a lollipop. Under Nellie's portrait Mrs. Blackstone wove, "Suffer little children to come unto me"; Mrs. Blackstone's youngest died in childhood. Into the portraits Mrs. Blackstone wove a bit of each child's hair. The stories woven into these rugs moved me, so after the York show I took a rug hooking workshop. I realized then—after spending eight hours to hook a sloppy-looking, pot-holder-size piece (which I never finished)—that Mrs. Blackstone's room-size rug is not just a work of art, but a masterpiece.

THIS YEAR AT YORK, there is only one antique show. The producers have joined forces, and instead of running two shows side-by-side, the Greater York Antiques Show managed by Jim Burk, and the York Country Classic managed by Barry Cohen, the dealers are in one hall. During the setup, there is grumbling that the high-end dealers from Jim's show don't want to be mixed with Barry's people, mid-level dealers like Avery and Tucker. "I'm a small fish in this place," Avery says. We overhear one big-time dealer say to his cohort, "At least we can bottom feed." I say to Avery, "You are fifteen years younger than most of the other dealers here." He laughs. "Yeah, but I don't feel like it." This November show is the thirtieth he's done this year, and at forty-six, he's feeling the wear.

Within ten minutes of arriving, Glen's contact stops by to look at Avery's rooster weathervane, which he's priced at $4,300. The man studies the weathervane briefly, then puts it down. "A crowing rooster is more desirable," he says. This must be a disappointment to Avery, though he keeps a poker face. There's still a whole show ahead. And there's a consolation prize. The man spots a theorem painting from 1835, a small, framed still life of fruit in a bowl. He's very excited about it and shells out $1,350. It's a fine start to the show, since Avery paid $150 for the theorem. After Glen's contact leaves, Avery says, "I still don't know what I sold." Theorems are paintings on velvet (or sometimes other fabric), which lends the image depth, a craft taught in women's academies from about 1800 to 1840. Theorems were typically painted using stencils, the nineteenth-century version of paint-by-numbers kits. The name "theorem" comes from Matthew Finn's 1830 book, *Theoremetrical System of Painting, or Modern Plan, fully explained in Six Lessons; and illustrated with Eight Engravings, by which a child of tender years can be taught the sublime art in one week.*

Avery doesn't have much of a chance to shop before the show, but even if he did, he might not be able to afford a prized piece. "The nice thing on the floor won't wait for the end of the show for me to have cash," he says. But a quick jaunt to the next aisle yields two small finds. One is a "firing glass" for $35. "She was selling it like it was a wineglass," he says. The glass looks like a largish shot glass with a squat stem, heavier than leaded glass, and cross-hatched with wear. From around 1790 to 1820, men in taverns pounded their glasses on the bar after drinking a toast, which sounded like guns firing, or shots, hence the name firing or shot glass. A few hours later, a customer picks up the firing glass. "I haven't had one of those in two years," Avery tells him. The man returns three times, perhaps between scouting the show for a cheaper one. It's axiomatic that the customer who takes up most of Avery's time is inevitably buying the cheapest object. Eventually the man buys the firing glass for $125. For Avery, it's a $90 profit for fifty feet of walking, almost two dollars a step.

The other find is a two-inch-tall snuff bottle for $60. Just as Avery pulls out bills to pay, another dealer, Richard, points to the snuff bottle and says, "I'll take this." The snuff bottle dealer points to Avery. "That guy just bought it." Richard's interest in the snuff bottle shows that Avery's instincts are good, on par with higher echelon dealers. In 2010, a single, eighteenth-century, enamel snuff bottle sold for a world-record price: $1,191,580. "With Richard," Avery says, "it's who you know more than what you know. I could have the same object, but the buyers know and trust him." Richard, an elegant older man, has enough real estate in his booth, catty-corner to Avery's, that he's designated a table just for wrapping, with white tissue paper and heavy-stock handled bags. Like almost all the booths, his is a "living room setting," arranged to look as if you'd walked into a nineteenth-century parlor—paintings on the wall, a chair or two, a small table, a vase filled with flowers. His booth contains a couple dozen high-ticket items, like a wall box—a plain wooden box that was mounted on a wall, used to store knives or candles—priced at $12,000. Avery's booth is crammed with antiques, as if he were at Brimfield. His packing material is rumpled newspaper, which he stores under the table, kneeling on the cement floor to wrap objects (there's a permanent callus on his knee), which he then places in plastic bags from Shaw's Supermarkets, Grand Union, or T.J.Maxx.

"There are so many fake snuff bottles, it's ridiculous," Avery tells me. "Snuffs were highly sought after, but they ruined the market with fakes."

"How can you tell this snuff bottle is not fake?" I ask.

"The color of the ivory on the bottom," he says. "And the orange top is from iron impurities that seep into the white jade. This one has a very soulful look to it."

During setup, Avery makes several sales, a pair of sterling silver salad tongs priced at $250 that he lets go for $215 to a dealer buying a Christmas present for her daughter. He sells a game board less than a minute after he sets it out for $1,250 to the dealer next door. The game board, built onto a wrought iron stand, is dated 1871. He tells the dealer, "You're on your own with that. I don't know anything about it." The market for game boards is strong. In 2007, a "snakes and ladders" painted game board from the cusp of the twentieth century sold at Skinner's for $64,625, a world record. "You can put it out at this show," Avery tells the dealer. "I don't mind." The dealer ups the price to $1,750, but in the end she sells it for $1,400. "The lady beat me up over it," she tells us, though she still earns $150 for dragging the game board ten feet over to her booth.

Avery sells a signed Bennington pitcher for $350, an ovoid-shaped redware jug for $1,050 to a big-time Maine dealer, and a Wedgwood plate with a gorgeous rabbit motif for $250. All told, before the show begins, he sells $5,000 worth of stuff, mostly to other dealers, who are, perhaps, "bottom feeding."

FRIDAY, OPENING DAY, we eat breakfast at a diner. Avery is the world's slowest eater. He stops eating to think, to talk. He tells me about a chest he's recently acquired. "I still don't understand the hinges," he says. "It should have plain snipes with cotter pins, but there are three different sets of hinges. It has a butt hinge now, but it's definitely eighteenth century."

"Uh huh," I reply.

"I was looking in this book about south shore Massachusetts furniture. There's a quote from the estate of where a guy had at the Waterman's Shop from about 1711, 'a trunk.' Now they would have said a 'chest' or a 'paneled cupboard.' I've only seen one other reference from these estate inventories where a 'trunk' was listed." He takes a bite, and continues: "European furniture tends to be bugged, but the 1600s stuff from America is more bug-safe. These little bugs, whatever they are, leave tiny holes." Powder post beetles—some species can live up to thirty years in a larval state before chewing their way out of the wood. Now Avery draws on a napkin an example of spline joint construction. "Stickley did it," he says. "It's a weird way to put two boards together, but it allows for expansion and contraction of the wood without cracking."

"The box doesn't fit any categories," he continues. "It's not a blanket chest or a Bible box." Boxes are tricky to identify; even experts make mistakes. At Plimoth Plantation, one of the oldest museums in the United States, there is a chest labeled "from Norway," which Avery is convinced is actually from Connecticut. "I'll go to the Museum of Fine Arts in Boston with you and show you the mistakes, the Mexican glass," he says. "But most of the display is good and right." Avery digs into his scrapple, a local specialty made from leftover pig parts, the offal, head, heart, liver, and other scraps mixed with cornmeal and herbs, formed into a loaf, sliced, and fried. He wants to buy a loaf to take home.

———

AT THE CONVENTION CENTER the doors are locked, so we stand in the parking lot in the chill November air. Another dealer, Greg Tierney, sits inside his station wagon clipping his fingernails. Behind his car he's set three Windsor chairs on the asphalt. One has a "continuous arm," a single piece of wood shaped into the swooping backbone and arms. "It has a bamboo turning on the legs, but the wood is not ash. Ash is more splintery," Avery says. He dates the chair to circa 1730. Tierney, who typically sells textiles, gets out of his car to ask Avery about the chairs. One chair has a blind socket, a "Connecticut feature," Avery says (the holes for legs were bored from the bottom and stop short of piercing through the surface of the seat). "This is so graceful," he says. "It's sexy." The second chair has "anthropomorphic knuckles"—the chair's arms end in a curve to look like fingers curled into a grasp. "It has a saddle seat," he points out. "See how they cut this out for your bum? Look at the ass wear. Three hundred years of sitting shows."

Tierney absorbs the assessment. "That might be a Philly back, but the legs are turned like a Rhode Island chair," Avery says. "I don't know enough about Windsors. Something about that fat back makes me think it's Philly." There is a child's Windsor, too. "That's nice and crusty," Avery says. He flips the small chair. "Nice mustard paint. I thought that was dirt, but it's paint. That means the price just went up." Tierney is asking $1,750 for the child's chair. Later, when we see another dealer carrying a Windsor chair, Avery whispers, "See that scallop on the front seat? There's not a rat's ass of a chance that it's real. Someone did that in 1940 to make it look good."

Inside, we fine-tune Avery's booth. There's a look to dealers at this level that denotes class, an Ivy League, corporate-executive casual, New York City art dealer look. Men in their sixties with neat gray ponytails, not hippie-ish, but every hair in place. Well-dressed older women with chunky jewelry and chic blunt haircuts, or the slightly outré gel-spiked hair. You can smell the money, see it in the shoes, the watches, the $300 sweaters. A dealer says to Avery, "A show like this quickly slots you—

what you can afford or not." There is an unspoken "no jeans" rule among the dealers. Most wear khakis or wide-wale corduroy. Only three or four dealers wear jeans, including Avery and Tucker. Avery's long-sleeved, blue and white striped dress shirt seems to choke him. He is chafing after five minutes, tugging at the collar.

The antique world is so Caucasian. Among the 125 dealers and hundreds of customers, I'll see three African Americans. What does that say about our relationship to this country's past? Owning an object from the past is claiming that past, or reclaiming it, honoring it. Why would you want an inkwell from a period when your ancestors were forbidden to write? Black Americana has been a neglected category, partly because some artifacts are offensive—"Mammy" and "Sambo" images, a tube of "Darkie" toothpaste—as well as painful reminders of slavery. But over the past thirty or so years, interest in black Americana has grown (a 2007 study estimated there were 50,000 collectors of black Americana), sparked by the designation in 1976 of February as Black History Month, by Alex Haley's acclaimed best-seller *Roots* (130 million people watched the 1977 television miniseries), and by the cachet brought to this category by celebrity collectors like Spike Lee, Oprah Winfrey, Branford Marsalis, Whoopi Goldberg, and Bill Cosby.

Amateur collectors have led the way in rectifying the dearth of African American material history. In *The Journal of African American History*, Dr. Elvin Montgomery wrote that scholars "lag behind collectors in their definition of what is worth collecting." James P. Hicks, a locksmith, began collecting black memorabilia in 1990. Hicks first took offense at objects that caricatured blacks, but later realized the importance of preserving even these things: "We have to tell the whole story, to learn what our American history books failed to report." His collection of over 1,100 objects was exhibited in 2004 at the Herbert Hoover Presidential Library and Museum. Mayme Agnew Clayton, a university librarian, spent decades of her life collecting African American artifacts, including 30,000 rare and out-of-print books, films, and documents—first editions of works by Langston Hughes, a signed copy of Phillis Wheatley's *Poems on Various Subjects, Religious and Moral* from 1773, handwritten slave documents—

and 75,000 photographs, 9,500 sound recordings. When she died at age eighty-three, her son established the Mayme Clayton Library and Museum in Culver City, California. "Culture is the measure of a civilization," Clayton's son said. "Without evidence of a culture, there is no proof that a people exists."

Avery has in his booth a framed sketch of a dandy in blackface, with the caption "Sally come up," signed *L.F.R.* Aside from the Topsy Turvy doll, this is the only black Americana I've ever seen among his wares. When I ask him what "Sally come up" means, he admits he doesn't know. Later, I learn that this is a song popularized in 1862 by an English performer named Frederick Buckley. The sheet music from the Library of Congress shows a black man similar to Avery's drawing. The lyrics:

> *Massa's gone to town de news to hear*
> *And he has left de o-ver-seer*
> *to look to all de Nig-gers here*
> *while I make lub to Sal-ly.*

There are several stanzas and a chorus—"Sally has a lubly nose, flat across her face it grows / it sounds like thunder when it blows." In the nineteenth century, you could buy this sheet music by mail order for five cents. Avery has priced the sketch at $119, a guess. In an antique store in York, I saw an early nineteenth-century charcoal sketch of a black girl priced at $16,000. Few portraits of African Americans exist from slavery. *Antiques Roadshow* appraiser Philip J. Merrill said that commonplace objects, like the sketch in Avery's booth, "tell the story of our sorrows, our defeats and our victories, in ways that no history book can."

Some people object outright to profiting from black Americana, especially from horrific artifacts. Lynching photographs—if you could stomach owning one—sell for more than $500. But Merrill said, "a picture of a boy with a noose around his neck," while controversial, "speaks volumes." Americans must confront this history. Others worry that collector demand will outprice museum budgets. In 2010, a receipt for the sale of a slave listed for $695 at the Black History Store in Chamblee, Georgia;

a small hooked rug, the size of a chair seat, made by Dr. George Washington Carver, was on sale for $9,500. In 1997, the Chicago Art Institute shelled out $185,000 for a daguerreotype of Frederick Douglass. But the controversy continues. In 2007, a Christie's auction of slave documents was halted by protesters, led by then New York State representative David Paterson and talk show host Tavis Smiley. Christie's has a policy against auctioning Holocaust-related objects, but prior to the protest, honored no such policy for slavery artifacts. After Christie's received a flurry of angry calls, the owners of the documents donated them to a museum.

Objects speak, tell a story. For some things, the storytelling is literal, a voice reaching across time. A slave born in 1780, called "Dave" and owned by Lewis Miles in Aiken, South Carolina, was a talented potter, and a poet of sorts, known for incising verses on his wares, proving his literacy at a time when most slaves were forbidden to learn how to read. One pot reads: "July 31, 1840. Dave belongs to Mr. Miles, where the oven bakes and the pot biles." (I like to read this verse metaphorically— his clay vessels firing in a kiln, the "pot" boiling is, perhaps, Dave himself.) At the time, Dave's pots sold for 10 cents a gallon; a twenty-gallon pot netted $2, or about $51 today. Dave produced an average of five thousand gallons of pottery annually, profit for his owner that today would be about $25,500 per year. "Dave the Slave" wares still generate profit for whoever owns them. In 2000, a signed, two-handled fifteen-gallon storage jar sold for $83,600. It's satisfying to imagine Dave having the last word, thumbing his nose at slave owner Lewis Miles, in perpetuity. On a pot dated June 28, 1854, Dave wrote: "L.M. says this handle will crack." After 150 years, the handle is still intact.

WAITING FOR THE SHOW to open, I count the objects in Avery's booth, slightly over three hundred. The trick to becoming a "living room" dealer is to know which ten or twenty objects to bring. Or to price antiques high enough that you only need to sell a few. Among the antiques in Avery's booth are two sets of andirons at $800 a pair, several yellowware bowls, several pairs of child-size leather gloves and mittens. There is a wooden butter press with a pentagon and flower design priced at $1,285. "Exceptional," Avery wrote on its tag. (A design pressed into butter was a dairywoman's signature, as butter could vary enormously in quality.) There's a child's sawdust-stuffed horse with shiny wear spots and missing its tail, and two huge blanket chests, one of which Avery has carried to ten shows—ten times unloaded this heavy chest, ten times packed it up again. This weekend, he will finally sell it and we jump for joy, not just to get rid of a large item—which supposedly will give us more room in the truck, but mysteriously does not—but because it was *about time*.

"That should have sold earlier," Avery says.

"What's the average number of shows it takes to sell an object?" I ask.

"It varies so much." He laughs. "I've had some stuff for ten years. Generally I get bored with something, so I'll put it away. Some of that stuff I tucked away ten years ago would probably be good now. You want your money out of something, but you don't want to fuck up with it."

A Skowhegan, Maine, ovoid jug is priced at $1,600, and five miniature pewter whale oil lamps, tiny enough to fit in your palm, cost between $150 and $350 each. The label, in Avery's New England vernacular, states the obvious: "Wicked small." There's a mint-condition Wedgwood chamber pot decorated with flowers and pagodas. Why would you make such a beautiful work of art whose function is so humble? The poorest of the poor did not have "a pot to piss in." Some chamber pots were decorated with verses: "Treat me nice and keep me clean / And I'll tell not what I have seen." I pick up a small wooden bowl priced at $395, and see tiny holes pricked in its well. "A sander," Avery says. "They used it to shake very fine sand on a letter to dry the ink." There are pieces of mochaware, many glass bottles and flasks, a daguerreotype, a sampler, and two redware pieces. (After perusing the floor, Avery says, "The redware at this show is better than any collection in any museum anywhere.")

There's a Victorian silver plate sugar bowl with its tiny sugar shovel for $175, an early American Indian bark basket, a beaded purse (possibly Indian), old signs (JOHNSON'S DRAPERY AND RUG SHOPPE), a "Pilgrim-century, New England youth's chair" for $1,295. Leaning against the wall is a seven-foot-long ladderlike thing in rough wood that has everyone guessing its function for two days. I speculate it was a form of stretcher. Avery thinks maybe buckets of milk were set on top. All this knowledge in the room, but nobody can say definitively what it was. One woman almost buys it for $700, but it won't fit in her car. (Avery will sell the ladder-thing at the next show for $300, where someone says it was used for drying tobacco leaves. Later, I see one in an antique shop called an "apple-picking ladder.")

In the glass case there's a $400 sarsaparilla bottle, a nineteenth-century "cure" for syphilis, and three tin candle snuffers for $100 each. There are two wooden canteens used during the Indian wars and the Revolutionary War. "How do you get a wooden canteen to hold water?" I ask. "When you put water into it, the wood swells and creates a seal," Avery says. The small canteen, more rare, is $795, the larger $595, but Avery will sell it for $550. There's a two-foot-tall clear glass hurricane shade, with Avery's handwritten note taped to it: "Rare! Actually Real." He's underlined "real" three times. Priced at $395, it sells for $350. There is a stub of wax—a beef tallow candle—worth $100. "I sold a candle box with six of those in it for the price of the box alone," Avery says, an early mistake, a $600 lesson. Beef or sheep tallow candles were expensive in their time. In the eighteenth century, the average New England household had fewer than three candles.

On the wall hang three oil portraits, one a handsome young Philadelphian who Avery thought might sell here in his home state. "You can buy a lot of men and women in their late thirties because by that age they had some money to get their portrait painted," he says. His second portrait is of an older woman. "She's so well done," he says. "I'd prefer she was twenty-two years old." The largest portrait is a fair young woman with large eyes and a delicate mouth, wearing a lace shawl over a black dress. "She's the youngest, prettiest girl I've ever had," he says, "except the one in college, which I won't tell you about." Across the aisle, Tucker has a few portraits, too, including a woman who might be the contemporary of Avery's, but Avery doesn't much like Tucker's girl. She has thin lips, which lend a sneer to her expression. "She looks like a nasty slut from the eighteenth century," he says.

He shows me an auction catalog with a group of six Prior-Hamblin School portraits, which sold for $391,000. "You can generally buy those," he says. "I bought one like this." He points to an example in the catalog. "These painters were the equivalent of today's sidewalk sketch artists. 'I'll paint your portrait for $1.50.' They were competing with the daguerre-otype market." He outlines the rules of thumb for portraits. "Men and women between nineteen and twenty-six years old are desirable. The worst thing is an old man, the second worst is an old woman. Kids are good, the younger the better, but not infants. You want a really attrac-tive kid." He points to the portrait of a little girl in Tucker's booth. "Tucker's kid looks bratty and spoiled. You wouldn't want to see that pudgy ornery face staring out at you every day."

Hanging on the exterior wall of Avery's booth is a four-foot-long cast-iron horse in full gallop. Avery's sign: MADE BY A WOMAN SHIPBUILDER DURING WWII IN QUINCY, MA. HEAVY! In 1943, at its peak, the Fore River Shipyard in Quincy employed 32,000 workers, including 1,200 women. Avery was going to put $300 on it, but asks my opinion. I suggest $900. I'd looked in several booths by then, and had seen a cigar store Indian for $55,000 (Jacob Garter Cigar Company, New York City—it sells on Saturday), a stenciled fire board for $24,500, a bull weathervane for $18,500, a single early fork for $875.

"My biggest problem is that I don't think big enough," Avery once said. *Think big*, I want to tell him now, but that's easy for me to say. I'm not trying to make a living here. He decides to split the difference and prices the horse at $600. When the piece sells fairly quickly to a man whose check says "something trust fund," Avery credits me with getting more money. He'd bought the piece at a house call. "The homeowner wanted $100. Now I'll go back and give her more." A day or so after the show, the man who bought the horse called Avery at home. He loves the horse. "He wants to be a customer," Avery says. "He can't be a customer if I don't have something impressive. How do you buy for that guy? Look at what he had to choose from just at York."

THE FIRST DAY of the show, business is steady for several hours, with six or eight people in Avery's booth at once, more action than other booths, though most booths are larger so perhaps this is an illusion of busyness. "I could never be one of those five-item dealers," he says. "I like the action in my booth." A man takes photos of Avery's paintings with his cell phone. I imagine someone at the other end is doing some quick research. A history professor from Indiana University is looking at the whale oil lamps; he is an expert on early lighting. "I got interested in material culture and it married nicely with my hobby of collecting antiques," he says.

J. Garrison Stradling, an *Antiques Roadshow* appraiser, comes into Avery's booth to look at a pitcher. "Could be early Limoges," he says. Even the guy who wrote the book on ceramics—*The Art of the Potter*—can't say for sure. I say to Stradling, "I saw you last night on *Antiques Roadshow*," a rerun I watched in my hotel room. He replies, "You see an awful lot of crap. Grandma's dish set. If I never see another set of Limoges china till I die, I won't care." Stradling started with nothing, he says. "I did Shupp's Grove in Pennsylvania. Old Shupp used to empty the Porta-Potties himself." Stradling moved up the ladder to the country's top shows, Philadelphia and the New York Armory show. "What I miss about not doing Brimfield is being out there among the people," he says.

A dealer comes into our booth to tell us a celebrity, Barry Nelson, is heading our way. This is exciting to older dealers, but Avery and I never heard of this guy. (He was the first actor ever to play James Bond, in a television version of *Casino Royale* in 1954, I learn later.) Nelson looks to be eighty, a tall frail man with small eyes and finely wrinkled pale skin. His sherbet-orange frizzy hair floats to his shoulders underneath a black cowboy hat. He still looks boyish, likely due to his small, pinched nose. He's accompanied by his wife, Nansi, who looks maybe fifty. Barry Nelson waits in the aisle in his ankle-length black oil coat, while Nansi studies a bottle in Avery's glass case, mumbling into a tape recorder. She points to a green, two-necked bottle, a "gemel," priced at $250. "Save this for Nelson," she says. The Nelsons slowly peruse every booth until the show closes. I wonder why Nelson is assiduously buying antiques. Don't most people at his age begin to de-access? Months later, Nelson died at the age of eighty-six. Not much later, thieves stole over $1 million worth of antiques from the Nelsons' country house, including two thousand apothecary jars, faience, majolica, and memorabilia from Barry's career.

During the last slow hour of the opening day, 6:00 P.M. to 7:00 P.M., Tucker watches Avery's booth while he and I walk through the show. We see dozens of folky watercolors in one booth, priced at a few hundred dollars. Avery suspects that the dealer has "made" these naive watercolors. When I ask why he thinks this, he says, "He just has too many of them. Nobody has that many at once. He's made me afraid to ever buy another watercolor unless it's never been out of the frame." In another booth, Avery points out an early lighting device with a tapered stem, which he says "for sure" is jury-rigged from a spinning-wheel part. The next day, the device sells. "It's frustrating to see people getting rewarded for knowing nothing," he says.

SATURDAY MORNING before the show opens, Avery and I preview a stoneware auction in another building on the fairgrounds. There are tables and tables of large grayish jugs with blue designs, three hundred lots for sale. "This all looks alike to me," I say.

"Don't feel bad," he says, "so much of it looks alike to me, too." He immediately proves this wrong when he asks the runner to retrieve from a case a redware cow with a calf at her udder. The vent hole—found in all ceramic figurines—is at the end of the cow's teat. "They normally put the vent hole in the arse, as the Irish would say. Definitely Euro, probably English, but nice," Avery says. He writes the lot number for "le cow" on his pad. Next he asks to see a redware pitcher with an incised flower appliqué. "A lot of stuff is French or Lithuanian. You have to watch out," he says. He shows me a spiral "watch-spring" design on a Jersey Morgan crock, then points out a repair, which I hadn't noticed. "The handle has a different sheen to it," he says. He teaches me the "knock test" for discerning hairline cracks in pottery. He holds a jug in one hand, puts his ear against its surface, and raps. "You can't see the crack, but you can hear it. It resonates."

The auctioneer starts selling. He sounds like a cattle caller, with a lot of hubbada-hubbada. The PA system is loud and staticky. Each piece, regardless of the price, is auctioned in the exact same manner, fifty lots per hour. "The guy is treating an $80,000 jar like a $50 thing," Avery says. Later, at the antique show, a twenty-something blond woman in painted-on, bubble-gum pink, corduroy hip huggers tells Tucker she'd come to see her grandfather's stoneware jug auctioned. It's the premier piece, estimated to bring $60,000. The jug is a four-gallon water cooler with cobalt decoration of a soldier and his wife, stamped FENTON & HANCOCK, ST. JOHNSBURY, VT, dating from 1858 to 1870. The soldier is thought to be Asa Peabody Blunt, a Union general. The pink-pants granddaughter says her grandfather fixed furnaces, and found the jug in someone's basement in New England in the 1970s. Later, we hear that the jug sold for $88,000, a new world record for New England stoneware.

AT THE ANTIQUE SHOW, dealers sit in chairs, reading trade papers. When the doors open at 10:00 A.M., there are virtually no customers. Around noon, the after-church demographic trickles in, well-appointed older couples looking for entertainment: "Honey, let's go to the antiques show." They stare blankly and walk slowly, like desert wanderers. Avery takes a trip to the men's room. While he's gone, two dealers from the show come over to inspect his tea table. The table is from New England, in original red paint, squarish, with cut-out corners, priced at $1,295. One dealer measures the table's height, then asks to see underneath. She studies the table closely. "The legs have definitely been cut down," she says to her partner. The couple thank me and leave. Tucker, who has drifted over, says, "Any table less than twenty-eight inches to thirty-two inches is no good." Avery's tea table measures about twenty-six inches tall. "It probably sat in the dirt in a barn and got ruined, so they cut off a few inches," Tucker says.

Before tea tables came tea, introduced into England around 1650. Samuel Pepys wrote in his diary in 1660 of having a cup of "tee," a "China drink" he'd never had before. In 1699, about forty thousand pounds of tea were imported into England, but by 1785, imports had risen to eleven million pounds. As people took to drinking tea, tax revenue from alcohol sales dropped. The British government placed a stiff tariff on tea, which led to wide-scale smuggling. In 1784, the new prime minister, William Pitt the Younger, reduced the tea tax from 119 percent to 12.5 percent. Cheap tea was then available to the masses, though elitists decried tea's ill effects on "persons of an inferior rank." Women neglected "the affairs of their families" for afternoon tea sipping. Since women were generally forbidden from taverns and coffeehouses, they gathered in homes around tea tables to discuss social issues, like slavery. An eighteenth-century poem by William Cowper was titled "The Negro's Complaint: A Subject for Conversation and Reflection at the Tea Table."

Well-to-do women organized elaborate tea parties with silver teapots, kettle stands, cups, saucers, "tea" spoons (before tea, only larger "table" spoons were used), strainers, "slop bowls" for the soggy leaves, trays to carry tea "geer" to the table, canisters for dry tea leaves. (Before tax reform, pricey tea leaves were locked in ornate chests to prevent servants from pilfering.) Women wore tea gowns and sat around elegant tea tables, perhaps like the one made in 1763 by renowned cabinet maker John Goddard for the wealthy merchant Nicholas Brown, who paid £90 Rhode Island currency. (A rough approximation in today's value might be around $2,000.) This same table sold 242 years later through Sotheby's for $8,416,000. A tea table was the first piece of American furniture to fetch over $1 million at an auction, in 1986.

Avery returns about ten minutes after the woman who'd measured the table had left. I tell him about the tea table incident, and watch his face fall. He tells me the table is all original, as he had written on the price tag. The legs have never been cut. "I hate having to go to the book," he says, "but that's what it's come down to." He opens *Warman's Ameri-can Furniture* and shows me how tea tables were usually twenty-two to twenty-six inches tall. (The $8 million tea table sold by Sotheby's in 2005 was twenty-six and three-quarter inches tall.) I feel terrible. I wish I could chase down the tea table people, but they are long gone. For Avery, it was a costly run to the men's room.

AFTER FOUR HOURS, I'm fading. The standing is deadly, and there are still five hours left. All day soft rock music plays, which I realize is a tape loop when I hear for the third time, "Brandy, you're a fine girl, what a goooood wife you would be . . ." The line sticks in my head like Chinese water torture, until a more fitting line takes its place: "Don't let the sound of your own wheels make you crazy." At 5:00 P.M. the show mercifully ends, but the joy is fleeting as the packing begins. Packing is a grind, worse than setting up, which, in an optimistic slant, can be like Christmas, a surprise in each box.

Even though Avery sold several items, including the large chest, the stuff will not fit in his truck. Everything has been decompressed. He asks Tucker to haul a couple boxes, but he still has four boxes left. He says, "Watch these disappear," and before I'm back from the ladies' room, miraculously the boxes are gone. He dismantled them and shoved individual items under the seat and behind the headrest. From the passenger seat, I can only see his two hands on the steering wheel, his knees, and if I lean forward, the tip of his nose. For the ten-hour drive home, I will sit with a box under my feet, on my lap, and several boxes stacked between us on the seat. If Avery were to swing hard to the right, I'd be struck by a flying object, killed by an antique. Avery says, "Note to self for next York show: Scale it down."

Driving home the next day, we can't resist a roadside flea market, where he finds an eighteenth-century hand-hammered iron spatula on sale for five bucks. He's amazed that a nearly three-hundred-year-old implement can lie in plain sight for hours. "Nobody cares," he says forlornly. The spatula is worth about $45, if he could sell it, that is. It's a foot long, with a thin handle and a small square face, good for flipping johnnycakes. I love the pockmarks and divots in the metal, can imagine the blacksmith pounding it into form, hear the ring of each hammer blow. The spatula feels rough and grainy from its forging, but smooth from three hundred years of use. It looks like it could last another three centuries. Avery buys the spatula and gives it to me. Later, I recognize his act for what it was: a thoughtful gesture, but also a rescue mission. He can't bear that something rare and handmade is ignominiously lost among flea-market junk, so he rescues the spatula and gives it to me to care for. I'm happy to have it.

At Avery's house near midnight, we sit around the kitchen table and debrief. Linda joins us. The York show is a step up and Avery has done well, having taken home over $10,000. We discuss his wrinkled shirt, the sneakers, his crowded tables, how a haircut might give him the sheen of a high-end dealer. Will these things really make the difference in sales? Why should they matter? I feel bad even making these suggestions, but Avery is trying to figure out how to jump to the next level. When I ask him which objects he might have left at home to "scale it down," he says he almost left the yellowware bowls. "I thought they were too low-end." But he sold two of them for $500. As is typical, Avery sold nineteen of the three-hundred-plus things he brought. It seems impossible to figure out which objects will sell. How can he cut back? Make his life more reasonable, be the "five-item dealer"? Avery has had moments of self-doubt. "I don't have what it takes," he said once. "I'm the middle-of-the-road guy."

Avery has come a long way from the early days of buying mistakes. In the years I've followed him intermittently, I've seen his steady rise, better merchandise, knowledge in new categories, success at higher-end shows, a growing roster of collectors and dealers who seek him out. Antiques dealers have a few options for selling their wares. Some own shops, or sell online, but that sedentary life would be too boring for Avery, sitting behind a desk all day in a musty shop. Selling online presents the same problem—Avery is too restless, and he thrives around people. He could try to sell at the top-tier shows—he has the knowledge—

but he chafed in his dress shirt after five minutes at York. He'd have to tamp down his rapscallion nature—the spirit of the kid who took a wild midnight ride on his sister's pony. Besides that, to design a "living room" booth at these elite shows, you need a flair for interior decorating.

Aside from a potentially higher profit margin and easier setup, there would be another benefit to "scaling it back," becoming a "five-item-dealer"—Avery's house wouldn't be so overcrowded. His house, he admits, has become "hoarder-esque." Lately, it has reached a critical mass.

Crowded House

Curt Avery tiptoes through his own backyard, ducking beneath the kitchen window so that Linda doesn't see him carrying under his arm a three-foot-long, custom-made sailboat weathervane. Like an inverse thief, he's stealing things *into* his house. Avery tucks the weathervane inside the door of the basement—the only space available now that boxes fill the entire room floor to ceiling, an impenetrable mass of stuff. Years ago, when I first began to shadow Avery, there was a pool table there, and a few boxes along the perimeter. Now, you open the door and face a wall of cardboard.

To antiques dealers, "stuff" is an occupational hazard. Once after visiting a colleague, Avery said, "Typical antique dealer's house, blanket chests two deep." Acquiring objects to sell means there's a surplus. As he did at the Hubley's auction, Avery buys a box lot and plucks the single gem—the Longwy candlestick—from the half dozen items. "That was my whole plan originally," he says. "I'd pick out the good candlestick and throw the rest into another auction, but it never worked out that way." If he takes the time to sell these $20 to $50 items, then he's not dealing in higher-ticket antiques. Avery attends one hundred or so auctions a year (not to mention other shopping excursions), and so over the course of nearly two decades, his house has filled with by-catch, the stuff he cannot sell, the "dregs." The things in the house are like the "misfits from *Toy*

Story," he says. "Stuff nobody wants." Even so, this chum is too valuable to simply toss.

The stuff in the house is like the plant in *Little Shop of Horrors*, growing and consuming and taking over slowly, year by year creeping from one room into the next, filling the two-car garage, then taking over the basement (a winding deer path to the washer), and filling a spare room. The stuff is like a geologist's core sample; the layers show the passing of time, Avery's learning curve over two decades. "I'm surrounded by mistakes," he says about the stuff. "They made me learn."

Over six years, I see the basement and rooms in the house fill, watch Avery try various solutions to clear out the crowded house. "I don't know what to do about all the stuff in the house," he says. "It's depressing. If I could get some value, or even wholesale, I'd sell everything today." To be successful, a dealer must have "fresh" goods, and must keep up with trends, which seem to shift each season. One year dealers were buying up all the wall boxes, another year paper bandboxes. *Country Living* annually lists its "top ten" antiques to collect, and *Martha Stewart Living* shapes the market. A high price at Sotheby's can create demand as quickly as an influx of fakes or reproductions can cool it. The best things sell right away, but lesser objects may take two or five or even ten shows to sell, or they never sell.

FOR COLLECTORS, storing their treasures is a perennial problem. From the fourteenth century on, wealthy collectors, like the Medici, built "studiolos" to hold their vast collections. The earliest studiolo on record is believed to be that of Oliviero Forza, a wealthy citizen of Treviso, north of Venice, in 1335. The collection of Prince Rudolf of Hapsburg, crowned Holy Roman Emperor as Rudolf II in 1575, grew so vast that he had to build new rooms, galleries, and entire new buildings. Catherine the Great, who inherited and then expanded the collection of her grandfather-in-law, Tsar Peter the Great, built new rooms, then whole buildings to hold it. The history of the sprawling Hermitage Museum in St. Petersburg follows her acquisitions: Catherine buys a collection (that of

Johann Ernest Gotzkowski, for example), then builds the small Hermit-age to house it; she purchases another collection (Count Heinrich von Brühl's), then builds the Great Hermitage; she splurges on more collections—Pierre Crozat's, Horace Walpole's, Count Baudouin's, John Lyde-Brown's—then adds more halls and galleries.

The home of nineteenth-century book collector Sir Thomas Phillipps was so overfull that a representative of the British Library wrote, "[T]here is not a room now that is not crowded with large boxes. . . . Lady P. is absent, and were I in her place, I would never return to so wretched an abode." When Phillipps moved in 1864, it took 103 carriage loads (involving some 230 horses and 160 men) to move his books, man-uscripts, prints, charts, maps, and other ephemera. A century later, in 1952, another bibliophile, Thomas Jefferson Fitzpatrick, left thirteen rooms of his Iowa house chock-full when he died. The dealer who sold Fitzpatrick's collection had to "inch" his way through "trails hacked into a bookman's jungle."

In the early twentieth century, Sir Henry Wellcome spent a fortune collecting objects related to the field of medicine for his dream of estab-lishing a Museum of Man. His team of agents filled eight warehouses in England, a former laundry facility, stables, and rooms in his company, Burroughs Wellcome. "But still there was not enough space," Frances Larson wrote in her biography of Wellcome. Andy Warhol's possessions filled all but two rooms of his five-story Manhattan townhouse when he died in 1987. According to Matt Wrbican, the archivist who, as of 2009, has spent eighteen years sorting through Warhol's collection, the only "normal" rooms were the bathroom and kitchen. Film director Guill-ermo del Toro, who has collected books since he was four, bought a second house "to lodge" his collection of comic book art, statues, paint-ings, movie props, and books. At the York antique show, I overheard a couple in Avery's booth say, "We've got two houses filled with stuff."

To be sure, "stuff" is an American problem, not restricted to collectors and dealers. In spite of larger houses and smaller families, from the mid-1990s to the mid-2000s storage unit rentals increased by 90 percent. In a 2009 survey of 1,500 Americans, 47 percent of respondents agreed with the statement "I wish my house were less cluttered."

For antiques dealers, the "stuff" can be an occupational hazard that edges toward hoarding. In *Objects of Desire*, Thatcher Freund describes the home of John Walton, a prominent antiques dealer in the 1950s: "So much furniture cluttered Walton's home that visitors had to pass through narrow alleys." Boxes and steamer trunks filled the home floor to ceiling of antiques dealer John Sisto, who was posthumously notorious in 2009 when it was discovered that he'd purchased over 3,500 historically important items looted from castles in Italy (documents handwritten by popes, kings, Mussolini). His son Joseph said, "At some point, you could barely move in the house." Avery's house is not this crammed, but he hasn't parked his car in his garage for a decade. When the stuff begins to creep inside the house, the problem comes to a head.

ONE MORNING before the York show, Avery is foggy-headed from poor sleep. "Too much on my mind," he says. He'd dreamed that Linda was sawing in half everything in the garage. "It's my livelihood. Does she want a clean garage at the cost of my livelihood? I understand the stuff in the house . . ." he trails off. Avery knows a dealer whose wife gave him an ultimatum: the stuff goes, or she does. The man chose his stuff. Another friend's wife sold her husband's entire collection while he was away, "for nothing," Avery says. She was sick of the stuff. "Now she's his ex-wife." William Davies King writes in *Collections of Nothing*, "My collecting continues to be oppressive to others and myself. When the breakup finally came in the three-year relationship that followed the end of my marriage, the woman remarked how relieved she was to have collecting out of her life." Even Warhol, the icon of material culture, envied his friend "B" who lived in a studio. "That's what I've always wanted," Warhol wrote, to "not have anything—to be able to get rid of all my junk . . . and just move into one room."

Every so often the stuff in Avery's house reaches a critical mass—

objects migrate into the living areas, or in hallways. "The stuff in the house was a bloody mess," Avery says. "Linda has just about had it with me. It's everywhere. It's just nuts, and it's embarrassing and I don't know what to do."

"I don't have the time," he says. "One week Linda was away with the kids, and I was like, *so this is what it's like to have time on your hands?* I got a wicked lot done that day. If I had forty of those days, I think I could straighten out my life." Like Moses on Mount Sinai or Jesus fasting, the magical number—forty days—would be transformative. "I really need that many days," he says. "I could get rid of the bad, sell off some stuff, make phone calls. I need forty days." But forty days of cleaning out the house means that Avery isn't selling antiques. "The reality is that I need the money coming in, and I have family obligations. That's the reality."

When antiques begin to occupy the living room like unwanted guests, Linda protests. "Who has stuff in their living room with price tags on it?" she says. She and Curt strike a deal. "The bargain is to cut the living room in half with a wall, one half for the family, one half for Curt's office and storage," Linda tells me. So Avery builds a two-by-four frame, hangs drywall, tapes and sands and paints, and moves stuff into his new office. But like the Disney sequence "The Sorcerer's Apprentice" in *Fantasia*, in which Mickey Mouse chops a broom in half, only to have it divide again and again, and thus multiply, cutting the room in half seemed to amplify the stuff. It was like the stuff was reproducing at night. Slowly objects began to repopulate the living room. "He hasn't removed the stuff from the family half," Linda says. "That was the bargain. I'm not being unreasonable."

AN ACT OF GOD, or nature anyway, forces Avery to deal with the stuff. "I had a situation where water ran off the house," he says. "The ground froze hard and then it poured three times in a week. I had a good inch of water in the basement." Avery lost some things, which was "a blessing in disguise," he says. "I salvaged some stuff and then I called the insurance company. The insurance guy said, 'Water that runs downhill is not covered.' When does water run uphill?"

When a species overpopulates, my biologist friend tells me, nature regulates the boom with a plague or disease or starvation. Checks and balances. Nature once again forces Avery to contend with the overpopulation of stuff when he discovers mold. He spends a day repacking boxes, but when he excavates further, he discovers that dozens of boxes are slimy with black and green molds. "I'm intent on cleaning up," he tells me. "It's not a healthy environment." One day he clears a large room in the basement and paints the walls with a waterproofing sealant. When he nearly faints from the toxic fumes, he calls the fire department, and they instruct him to shut off his furnace—in the dead of winter—and open windows for three days. The family sleeps in the master bedroom while the house airs out. This time he calls the main office of the insurance company. "Those assholes don't want to pay anything," Avery says. "I asked the guy about the mold and he went into a sinister laugh."

Next, Avery tackles the two-bay garage. If he clears up space here, he can relocate things from the house and the basement. "The stuff is doing him no good," Linda says. "It's been moldering in the garage for five years." Avery takes a few weeks off from the business of antiques. "In the last month I haven't been to two auctions. I haven't made any money in a month or two." Linda says, "He's been spending whole days in the garage, into the night. He gave a truckload of stuff to Marion, and there have been huge piles of trash at the end of the driveway." Marion, Avery's neighbor, is the bottom-most of the resale ladder. A school bus driver, she spots castoffs on her route (her fellow drivers alert her to sidewalk treasures over their CB radios), and she hauls discards out of the dump to sell at yard sales. (Avery's daughter, Kristina, overhears us talking about Marion, and she volunteers that she found a roll of wallpaper trim at the dump. "That's a $9.99 value for free!" she says. Avery smiles. "That's my girl.") The stuff that even Marion can't use, Avery heaps into a pyre in his backyard and burns, a personal bonfire of the vanities. "It's mostly boxes and really bad things that I was going to fix someday," he says. "But even if I fixed something and it's worth $100, better to burn it."

After days and days of purging—cleaning, hauling, and burning—
Linda was afraid to look inside the garage. "There was a tiny space
open," she says. "I knew I'd be disappointed. I just say to him, 'Keep
going. Keep going.'" After three months, though, Linda admits there is
a dent. When I arrive at Avery's house one day to accompany him to a
show, I say, "Can I see the dent?" He cut his hands through the air like
an umpire calling safe. "There's no fucking dent," he says. "It's a mon-
strous job. I had no idea how bad it was. It's a year-long problem."

WHEN I NEXT TALK to Avery, he's found another possible solution to
the house problem: renting space in a group shop. "I've never done this
before," he says. "It's kind of like a little old lady thing—they check their
booths two or three times a week." He knows other dealers who sell
merchandise through group shops. "Lee Massey has stuff in seven shops.
He's successful because he works it hard," Avery says. Avery managed to
finagle two spots for a package deal, $550 a month, at a large group shop
in Rhode Island. "If I sell $550, then it's just like throwing the stuff
out. At $1,000, I'm probably breaking even," he says, factoring in his
costs for the inventory. "I'm going to put low-end items in—teacups and
crap like that. I don't know what I'm doing. This is new to me, but if this
works, there goes the house problem."

Avery spends a day pricing objects, and then moves the "first wave" of
stuff into his space. "I put a cherub bowl in there for $150 and a Staf-
fordshire platter. I paid $200 for it, but I damaged it so I put it at $169.
I'm just going to inundate it with crap." A month later, I call Avery to see
how the group shop is going. "The booth has more than six hundred
items," he says. "It's the mega-version of a booth. I have shit everywhere,
but it's good looking. Another dealer said, 'You have a very impressive
collection.' I thought, *Collection? This is stuff I want to get rid of.*" In
the first three weeks, Avery took in $2,700. "If I can keep doing that, I'll
be happy," he says. But then again, "They only took the good stuff, the
no-brainers."

Avery stocks the co-op space mostly with things that "no one will buy in real life," he says, his "ankle level" stuff. "You can't put anything good in there because it might get stolen. I'm in the worst place in the room for theft. That area is awful, a warehouse district." Still, the group shop is part of the "answer" to the house problem.

PERIODICALLY, I see improvements in the crowded house, a pathway in the basement where there was once a wall of boxes, but in spite of the trips to the dump, the truckloads donated to Marion, the bonfires in the backyard, and the group shop, there is still a superfluity. "This is out of hand," Avery says. "It's a good thing I didn't know. I'm only halfway through the stuff."

Auctions—partly the cause of the problem—become part of the solution. "If I put stuff in an auction, I'll get killed," he says. "I'm going to have to bite the bullet and take a loss." Avery builds several "lots"— mixing the good with the bad so that a local auctioneer will take the stuff. "Probably it will die a horrible death, but I'm going to keep doing it. Everything must sell at $20. That's my rule. Hopefully each thing will bring $50 or $100." That winter, with full houses at auctions—dealers stocking up for the summer shows—what sold and what didn't was "comical," Avery says. "I gave them three oil paintings by the same artist. I wanted $100 apiece. He hands them back and says they did not sell with a $20 opening. How could they not sell? There are 110 people there. Of the three, one sucked, but the other two were beautiful landscapes. If I give stuff to an auction house, I don't want it back. I'll take my hits, but I don't want this shit back," he says. "I'll be able to ride this place for a while. It's a shitty place, but it's part of the answer."

An older dealer Avery knows dealt with his overload by having "five enormous yard sales," so Avery and Linda try that. For his yard sale, Avery hires Joan Christianson to help, and lets her pick the stuff first. Twenty-dollar dishes sell for a buck or two. Fifty-dollar plates for ten. Other dealers clean up. Avery netted a couple thousand dollars, so he held two more sales, though the yard sale crowd is "fucking brutal," he says. "I was so depressed dealing with yard sale people. At first it was kind of fun, but now there is hardly anyone who'll spend fifty bucks. They buy the toys off of Kristina's card table. I had fifteen tables full of stuff. For every sale I made, Kristina made three. That's what people want. The fifty-cent jewelry box." He continues, "I've had three yard sales. I should say, 'Wow, I'm proud of me. Like, *yes!* I got rid of stuff!' But I didn't. There's no answer for the crap."

When the economy crashes, Avery works harder to make the same amount of money, which means he can't take time off to clean out the house. In the down economy, business is slower, so theoretically there might be fewer objects to contend with, or more time to deal with the house. But Avery's strategy in the recession—of necessity—is to work more, buy more, try harder. He's trying to be more selective about what he buys, but as long as he's still earning his living by setting up at close to forty shows per year, with an antiques market in flux because of changing aesthetics and an unpredictable economy, he's going to have more inventory than he can sell. If he takes the year off he needs to clean his house, as a self-employed merchant he'll earn no income. He's about to send his son off to college, so this is not an option.

After Avery tries several "answers" to the house problem, I ask him what he unearthed in the boxes. "Everything," he says. "The good, the bad, and the ugly." The bad he pumps through auctions, loads into the group shop, or donates to Marion. The ugly—the moldy or broken stuff—he burns. But there is still too much stuff. "There's just no answer," he says. Henry Wood Erving, collector and author of *Random Notes on Colonial Furniture*, found a creative answer for his "stuff" problem—he blamed his house. "I've been conscious at times that my home was cluttered, but that's entirely the fault of the house and not what's in it." Avery's house is small by American standards for a family of four, so the house might be partly to blame. But that doesn't solve the problem. It took two decades to accumulate the stuff—it will take a heroic effort to clear it out.

CHAPTER 12

Two Heads Are Better Than One

Throughout history collectors have filled their homes with stuff; that much is well documented. But *why* we collect is still a conundrum. The impulse to collect begins as early as age three, a tendency that fast food restaurants and toy manufacturers exploit by marketing sets of toys and urging kids to "collect them all." In fourth grade, I had a shell collection, which was about the hunt for a whole, perfect specimen from the beaches of Massachusetts. I kept the shells—whelks, limpets, periwinkles—in a shoe box. One summer, my family visited Provincetown at the tip of Cape Cod, where in a souvenir shop I saw bins overflowing with enormous conchs and shiny abalone and dried starfish, a spectacular warehouse of exotica that shamed my tiny collection. I remember feeling thrilled by the gorgeous abundance, but then quickly deflated. Collecting had lost its appeal, for it wasn't the objects as much as it was the search. "What is sought with difficulty is discovered with more pleasure," St. Augustine wrote.

Like boys for generations who avidly collected baseball cards, Avery's son, Dylan, collected Pokémon cards. Dylan kept each card tucked into a plastic sleeve in a loose-leaf binder. One day he walked me through his collection, annotating each card, its value and desirability. Seemingly overnight he outgrew the Pokémon cards and gave the entire collection to his younger sister, Kristina. Then he started collecting cruets. "He's probably the only kid in America to receive an antique cruet for Christ-mas," Avery says. Why cruets, I wondered. A container for vinegar and oil. A ten-year-old boy. What's the connection? The cruets are beautiful, in leaded and cut glass, and perhaps that alone attracted Dylan, the spar-kly refraction of light. Avery says, "As long as he's collecting something."

I wondered why Avery wanted Dylan to have a collection. Does col-lecting demonstrate an aesthetic radar, a refined sensibility? JFK col-lected scrimshaw carvings, which decorated the Oval Office, but Saddam Hussein was a collector, too. He owned sixty cars, including a 1917 Mer-cedes, a 1930s Packard, and a V-3 Woody. Napoleon collected books, and Augusto Pinochet collected Napoleana—now exhibited in Chile's largest museum. John Lattimer, a urologist, literally collected Napoleon—he owns Napoleon's penis. (Allegedly, it was snipped off by the priest who administered last rites.) Andy Warhol collected everything, and now people collect Warhol—for a very high price: $71.7 million for a paint-ing, *Green Car Burning 1*.

Malcolm Forbes, who spent millions on his collections, wrote, "A collection—any collection—reflects a personality," a certain "quality of mind." A man named Steve Jenne collects celebrities' half-eaten sand-wiches. It started when Richard Nixon visited his hometown, ate some of a bison barbecue sandwich and left the remainder on a picnic table. Jenne took the sandwich home and froze it. The story got out, and he was in-vited on *The Tonight Show*, where he then collected leftover sandwiches from Johnny Carson (barbecue again), and guest Steve Martin. This is called "contagious magic"—the object is "contaminated" by its illustrious owner—saint, hero, or celebrity—and that infects the collector.

At lunch a colleague tells me one of her students collects aprons, how the design of aprons tells the story of the changing female form over centuries, the evolution of our notions of feminine beauty. My friends Jason and Heather have a friend in his forties who has collected his toe-nail clippings since he was a child. This is not as uncommon as you would think. Photographer Amy Kubes has collected her toenails since 1995. "I've never missed a cutting," she wrote. William Davies King, author of *Collections of Nothing*, has "seventeen to eighteen thousand labels," including labels from forty-four brands of canned tuna. "I'll spare you the clams, crabmeat, mussels, oysters, sardines, snails, herring, salmon, and kipper snack" labels, he writes. Briefly on my postcollege backpacking trip across Europe, I was a tegestologist (from the Greek *tegestos*, a small reed mat)—a collector of beer coasters.

PSYCHOLOGISTS POSE A RANGE of theories for collecting: anal retentiveness (people collect to control—"All collectors are anal-erotics," wrote a Freudian theorist in 1912); attachment issues (objects as substitute for mother, or for a lover—"A passion for collecting is frequently a direct surrogate for sexual desire," a psychoanalyst opined in 1927); as an extension of self, to combat a sense of "nothingness." It has even been postulated that men, who are collectors in higher numbers than women, collect to compensate for their inability to bear children. Freud theorized that women collectors used objects as substitutes for mates, while men collected as "conquests," like mountain climbers bagging peaks. Freud wrote that the collector "directs his surplus libido onto an inanimate object: a love of things." Freud should know; he collected over two thousand antiquities, Egyptian, Greek, Roman, and Asian figurines, and phallic amulets and objects. Freud greeted his beloved statuary each morning. His maid even observed him petting his Baboon of Thoth statue, an Egyptian deity, the same way he stroked his chow dogs. This link between libido and collecting was echoed in a 2010 Viagra ad. The actor says, "My wife and I couldn't control our antiquing—porcelain figurines, oil lamps, those tiny spoons. Antiquing took over our lives. So I tried Viagra, and now my antiquing is pretty much gone." The ad, pulled by Pfizer after a short run in Canada, is "pretty much gone."

Psychoanalyst Werner Muensterberger wrote in *Collecting: An Unruly Passion*, that collectors collect to "ward off undercurrents of doubt and a dread of emptiness," a sort of balm for existential woe. William Davies King attributed the impulse to collect to "a wound we feel so deeply inside this richest, most materialistic of all societies, and partly from a wound that many of us feel in our personal histories." Simon Garfield, in *The Error World: An Affair with Stamps*, wrote, "Collecting fills a hole in a life, and gives it a semblance of meaning." Curt Avery says, "There's security in acquisition. That's what drives this business." But as Russell Belk notes in *Collecting in a Consumer Society*, "It is not material security, but psychological security" that a collection provides.

Dread, loss, desire, conquest, attachment, substitution, security— whatever the explanation, there has been a want to pathologize collecting, to see ardor for objects as suspect. "Today we tend to think of collecting as an eccentric pastime that suggests a need for psychoanalysis," wrote anthropologist Frances Larson in her biography of Sir Henry Wellcome. "Collecting can be a sort of love sickness," Susan Orlean wrote in *The Orchid Thief.* In the first century B.C.E., Cicero accused Caius Verres of "insanity" for his rapacious collecting, and in the mid- twentieth century, thirty-two-year-old Ralph Ellis was committed to a mental institution by his mother because of his voracious collecting of books on ornithology. When Ellis was released, he resumed collecting. By 1945, he'd shipped two railroad cars loaded with 65,000 books and ephemera to the University of Kansas, where they are housed.

Some psychologists consider collecting a sign of Asperger's syndrome, a mild form of autism. One academic article even links collectors and serial killers. "[T]he serial killer as collector represents, in a way, the logical conclusion (or limit) of collection as pathology in consumer culture." Collecting is sometimes conflated with hoarding, a symptom of obsessive compulsive disorder, or obscene greed, like Imelda Marcos's 1,060 pairs of shoes, 200 size-42 girdles, and 500 size-38 bras (one bulletproof). But the difference is obvious, as one sociologist wrote: "The hoarder is interested in quantity, the collector is interested in quality." Collecting can even be therapeutic, a way to "improve concentration and reduce isolation." Collecting, Paul Ackerman wrote in, "On Collecting: A Psychoanalytic View," can "defend against depression and loneliness."

In these formulations, collecting is not about the object as much as it is about the collector. But collectors often speak in terms of love, like the dealer at Brimfield who said, "I got weak in the knees when I saw that," and Malcolm Forbes, who wrote of his Van Gogh painting, "I love it dearly." True collectors "persevere," Simon Garfield wrote in *Error World: An Affair with Stamps*, "because they are in love."

Collecting is not necessarily about filling a gaping hole in one's psyche, but about expansion—seeking to understand, even own, the world through objects. Susan Stewart, in *On Longing*, calls this "the homemade universe." Collections take on a life of their own, have a magnetic force. Like attracts like. A single thing is an oddity, lonely. One object with its twin is interesting, a pair. Three is a crowd, four is a family, five or more a community—then a village, a world, a universe, and now, the collector is its ruler, its god. At the Rotary flea market, Avery bought his daughter, Kristina, then eight years old, a cat puppet on a string, which she manipulated as she walked along. "We're the dolls of God," she'd said. Perhaps that fuels the desire to collect—to be the god of our dolls. "People collect to have a controllable world," Joan Christianson, said, "especially the doll people." Collecting has its etymological root in Latin, *collecta*, a gathering, but a "collect" is also a short prayer, and there seems to be a link—collecting can be a quasi-spiritual act. Christianson, who started antiques dealing when she lost her office job, admitted she never attended church, but "religiously" woke at dawn each Sunday to comb the flea markets. Collectors, Russell Belk writes, "may act as sacred priests" who transform something ordinary into a "sacred object in a collection." Collectors and dealers speak of seeking the "Holy Grail" of antiques. "There's a whole cult of chair people," Avery said once.

"Cult," by definition, might fit: "A system of religious worship directed toward a particular figure or *object*." But "club" is more accurate: collectors collect themselves. For every object, for every category, there is a club. The American Philatelic Society was founded in 1886—just two decades after stamps were first produced. Today there are over 44,000 members in 110 countries. The Uber-Club, the mother ship, is the Association for All Collectors. "Most people collect and display something during their life time," the Web site says. "People love to collect . . . and many are very good at it!" The Association for All Collectors links its Web site to the Association of Collecting Clubs, which in 2009 listed 6,082 member clubs from A to Z, like the Airline Spoons Club, the Alice in Wonderland Collectors' Network, the Buttonhook Society, the Chatty Cathy Doll Collectors Club (featuring a bimonthly twenty-four-page newsletter called *Chatty News*), and the Zippo Club (tobacco collectibles and lighters), which has branches in Austria, Holland, South Africa, and Poland. Perhaps one of the strangest clubs is the Hawkeye Barbed Wire Collectors Club, "supporting barbed wire collectors and enthusiasts in the greater Iowa area." There are over five hundred patented types of barbed wire, enough to keep a collector busy for a lifetime.

IN COLLECTING ANYTHING, there is the whiff of mortality and immortality both. "Collecting," wrote the director of London's Design Museum, "is best understood as an attempt to roll back the passing of time . . . to defy the threat of mortality." Henry Wood Erving, author of the 1931 book *Random Notes on Colonial Furniture*, wrote that antiques "lengthened my life and greatly increased my happiness." Sir Henry Wellcome never completed his ambitious goal of collecting objects for his "Museum of Man" before his death at eighty-two. "He never thought he would die," one of his employees wrote. But rather than denial or defiance of mortality, some objects serve as reminders, like "postmortem" photos, or *ars moriendi*. In the nineteenth century, when the death of children was common, families memorialized their lost children in photographs, which look like sleeping babies but for certain symbols— a rose held downward, or a morning glory with its blossoms that last only a day.

Human body parts are, perhaps, the starkest memento mori. William "Billy" Jamieson, a Toronto-based dealer and collector of tribal arts and the macabre, owns one of the world's largest collections of shrunken human heads. Jamieson has no qualms about his collection. "People don't want to look at their own mortality," he says, "but I'm a Buddhist and I believe when you are dead you are gone." I learned of Jamieson through his ads in trade magazines: "Collector seeks objects of the macabre, and oddities and curiosities from around the world—coffins, shrunken heads, torture devices, Victorian death/spirit photos, anything weird or strange." His list echoed the duke of Buckingham's wish list in the seventeenth century—"anything that is strang."

"I love the macabre, weird stuff," Jamieson tells me. "I'm just buying a shrunken body from Ecuador. I have over five hundred photos of prisoners, and over nine hundred inmate records from the turn of the century. Remember that novel *The Great American Tragedy*? It was made into two movies—Elizabeth Taylor was in one—about that fellow that murdered a pregnant woman? I have his death certificate, and photos from the execution chamber. I'm just trying to buy a nineteenth-century guillotine owned by one of the last executioners in France." Jamieson speaks rapidly, pausing occasionally to ask, "Do you understand?"

"I own one of the first electric chairs, the same one Warhol made famous," he says. "The first electric chair fell over, so they had Gustav Stickley design another one." Before he was a well-known furniture maker, Stickley was director of manufacturing operations at the state prison in Auburn, New York, from 1892 to 1894. In Stickley's prison shop, inmates fashioned chairs that were sold to the public. "The back is beautifully made, you can't believe it," Jamieson says of the electric chair. "He put designer grooves on it. Who's the buyer for it?" he asks. "It could be some sick collector like myself. Or is it a Stickley collector?"

As a boy, Jamieson collected two-dimensional heads—baseball cards (a $500 million market in America annually)—but he bought his first real human head in 1992. Since then, he's consigned shrunken heads to a "major designer shop in Beverly Hills." (A shrunken human head today costs $15,000 to $20,000.) He counts a number of celebrities as clients for tribal arts and objects of the macabre. "I don't want to mention their names," he says, though in several newspaper articles he named Mick Jagger, Nikki Sixx, Tim Burton, Danny Elfman, and Steven Tyler. (Nicolas Cage sold his collection of shrunken heads in 2009, among other assets, to pay back taxes.) I ask Jamieson, who has transformed part of his seven-thousand-square-foot Toronto loft into a modern-day cabinet of curiosities, why the shrunken heads sell well in the Beverly Hills boutique. "These people are wealthy beyond anything," he says. "So what do you get somebody like that?"

Jamieson sends me a press release about a display of shrunken heads in Ripley's "Odditorium" in Times Square, and curiosity gets the better of me. On a rainy February morning, "Don't Go Breaking My Heart" playing in the museum's lobby, I pay $25, pass through the museum's heavy curtains and am confronted with an enormous stuffed Holstein with a dwarfed fifth leg protruding from its shoulder, at its feet the world's largest hairball, like a ten-pound beach ball. I'm here for the shrunken heads, but the layout forces you through gallery after gallery of grotesqueries, a sepia photo of the world's smallest couple—Martha and Juan de la Cruz, twenty-one and twenty-four inches tall respectively—juxtaposed with the largest sneakers ever made for seven-foot-tall Bob Lanier of the Detroit Pistons; Lanier's twenty-four-inch shoe is as long as Juan de la Cruz was tall.

No heads yet on the second floor as I pass a plastic replica of the world's fattest man—Walter Hudson, who weighed 1,400 pounds—suspended by chains from the ceiling. I walk through chambers with nineteenth-century whalebone canes, a large collection of cigarette lighters, a stuffed alligator, a section of the Berlin wall, framed hair-wreaths from Victorian England—trying to find the shrunken heads—past an entire room of medieval torture devices, with a creepy soundtrack of groans and chants, past an electric chair called "Lucky 21," through a room given over to a family suffering hirsutism, the "wolf brothers" from Mexico, and beyond that locks of hair from Elvis, JFK, and George Washington. I walk faster, anxious to find the shrunken heads, and arrive finally at the last gallery, the pièce de résistance of the "odditorium," the collection of twenty-four shrunken heads, "more shrunken heads on display than the American Museum of Natural History," including heads formerly owned by Andy Warhol and Ernest Hemingway.

The gallery is dimly lit, with sand-colored walls, bamboo and palm fronds, a "jungle" soundtrack of random grunts, snorts, bird shrieks. Most jarring about the heads, each in a glass case, is their size, some as small as plums, faces with tiny features. I'd imagined they'd be wrinkled, like dried apple sculpture, but the skin is taut, like leather stretched on a baseball. (Generally, shrunken heads were filled with sand.) There is one head of a child, which is the size of a large walnut, with fluffy reddish-brown hair. The heads look almost adorable, perfectly proportioned miniature faces—but it's suddenly horrifying to realize they are real human beings, not dolls. You can see each individual's features sharply, the delicate flare of nostrils, the fine cilia of the eyebrows, the outline of lips, stitched shut to trap the spirit of the fallen warrior or victim.

Since hair does not shrink along with the deboned head, the eyelashes are long, like horses' eyelashes, and the hair is big—six inches long on a cue-ball-size head. One hairdo resembles the "flip" curls my babysitter made in the 1960s with Campbell's soup cans. A plaque reads "How to Shrink a Head" and offers a ten-step recipe, the final step, "style and decorate hair to taste." A curly-haired shrunken head is called "Goldilocks." Her nameplate reads, "If the broth was too hot, the hair would fall out. Too cold, and shrinking would suffer." Some of the heads have noses pierced with bone, or feathers in the hair. The tiny faces are vaguely simian, like lion monkeys or howler monkeys. In the early part of the twentieth century, there was a healthy trade in fake shrunken heads made from monkey heads. But these faces are so clearly human, with heart-shaped lips and delicate folds in the ears. One small head sporting a huge Afro and headband looks like Jimi Hendrix, with large lips and wide eyes (the eyes are all shut on the heads), a straight broad nose and high cheekbones. Handsome. The museum's founder, Robert Ripley, said, "I have traveled in 201 countries and the strangest thing I saw is man." Maybe that's why the shrunken heads are so affecting; they are so clearly like me.

"IT'S WEIRD TO SURROUND your life with objects of death," Curt Avery says, but Billy Jamieson is blasé about living with shrunken heads. "Before sports trophies came human trophies," he told the *Toronto Star*. "It goes back thousands of years. David in biblical times brought back the head of Goliath. . . . Now we've calmed it down, and you get a little bowling trophy. My teenage boy has a wall covered with hockey trophies;

he loves them. In a head-hunting culture, he'd be preparing to take his first head." Head hunting was a rite of passage, Jamieson said. "In a lot of cultures, you couldn't get laid until you took a head."

Sex and death. Maybe collecting is linked to basic primal urges. Some researchers think collecting is wired into our DNA, a biological instinct reaching back to our hunter-gatherer ancestors. One scholar wrote that in collecting, "one locates the prey, plans for the attack, acquires the prey in the presence of real or imagined competition." Collectors commonly speak of the "thrill of the hunt." Collecting may be rooted in the Darwinian notion of "survival of the fittest." Early humans who cached food and tools were evolutionarily successful. In this way, humans are like rats, surviving over eons because of an "urge" to hoard. In addition to *Homo sapiens*, up to seventy other species collect or hoard, and not just food. American crows and northern ravens have been known to collect "aluminum foil and brightly colored objects," and hamsters in laboratory studies chose to hoard glass beads over food.

A 2004 study, "A Neural Basis for Collecting Behavior in Humans," located the collecting instinct in the limbic system, our "mammalian brain," the locus for emotions—anger, fear, love, hate, joy, sadness. The study showed that damage to this part of the brain resulted in "abnormal" collecting (indiscriminate hoarding of useless objects), and located the "drive to collect" in the "limbic subcortical and mesolimbic cortical structures," with higher brain functions modulating "the drive toward objects." Greatly simplified, the urge to collect derives from a more primitive region of our brain, with the more recently evolved rational part organizing the collecting impulse. "The normal operation of this multitiered system [the primitive and advanced levels of the brain acting in concert]," the researchers wrote, "probably underlies the ubiquitous tendency of humans to create socially acceptable collections."

Philosophy professor William Irvine writes, "When it comes to desire formation, our intellect typically plays second fiddle to our emotions." Desire, he says, is rooted in our "biological incentive system." Desire is insatiable. Once we gain the object of our desire, we begin to lose our desire for it. This dissatisfaction catalyzes a new desire. The collector's dilemma: you can never be finished. As Philipp Blom writes in *To Have and to Hold*, "The most important object of a collection is the next one." Neuromarketing guru Martin Lindstrom, who uses functional MRIs to map the brain's physiological reactions to objects and images, wrote in *Buyology*, "When we first decide to buy something, the brain cells that release dopamine secrete a burst of good feeling, and this dopamine rush fuels our instinct to keep shopping even when our rational minds tell us we've had enough." He concludes, "The more dopamine surges through our brains, the more we want, well, *stuff*."

Whether it's some atavistic biological drive, like swallows returning to Capistrano, or a spiritual calling, like the faithful making an annual pilgrimage to the holy land, or a quest of another kind, every May for over fifty years some 250,000 people gather from all parts of the country, and the world, and descend upon a village in western Massachusetts, seeking the objects of their desires. The May show at Brimfield—the mecca for collectors—marks the opening of the antiques and flea-market season, a springtime ritual. The busiest show of the three annual events, the May show "is like the trading floor of the stock market," Avery says, "or a Who concert." My first time there last July, the slowest show, was a practice run. You haven't truly experienced Brimfield until you've been there in May.

CHAPTER 13

Stump the Dealer

Brimfield ages you, like dog years. Life passes in "Brimfields." In human years, Avery is forty-seven. In Brimfield years—the number of times he's set up there—three times a year for nearly twenty years—he's approaching sixty. The May show has the highest attendance of the three annual events; on Interstate 84 a giant flashing marquee warns, ANTIQUE SHOW ... EXPECT DELAYS. In town, you can feel the buzz of energy, bumper-to-bumper traffic, overflowing fields, swollen crowds. The sidewalks are clotted with people elbow-to-elbow, a mile-long block party—tents and booths and piles of things as far as the eye can see. It reminds me of the crowds that pour into Boston's "Little Italy" each August for the Festival of St. Anthony, patron saint of miracles, the poor, and lost things. St. Anthony would be the perfect deity to lord over the flea market, too, where antiques dealers pray for the miraculous find—the "Holy Grail"— the poor seek bargains, and the nostalgic search for their lost childhoods in objects from the past.

This time, I join Avery only for the weekend J&J show. On Thursday at 4:30 P.M., we park our cars among the hundreds of U-Hauls, pickups, Penske trucks, vans, and campers lined up for entrance to the J&J field at 6:00 P.M., an hour earlier than last year. The locals have a conflicted relationship with the flea market. Some people abhor the chaos, others appreciate the revenue, up to $50 million annually for the town

coffers. This year every dealer must have a license from the town of Brimfield, another $30 added to show costs. It seems only fair. After all, cops
are needed to direct traffic, manage crowds, and respond to emergencies.
Still, the dealers grumble. Profits are down, but the weak economy has
an inverse effect, too. "Every field is full," Avery says. "Nobody has been
selling all winter. Sellers are desperate."

While we wait in line, we play "Stump the Dealer." I trot out objects
I've purchased at yard sales and flea markets since I last saw Avery, a tole
tray that he says is one hundred years old (he points out hand-cut tin),
and maybe worth $50 (it was painted in the 1950s, unfortunately), a
Diehl police candle lantern from the nineteenth century, which I bought
for $20 and is worth maybe $80. So far I'm doing pretty well. I pull out
the last two items—stoneware! My friend Nancy and I had bought two
pieces after watching a videotape of Avery on a local cable show, *On the
Antiques Trail*, an episode called "What a Crock!" Avery showed the
audience how to date stoneware. Mid-eighteenth-century crocks were
plain, but by the nineteenth century cobalt oxide was used for decoration.
He explained how vaporized rock salt created a sheen on the surface, and
pointed out an Albany "slip," a thick brown coating that sealed the inside
of the crock. He warned, "A white color signifies the piece is not American." Stoneware can bring extraordinary money, like the $88,000 for the
stoneware cooler at the York auction. Or $148,500 for a 1773 William
Crolius heart-shaped inkwell.

Such riches Nancy and I dreamed of after we watched "What a
Crock!" I show Avery a bean pot I bought for ten bucks, which he says
is worth about $25 (though I sense he's being generous so as not to de-
flate my pride), and a smaller wine-jug-like vessel Nancy had purchased,
which looked very old. Nancy was already fantasizing about the new
guitar she was going to buy with her profit. Avery looks at the jug.

"What did Nancy pay for it?" he asks.

"Eight bucks," I reply. "What's it worth?"

"Eight bucks."

We laugh. That's what the antiques business can do: make you feel
hopeful, then greedy, then ignorant and embarrassed. Avery says that the

crock is not ovoid, and the smooth bottom indicates it was factory made. Another lesson, this one cheap, just eight bucks. No new guitar for Nancy.

Finally, the line moves and an hour later we drive onto Avery's space. We erect the tent, cover the tables with cloths, and begin the familiar routine. I remove objects wrapped in shirts, towels, shorts. "That's when you know you are unpacking the third show of the week," Avery says. If it rains at a show and your boxes and wrapping paper get soaked, you have to improvise. I start unwrapping another bag, then I realize it's Avery's clothes for the week.

In May, the field is covered with patches of bluets, tiny lavender flowers that from a distance look like snow. In the woods and vernal pools beyond the chain link fence, peepers serenade us, a thousand frog voices, a melodious symphony of amphibian lust. The sodium lights haze the field with purplish light. At 9:30 P.M., we are still unpacking by the glow of a battery-operated lantern, our hands blackened with newsprint. Chop wood, carry water. That's the best attitude toward this task. Unwrap one item, then the next, and the next, and keep going without looking up or else you'll feel overwhelmed and almost like crying.

It's discouraging to see the threadbare, tail-less stuffed pony I've seen at a couple of shows now. "I'm too high on that," Avery says. "I'll just mark it down and get rid of it." The price of an antique should not be based on the market, it seems to me, but ideally should reflect its intrinsic value; it's an insult to the little horse not to dignify its age and rarity with an appropriate price. After 11:00 P.M., we leave the remaining four boxes for the morning. We carry the outside tables into the tent, roll down the tent-flaps and bungee the entire setup. Avery and I walk around, peek into booths, shop by flashlight. He points out a Pilgrim-century child's toy bed. "A Victorian copy," he notes from six feet away in the dark. We see many large wooden burl bowls. "I don't know what to think about these anymore," Avery says. "The fakes ruined it." Ancient-looking hand-carved wooden bowls are ubiquitous these days—imports from Africa.

Overhead, killdeer screech and a delicious breeze washes over us. At Ken Hartwell's booth, he's unloading bins of washers and metal parts from a cellar-load he bought. He has dozens of bottles he's turned purple with his "process." Between the 1880s and 1915, manganese was used as a stabilizer and clarifying agent in glass-making. When sunlight interacts with manganese, clear glass tints lavender. Since lavender bottles fetch a higher price, bottle dealers set old glass in the sun, or use black lights to hasten the process. Hartwell found a connection at an irradiation facility, where he "purples" large batches overnight, like alchemy, turning $1 into $10. Glass-collector purists hate this practice of "nuking" bottles. Elaine Henderson, in *The Antique Trader*, issued a cri de coeur to "reject" glass that has been "ultraviolently [sic] tampered with." Hartwell once told Avery, "I'm going to make a million dollars, one dollar at a time." With his "process," he accelerates his progress tenfold.

Leon, the dealer in the next booth, shows Avery an old bottle. I don't quite get the exchange, until Leon says that he used glass dust to fake age on the bottom. He's done a good job, put the "wear" in the right places. Avery can tell the bottle is a reproduction, but someone else might be fooled.

At midnight, I head to my tent, the only tenter on the field among hundreds of campers and vans. One of Avery's friends walks by, teases, "This is not the sixties, you know." My tent is a throwback to when the atmosphere at Brimfield resembled a rock concert or a love-in.

FRIDAY AT 5:30 A.M., after a hasty tooth brushing and face washing, I head to Avery's booth to pull out tables, wipe condensation off objects. The concession lady whirs by in her electric golf cart, dispensing free coffee to dealers. "Hey, Babe. How do you take it?" her suggestive offer. "Yankees rule!" she teases a dealer wearing a Red Sox cap, then whizzes down the lane. You can hear her for several more stops, her voice at first cheerful, then grating. Before the gates open at 6:00 A.M., Avery takes ten minutes to cruise the show, returning just before six. "There's something good on the field," he says, a little breathless. By "good" he means spectacular, singular, special, the best thing he's seen all week. "In that booth right over there." He points to a booth catty-corner, and asks if I can see the "family register" hanging on the wall. "It's a bone-crusher," he says. "It has ships, eagles, little sayings. It's over the top. Someone should buy it. I should buy it." The price is $3,000.

My eyes aren't good enough to spot it from this distance, but from the York show, I know what a family register is, a hand-lettered, decorated manuscript that records births and deaths, or baptisms, confirmations, marriages. Family registers were kept by New Englanders in the nineteenth century, but were especially common to German immigrants, many of whom settled in rural Pennsylvania, the "Pennsylvania Dutch," who called these documents "fraktur." *Fraktur* means "broken," like fracture. The term originates from a type of German decorative lettering. Hitler briefly revived the use of Fraktur lettering since it was a purely German form, but reverted to Roman typeface so that the world could more easily read Nazi propaganda. Early Pennsylvania Dutch fraktur were hand-drawn or painted. Later, templates were printed with blanks for artists or scriveners—called "ausfullers" (filler-outers)—to complete with dates, or embellish with color and images: tulips, zodiac symbols, angels, flags, hearts, and birds. Ausfullers traveled from farm to farm with their goose quill pens, or later steel pen nibs, cakes of pigments, inks, resins to fix the colors, compasses, straight edges, blotters, brushes. A skilled ausfuller could earn 10 cents per word in the late eighteenth century, about $2.40 today.

Fraktur and family registers are considered "naive" or folk art. In 1999, a fraktur by an artist named Daniel Otto, with a "dog-faced alligator" drawing and two parrots, sold for $181,500, and in 2004, a dealer paid $366,750 for a fraktur dated 1801, painted by Reverend George Geist-weite. I've rarely seen Avery so excited about an object as he is about the family register. "If it's so good, why *don't* you buy it?" I ask. He cites various reasons—cash flow; and who would he sell it to? He mentions the piece several times throughout the day. Later, he walks over to the booth of a high-end dealer, Bert, to tip him off about the piece; he thinks Bert would be interested, but he's busy with three customers so Avery leaves.

AT 6:00 A.M. when the gates open under darkening skies, shoppers fill the aisles. "Do you have any postcards?" a man calls into the booth. "No, sir," Avery says. "Anything on magic?" another man asks. "Brass luggage tags?" One of Avery's first sales is a plain wooden drying rack to Stephen-Douglas Antiques, a tag team from Vermont with an excellent reputation. Avery has placed a pair of baroque-looking tin sconces on the hood of his truck. Behind the sconces, his Rolling Stones boxers are spread on the dashboard, red lips on black fabric. He must have gotten them wet swimming earlier in the week and is drying them out. Several buyers like the sconces, but walk away at $900. A few hours later the price drops to $675, and a young woman with a lighting store in Houston loves them, buys them. I wonder what she'll charge her wealthy customers for them.

The three geometric-patterned shirred rugs are here. I wish someone would buy them. "The shirred rugs," Avery says, "those are a loser." (Avery will eventually sell these rugs to a "very good" Maine dealer for $350 each. "It took me a year and some change to sell them for what would be considered a fraction of their price a few years ago," he says.) But mostly there are new, interesting items, like an early wooden hand-lettered Ouija board. "The first Ouija board was published in 1890," Avery tells me. And I thought they were invented during my childhood in the sixties. In 1967, the Ouija board outsold Monopoly, and in 1994, it ranked second in popularity of games (behind Monopoly) in a survey of seventeen thousand kids. But before Parker Brothers took over the patent in 1966, William Fuld owned the rights. (Fuld claimed that "ouija" was a portmanteau word from *oui*—French for "yes"—and *ja*—German for "yes.") In the 1890s, there were several divining boards, but Fuld filed legal actions against his competitors, even his own brother, Isaac, who sold the "Oriole Talking Board."

In sixth grade, my friends and I used our Ouija boards to ask if certain boys liked us, or to spell the names of our future husbands, a long-standing tradition, it appears. The *Kennebec Journal* in Maine reported in

1903 that "a young couple in Portland are about to be married as a result of the work of the wonderful ouija board. . . . the ouija board gave her his name as that of her future husband." But things didn't work out so well for Mrs. Eugenia Carpenter, according to the *Boston Daily Globe* in 1891, after her oujia board predicted that "her suitor would not return to her." She was discovered "wandering almost nude in the streets." I love this early Ouija board in Avery's booth, not for its ability to predict the future, but for its power to summon the past.

AN OLDER DEALER ENTERS Avery's booth and studies a pewter teapot. He and Avery settle on $400, and after the sale, Avery says, "Now tell me what I just sold." The man downplays the piece. "Well, it's dented in a few places so it's not that great." After the dealer leaves, Avery turns to me and says, "I just made a mistake."

"How do you know?" I ask.

"I can tell by who bought it," he says. He hadn't researched the teapot, just put it out for a quick turnaround. He could tell he'd priced it too low by the man's reaction as soon as the money was in his hands. For the rest of the weekend, Avery refers to the deal as "the pewter fuckup."

Avery's friend and mentor, Edward, stops by to say hello, a quiet, respectful, knowledgeable dealer. He's a handsome, compact man with leonine gray hair. He sees me taking notes, says, "What are you doing? Catching the antiques trade in its death throes?" As if on cue, thunder booms overhead.

"Has anyone ever been struck by lightning at Brimfield?" I ask Avery.

"Yeah, me," he says. "The first time I bought a chest. Death by Pilgrim-century chest."

Minutes later the sky tears open and torrential, biblical rain drives us under the tent. Avery lowers the front flap against the whipping winds, sheltering us with five patrons as we wait out the gully washer. Trapped under the tent, people look at objects. "You could be stuck in a worse booth," Avery jokes. He picks up a gorgeous, 1780s sugar bowl, silver plate over copper, "but the silver is so thick in all these years the copper doesn't show through," he says. For comparison, he shows me a silver plate candlestick that is nearly all copper, just traces of silver on the surface. He admires the feet of the sugar bowl, the curved top that fits snugly, the delicate smithing on the bowl itself. "Silver is so high right now. They come into the booth with their scales to weigh it. They don't care about its antique value, they just melt it down."

The rain keeps up steadily for four long hours. A belly of water bulges in the tent ceiling. Avery grabs a four-foot-long Shaker-made coat rack and pokes the ceiling, draining the puddle. Afterward, he refers to the coat rack as "the Shaker puddle-poker." Tired of being trapped, people dash from booth to booth in garbage-bag raincoats. Finally the rain stops and the sun shines, but the air is instantly blazing hot and sticky in that depressing *oh-no-global-warming-is-here* way. And now the aisles are mud. Luckily, we are on the upside of the field. The people in the booths downslope—and their objects—stand in three inches of muck. Some dealers trenched their perimeters to channel the water, lifted furniture off the ground, laid down cardboard and lumber walkways. In the past, the muck has been so thick that vehicles had to be winched free. Every site has shortcomings. Our ground is dry, but by late afternoon, the sun glares directly into our booth, frying us, erasing all shade, making anything with metal—pewter plates, brass candlesticks, mirrors—third-degree-burn hot. Weather can make or break a show. "We got weathered," one dealer says. Another dealer adds, "Everything was going so well and then the rain killed the show."

At the end of the day, Avery checks on the family register. He's amazed that it hasn't sold after an entire day on the field. When the show closes at four (mercifully—after ten hours), we wrap up the booth, drive to a pond, then plunge into the cool, reviving water. Avery rinses his dirty socks in the shallows. It's Friday and he's been here since Monday, sleeping in his truck, bathing in this pond, laundering clothes the old-fashioned way. Afterward, we wander over to Avery's friend Alex's booth, where a few dealers are telling stories over burgers and beer, like cowboys around a campfire—Avery's bid for a piece of redware at an auction that he was "all hot and horny for," Alex's gaffe on a fire grenade that he picked up and put down. He later learned that underneath the crud was rare red glass; he'd passed up a $3,000 profit. Fire grenades are glass orbs filled with a saline solution (or in the early twentieth century, carbon tetrachloride—"the latest triumph of chemical science," read an ad), that you smashed into flames to douse a fire. Because the purpose of the object was to break it, intact fire grenades are rare.

As the night wears on and a half dozen dealers drink beer and smoke "fatties," Alex turns theatrical. He's boyishly handsome, with dimples and a cleft chin, a cool, blue-eyed stare that can make you uneasy at first. For many years he played guitar in a band, and so he has a stage presence. All the world's a stage, even this plot of grass under a starry spring night in Brimfield. Alex stands, pauses for a beat as his body becomes inhabited by a crusty sea captain, smoking an invisible pipe. He recites verbatim Quint's speech in *Jaws*. "They tore apart about a hundred men, the first night . . . And pretty soon, when they stepped it up, and you'd feel 'em bump you . . . Sharks averaged six men an hour." *Platoon* is next for re-enactment. Curt and Alex have both memorized lines from the film. Alex asks the title of the book I'm writing, and I say I need one. He suggests "At the Flea Market." He and Curt invent a talk show, "At the Flea Market, with guest Curt Avery," Alex says. He picks up an old broken oar with a mermaid carving from his $5 bargain table. "Curt Avery, tell us what this was used for?" Curt grabs the oar, and speaking with an exaggerated seriousness, says, "Well, Alex . . ." He says the oar was used to hunt seals, and he starts whacking a set of tiny vintage stuffed seals on Alex's bargain table. Then Alex parodies an auctioneer and conducts a "mock-tion." Avery is Opie, a runner who can't identify a pair of sugar snips to bring up for sale. Alex grabs a 1930s phone and says, "I have an opening bid of $200," and everyone cracks up at the obvious phantom bid, antique-dealer humor, necessary decompression after six arduous days buying and selling at Brimfield. Flea-market nightlife. Their voices echo as I drift over to my tent.

ON SATURDAY, "RETAIL DAY," the show opens at nine, but there's no sleeping in when you are camped on the field. At dawn, car doors slam, a truck in reverse beeps, people yell, a man loudly hucks and spits every fifteen minutes. But the day is gorgeous, with crystalline skies and perfect puffs of cloud. Avery has been shopping, and returns carrying a Civil War sword with a gilded handle. Right after the show opens, Bert, the high-end dealer Avery attempted to alert to the family register yesterday, walks into the booth and says, "Look what I just bought." He unveils the very same family register. The document has a small tear on one edge, but it's real, dating to about 1780, and is ornately decorated with eagles, ships, proverbs—"United we stand, divided we fall." The colors are vivid, the last entry around 1908. Bert paid $2,000; the price dropped by a thousand overnight. Avery asks Bert what he thinks the family register is worth. "Ten thousand dollars to $15,000, maybe $16,000," Bert says.

Bert admits that he used to write uncashable $50,000 checks if he saw something good, and then he'd pray and hope and network to find a buyer quickly, recover his money, and make a profit when he sold the piece. He knew he had a few days between the ink drying on the check and the bank cashing it, and he trusted his knowledge, trusted his ability to find a buyer while the clock ticked. This method has worked for him and now he routinely writes checks for up to $70,000, he says, money he doesn't always have, but money he *knows* he'll find. His gambles have paid off so far, he says. Risk. Courage. Faith. Confidence. Chutzpah. Most important, knowledge. After Bert leaves, Avery says, "That guy is one of the biggest dealers in the country." I sense a tinge of regret in Avery, but Bert buying the register is also a good sign. It gives Avery confidence in his eye and his gut.

Throughout the rest of the day, Avery mulls the situation. "If the guy in the booth over there could only sell it for $2,000 on this field, how would I sell it?" he says. Still, he takes comfort that he was right, even if it was a practice round. He tells me his friend Jimmy bought a piece of stoneware from an online dealer for $10,000, how Jimmy drove to Indiana to pick up the piece, which turned out to be Belgian and worthless. This is the cautionary tale, the $10,000 mistake. In the end, Jimmy got his money back, but that's not always the case. A $200 mistake is routine in the learning curve, a $1,000 gaffe is a bummer, but a $10,000 mistake is an exponentially more painful lesson. "The higher the price, the easier it is to make a mistake," Avery says. A high price implies that an "expert" has given a stamp of approval. You can become complacent, less than rigorous in your own investigation. But the "mistakes" cut both ways. You can make a mistake buying a thing, or you can make a mistake *not* buying it.

Avery once witnessed a dealer lose a million dollars by *not* buying something. At an auction one night, a darkish "marine scene" painting came up for sale. Two dealers suspected it was a Mary Blood Mellen, a student of Fitz Henry Lane, who was "one of the first great luminists from this area in the late 1800s," Avery says. "He painted harbor scenes. They are very powerful, very detailed, and gorgeous. They bring three to five million." In 2004, Skinner's hit a world record with a Fitz Henry Lane oil, *Manchester Harbor*, which sold for $5.5 million. "This guy—call him Joe—has been on this painting kick," Avery says, hoping to "hit a winner." The auctioneer started the bidding low, around $300, but once it approached $1,000, only two dealers fought for it, "Joe" and "a clock guy," who was a decoy for another dealer. The bidding was spirited, "real fast and furious and mean," Avery says, "but at $14,500, suddenly Joe and the clock guy tried to deny the bid. Nobody knew who had actually made the last bid, but neither wanted to get stuck with a Mary Blood Mellen, which is worth $15,000 at best." Finally, the clock guy stepped up and bought the painting. Later, the art dealer, for whom the clock guy was a decoy, brought the painting before the Fitz Henry Lane Society, which authenticated it as a work of Lane's, and not a piece by his student, the minor painter, Mary Blood Mellen (as Joe and the "clock guy" had thought). The dealer then sold the Fitz Henry Lane painting for about $960,000.

"Joe wouldn't take the painting for $14,500 and got burned," Avery says. "I felt sorry for him. We are only going to be presented with these things a handful of times in our lives, if we are lucky. Like a lottery ticket." The story was a lesson for Avery. "I went to the Museum of Fine Arts in Boston to look at the Mary Blood Mellens," he says. Compared with the work of her mentor, Fitz Henry Lane, he thought Mellen's work "looked like cartoons."

Three months after Brimfield, Avery tells me that Bert sold the family register at a high-end show for $7,000, half of what Bert thought it was worth, but triple what he'd paid. "I saw it at six A.M. for $3,000," Avery says. "Bert bought it the next day for $2,000. If it had been offered to me for $2,000 when I saw it, I would have bought it."

SATURDAY IS SLOW but steady. Avery talks with Jane, a dealer in her early sixties with an infectious optimism. They are discussing an eighteenth-century cupboard made of a wood called "butternut," a type of walnut. The cupboard is two feet high, with three shelves, and visible traces of original reddish paint. The cupboard looks like it once had a door, but Avery is adamant that it was built as an open shelf. He gets irritated when the first thing people say about the piece is, "That used to have a door."

Avery is worried about his reputation because he recently sold Jane a candle stand for $50 that he told her was "*Not right!*" Jane sold it to another dealer, who sold it to a third dealer. Now the piece is on sale in a booth for $1,500. Avery is worried because the provenance of the candle stand as originating with him may have followed it from dealer to dealer, but not the fact that Avery said the piece was *not right!* "Somewhere down the line, someone believed that thing was real," he says, based on the $1,500 asking price, "some dealer who probably thought everyone else was missing the boat." This haunts Avery. "I don't want my name attached to that thing," he says. "Because of the chain of ownership, my name might be tainted as contributing to the illusion that it's real."

"I stand behind everything I sell," I've heard him say many times. "I guarantee my merchandise." If he doesn't know something or can't vouch for an object, he discloses this. "You're on your own with that," he'll say, or "Your guess is as good as mine." If he's unsure, his tags will note that a piece is "possibly" this, or "maybe" from a certain period. Jane buys the butternut cabinet, but at least Avery is sure it's real.

WITH AN HOUR to go before closing, a dealer spots Avery's netsuke in a glass case, which he calls "net-ski." He has a set of seven that he bought at Skinner's, two-inch-tall, signed, carved figures—tiny potbellied Japanese men wrapped in robes, pointing to the heavens or laughing, with a mouse crawling up a cloak or a bird on a shoulder. In seventeenth-century Japan, artists called *netsukeshi* carved figures to serve as toggles that secured pocket-appendages to the sashes of kimonos (kimonos were designed without pockets). Netsuke were carved from wood, ivory, clay, coral, bone or antler, walrus or narwhal tusk, bamboo, amber, or made of porcelain, and come in a wide range of subjects—warriors, priests, animals, gods and goddesses, mythical characters, and erotic figures called *shunga*.

The woman, a new owner of an antique shop, hesitates about the netsuke, though she's clearly fascinated by the little guys. She says she'll be back, and we think we'll never see her again, which is typical, but a half hour later she returns. She's never carried anything like them and she's nervous. Avery tells her she can ask $150 each. He wants $100 apiece, but maybe because she's a nice lady and a newish dealer, he gives her a knock at $500 for seven, and she buys them.

Ten minutes before the show closes, an elementary school teacher fingers Avery's clay marbles, says she wants them for her class. Avery offers to sell one hundred for $20. She patiently picks through the bowl, choosing the brightest colors. After she leaves, he says, "Good. One less marble to pack." Probably it's the heat and sleep deprivation and exhaustion from three long days, but Avery's comment strikes me as hilarious and I double over laughing. His truck is filled to capacity, every nook and cranny stuffed with antiques, hundreds of items to repack and take home for the next show, but one—or one hundred—fewer marble to pack. Good.

At 4:00 P.M. we pack, working silently and methodically for three hours. The last act is Avery lashing the bundle of metal tent poles, which must weigh a hundred pounds, and lifting them onto a table he positions next to his truck. He climbs onto the table, stands, and then clean-jerks the poles onto the cab of his truck, like an Olympic weightlifter. "This will kill me some day," he says casually. I'm not sure if he's referring to the lifting, to Brimfield, or to his nomadic life. At 8:00 P.M., in the fading twilight, we part ways.

Brimfield is an imagined city, here one day, gone the next. In a week, the crowd expands to 250,000 people, with probably 8,000 temporary residents in tents, cars, vans, campers, motor homes. Four thousand small businesses open up, offering an inventory of millions of objects, and then—though the packing feels long and miserable—in a relative flash the city is gone. Vanished. Like Oz, a mirage, the fields empty but for bits of litter, ready again for cows.

CHAPTER 14

Shop Victoriously

One day at Brimfield, as Avery and I approach a pudgy, middle-aged dealer, he whispers, "Body by eBay." He's seen many dealers who "ballooned out" when they began to sell on eBay. "I, too, put on fifteen pounds," he says, "but then I started leaving free weights around." When Avery took a break from selling on eBay and added more shows to his circuit, he lost twenty pounds. "The stress diet," he says. eBay changed more than the physiques of antiques dealers; it changed the nature of the business. "The stuff I was good at—the small stuff—eBay helped with at first," Avery says. "Everything was suddenly very saleable. Instead of dragging the inkwell to four shows, it would sell in a week." For the first few years, eBay expanded Avery's audience worldwide. But eventually, the listings caught up to the buyers. "A Stoddard umbrella ink used to be hard to find," he says, speaking of a rare inkwell from the Stoddard, New Hampshire, glass factory, "but with eBay, every Stoddard ink came out of the closet. They used to bring $425, but one just sold on eBay for $200."

eBay changed the nature of "rare" in antiques, and rendered dealers' esoteric knowledge less important, at least for some objects. "eBay leveled the playing field," Avery says. "Anyone can find out about a piece of Meissen pottery. They can't pronounce it, but they can have it sold in a week. Once everyone caught on, it tanked." At the York, Pennsylvania, show, a woman picked up one of the emerald green Wedgwood plates that Avery had marked at $125 each. She told me she'd bought a stack of them for a buck apiece at a yard sale. She knew nothing about them, but listed them on eBay. "I was shocked when they sold for hundreds to a buyer in Australia," she'd said. "All the dues we've paid earning knowledge in this business and the stuff ends up on eBay and it doesn't matter," Avery says. "Any idiot with a computer and an attic full of stuff can sell on eBay."

IN 1983, a Manhattan business consultant named Howard Davidowitz said, presciently, "The next great retail fortune is going to be made in the institutionalization of the flea market." Just over a decade later, software engineer Pierre Omidyar founded eBay. When the company went public three years later, the stock hit ten billion overnight and Omidyar instantly became the world's wealthiest thirty-two-year-old. In its first decade, eBay was the fastest-growing company in history. With more than 88 million active users in 2009, eBay is the world's largest Internet marketplace, claiming one quarter of all online sales.

"If we were a nation," former CEO Meg Whitman said, "we'd be the ninth most populous." By Whitman's calculus, eBayland would have more citizens than Germany.

eBay's original tagline showed its founder's democratic intentions: "The power of all of us." Pierre Omidyar hoped eBay would represent the best of human nature—recycling, reusing, people connecting with people. But eBay has changed. Its tagline in 2007 conveyed a more mercenary capitalism: "It's better when you win it. Shop Victoriously." Perhaps because of the auction mentality or the anonymity of the Internet, eBay has inspired greed, fakery, immorality, stupidity. Within minutes of the September 11, 2001, attacks on the World Trade Center, people listed chunks of debris for sale. After Hurricane Katrina, people tried to auction MREs (Meals Ready to Eat), military rations issued to hurricane refugees. Over the years, people have tried to sell things that are illegal, weird, or just plain sad: three grams of plutonium, AK-47s, a Russian-made rocket launcher, tickets to a death row execution, breast milk (the auction was pulled because it was not packaged to government standards), a "ghost" captured in a jar, a human kidney. A kidney stone—William Shatner's—sold on eBay for $25,000 to GoldenPalace.com, an online casino. An eighteen-year-old boy auctioned himself off for a prom date, and another teenager posted "Young Man's Virginty." Anyone who cannot spell "virginity" correctly should not be having sex, let alone selling it.

People have tried to sell newborn babies, and a man put his wife up for sale on a Brazilian auction site partially owned by eBay. In 2005, an Israeli couple living on the West Bank tried to sell for $40,000 advertising space on the house from which they were to be evicted. They wrote: "We (among hundreds of others) will entrench ourselves in the houses . . . and fight as hard as we can against the soldiers. This event will be filmed by international news stations and will reach MILLIONS OF VIEWERS AROUND THE WORLD. . . . We will hang a big flag with your company name on it!" Perhaps worse than selling a body part, your child, your maidenhead, or your betrothed is to sell your soul. A Massachusetts man sold his soul for $1,325.

eBay forbids certain categories, and they'll instantly pull auctions of banned items: bootleg music, Nazi paraphernalia, live animals, and endangered species animal parts, like tortoise shells or ivory. "You have to be careful how you describe things," Avery says. eBay deleted his listing for a box that contained "whalebone," even though the bone was inlaid a century earlier. He listed an antique fur bonnet, but did not say "seal fur." When Joan Christianson listed "codeine apothecary jars," her auction was deleted.

A decade after eBay's birth, Pierre Omidyar said that eBay showed "more than two-hundred million people that they can trust a complete stranger." The reality has not lived up to Omidyar's ideal. eBay's largest legal problem is the sale of fakes. "Online selling is a comedy," Avery says. One dealer he knows "embellishes the hell out of things" and has been very successful. "He lists something as an American Betty lamp and gets the price as if it were authentic when it's Lithuanian. People in Arizona and out west don't know. The New England buyers aren't buying that crap," he says. "Anyone who is willing to lie, or is ignorant that they are misrepresenting stuff, does well online. They are winning big."

Fraud on auction sites like eBay is the second most common complaint made to the FBI's Internet Crime Complaint Center. The center received 275,284 total complaints in 2008, 33 percent more than in 2007. Over 70,000 of those were for auction fraud. (Because of underreporting, these figures may be a fraction of the actual number.) In 1997, the Federal Trade Commission received 107 complaints about online auction chicanery. Less than a decade later, in 2006, it logged 30,837. (There is an upside to eBay fraud: an anthropologist claimed that eBay made it easier for "tomb raiders" to fake artifacts than to raid burial sites.)

Lawsuits against eBay have escalated over the years. In 2000, a man sued eBay after buying a baseball bat for $367 that was advertised as signed by Ted Williams. In 2004, Tiffany & Co. sued eBay for counterfeiting after Tiffany agents secretly purchased 186 pieces of "Tiffany" jewelry from sellers with positive ratings, 73 percent of which turned out to be fake. (In 2006, about $1.5 million worth of Tiffany products sold on eBay *monthly*.) Louis Vuitton and Christian Dior also sued eBay for $47 million for its failure to stop counterfeit products from being sold. An eBay spokesperson countered the charge: "We never take possession of the goods . . . and we don't have any expertise." The lawsuits could have fundamentally changed eBay's practices, forcing them to police millions of items, but in 2008, eBay prevailed in a U.S. court against Tiffany. Weeks earlier, however, eBay lost two similar suits in French courts, and and was ordered to pay $61 million in damages to Moët Hennessy Louis Vuitton, and $30,000 to Hermès.

BY THE MID-TO-LATE 2000s, Avery, like many dealers, had soured on eBay. "They killed the golden goose," he says. "eBay is saturated. My friend put fourteen items on and two sold." It's not just that eBay is flooded with merchandise, but changes to the system favored buyers. "eBay shot itself in the foot," Avery says. "They offer dealers less and less. They raised their fucking fees so much, the greedy bastards." eBay, or as some dealers say, "FeeBay," charges fees for listing objects ("insertion fee"), reserved prices, bold text, using the "Buy It Now" option, enlarged or multiple pictures, longer listing time, and final value fees, among others. On any given day, eBay customer support receives 100,000 contacts in North America, which might be why connecting with customer support is "like trying to get to the Wizard of Oz," Avery says. Fed up, Avery, once a "power seller," quit eBay. "It's everything," he says. "The scams, the crappy sellers." eBay's 2009 slogan—"Come to think of it—eBay"—suggests that others, like Avery, abandoned eBay and now need a reminder. "It's too bad," he says, "because there's a lot of good honest people out there who'll sell you a nice product. Now would be the time for somebody else to come in and really try to run a nice honest business."

"Crappy sellers"—a bane to Avery—are a boon to his friend Jimmy Desjardins. "My angle is a little different from other dealers," Jimmy tells me. "Most people on eBay are selling. I make a living *buying* things on eBay." Jimmy's a high-tech picker, a cyber-picker. Each morning, he rises from bed, greets his dogs, fixes a cup of coffee, selects some music, and settles himself in front of his computer for a day at work—shopping for antiques. Or, more accurately, for "mistakes"—objects that sellers have misidentified, misspelled, or miscategorized—mistakes like the early eighteenth-century glassware that Jimmy won on eBay for $305 and sold for $50,000. Jimmy is the poster child for eBay's slogan, "Shop Victoriously."

I meet Jimmy at a high-end antique show in Hartford, Connecticut. He walks out of the show carrying a plain cardboard box that contains a stoneware sconce worth $12,000. He's average height and build, sandy hair, charmingly self-deprecating. When I asked him to describe himself so I could find him, like what color hair, he laughed. "Well, there's not too much left." Jimmy and I sit in my car and talk. "The computer has completely changed my life," he says. "I'm making triple what I made doing it the old-fashioned way, driving to auctions and shops, having to go everywhere to see everything. Now I can see it all from my den."

In 2008 on eBay there were, on average, over 133,000,000 items concurrently listed for sale (a pair of shoes sold every three seconds). Imagine laying out all of these items at a huge flea market. Now imagine you're a dealer or collector trying to find something good the "old-fashioned way"—the 90-degree heat of Brimfield, the miles and miles of walking in circles. "Or getting up when it's five degrees and having to go out to work," Jimmy says. It would take a lifetime. Theoretically, Jimmy is searching through these 133 million items, like panning for gold, but from the comfort of his home. "I'm in a nice comfortable chair, I've got my music playing—I love classical Indian music as much as I love jazz—I'm sitting there listening to Bill Evans play his piano and I'm searching eBay." Like the old-time slogan for the Yellow Pages, Jimmy lets his fingers do the walking. "I have a lot of techniques I use to find mislisted things. I search for misspelled words. If you search the way something is properly spelled, then all the competition can find the thing. If it is mislisted, then eighty percent of the people who would bid on it would never find it." Jimmy was trawling eBay for mistakes before the proliferation of services now available to search for mislistings— Fetchbid.com, Oktshun.com, or Branica.com.

"Believe me, it works," Jimmy says. "I've made so much more money on eBay than I did doing it the old-fashioned way. And I'm saving money on gas from not driving all over creation." For the $50,000 glassware hit, Jimmy had no competition. "I was the only bidder, and the auction ran a full week. Their minimum bid was $305. I bid $16,000, hoping that I wasn't going to be outbid, but nobody else bid." I didn't understand why Jimmy didn't have to pay the $16,000 that he bid. On eBay, he explains, bidders only see current bids, not the amount a buyer fixes in his mind. "Say you're sitting in a traditional auction and up comes a piece of furniture," Jimmy says. "In your mind you say, 'Well, jeez, I'm willing to go to $20,000 on that.' But you get it for $10,000. No one knows you were willing to bid up to $20,000." Like Avery's scrawled notes on the pages of his auction catalogs, eBay confidentially stores the bidder's secret high bid. "You bid your max," Jimmy says, "because the only way your bid can be advanced is if someone else bids against you. If you put a million-dollar bid, and someone else bids $100,000, then the eBay system will put me on top at like $101,000, or whatever."

For the glassware Jimmy bought for $305 and sold for $50,000, the seller was an eBay storefront, one of over 500,000 nationwide.

"The sellers were probably like, 'Woohoo! Three hundred bucks!'" I say.

"I tell you I never expected to get a $50,000 thing," he says. "I rented the most unbelievable house on the ocean. We ate lobster every night. We just lived like royalty for two weeks."

LIKE CURT AVERY and Ken Hartwell, Jimmy's interest in antiques began from the ground up—he too was a bottle digger. "My friends and I found this old cellar hole in the woods. We started digging out the rubble. I found a rusty part to a musket. You wonder who lived there. When you are a kid, in your mind, it was Daniel Boone." Bottle digging fostered Jimmy's curiosity about the whole spectrum of antiques. After college, he worked as a cabinet maker for a company that moved old houses. "If there was a great eighteenth-century home in the way of a new school, my company would dismantle it, sell it to some wealthy person, take it apart, number it, and reassemble it on their lot. I made all the interior millwork, the moldings, the raised paneling, all authentic." When New England suffered a recession, "out of necessity," he began to set up at antique shows. "I thought maybe I could supplement my income, but that just took off. I never went back to the cabinet making." Like Avery, Jimmy has the antique fever, especially for figural pottery. "I'm not just a dealer," he says, "I *love* this stuff. I'm an addict with a habit."

The very first object Jimmy bought on eBay, around 1999, was a piece of redware listed as an "old drip glazed pot." It was a piece that Curt Avery had been watching, too. "They didn't use the term *redware*," Jimmy says. He didn't know for sure what the pot was, only that it was "very early" and had an "interesting glaze." He bid $350 and won the piece for

$140. "As soon as I got it, I e-mailed the auction to Curt, and said, 'Hey Curt, my first eBay purchase, what do you think?'" Jimmy sold the pot to Curt for $500. A while later, Jimmy saw a photo of the same pot, only missing its lid, at a Virginia auction. He called the auctioneer to find out the sale price. "The guy goes, 'Oh, you mean the Great Road crock?' There was a potter, I believe his last name was Cain, who had a pottery on this Great Road in Tennessee."

The Great Road, originally part of an Indian trail called the Great Warrior Path, was a major route from Philadelphia across Virginia, dipping down into northern Tennessee. Horseback riders and pioneers towing handcarts loaded with their worldly possessions followed the path to the new frontier. By the late eighteenth century, the Great Road and its tributaries were crowded with horse- (or cow-) drawn wagons. Potters set up shop to sell necessities—preserve jars, liquor jugs, tableware— to the westward traffic. The 1850 census recorded thirteen potters in counties along the Great Road in Virginia and Tennessee. The Cains were a pottery dynasty, started by Leonard Cain around 1814. His sons, Abraham, William, and Eli, continued the family vocation. His grandson Martin Cain potted until the early 1900s, the last of the Cain family potters.

The Great Road pottery Jimmy had seen in the paper had sold for $12,500 at the Virginia auction. "Curt kept the piece for a number of years," Jimmy says, "but then he called me and asked if I wanted to buy it. I gave him $10,000. So I bought it on eBay for $140, sold it for $500, and bought it back for $10,000." Jimmy thinks the piece is worth double that, which may be conservative. A six-and-a-half-inch redware pitcher attributed to the Cain family, with a chip in the rim, sold in 2009 at a Knoxville auction for $22,500.

Avery's recollection ends the same way, but the particulars vary. He'd been watching the auction on that redware piece all week. "It was listed wrong," he says. "The guy never used the word 'redware.' The jar looks like it has tar on its sides, orange, with a black streaky glaze, maybe used for storing pickles or preserves." Great Road pottery is orange from the iron-rich clay; as you move north and east, the soil darkens, and pottery looks more reddish. The Cains used lead and manganese glazes, which under intense heat turn brownish black.

Avery was waiting until the last minute to bid on the piece. "I didn't want to bid early because people used to search me to see what I was bidding on, I learned that real quick," he says. (This practice is called "shadowing," according to *Snipers, Shills, and Sharks: eBay and Human Behavior*.) Instead, Avery was going to "pound the crap out of it" just as the auction closed. These were the early days on eBay before "snipe" programs, like Auction Stealer or Auction Defender, which bidders can set to automatically top any bid just seconds before the auction closes. Before snipe programs, you had to watchdog each auction. "I'd be sitting there on a Sunday afternoon waiting for this auction to close," Avery recalls. "I remember this big important buyer from New York came to my house one day to look at some stuff, and I said, 'Wait a minute, Dave, I gotta get this eBay thing.' He watched me nail it in the last ten seconds." Toward the end of the auction for the redware piece, Avery noticed Jimmy's bid. "I was like, *ah fuck*." Avery called Jimmy and they made a pact: Jimmy would buy it, but offer Curt first refusal. "He nobly agreed to sell it to me," Avery says. Avery paid Jimmy $800, and kept the piece in his collection for a couple years. He later learned that a similar piece sold for $16,000, but when Jimmy called (in Avery's recollection) to offer him $10,000, he sold it to him, remembering the favor Jimmy had done for him originally.

EVEN IF MORE PEOPLE catch on to the mislisted strategy, Jimmy isn't worried. "While the number of competitors—so to speak—who have knowledge has increased, so has the volume of listings. I could be on eBay twenty-four hours a day and never complete all my searches." Jimmy's secret weapon is not searching for mislistings: it's his knowledge. "I don't look for things that can be easily looked up in a price guide. If you have a Mickey Mantle baseball card from 1955, you can find out what it's worth in five minutes. Free blown glass, handmade pottery—if you own one of these things and you don't know what it's worth, you have no means to look it up. There's nothing written about it. I focus on those types of items."

Assessing antiques is a process of piecing together information from a variety of sources, except, Jimmy says, the most obvious source. "The one type of book you should avoid is price guides," he says. I laugh, since those are exactly the books I consult. "They keep you stupid. You don't learn how to value things in your own mind." Price guides often use auction sales to value items, unreliable information at best. "What you don't know is who was at the auction for that sale," Jimmy says. "Does the price reflect irrational exuberance, or a slow day? Was the piece pristine or damaged?" Price guides "do more harm than good," he says. "I know people who have been doing this for thirty years who still can't price something without using a price guide. It's like they don't have a mind of their own. It's robbed them of their mind."

Jimmy's strategy is to buy specialty reference books. "I spend at least $1,500 a year on my library. The type of books I buy are very focused," he says. "They generally go out of print. The pottery of eastern Tennessee, or the glass of John Frederick Amelung." Reference books offer history and background. Using that information, combined with auction and show sales results, you develop your own sense of rarity, authenticity, age, and value. "I bookmark a lot of things just to follow what they sell for, just for the knowledge," Jimmy says. "You know, things that are listed correctly."

"If you focus on quality reference books," he says, "when you see a piece, you are going to know how to value it." He gives an example. "I bought a book by H. E. Comstock, *Pottery of the Shenandoah Valley Region.* This book is worth its weight in gold." Jimmy read about Anthony Bacher, a German immigrant into Virginia around 1849. "I don't think I owned that book six months when I saw this pitcher at Brimfield," he says. "The booth was full of crap, 1950s toys, Barbie dolls, and this one piece of pottery." The pitcher had twenty-four applied flowers, a design

Jimmy recognized from the Comstock book. "I flipped the pitcher over and it was signed, 'Anthony Bacher, 1852.'" Jimmy thinks the pitcher is the second-oldest known after Bacher's arrival in the United States. He paid the dealer $500, and sold the piece for $8,500 "in one phone call," he says. "Today that piece is worth $25,000."

One of Jimmy's friends complained that he didn't have time to read reference books. "I'm thinking, *you don't have time not to read them.* You can work hard or you can work smart. It's like this piece of pottery in this box," he says. "I paid $12,000. I showed it to my friend and he said, 'Jeez, I wouldn't have had the balls to pull the trigger on that.' But if you had the knowledge, you would. Confidence comes with knowledge."

IN SPITE OF JIMMY'S "victories" on eBay, he's made mistakes. "Some people use cheaper digital cameras and the resolution is low. Or they didn't super-size the picture, which costs more with eBay. That's what kept a lot of the traditional antiquers away from eBay. They didn't like this long-distance, picture, send-in-money-to-strangers whole thing. They are used to picking it up and looking at it," he says. "I got over that." Early on, Jimmy would risk $50 or $60 on something that turned out to be a reproduction. "Whenever I get something in the mail, I always open it at the post office so Margaret can see it," Jimmy says. Margaret is the postal clerk in Jimmy's small town. "I'd open the box and say, 'Oops, this one's for you.'" Margaret displayed all the objects on a shelf. "Every time I go in the post office, I'm reminded of my mistakes," he says. "From a distance, it's all this great-looking stuff, but everything up there was piece-of-crap repro." The mistakes don't bother Jimmy. "The few things I lose on—you know, I get something for $50 or $75 that's not right—that's just the cost of doing business."

Jimmy admits that there can be a disadvantage to being removed from a tactile, three-dimensional relationship with objects. "There are very sophisticated fakes out there. There's tons of repro glass, just tons of it. It's been faked for seventy years so even some of the fakes are almost antique now." Aside from his $50,000 hit, most of Jimmy's profits are in the $3,000 to $10,000 range. From his years of selling antiques the "old-fashioned" way, Jimmy has established a network of buyers. "I know the top collectors of early American glass, and a lot of the pottery collectors. I can get the stuff so cheap so I sell to dealers. I just bought a redware dog for $170 that is worth $4,000. I'll sell it for $2,000 to a dealer and he's happy, I'm happy."

For some people, turning your hobby into your vocation saps the joy. Not for Jimmy. "Oh!" he says. "The thrill of the hunt. I've bought wonderful things from around the world I would have never come in contact with otherwise," like a "mislisted" piece of Sandwich glass. "They made these little figural bear jars that contained bear grease," he says. Bear grease, or rendered bear fat, was used as a baldness cure for ages. Supposedly Cleopatra recommended to Julius Caesar a hair-growing potion of bear grease mixed with charred mice, horse teeth, and deer marrow. In 1795, perfumer Alexander Ross published "A Treatise on Bear's Grease, with observations, to prove how indispensable the use of that incomparable substance to preserve the head of hair, in that state of perfection."

By the 1830s, bear grease was widely sold across the United States, infused with herbs to camouflage the odor. Bear grease was sold in dark bottles. "They always turn up in amethyst glass, almost like black. Or opaque white," Jimmy says. "I'm sure the product wasn't too appealing, like Crisco or something." The bottle Jimmy found on eBay was honey-amber colored, in the shape of a bear, and made by the Sandwich Glass Factory, founded in Sandwich, Massachusetts, in 1825. Once employing five hundred workers, the factory was renowned for fine pressed and hand-cut glass. As first lady, Jackie Kennedy bought an antique Sandwich glass sugar bowl as a gift for Nina Khrushchev. "So now you have a desirable form, in the rarest color," Jimmy says. The eBay seller called the bottle a "dancing bear ink pot." The mislisting threw collectors off the trail. "All the ink people look at it cross-eyed because it's not an ink," Jimmy says. He won the auction for $600 and sold the bottle soon after for $4,000. "It came from the Orkney Islands north of Scotland," he says. "It blows my mind sometimes where these things come from." The seller had found the bear grease bottle at a rummage sale. "You wonder," Jimmy says, "what's the story behind this little bear?"

TO MAKE MONEY BUYING and selling antiques Jimmy's way, you have to have patience. And faith. Weeks can pass without a hit. "Sometimes I get three things in a week, sometimes I go a month without a single thing," he says. He's not anxious when he doesn't find something right away. "If I look at it in year terms, every year I do fantastic." Recently he bought a rare flask made in Edgefield, South Carolina. The dealer's listing said that he'd found the piece at Brimfield, but didn't know who made it or how old it was. This seems strange, advertising your ignorance. "I think I got it for about $110," Jimmy says, but he "immediately threw it right back on eBay in the southern pottery category," where it sold for $2,600 to a museum in South Carolina. He found another Edgefield piece on eBay that was not listed as stoneware, nor as southern pottery. "They just put 'old crock' under 'general ceramics.' I mean, that's a huge category." He recognized the piece as made by Thomas Chandler, an 1850s potter. He won the auction for $200. "When I opened it up, the first thing I saw was 'Chandler, maker' stamped right under the handle. Not only was it marked, but the decoration was so well executed, and it was pristine." Jimmy thought the piece was exceptional, so he contacted the Winterthur Museum, and it "grabbed it" for $5,000.

I asked Jimmy if he missed the days of selling antiques outdoors, the gypsy life. "It's a little lonely," he says, "but it's a trade-off. I love being able to stay home all day. I don't consider what I do work. If I worked doing cabinetry, this is what I would be doing for fun, so I consider myself fortunate." He pauses. "Hopefully these rarities will continue to be listed by people who don't know what they are," he says. "Sometimes I sort of feel sorry for these people in one respect, but in another respect, the whole world could bid against me and they don't. These pieces are there for the taking. If I don't take them, someone else will."

CHAPTER 15

Gold Is Where You Find It

Shopping for antiques online, I imagine, is like virtual dating. You are removed from real-world experience, from the intimate, physical encounter with objects. At antique shows, people run their fingers through Avery's marbles, touch fabrics, ping glassware, rub woodwork, sniff rugs. They caress the smooth plains of an earthenware vessel, feel the heft of a pewter charger. According to marketing consultant Paco Underhill, "We buy things today more than ever based on trial and touch." Nearly 90 percent of new items in the grocery store fail, he found, because customers "never tried them." This is primarily why Underhill contends that "the Internet, catalogs, and home shopping on television will . . . never seriously challenge real live stores." In spite of the efficiency and comfort of hunting for antiques using the Internet, there is a physical and sensual pleasure, and a satisfying immediacy to shopping "the old-fashioned way." As Avery says, "Shopping is the fun part of this business."

Avery's motto for shopping is, "Gold is where you find it." You never know where you'll turn up a great antique: flea markets, yard sales, junk stores, auctions. "The greatest things can show up in the worst, the most shittiest, crappiest places," he says. One day, he took his daughter to the zoo and along the way passed a small flea market. "There were like five dealers with the worst garbage in the world, wrapping paper, spoons, socks, just crap." One table had a pile of tools, in the midst of which Avery spotted a pair of late-eighteenth-century sugar snips. "They look like pliers with little blades on the end. It's an unmistakable form. Sugar was sold in a cone, which sat on your table under a dome so flies couldn't get it. When you wanted a piece for your tea, you'd snip it off with these things that look like garden shears." Avery bought the "sugar shears" for two bucks. "These things sell for like $125," he says. "Probably somebody died, and maybe the wife said, 'Oh, a pair of pliers,' and threw them in the tool box. Stuff travels, gets mixed up. When you see something that old show up in that way, it's very cool." Another day, he found an eighteenth-century box at a flea market in Rowley, Massachusetts. "As I was walking out, I saw a chest full of axes and hammers. I thought, *that doesn't look right*. It looked wicked early." He emptied the tools and inspected the old chest. "This was no tool box," he says. "This was a fucking 1740s storage box!" He bought the box for $20 and sold it for $150.

Avery says he rarely goes to yard sales, but if he happens to drive by . . . One day he found an eighteenth-century Liverpool pitcher for $10 at a yard sale. "I just scooped it up and left," he says. He sold the pitcher for $450. The same day at noon—late for a yard sale—he found a Chippendale tea caddy for $15, worth an "easy" $200. "How does this happen?" he says. "It was on the table where you check out, with a big pink sticker. Nobody knew what it was, they just didn't know." From these stories, I thought that yard sales and flea markets were the best hunting grounds, but Avery says, "I do my best in high-end antique stores." Jimmy Desjardins agrees. "Before eBay, all my best scores came from the highest-end dealers and the best-quality shows. The myth that the flea market is where you find great scores is wrong. You get your best deals from the best dealers."

I wanted to see that principle in action, so I accompanied Avery on a buying excursion to some fancy antique stores. Given the drudgery of setting up for a show and repacking hundreds of objects afterward, shopping truly is "the fun part" of this business. Besides that, I hope to be there if, or when, Avery finds "the big one." This is how it happens—on any ordinary day.

On a January weekday, I meet Avery in the seaside city of Portsmouth, New Hampshire, two hours from his house to the south, and two from mine to the north. We grab a fast-food lunch—time is of the essence—and hit an antique shop next to the burger joint, but leave after fifteen minutes ("A bunch of swill," Avery says). We drive a half hour to "Antique Alley," a stretch of New Hampshire's Route 4, which claims to be the oldest antiques shopping district in New England, with more than five hundred dealers. We pull into the parking lot of a shop, but Avery recognizes another dealer's car, so we drive farther down the main strip in the town of Northwood, which is crowded with antique shops. We stop at a large group shop where it's quiet, just a handful of people perusing the dozens of booths. I see a wooden object in a glass case.

"Is that a pestle to a mortar?" I ask.

"Probably," Avery says. "Tucker sold something like this as erotica. Some lady paid $125. It was worth five bucks."

We see a pair of Hessian soldier andirons, which Avery has sold before, but andirons are not selling like they used to. We see many iron doorstops, which can be valuable—a "Halloween girl" holding a pumpkin sold for $39,200 in 2006. But most doorstops are less than one hundred years old, and the market is fraught with reproductions. Avery points out a Sandwich glass sugar bowl, priced at $140, with beautiful patterns. "I just bought one like this out of a shop for $12," he says. The dealer thought the rim had been "ground," which would have devalued the piece. But that dealer was mistaken. "This is pressed glass, but sometimes they didn't put enough glass into the mold," he says. "They call that an underfill." Avery sold the $12 sugar bowl for $140. "I immediately went out and treated myself to a nice lunch."

Next he picks up a small yellowware pitcher, palm size, with silver luster on the embossed design. "People don't like the silver luster, but you could take steel wool and scrape it off, then you'd have a regular piece of yellowware worth $195." This piece is priced at $40, but Avery sees a fine half-inch line that penetrates the vessel. If the crack was only in the surface glaze, "crazing," it wouldn't be worrisome. He passes on the piece. "It's marginal," he says. "Everybody is getting laden with crap." He paraphrases an aphorism from his hero, Benjamin Franklin. "Small leaks can sink a boat. That's a small leak."

"Death by a thousand cuts," I add.

"You can buy everything because it's all priced less than it's worth," he says, "but you tie up all your money in a perfume bottle that you get for $35 and sell on eBay for $100. I don't want to be dealing with that."

It has been three years since I worked that first Rotary Club flea market with Avery, and I can see how far he's progressed from actually buying the perfume bottles. Avery picks up a wooden wall box, used for storing candles or knives, priced at $285. He looks at it for ten seconds. "This rocks," he says, using the code words for "worthless." He points out square-head nails, which look old to me. Original nails bleed rust into the wood over time. This box is too clean, no telltale stain from the new "old" nails. After an hour or so, Avery thanks the attendant, and we drive to another group shop down the road, wander the aisles. Avery stops at a stoneware chicken feeder, which is shaped like a tiny igloo. "Peep-o-day" is incised into the feeder's surface. "This is a rare piece of stoneware," he says, "but will anyone care?" He seems slightly demoralized. "That could be the type of thing that goes well on eBay, but do you buy it?" He answers his own question: "No," he says. "It's not that strong. I'm not going to get involved." I joke that it's one of those tiny cuts. "That's a big cut at $122," he says. "That's a bleeder."

We move along to the next booth, and Avery kneels in front of a straight-edge stoneware vessel. "If you ever see 'bitters' written on it, it's good." This one does not say bitters. "Canadian stoneware has really kicked in," he says of a three-gallon crock by Farrar, priced at $145. "That could be a good one," but he passes. He summons the shop manager and asks her to open a case. He thinks he's spotted a "pick wick," a small toothpick-sized metal instrument for taking up the wick in oil lamps. "I've never owned one," he says. "They are extremely rare. They can bring $300 to $600." This piece turns out to be a thread holder, not a pick wick after all. In another case is a pair of "heavy duty" Arts and

Crafts sconces for $395, made of sturdy-looking metal. After looking in dozens of booths at hundreds of objects, Avery says, "That's the only thing I've seen today that I really like." Still, he passes on the sconces.

We move to the basement where there are another dozen or so booths. Avery sees a pair of mid-eighteenth-century andirons. He sets them on a table for closer inspection. "The striations in the wrought iron are good," he says. The andirons are tall spikes capped with a brass ball. No fancy hound dogs or clowns or Hessian soldiers. The brass balls must be "seamed," Avery says, and looks. "Yup." It takes me a while but I finally discern the fine seam in the metal. "The dogs are real," he says, referring to the back legs of the andirons. He buys the andirons for $125, in spite of saying, "I need another pair of these like I need a hole in the head."

"How much will you try to get for them?" I ask.

"The short money would be $250," he says. "These are going to be a hard sell, but I like them."

We walk by a sundial held up by a cherub. "Instead of these andirons, I should be buying naked putti," he says. "People like naked putti. I hate to say it, but I like naked putti, too." In the backroom, where a large open area houses a dozen or so dealers, Avery walks along a wall of shelves: "Nothing, nothing, nothing, nothing, bad cast iron, nothing, probably nothing, nothing." I admire his laser eye, his bionic antiques vision.

"There are people out there a lot better than I am," he says.

"You remember so many details."

"It builds on itself. I don't consider myself that clever. Between living through the seventies and the eighties, it's amazing that I have any retention at all. My biggest asset is being able to figure things out from context. Just being able to put two and two together."

Assessing is an analytic process, a synthesis of multiple pieces of information, a way of thinking. "I miss stuff," Avery says. "For a guy who does what I do, for some reason, I don't see things. I don't concentrate well. I look through a booth, and I'll be like, nothing there, and I'm in a hurry, but I say, wait, go back and look. So I go back and look again, and shit, I didn't see that thing, I didn't see that piece of furniture. I do it all the time." I hypothesize that there is visual-spacial field aptitude necessary to spot the prize among the dross, a sort of "Where's Waldo" skill. "I'm real good at assessing things when they are right there, but I just miss stuff. It's kind of a handicap," he says, "but I find my fair share." He picks up a green glass pig, about eight inches long. "Fake," he says. "If that was real, it would be worth ten thousand and I could sell it in one phone call."

He points to a cream-colored Wedgwood pitcher with black lettering that reads: "Success to the crooked but interesting town of Boston." It's unclear if crooked meant morals or city streets. "They call this Liverpool pottery," he says. One of the most famous English potters supplying the colonies was Josiah Wedgwood, pen pal to Benjamin Franklin, grandfather of Charles Darwin. (Darwin married his first cousin, Emma Wedgwood; the couple shared the same granddad, Josiah). Born to a poor family of potters in Staffordshire, crippled by smallpox, and never educated, Wedgwood spent years conducting hundreds of experiments until he finally created the first "pure white" glaze in trial #411, a formula that brought him vast riches.

Around the mid-1700s, potters developed a process for transferring printed images onto ceramic using engraved copper plates, much less laborious than hand-painting or incising. Factories produced large quantities of cheaper "transferware" for the colonies. Since much of the pottery was shipped through ports at Liverpool, it became known as "Liverpool" pottery. The transferware served as a medium for political sloganeering. Wedgwood, a proponent of American independence, and a founding member of the Society for Effecting the Abolition of the Slave Trade, imprinted political statements on his wares, like a coiled rattlesnake alongside "Don't tread on me." Other potters followed suit: "The Negroes Complaint: Skins May Differ but Afflictions Dwell in Black & White the Same" and "Am I Not a Man and a Brother." Avery owns a piece of this eighteenth-century Liverpool pottery, the "real deal," he says. "Liverpool is so good, it's okay if it's broken." This piece he's holding is in mint condition, but it's a worthless reproduction.

It's 4:50 P.M. and the shop is about to close when Avery sees a lamp font in a glass case by the exit. He knows the dealer who owns the stuff, a man he respects, but who—he whispers to me—"doesn't know glass." Avery buys two "peg lamp" fonts for $60, which are worth about $250. The peg lamp fonts look like glass blobs with a stub or "peg" at the bottom. The peg fits into a candle holder, converting it to a portable lamp.

Five hours of shopping and two small hits—the andirons and the lamp fonts. Not a banner day by any means, but not a total washout. No gold, but bread and butter. Every day Avery—and all antiques dealers—hope for "the big one," the deal of a lifetime. "Only a handful of dealers have educated themselves enough to do that," he says. He quotes his friend Jimmy. "Luck is when knowledge meets opportunity." Avery's earned the knowledge, and he puts in the time. Now all he needs is luck.

CHAPTER 16

Roadshow Rage

Antiques Roadshow is a celebration of luck without knowledge. On the *Roadshow*, finding great antiques seems as easy as looking in your attic or a nearby dumpster. Along with eBay, and the flood of reproductions from China, *Antiques Roadshow* has profoundly affected the antiques trade. I asked Avery about the *Roadshow* effect. "People are buying with their wallets now, not with their hearts," he says. Entrepreneurship is eclipsing connoisseurship. "They used to collect for the love of it. Now they are doing it for an investment. It's all changed."

"But isn't it good that *Antiques Roadshow* has made antiques more popular?" I ask.

"That's the problem," he says. "Antiques have become popular, but not in the way that people will want to go out and buy them. They are popular in that everybody thinks that everything they have is worth a lot of money."

Executive producer Marsha Bemko admits as much. "Antique dealers praise us generally for raising the interest in antiques, but criticize us because now everyone thinks what they have is worth thousands of dollars," she says. "We have unrealistically raised expectations."

Antiques Roadshow, in its fifteenth season in 2010, has attracted more viewers than *60 Minutes*, *Sex in the City*, and *The Sopranos*. The show's pilot, *The Great American Treasure Hunt*, was taped in 1992 at Skinner's auction house in Boston, hosted by Monty Hall from *Let's Make a Deal*, but the pilot found no takers until 1996 when Boston's public broadcasting station, WGBH, picked it up. The first season was "sketchy," publicist Judy Matthews recalls. "Some of the people that get on television, you wonder what they were thinking when they dressed that morning. In the early years, we got a lot of wolf T-shirts." But after the first season, the show reached eight million viewers. In Los Angeles that year, the taping was "like a rock concert," Matthews says. "Thousands of people lined up at the box office. They slept on the sidewalks overnight. It was scary." In Richmond, Virginia, a woman fainted in the 100-degree heat as she waited in the line of five thousand people, but when the ambulance arrived, she refused to give up her spot. "I like to compare it to Lourdes," Matthews says. "People come to get their object anointed."

WHEN I WATCH *Antiques Roadshow*, I envy the guests clutching heirlooms or telling poignant stories about a great-great grandmother who offered some famous Civil War general a glass of water and was rewarded with a trinket now worth thousands. Or the family silver or a highboy passed down for seven generations. Hearing these stories, I long for a tangible past, a record of my family in objects. My paternal grandparents grew up in Ireland and were "dirt poor" (dirt: the floors of their stone houses, and burned in the form of peat). My maternal grandparents, Italian, the same: peasant farmers who even in America remained poor. Neither of my parents' parents had much more than the clothes on their backs when they arrived in New York and Boston in the 1910s and '20s. I have very few artifacts from the lives of my grandparents or their parents, and thus I know little about my ancestry. Objects tell stories of human lives, testify. As a farm woman in Steinbeck's *Grapes of Wrath* said when forced to sell her family's possessions, "How will we know it's us without our past?"

As common as the family heirloom narrative on the *Roadshow* is the rescue story. Someone yanked an interesting object out of a dumpster or found it at a flea market for a buck, and it turns out to be a signed Tiffany vase or Hudson River School painting. Between the heirloom and the lottery ticket narratives, there are no losers on *Antiques Roadshow*, which no doubt contributes to the show's enormous success.

PHILADELPHIA IN JULY IS a steam bath, the temperature in the eighties by 6:00 A.M., the air cloying with humidity and palpable city grime. I ride an escalator to a second-floor auditorium of the Convention Center, a three-story, block-wide and -long building, where an entourage of forty or so WGBH employees and a hundred local volunteers are preparing for a *Roadshow* taping. The volunteers are a group of well-groomed, middle-aged white folks—the khaki crowd—in this racially mixed city, recruited from among the viewers of the local PBS affiliate. For their fourteen hours of labor, the volunteers receive a pen, a blue polo with the *Antiques Roadshow* logo, and an opportunity to have two items appraised. (The day before at the volunteer briefing, a WGBH employee got a big laugh when he said, "You can keep this pen, along with your shirt, which could be collectible in about ten years.")

By 7:00 A.M., ticket holders stream in steadily. Volunteers at the entrance yell, "Have your ticket out," and "Keep moving," and, "If you have firearms you need to register them." Two cops from the Philadelphia Police Firearms Identification unit stand before a table arrayed with screwdrivers and wooden rods. The officers have had two years of training in ballistic and forensic science, which included a history of firearms, "from muzzle loaders on . . . but we don't see a whole lot of those type of guns," one cop says. A man steps up to the table and presents a pistol. "I got a kid to put through college," he says. The officer cocks the hammer, stares into the barrel, and rotates the chamber to check for bullets. Then he affixes a trigger lock, a white plastic tie.

"We can identify single action, Army Colts, Old West style, and gas guns that are filled with a reservoir of compressed air to fire projectiles," one cop tells me. The ingenious history of killing. These are not guns criminals use, not anymore anyway. I watch as one officer inserts a dowel into the bore of a muzzle loader. "If the dowel is the same length as the barrel, the gun is empty," he says. In the first ninety minutes, the two cops inspect thirty-five firearms. If that number is any indication, the cops might handle nearly three hundred weapons that day. Indeed, the Arms and Militia table will be one of the busiest on the set. I asked one of the cops if he was interested in antique armaments. "My hobby is baseball cards," he says.

Once past the lobby, ticket holders enter the huge convention hall, which has been sectioned off with yellow caution tape, like a cattle chute. About seven thousand people will pass through the hall today, pulling Radio Flyer wagons, garden carts, furniture dollies. An older woman pushes two dolls in a wheelchair. There is no seating, but one well-organized woman has strapped two beach chairs to her cart. At the volunteers' briefing, an employee in charge of "crowd control" asked the volunteers to report people cutting in line and other rambunctiousness. "If you see a sword fight, or anyone being stupid with their weapon, tell us," she'd said. I ask Matthews if the people mind the wait. "They are happy as clams," she replies. "I can't imagine why. I would never do it."

IF THOSE WHO MAKE the pilgrimage to the *Roadshow* seek anointment, as Matthews says, the appraisers are the high priests and priestesses. Of the seventy to eighty experts tapped for the event, a few have the sheen of the highly educated, with degrees in art history, the crème de la crème of auction houses, Bonhams & Butterfields, Christie's, Sotheby's, a team of six from Skinner's. These pedigreed appraisers have a supercilious air, like academics or museum types. The autodidactic appraisers are spit-cleaned in their Sunday best, but upon closer inspection look a bit rumpled.

In the auditorium, I talk with pottery and porcelain appraiser J. Garrison "Gary" Stradling, a tall, lumbering man; he's one of the four appraisers who have appeared on the *Roadshow* since its first season. Stradling worked for network television in New York City, he tells me, but quit after his boss told him to cut his staff. He turned his hobby of antiquing into a full-time vocation. In a non sequitur, he suggests that I talk to an auctioneer in New Jersey, who Stradling claims played guitar with Led Zeppelin. "He's mafia," Stradling says. "His stepfather is serving three life sentences."

You wonder why Stradling continues to participate in the *Roadshow*'s grueling cross-country tour of marathon appraisal events. In one day, he might examine two hundred items. Appraisers receive no compensation, pay their own expenses, and aren't allowed to hand out business cards. Signs warn: "There is absolutely no buying or selling of any items at *Antiques Roadshow* appraisal events." When I ask the producer, Marsha Bemko, if it was worth the trouble for appraisers, she says, "Have you ever heard of Leigh or Leslie Keno before *Antiques Roadshow*?" The show *has* brought the Kenos fame—and a National Humanities Medal for each, bestowed in 2005 by George W. Bush. They hosted a spin-off show, *Find!*, in which they "find" a painting in a Boston attic, which was later sold for over a million dollars. But few of the other appraisers have achieved this degree of renown, which is perhaps why only four have stayed from the start.

AT THE FRONT of the holding area, guests are issued "category" tickets: Arms and Militia; Books and Manuscripts; Metalwork; Decorative; Clocks and Watches; Musical Instruments; Silver; Pottery and Porcelain; Glass; Science and Technology; Collectibles; Dolls, Toys, and Games; Photographs, Prints, and Posters; Paintings and Drawings; Asian Arts; Tribal Arts; Antiquities; Rugs and Textiles; Folk Art; Jewelry; and Tools and Implements. There are no tickets for coins or stamps, the most popular collecting categories. "They are too easily faked," Matthews says. "It's not worth it. We'd have to keep disappointing people over and over." This strikes me as odd, given that disappointment will be the outcome for the majority of people here.

At 7:45 A.M., the first wave of hopefuls rushes onto the set, a curtained ring, which creates the look of a bustling crowd. I hear a woman say loudly, "Oh, there's one of the twins." Fans line up seeking the Kenos' autographs. The crowd thickens with excited people. A guy carrying a small metal elephant mutters, "Wow, wow, wow!" Some sad sack has brought a bagful of Beanie Babies, and it's almost poignant to see an out-of-shape, middle-aged man, sweat beading on his forehead, lugging a dresser with a marble top that even I can see is common, probably worth $300 at best. A man named Sam from Philadelphia carries a beach-ball-size papier-mâché head, a puppet with a leering toothy smile and real human hair, circa 1920, probably a parade piece, worth $800 to $1,000, he learned. The scary puppet is a cross between the horror film doll "Chuckie" and Alfred E. Neuman. You pull a string and the mouth opens to show yellow lacquered teeth. The head has been in this man's family for generations. "I'm the keeper of the head," he says.

At the Tools and Implements table, a lady unloads from a huge suitcase fishing poles, bait cans, angling paraphernalia. She pulls pole after pole from her bottomless bag, even a couple of old golf clubs. Two old fishing reels are quickly valued at $60 each. I overhear a man ask a *Roadshow* employee—identifiable by green polo shirts—how many people get on television, and he is clearly crestfallen when he's told that it's only fifty. The chances of having your object on the show are "very rare," Matthews says. Each of the seven thousand ticket holders is allowed to bring two items for appraisal, which means that as many as fourteen thousand appraisals take place in a ten-hour period. Over the course of the day, the producer will select about fifty objects to showcase. At these odds, a guest may have less than a one-half of 1 percent chance of owning an object that is rare or valuable or interesting enough to appear on television.

At the Musical Instruments table, where there isn't much of a crowd, a man presents a National resonator guitar painted black and red. Ugly, but still valued at $3,000 to $5,000. At the Books and Manuscripts table, another low-trafficked category, a woman has brought a beautiful edition of *Cinderella*. The appraiser from Christie's identifies the book as chromaphotography, which he values at $50 to $75. There is a huge line at the "collectibles" table, which seems to be a kind of catchall—the Beanie Baby lady winds up here. Prints and Posters and Tribal Arts are slower tables, sometimes completely vacant, with the appraisers looking forlorn, like wallflowers at the prom.

At the Toy table, a woman presents a metal dime bank, with a nut and bolt on the bottom, about six inches long. The appraiser, Noel Barrett, with glasses, his hair in a ponytail, one of the four original appraisers, turns it over, squints, looks around aimlessly, then says, "What did you want to know about it?" The answer seems painfully obvious—she wants to know the value, its age and background. The woman seems stymied by his question, and finally Barrett says, "Well, we see a lot of these banks, but the most valuable are the ones where the arms move. This is a nice piece, but not what we call 'very expensive.'" The appraisal takes less than thirty seconds, and he doesn't give the woman a monetary value. She sheepishly puts the bank in her tote bag as if she has failed at something, and Barrett yells, "Who's next?"

IN 2001, the sixth season of the show, an elderly man, Ted from Tucson, showed up with a rather plain, broad-striped cloth. The blanket, Ted believed, was given to his grandmother's foster father by Kit Carson, a government agent to the Ute and Apache tribes in Taos, New Mexico, in 1854. The appraiser, Donald Ellis, identified the blanket as an early-nineteenth-century, Ute-style chief's blanket. When the red dye in the blanket was analyzed later, it was discovered to be cochineal, extracted from a tropical insect, which the Navajo began using around 1840. The dye dated the blanket as one of the oldest surviving, fully intact Navajo blankets, which Ellis valued at $500,000 "on a good day."

The old man, in his tucked-in striped shirt and greased hair, choked up on national television. "Oh my God," he said, his mouth agape. "I had no idea," his voice shaky. "It was laying on the back of a chair." He put his hand on his heart. "I can't believe this." He removed his glasses to wipe his moistened cheeks. "My grandmother and grandfather were poor farmers," he said. "There was no wealth. No wealth in the family at all." He grew more emotional as the appraiser shook his hand, said, "Congratulations."

"I'm flabbergasted," Ted said, and indeed he was the perfect picture of flabbergastedness. I was genuinely moved by this ordinary, working-class man who had lived all his life among a richness he failed to recognize. Because of the value of the blanket, security guards escorted Ted and his wife off the set. Two years later, the same appraiser, Donald Ellis, sold the blanket for Ted. With the proceeds, Ted and his wife bought a "modest" retirement home. In the end, the couple admitted, they weren't "in love" with the blanket.

In January 2010, after thirteen seasons, *Antiques Roadshow* aired its first million-dollar appraisal. A woman inherited several Chinese jade and celadon pieces from the Ch'ien-Lung Dynasty (1736–1795). The appraisal—based on a "conservative auction estimate"—was $1.07 million. "*Roadshow* finally captured this elusive trophy," Marsha Bemko said.

OF THE FOURTEEN THOUSAND objects that will be appraised on this day, Bemko, the executive producer, decides which deserve to be on camera, relying on the appraisers to pitch ideas. Bemko is a tall, thin, energetic woman in her early forties, with large brown eyes and a commanding yet easy-going presence. She came to the *Roadshow* in 2001 from a film background, but finds the *Roadshow* more dynamic. "This is one of the smartest shows," she says. "I call it guerrilla TV." Within the first half hour of the taping, one of the textile appraisers calls Bemko over, says he has a rug that is worth $2,500, that the rug could show issues of repair. The appraiser and Bemko huddle out of earshot of the rug's owners. "Let's hold off," she tells the rug expert. The appraiser is new, so Bemko is gentle in rejecting his pitch. "It's early yet," she says. "I know you are going to see a better rug today. But we'll do it at the table." In addition to the fifty objects showcased, a roving camera crew tapes thirty to forty "over the shoulder" appraisals.

In the first hour or two, the crew tapes a set of cigarette cards, a painted Pennsylvania Dutch chest, a pair of carved scrimshaw powder horns. The production stations shoot out from the center to capture the milling crowd and the tables that ring the perimeter. On this day, they had to change the jewelry banner, which had an image of an open necklace, because the curving ends of the necklace turned into devil horns when someone stood in front of it. Lint on the set is a problem, too. "We spend a lot of time picking lint off the tables, floors, the velvet-covered display racks," Matthews says. And derrieres cause trouble. The crew often films an object set on a waist-high table. "Many times we cannot use the shot because in the background is someone's ass," Matthews says. "The *Antiques Roadshow* butt shot. That's a phenomenon in this business."

ANTIQUES ROADSHOW has been called "soft-core porn for antique fetishists." The comparison can seem apt. Each vignette is carefully stage-directed to elicit a frisson. The first step is screening for innocent guests. "We want people who are ignorant of the value," Matthews says, virgins, if you will. Once the film crew is ready (all lint removed, the object posed for the cameras on the plush velvety surface), they usher the guest onto the set, the camera zooming in close enough to show the appraiser's immaculate cuticle care as he lifts the object and peeks at its undersides. Then the appraiser strokes the guest, building excitement with sweet nothings—"very rare" and "untouched" and "pristine" and the ultimate teaser, "I've only seen one other piece and it's in a museum." You can feel the excitement building, see it in the guest's face, imagine her heart fluttering, sweat beading on her forehead, eyes glazed as she waits—with halted breath—for the climax, the tantalizingly withheld *dollar value of the object*, the literal "money shot."

"It's a live moment thing," Bemko tells me, though the spontaneity is artfully managed. "We've changed the way we ask the appraisers to say the price. Instead of saying 'twenty-five hundred,' we ask them to say 'two thousand five hundred.' We were watching our guests on the monitor and we saw a reaction between 'twenty-five' and 'hundred'—their faces dropped." In that split linguistic second, guests were mentally anticipating twenty-five *thousand* instead of *hundred*. "You can literally see the change in their expressions," says Bemko.

The money shot is the abiding principle of the *Roadshow*. "Aesthetic education is not really the point," critic Alain de Botton wrote of the original British version. (PBS licensed the British show, which in 2010 entered its thirty-third season.) "The experts, for their part, are singularly inept at telling us anything genuinely interesting about the objects," de Botton wrote. "They give us no clue about why an object might be considered beautiful; the price tag is everything." Curt Avery has a similar take. "*Antiques Roadshow* does not educate people at all. I try to pay attention to little tips, but it's so eclectic. Ninety percent of the show is useless information. Ten percent is useful, but how much of that do you retain? It is really not about educating people." Bemko seemed sensitive to such criticism. "It is most entertaining to our viewers and useful when we talk about objects," she says. "It is beyond elation or disappointment." At best, the *Roadshow* painlessly introduces history—small spoonfuls—to Americans the way Oprah delivered classics, Steinbeck and Tolstoy, to an audience who otherwise might not take that initiative.

But the money-shot mentality skews the "reality" of antiques in the real economy, or more troubling, shifts the emphasis from the aesthetic and historic to the economic. One would hope that an interest in old things via *Antiques Roadshow* corresponded to a population weary of the glut of mass-produced, disposable items, or nostalgic for beauty and craftsmanship. But the show can inspire the worst of our capitalist culture, hitting a Vegas-style "jackpot," or the capitalistic tendency to measure the value of anything in dollars. As one appraiser said to a guest that day, "I guess everything comes down to dollars and cents."

AFTER THE CLIMAX of each vignette, there is the denouement: tears, gratitude, sometimes a pretend-blasé, a triumphant "YES!" or a crass "Cha-ching." A comment I overhear in the Philadelphia farmers' market, where a number of *Roadshow* guests from the early time slots were dining, captures the zeitgeist of the event: "Did you get rich on the *Roadshow*?" Certainly there are people who demonstrate a genuine love and interest in the objects, and many who will clearly pass down the family treasure, but for some of the guests, their next call is to the auctioneer. After a high appraisal in one episode, a guest admitted, "It's as good as gone."

And who can blame them? Antiques dealers buy and sell precious objects all day long—exchanging historical artifacts for a car payment, the mortgage.

While the chosen few hit pay dirt on *Antiques Roadshow*, for the majority, the experience seems anticlimactic, a dud date. Many guests were no longer "happy as clams." After driving from all points in Pennsylvania and beyond, carting their objects for blocks, waiting two hours, they finally make it to the appraiser, who, 99 percent of the time, dispatches a cursory summary. Some guests leave immediately, but others stand around stunned, a bit dazed. It's over so quickly, and they did not "get rich" on the *Roadshow*. For these folks, there is the consolation prize: the "Feedback Booth," a sort of post-traumatic debriefing station, a "last-ditch effort to get on TV," Matthews says. The Feedback Booth looks like a beach changing tent, a small curtained area away from the main set. People step inside and position themselves in front of a little peephole that frames them. They have ten seconds to audition for a cameo. Anyone leaving the appraisal area can stop by the Feedback Booth, and as the day progresses the line grows long. "We get hundreds of these," Matthews says.

A guy wearing a Civil War hat and carrying two handguns poses them across his chest. A woman steps in with her porcelain pot, worth very little, asks the camera guys, "Should I do a Vanna?" One of the two camera technicians, local contractors, gives her the signal, and the woman says, "Our item wasn't worth very much, but we had fun anyway." The other camera tech—out of view of the people being taped—cracks up. "The people with big money are all happy, the others are all frowning. 'Yeah, we had fun *anyway*. Yeah, we drove four hours and stood in line for another two and this thing is worth fifty cents, but we had fun *anyway*.'" The camera guys position and tape more people, joking all the while. "Yeah, the stuff is worth 'sentimental value.'"

A fiftyish, well-appointed woman stands in line for the Feedback Booth with her genuine whalebone lampshade, which looks like a birdcage made of bone, or an elaborate corset. The appraiser told her nobody collected those anymore, but she didn't believe him. She tells me that one of these lampshades "sold for $40,000 and here it was appraised at $4,000." I say, "That's not bad," and she says, "But it's not $40,000!" I ask her how much she paid for the lampshade. "Nothing," she says. She'd hauled it out of a trash can. The bitter woman lines up for the Feedback Booth, following a man who holds a calendar from the desk of Fidel Castro, valued at $1,500. "Any minute now this could be worth a whole lot more," he says.

When I ask Judy Matthews if she thinks most of the people are disappointed with the *Antiques Roadshow* experience, she says, "They don't seem to mind. It's like everyone was toking up before they got here." Certainly at least a few people are still clam-happy. In one Feedback Booth cameo in 2007, a woman gushed, "This is our lifetime dream. I've waited ten years to come to *Antiques Roadshow*." Perhaps Matthews is right; perhaps the disappointment I sense is my own. I expected to witness a transformation like at Lourdes, an exaltation. But as appraiser J. Garrison Stradling said of the *Roadshow* when I saw him at York, "You see an awful lot of crap."

An even cheesier final hurrah for disappointed guests is the "Wheel of Fortune" by the exit doors. The show's sponsor, Liberty Mutual, has set up the wheel to give away promotional items. It's surprising (or maybe not) how many people (including me) stand in line to spin the wheel—a winner every time!—to get a Liberty Mutual T-shirt, chip clip, pen, mug, the most craptacular of advertising garbage, the very antithesis of antiques, but in the end, something for nothing.

CHAPTER 17

Wilmington, aka the John Malkovich Show

The Wilmington Show, officially known as the Greater Boston Antiques Festival, held in January, has been an important venue for Avery, "the first time I cracked $5,000 at an indoor show," he says. "Last year at Wilmington, I put two huge cement dog ornaments on a cart and forty feet into the hall a guy bought them for $1,300. When you have a show like that, you work it real hard." Wilmington is one of Boston's most well-attended, reputable indoor shows. In 2006, Barbra Streisand showed up with an entourage of body guards and assistants (her helpers took pictures of objects and asked dealers for "bulk prices"). The show—with 160 dealers—was kept open an extra half hour for Streisand, who spent some $10,000 on antiques, including an eighteenth-century Betty lamp, priced at $2,400 (sold for an undisclosed lesser amount), Art Nouveau vases, and a circa 1930 carved wood and gilt eagle, clutching in its talon a "God Bless America" banner, priced at $2,100.

The Wilmington show is produced by Marvin Getman of New England Antique Shows. Avery's had a couple run-ins with Getman. Once, Avery shared a booth at Getman's outdoor show with another dealer, who hadn't read the fine print in the contract stating that tents must cover the entire twenty-by-twenty-foot space. Avery's tent covered only ten by twenty, so Getman wasn't going to let him set up. At the last minute, Avery was able to rent another tent. "Marvin threatened to throw me out more than once," Avery says. Other dealers have complained about Getman's restrictions, like requiring white tents at a summer show, but those "doubters," Getman told a reporter, "became believers after the show."

Still, Avery respects Getman's business acumen. "He's a great promoter," Avery says. "Fucking promoters. Some of them will take your money and keep it all. They don't advertise and the shows bomb. Marvin charges an arm and leg, but he puts a lot of money into advertising." Getman has a "border collie work ethic," the *Maine Antique Digest* said, and a "willingness to spend ad dollars." A "Getman gate," the paper said, "even when it's down, is big." The bone of contention between Avery and Getman has been about booth style. "My stuff is tchotchkes to him," Avery says. "You could hand him a seventeenth-century brass candlestick and it means nothing. He even pointed to a nearby booth and said, 'Now this is the type of booth I like.' But it was a bunch of horseshit, a carved, tobacco store Indian, not a real one, but from the 1970s. He wants big, easy-to-understand, impressive things. They just have to look impressive, not really *be* impressive."

I MEET AVERY at the Shriner's Auditorium in Wilmington, a suburb north of Boston, in the Fez Room, annexed to the larger hall. Dealers in the Fez Room are complaining that their booths have shrunk. The chalk lines on the red floral carpet are three feet shorter; two of Avery's tables won't fit this year. As I unpack boxes and set items on tables and shelves, Avery shops. Several dealers are here during setup just to shop; one dealer tells us he paid the $300 booth fee in order to get in early and gave away his space. After his first shopping round, Avery returns with a small table that he's excited about. "This could be a lottery ticket," he says. It's a period game table, probably 1780–1800, he thinks, with inlay on the surface and delicate curved legs. "On its worst day it's worth $400," the price he paid. The surface has slight water damage, but he can fix that. "The guy bought this at an estate sale. He was number *sixty* in line. A late eighteenth-century European game table and everybody passed it by."

Avery's merchandise is wildly disparate. A Nantucket basket woven with strands of black baleen is priced at $1,800. Baleen is coarse, hairlike fiber that grows in the mouths of filter-feeding whales—right whales and gray whales—a brushlike surface that traps plankton. Baleen is made of keratin, the protein in hair and fingernails, so it's flexible enough for weaving. There's a bowl of eighteenth-century clay marbles—vivid red, blue, and yellow—for a buck each. For $500, Avery bought someone's lifetime collection of two thousand, and he's piecing them out. "It's slow money," he says. (He will sell twenty at this show—slow money indeed.) Another higher-ticket item is a portrait of a boy about ten with big bright eyes, in a gilded oval frame. Avery writes on a placard: "American School, circa 1840. N.Y. lable." I point out that he has misspelled "label." He starts speaking in a French accent, reaches up with his Magic Marker to put an accent mark over the "e": *lablé*. He doesn't seem to worry that his joke will confuse a buyer.

I am nearing what I think is the end of unpacking—I've started to stack antiques on top of each other, smaller items in bowls, candlesticks crowded on top of an art deco mirror—when Avery strolls in with one more box. (The next day, he brings even more boxes, puzzled himself as to how he will get one and a half trucks' worth of stuff home after the show.) I decide this trait of bringing too much is a sign of optimism; he wants there to be enough space, almost *wills* there to be more space.

After setting up, Avery and I walk around and peek in booths. There's a large booth catty-corner from his that's arranged like a nineteenth-century parlor, a "living room" booth, with a table in the center. A few high-priced items are set on shelves, maybe thirty items total. With so few things to unpack, the dealers went home hours ago. "I'm going to clobber this booth," Avery says. He points out a detail on an open cupboard that he says was "never done" in the period listed on the price tag. "It just wouldn't be like that." It's a later repair, but the piece is priced as if it were untouched. "These are the type of dealer that 'major collector' will buy from," he says. Since the early lighting device incident, that "major collector" has become the exemplar of the wealthy dupe who can fall prey to unscrupulous or simply ignorant dealers. Avery points to a ceramic bowl with a yellowish-swirl glaze. "I'm sure that's not real. I'll pick that up and it will have a hollow spot underneath." When he lifts the bowl, we see a big indentation in its bottom. "Lithuanian," he says, then checks the tag. "Priced as American."

THE WILMINGTON SHOW OPENS on Saturday at 10:00 A.M. Very old men—octogenarians all—stroll the floor in cherry red blazers and six-inch-tall cylindrical hats with black tassels and sequined script that reads, "Aleppo Boston." They are the security. I can't imagine they could prevent any crime. They are just old guys in silly hats. Actually, they are members of the Ancient Arabic Order of the Nobles of the Mystic Shrine for North America—Shriners. The hats are fezzes, and this is their convention center. The men are old, the order is ancient, and so perhaps the perfect backdrop to the antiques show.

The gate is huge. Getman draws a crowd, that's for sure. Unlike the typical one-hour rush, it is bumper-to-bumper traffic in the aisles for five hours. Within the first thirty seconds, a dealer sorts through Avery's Staffordshire plates—"This one, this one, no on that, this, yes, yes, no"—and spends $2,400. In the midst of the crowd, the actor John Malkovich walks into Avery's booth, dressed in what is perhaps his incognito outfit, baggy jeans, nondescript jacket. He scans the tables, but doesn't buy anything. As he leaves the booth, I give him a Mona Lisa smile, trying not to blow his cover; he nods. "He collects toys," Avery says.

Avery gets many compliments on his booth. I overhear a woman say, "I love this guy's stuff." He has a good eye for unusual and interesting objects. Quality. The booth next door has 90 percent silverware, another booth down the way has nothing but textiles. Fly-over booths, in my mind. (I love textiles, but giant piles of fabric overwhelm me.) Many booths are "living room" arrangements, which I find off-putting, as if you were walking into your grandmother's fancy parlor, and will be scolded if you smudge something. Or like a museum display, to look but not touch. You hate even to step on the oriental carpet they have laid down.

A short man with a French-sounding accent asks if we have any watch fobs. Fresh out. Another man inspects a tintype photo in a "union case." The case is gutta-percha, Avery says, one of the first resins developed in the mid-eighteenth century. Gutta-percha was used for buggy whips, toys, handles. "I've dug it up," he says. "It lasts in the ground." Avery's booth is a buzz of activity, and his neighbors across the aisle look on with envy. Shop owners from Maine, they have only worked one other show. Their merchandise is weird—a huge, five-foot-long grass-woven fish sieve, "possibly for alewives," I hear the guy say. They have other large, historically interesting things, but not things you would put in your house. That's what the Wilmington show is all about—decorative arts. Early Americana does not sell, but lamps and china and Italian papier-mâché tables, plant stands and rugs and delicately woven table runners do. "We're looking for a huge painting to go over our fireplace," a middle-aged woman says. Later, I overhear the dealer from Maine talking into his cell phone. "My antique business is going well," he says, "but not this show. We laid an egg at this show."

AFTER A NINE-HOUR SETUP on Friday, and a busy ten-hour opening day on Saturday, we could sleep late on Sunday because the show doesn't open until 10:00 A.M. But Avery wants to shop at a nearby flea market, so we meet at 7:30 and spend an hour and a half walking around a warehouse that used to be a discount store called Frugal Fannie's. It's 11 degrees, but there are a handful of dealers set up in the parking lot, cloths spread on the ground, card tables loaded, dealers standing and shivering. It costs $1 to get into the musty warehouse, where there are a few dozen low-level dealers. Mostly this is used junk, a good place for college students to furnish an apartment. Avery examines a toy cradle priced at $25. "It's old," the dealer says. Avery passes on it when he notices some damage, but takes a minute to educate the woman. "This is Victorian," he says, "from about 1880." She thanks him for the information. At another table, he buys two vases. "Bud vases," the woman says, "they have some age." They are deep blue, with a bulbous bottom and straight top, about six inches tall. Avery buys them for $20. Later, when we return to the antique show, he'll pop them in his display case with a tag of $275 for the pair. They are hyacinth vases, highly collectible, used in Victorian times to force hyacinth bulbs into bloom. I almost feel bad for this level of dealer. I want to grab them and say, *Do your homework! Find out what you are selling!* Avery buys a large tole tray with a floral decoration. "A lady slayer," he remarks, and as we walk around, three separate women comment on the beautiful tray. At the antique show, he'll sell it to Joan Christianson. He paid $20, charged her $50, and she'll ask $100. It's low-level dealing, pocket change, too easy to pass up, I suppose.

On Sunday as the show opens, a dealer named Chip asks Avery for his opinion on two bottles he's been offered, a green Griffith and Hyatt liquor bottle with a partial clipper ship label, and an early green flask. Avery shows me the pronounced, thick-lipped pontil on the liquor bottle. "That's what bottle guys get excited about," he says. "That's the equivalent of a girl with big boobs." Avery tells Chip they're worth $1,500. Chip buys them for $500 and then comes back and flips them to Avery for $600, a quick but small profit. The bottles are a specialty item, so perhaps Chip doesn't have the connection to sell them. Avery does. "It's so easy to sell this shit," he says. "I can even be a little mean with it." Within a couple of weeks, he sells one bottle for $1,000. "I tried to give Chip some more money, but he wouldn't take it," he says. Avery's done that, too, refused kickbacks. "You end up in this argument when they insist on giving it to you." Still, the gesture is fair-minded, and helps with future deals.

In the afternoon on Sunday, when the crowd wanes, two guys in leather overcoats with strong cologne ask Avery about some old medicine bottles one of them inherited. Avery explains poison bottles, labels, apothecary jars. "If you see the ingredients opium or heroin, you can date the bottles as earlier than 1906," he says. This is his métier; he seems to enjoy educating these people, and they seem grateful to learn. He gives them his phone number and invites them to call with questions once they get home and have a chance to look more closely at their bottles.

In the final hours of the show, the producer, Marvin Getman, is quietly approaching certain dealers to invite them to participate in a very high-end Boston show he's setting up for the first time, but he skips over Avery. "He's creating this really vetted show, and he doesn't want me there," Avery says. Getman is selecting the dealers with the sparse "living room" booths, including the one full of mistakes, the booth Avery "clobbered" on Friday. The process reminds me of elementary school, when kids handed out Valentines only to a select group. Avery is laughing because he's not being asked to join the elite Boston show, when dealers who haven't sold much, or dealers whose merchandise is terrible though *arranged* nicely, are being selected. "Marvin's a great promoter, but he doesn't understand anything about antiques," Avery says. "He vets it—who he wants and who he doesn't."

The online application for Getman's shows winnows out dealers with questions like, "Other shows you have done in the last year" and "Dealer or promoter references" and "Do you display in a room setting booth?" For Boston Antiques Weekend, his new "juried" show aimed a "notch" above Wilmington, Getman appointed a "selection committee" to hand-pick participants based on how dealers display their merchandise, like a beauty contest. (They asked new applicants to submit photos of their typical booths.) The best dealers would earn spots in "The Gallery" at the front of the hall. "Tabletop dealers will be at the back," Getman told *Maine Antique Digest.*

Avery is laughing, but he's clearly bummed about being snubbed by Getman. It must be frustrating to see less knowledgeable dealers with worse merchandise being invited to the ball, while he's left to clean cinders from the fireplace, so to speak. It's analogous to people who buy reproductions, satisfied with corner cupboards and benches that *look* like valuable antiques on the surface, but lack substance and authenticity. More important, Avery has done well at Getman's shows, both buying and selling, so he'll miss an important opportunity if he's not selected. "At the Wellesley show last year," Avery says, "I bought a child-sized Uncle Sam parade costume for $38 and sold it for $1,000 at the Deerfield Americana show." At this show (aka the John Malkovich show), Avery surpassed his target of $5,000, a good start to the year, especially in a recession. "There's a look Getman wants," Avery says, "but he doesn't understand what he is sacrificing to make it look nice. At his Wellesley show, the dealers who did well were people like me, middle-of-the-road dealers. The dealers with fancy room settings did not do well."

Two weeks later, Avery tells me that Getman still hasn't invited him to the high-end show in Boston. "He doesn't know anything about antiques. All he knows is what he likes and he knows how to promote shows." After another week or two of stewing, Avery decides to call Getman to ask why he wasn't invited to Boston Antiques Weekend. Getman tells Avery that his booth is "too cluttery," that 75 percent of the booths in his Boston show will be "room settings" or a "wall show." (A wall show is just as it sounds; the booths are divided by temporary walls, on which dealers can hang paintings.) This happened once before to Avery. He didn't receive a renewal application from a Vermont show he'd worked for a couple years, and when he called the promoter to find out why, he told Avery that his booth didn't have the right look.

Now, Avery has to lobby Getman for an invite to his swanky new show. He tells Getman about the Wistarburgh bowl he sold for $12,000. Avery bought nine glass bowls at an auction for $1,100, sold one for $800, and had several other valuable pieces, including one he called an "enigma bowl." Very small, ribbed, slightly green. He thought the bowl was Mantua or maybe New Geneva, two early glass factories. He mentioned the bowl to one of his online customers, who told him twenty ribs indicated a "South Jersey house, generally Wistarburgh." In 1739, Caspar Wistar, a Philadelphia brass button maker—his buttons were "Noted for their Strength and Warranted for 7 years"—passed through New Jersey on a button-selling trip and saw the perfect conditions for a glass factory, wood for the furnace, abundant white sand. The Wistarburgh Glass Manufactory is considered the first successful glass house, but also the nation's first successful factory of any kind. A single Wistarburgh mug, with a nearly three-inch crack, sold for $55,000 at auction in 2010. Through Avery's online customer, he found a buyer for the rare Wistarburgh bowl, netting $11,000 after he paid $500 to his friend and another $500 to the friend's friend for making the connection to the collector.

But the Wistarburgh bowl doesn't impress Getman. "I told him I did the York, Pennsylvania, show and *that* got me into his show." He's in! Still, Getman has placed Avery at the rear of the hall. "That's fine," Avery says. "I do very well in the back at the Nan Gurley show." Boston Antiques Weekend will cost him $1,000 for a small, back-of-the-hall space. "There is a dress code. No jeans, no sneakers," Avery says. The dress code, Getman told a reporter, was necessary to "complete my vision of this world-class show." Avery's first purchase to prep for the high-end Boston Antiques Weekend, coming up in two months, is not a nineteenth-century game board or a rare piece of stoneware, but a pair of leather Florsheim shoes.

CHAPTER 18

Living the Pilgrim-Century Life

I once asked Avery to name his "Holy Grail," the object he would most love to own. "In glass, it's a lily pad pitcher," he said, "but in all else, a seventeenth-century six-board blanket chest." Pilgrim-century furniture is "the greatest stuff on earth," and six-boards "the greatest Americana anything." Avery has about a dozen blanket chests at home. "I can't get enough blanket chests," he says. Six-board blanket chests are just as they sound—a box constructed of six planks of wood: top, bottom, four sides. Love for six-board chests is an acquired taste. "There are limits to the charms of the New England six-board chest," wrote art critic Robert Hughes in *The New York Times*. "Early American furniture, Puritan furniture, has a homemade, Jacobean coarseness, and when decorated—either by turnery or painting—was apt to be clunky." This is what appeals to Avery. He said of a Portsmouth, New Hampshire, six-board blanket chest, "I love it for its simplicity and awkwardness."

Wallace Nutting, in his encyclopedic *Furniture of the Pilgrim Century, 1620–1720*, wrote that the blanket chest was the "central symbol of house furnishing . . . the first effort at joinery, and the last achievement of art." Nutting waxed poetic: "Romance, tragedy, the joy of the bride, the last memory of a long dead owner, all gathered about a chest." Blanket chests, he wrote, were "the one indispensable piece of furniture in an old civilization, or in a new country." The earliest immigrants to New England arrived with nothing more than a blanket chest filled with their worldly possessions, often textiles, which were extraordinarily valuable. In a seventeenth-century Massachusetts estate inventory, one linen napkin was assessed at three-quarters the value of an acre of the owner's land. Blanket chests were used for storing a family's few possessions, or as seats. People even ate from or slept on chests.

Because of a six-board blanket chest "emergency," I am driving five hours to the Cudworth House, a historical home in Scituate, Massachusetts, where there is an important seventeenth-century six-board chest with impeccable provenance. Avery's mission is to relate the Cudworth House chest with one he has just purchased. If he can prove that his chest was crafted by the same maker, Joseph Tilden, the historic and possibly financial value of his six-board will soar.

THE SIX-BOARD BLANKET CHEST emergency started as a six-board blanket chest accident. Avery bought the chest at an auction held in the middle of a two-day antique show in Marlboro, Massachusetts. "What an adventure," he says of the weekend affair. "There was a lot of action in the parking lot before the antique show. People open the backs of their trucks seductively. Dealers are not supposed to sell, but if they just *happen* to pull something out and if you *happen* to make an offer—it's all underground, like 'Spy vs. Spy.' A guy furtively follows you to the back of your van. . . ." After setting up his booth, Avery hurried over to the auction, which featured country Americana from a collector "thinning" his collection. "I got there at six-ten P.M. and the auction started at six-thirty P.M. so I didn't have much time to preview," he says. With only minutes to look over hundreds of objects, serendipity brought the trunk to his attention. "I heard a big crash. An older woman had lifted the top off this blanket chest—a big clunker of an archaic-looking chest—and it fell and made a wicked lot of noise." He went to help the woman, and when he placed the lid back on the trunk, he noticed saw-tooth decorations, "a serrated edge, two lines, like someone scratched it with a screwdriver," a Pilgrim-century feature. "I thought, *Holy shit, this could be Marshfield area*," he says, referring to a town south of Boston.

The catalog estimated the chest at $1,000 to $1,500. "I had ten minutes to make up my mind," Avery says. "The auctioneer said, 'This thing is ancient. I don't even know what to tell you. Somebody give me $300.'" Silence. Afraid the auctioneer would pass, Avery raised his hand. Then the bidding volleyed between Avery and a mystery man. "Nobody knew who he was," Avery says. "Some guy with white hair and bald. He bid on all the early stuff and left." Avery won the chest for $2,500, almost double the estimate, "plus the juice," the 17 percent buyer's premium. "It's emotional. You just want it." The chest was one of the highest-priced items sold at the auction that night. "People were flipping out when they saw what this went for," Avery says. "If that woman hadn't dropped the lid, I would never have noticed this thing." Or if he hadn't been the chivalrous sort to offer her assistance.

MAYBE FEELING A LITTLE buyer's remorse—the trunk was in rough shape, the lid "cupped" or bowed from the sun—Avery "crashed stuff out" at the antiques show the next day to pay for his new acquisition. At the show, he saw the trunk's former owner, the "kid" who was "thinning" his collection. He told Avery that he'd purchased the trunk for $100 twenty years earlier at a flea market from a guy "with all this shit hanging off the back of his truck." The story tells Avery that the original seller did not know much about the trunk. "He probably picked it up from some clean-out job and it had never been on the market."

After packing up from the Marlboro show, Avery arrived home at midnight, but he immediately hit the books. "I was so excited," he recalls. "There's a small box in the Museum of Fine Arts in Boston with this decoration." The next morning, he called the museum, but was put on hold for twenty minutes. "I couldn't get through to an actual person, so I hung up and called the emergency number."

"A six-board chest emergency," I joke.

"Haven't had an emergency like that in three hundred years," Avery says.

(The fact that the Museum of Fine Arts has an emergency number fills my mind with absurdities for which one might need this number. "Help . . . dying. Must see art.") Avery spoke with the assistant curator of the American Collection, who said the trunk was in deep storage at some outlying warehouse, and not accessible. She promised to send him information. "The one in the MFA is attributed to Joseph Tilden," Avery says. "The only examples I'm aware of are in the MFA, and there's another one known. If I can relate my trunk to the MFA trunk, mine could be one of the only examples around and it will be important." On the MFA Web site is a photo of their trunk, labeled "Little Board Chest, circa 1675–1700, pine and white cedar, tin plated iron and lock and hinge." The key to linking Avery's six-board chest to the museum's chest was whether or not the saw-tooth decoration on the side carried onto the lid. "The picture teases you," Avery says. "You can see the lid but not the sides."

Much rests on such small details. A seventeenth-century six-board chest was attributed to Ipswich, Massachusetts, maker John Knowlton by its waffle scratch-carved design. The distance of the waffle squares from each other, and the number of protrusions in each square, were identical to the pattern on a fireplace lintel in a house Knowlton built. If Avery can relate his chest to a known maker, he can establish provenance. "If the sides are decorated on that thing, it's going to relate it to mine, made by the same guy. I *have* to see that one in the MFA."

"This is an exciting find," Avery says. "The feet are shallow as if they'd lost four inches in height," common in three hundred years of use. Avery's trunk has some problems. "There's a drawer missing from the till box. The lid is original, but it's broken off. It's a train wreck, but nobody has put two and two together." The details on his trunk, and the one in the Museum of Fine Arts, are noted in two important reference books, *The Wrought Covenant: Source Material for the Study of Craftsmen and Community in Southeastern New England 1620–1700* and *A Cubberd, Four Joyne Stools & Other Smalle Thinges.* "Both places mention the till is held in by tiny wooden pins," Avery said. "When I looked at this thing, I said, 'Holy shit, there's the wooden pins.' They're slightly bigger than toothpicks, holding in these big boards." The six-board is "a battered thing," Avery said, "but in the end, this will be a winner."

I CALLED AVERY a week later to see if he'd learned anything else about the chest. As promised, the MFA contact sent information, which revealed that the original curator who'd acquired the MFA's trunk in 1981 authenticated the piece through a larger "Tilden" trunk at the Cudworth House; this trunk had impeccable provenance—it was donated to the Scituate Historical Society in 1979 by Charles Tilden. Until it was donated, the trunk had never left the Tilden family. Nathaniel Tilden, born in 1583 in Tenterden, England, arrived in Massachusetts in 1634 with his wife, Lydia Huckstep, and four children. Nathaniel died only seven years after immigrating, but he spawned several generations of "joiners." The MFA curator's report noted that there were only five Tilden pieces known. "Mine is the sixth," Avery says.

"It may not be a huge money thing, but it will have historical value," he says. "The Museum of Fine Arts won't buy it, though. They'll buy some pigeon shit on tinfoil," he says, referring to an exhibit of contemporary art, "ten huge photos of people being shit on by birds."

"They had a huge room at the front dedicated to that, while the Pilgrim artifacts are stuffed into the basement at the end of this bleak, dimly lit hall." As Avery left the American collection one day, he passed a woman lecturing about the bird photos. "She was explaining that this was art," he says. "I was appalled. As I walked out of the room, I muttered, 'This stuff sucks.' It was my little rebel stand."

NOW AVERY HAS to see the Tilden trunk, so a couple weeks later, we visit the Cudworth House. With an hour to kill before our appointment, Avery teaches me about blanket chests, using an example parked in his son's room underneath posters of Bart Simpson and *Family Guy*. We sit on the floor in front of the trunk. "The earliest trunks have intaglio design—incised or engraved into the wood. Later they applied decorations. Scratch decor was the poor man's way of getting a decorated chest. Anyone with a screwdriver can make the scratch decor," he says. The trunk in his son's room is a panel chest, with stiles (vertical planks) and rails (horizontal planks). "In fifteenth- and sixteenth-century Europe, when wood became scarce, they had to use smaller pieces, so they made panels," Avery says. "Here in America they had eighteen-foot-wide trees, but for a hundred years they still did the joinery with the stiles and rails. Maybe they wanted to show their skills, or maybe they made them this way out of habit, but it was close to a hundred years before they started to make the standard six-board chest, which was so much easier. Top, bottom, four sides."

We move on to the hinges. "A snipe hinge looks like cotter pins. Metal was precious back then. First-growth pine was very heavy, but these lids were held together with a piece of metal about the thickness of a coat hanger. This trunk has a sizeable piece of metal, and an elaborate lock. But where the snipes usually are, it's notched out. That's very unusual." Now we examine the lock. "On these older trunks, the lock is attached from the inside and folds down, and the hasp folds into the lock. If you think about it, locks are not usually made this way. This is a seventeenth-century lock. Shortly after this time, they changed the way they made locks, with the hasp folding over. This other style came back around 1800, but this type is only on trunks from the seventeenth century." My mind is swimming with hasps and hinges.

An antiques dealer's time is spent mainly in three activities: buying, selling, and researching. (Maybe four, for itinerant dealers: packing and unpacking.) Avery seeks every opportunity to further his education. "I went to a yard sale at a house built in 1680," he tells me. "The owner didn't seem in the mood for inviting anyone in, but I Eddie Haskelled my way in there. You have to see the architecture, how the fireplace was laid out." Avery studied the interior craftsmanship of the three-hundred-year-old house. "I noticed the beaded molding on the beams. It was simple—they planed the molding with this unique tool until it left a design." Two years later, Avery saw the exact same molding on a dresser. "I knew it was Pilgrim century and from that area," he says. Another time, he just knocked on the door of a historic home and told the owner he was interested in old houses. "A state trooper lived there and he took me through every room in the house," he says. "I was looking for clues." One clue was the staircase. "The people who built houses then were ship builders, so the staircases were steep and narrow. The banister was original, the rungs were turned inward. I've since seen that type of turning on table legs." When a house built in 1685 in Avery's town went on the market, he called the realtor for a showing. "I had to see it," he says. "I had no intention of buying it, so I felt a little guilty, but I had to see it."

His years of research have made him an autodidact. "My forte is six-board chests," he says. It would seem that a basic box might be simple to understand, but even experts are unsure sometimes. In 2010, Avery bought a decorated chest listed as "Provincial Carved Oak Storage Chest," with an estimate of $300 to $500. He won the chest at auction for $1,126, which was a "puzzle," he says. That amount tells him that bidders "took a little poke at it," but weren't confident enough to really chase after the piece. "If it was American, it should have sold for $20,000 to $30,000. But if it was English, it should have sold for $200 to $300." The box "could be something," he says. "It has this weird dentil molding, but this is where it gets confusing because it's probably not really dentil molding." ("Dentil" molding resembles rows of teeth.) "In the Chippendale era," he continues, "they scribed lines in the legs. With Pilgrim, they did the same thing only it's called channel molding. They did that from 1650 to 1700 and then stopped, and then it came back with Chippendale." At a Boston auction, Al Whitmore, who Avery said is "a major buyer for top New York City dealers, a scout, a picker," confused these two features on a table, which he dismissed as country Chippendale. Avery explains. "In other words, not from the 1770s, but made by some country bumpkin. He interpreted channel molding from the seventeenth century as country Chippendale from late eighteenth to early nineteenth century. He missed by a hundred years and three styles."

Another box that Avery recently bought—smaller, with two carved "folky" birds—also confused "a room of experts." But a tiny chip in the box spoke to Avery. Like the other chest, this piece sold for the "wrong price"—$3,500. "It's worth five to ten times that or else it's fake," he says. The night before the auction, Avery was too excited to sleep. "This was the coolest thing I saw in my life. I had it written down for $5,000. It was fun, but anxiety provoking. The whole way there, I was thinking, *how high am I going to go?*" When the box came up, he expected it to take off, but everyone "negated" it. "Lee Massey said, 'What the fuck are you looking at that for? That is a piece of shit, Curt.' He thought it was nothing, a foreign thing. I negate people like him because they don't deal in this stuff. They look at me, and say, 'He's living the Pilgrim-century life, and winging it and missing.' But I come in under the radar. They don't know I do all my studying at home."

Like a lawyer in a courtroom, Avery dismantles each objection to his belief that the $3,500 box is American. Argument #1: "Everyone thought it was recarved and fake, but there is no question about the age of the chip. The chip is ancient. And in that chip, there is no carving. If this was a fake, they would have continued carving into the chip. The carving breaks off right where it should." Avery had studied the box with a magnifying lens. Argument #2: "Then they'll say, 'It's foreign, look at the size.' Everyone assumes that these boxes have to be larger, but Americans made little boxes." As proof, he shows me a photo of a similar box owned by the Winterthur Museum, pictured in *Neat & Tidy: Boxes and Their Contents Used in Early American Households* by Nina Fletcher Little. Argument #3: "You could argue that someone brought it from Scandinavia around 1820, but what are the odds of that? Underneath the lid, written in the late eighteenth century, in green ink from an inkwell, someone wrote something about 'dry fish.' Nobody noticed that. It means that the box has been in this country since someone wrote on it in English." Argument #4: "They'll say it's English, but it's not. The wood is wrong for England. It's true that we shipped wood to England—they were desperate for wood. But this came out of a collection of a guy who collected Pilgrim." Without provenance, Avery will have to marshal these arguments, and perhaps more, to convince someone else of the chest's authenticity. That is, if he ever parts with it.

THE CUDWORTH HOUSE was closed for repairs, but the Historical Society gave Avery special permission to examine the Tilden chest. Built in 1728, the Cudworth House looks out of place in the suburban neighborhood that sprang up around it, the way the Old North Church looks lost in the shadow of Boston's skyscrapers. From the outside, the clapboard house appears small, though it was home to twelve people, including two "spinster sisters," says the docent, a tiny frail woman who looks like she could have been one of the spinsters. In the main room, there is a massive fireplace, big enough for two or three small fires to cook the typical Pilgrim meal, a bland stew that bubbled in a cauldron like the one here, forged by Mordecai Lincoln, ancestor of the future president.

The floorboards throughout the house are eighteen inches wide, cut from first-growth white pine. "They were taxed on the width of their floor planks," the docent says. "The biggest trees were the king's property, so if you had these wide floor planks, you were taxed at a high rate. Sometimes they used the widest planks in the attic to hide them from the tax assessor." The windows have twenty-four tiny panes of glass on each sash, the ceilings are low, the doorways narrow, the floors slope. The house has eight fireplaces, and a steep staircase leads to the upper level, but no closets, and no bathrooms—only chamber pots or outdoor privies.

The building is under repair, so the furniture is draped with sheets, like a haunted house. The trunk that Avery has come to see has been set in the middle of an empty, sunlit room. The docent hands him a paper with a paragraph of text, and he can see how little they know about their chest. He has prepared a packet to give them, and as he hands the docent the sheaf, he tells her how unusual it is for the snipe hinges to be so sturdy. "These huge chests from this period were held together by wire as thin as a coat hanger," he says, which is why so many lost their lids over time. The woman says, "When you think of a blacksmith making a nail and hammering the metal, it took a while." Until the turn of the nineteenth century, each nail was wrought by hand, no two nails alike. The local "smithy" bought square rods of iron from an ironmonger, or from a nearby iron mill. The blacksmith heated the rods, then tapered them, cut a length off and wedged it into a slot in his anvil. He hammered the protruding bit of iron to fashion the flat head, a shape that loosely resembled a rose. The process was laborious, so nails were used sparingly, sometimes just one nail to attach each board. When houses burned down, people sifted through the ashes for the precious nails. Around 1800, blacksmiths began to use foot-powered machines with blades that could cut nails from cold iron plates, enabling them to bang out 150 "cut nails" per minute.

Avery points out the rose-head nails. "Feel the flatness," he says, running his finger over each one. "You don't see T-head nails because they came later." The date carved into this box is 1689. This box is the "primary" piece used to authenticate others made by Joseph Tilden, the grandson of Nathaniel, the original immigrant.

Avery examines the feet, pointing out the smooth groove in the base. "Wood joiners sometimes used shark skin to sand surfaces," he tells us. He takes off his coat and kneels on the floor, snaps photos from several angles. He suggests that the chest was once painted black. "Black was a seventeenth-century color," he says. The old woman interjects, "I hope you don't mind if I differ with you, but I think that's dirt." Avery responds good-naturedly, "I hope you don't mind if I differ with your differing." He takes out his loupe and inspects the surface, sees the evidence of black paint. After the docent peers through Avery's loupe, she agrees. "Nowhere in the documentation is it noted that the trunk was originally black," he says. The saw-tooth carving on the side of the box carries onto the lid, which is "very, very unusual," Avery says. "That normally doesn't happen with six-boards, but Tilden did that." The carving is "one of the more convincing factors" that indicates Avery's box, too, was made by Tilden.

After a half hour, Avery finishes his examination. He picks up the chest and carries it to the storage room, and covers it with a sheet. He tells the woman how important the chest is, and she asks what its value might be. "Conservatively, ten to twenty thousand," he says, "but it's so unique and rare, you really can't value it. At auction, it could do anything. In an auction, it's only the last two guys that matter." She nods appreciatively. "With the right surface, it might go for fifty to a hundred thousand. They'd fight like dogs for that," he says, "but you aren't going to sell it." An edict, almost. The right blanket chest, with the right decoration, can bring big money. In 2001, a Connecticut heart and star-flower carved six-board blanket chest sold for $170,000. In 2007, a painted, decorated, "possibly Virginia" blanket chest circa 1797 sold for $288,000.

Driving away, Avery worries that he hasn't conveyed to the docent the historical importance of the trunk, how rare and unusual the piece is. And he'd forgotten to examine the wooden pins holding in the till box. I ask Avery if—after all is said and done—he is satisfied that his trunk, too, was made by Joseph Tilden. He is sure, he says, but the bottom line? "Nobody cares."

ABOUT A YEAR after this trip, at the Montsweag Flea Market in Maine, I see what looks like a Pilgrim-century blanket chest. My heart skips a beat. I move closer to the chest perched on a table top. The chest is constructed of six huge, wide planks, the feet have the V-cut and have lost inches from wear, the top has what look like original snipe hinges. The dealer says, "That's very old," and I say, "Yes, I can see." The price is $250. Should I buy it? Should I make my first $250 mistake? What if it's not a mistake, but is worth ten times that? I understand Avery's words from his early days as a dealer, how breaking the $100 mark was "traumatizing." This six-board looks real to me, looks *right*.

But I'm not an expert. Maybe the top has been replaced, or it's not as old as it looks. If it was real and valuable, wouldn't someone more knowledgeable have plucked it off the field? After all, buyers are here at dawn and I'm waltzing in at nearly noon. But then again, as Avery says, nobody knows the Pilgrim-century stuff anymore; they don't recognize it, or they don't care. Maybe that's why the piece is still here at this flea market instead of a high-end show. It takes enormous willpower to pull myself away from the trunk, to walk away and not look back. For days, I'm haunted by the blanket chest. How could I leave it behind? Weeks later, it's still on my mind.

A few months after that, I tell Avery about the chest. He draws pictures of seven different types of foot cut-outs on six-boards, from the most common to a couple quite rare. Just seeing the variety makes me realize how little I know about blanket chests, that just because you can tell something is old and you recognize the hinges doesn't mean you can put together the whole story: the feet, the wear, the lock, the wood, the nails, the lid, the decoration or lack of it. An antique shows up in a booth once, but typically it's gone the next day; the dealer moves on, or perhaps someone else bought it. Antiques are often one-of-a-kind—if you see something good, you have to act. When I walked away from that six-board blanket chest, I may have saved myself from a $250 gaffe. But then again, maybe the six-board was "the one." I'll never know.

CHAPTER 19

Red Carpet Affair

It's the last weekend in March, and here we are at the much-ballyhooed Boston Antiques Weekend, crashing the party, as it were, the show Avery talked his way into. Boston Antiques Weekend is Massachusetts' version of the country's top shows, like the Winter Antiques Show at the Armory on Park Avenue, the "Grande Dame" of a cluster of January shows that add up to "Americana Week" in New York. The Armory show, which bills itself as the "most prestigious and profitable" antiques event in the country, has run for over fifty-five years, with about seventy-five elite dealers, like Leigh Keno. The setup costs, including extras like corner locations, lighting, and glass cases, might amount to $30,000. On par with the Armory show is the Philadelphia Antiques Show, operating each spring since 1962. The admissions schema for the Philly show's "preview party" reveals how time is money: tickets to enter at 4:30 P.M. start at $600, and drop as the clock ticks. At 5:30 P.M. they're $300, and by 6:00 P.M. the bargain rate of $125. "The New York City and Philadelphia shows are about confidence and credibility," Avery says. "People will buy a fraktur from David Wheatcroft because he stands behind it. The doctors, lawyers, and Indian chiefs trust that."

BOSTON ANTIQUES WEEKEND is not as elite as the New York and Philly shows, but it's promoted as "a world-class event for a world-class city." It's a chance for Avery to see how he'll fare at a top-tier venue. In the past, Boston's best show was the Ellis Memorial Show, which Avery says was "very fancy, very high-end," but the Ellis show is defunct. This happens over time; shows wither, or are reinvented elsewhere. At the Ellis show, the high-end dealers weren't successful, Avery says. "The fancy schmancy stuff didn't do well. The grounds were beautiful, but bronze statues for $6,000? The Boston market has a reputation for being exceedingly cheap. Cheap old Yankees."

For this show, the big-ticket dealers are at the front of the hall, with large double- and triple-sized booths on blood-red carpet, bright papered walls hung with paintings, lit by tasteful track lighting. Tall glass cases are full of china, statuary, silver. One booth features a pair of Elmer Crowell decoys for $14,500, in another a sixteenth-century Madonna painting for $50,000. These "living room settings" look like life-size dioramas, three-sided rooms furnished with tables set for twelve, towering grandfather clocks, desks. The neighborhood changes as you progress toward the back of the hall; the booths are smaller but still carpeted, still lit, still walled, until you get to the very back. The red carpet abruptly ends. Now you walk on bare cement floors, and there's no lighting in the booths, so the whole area is darker. There are no walls—just curtains to separate dealers, so you can't hang anything. The change is sudden, like crossing the tracks to the wrong side of town. This back section is the equivalent of "the projects." This is where Getman has placed Avery.

The main show is flanked by an antiquarian book show and a vintage textile show, 231 dealers total. Besides the royal red carpet for the bigwigs (the booksellers and the textile people don't get red carpet either), there is a live piano player, and for $10 admission, twenty free seminars billed as "Learning with the Pros," including "Everything You Wanted to Know About Collecting Old Maps of New England" and "Five Hundred Years of Dolls."

There's heavy security here. The Expo Center is in Boston's high-crime Columbia Point neighborhood. There was a murder in this neighborhood the night before, I hear on the news. By the time I arrive from Maine for Friday's setup, Avery has already sold his best piece to another dealer. There is still plenty of unpacking left, but we take a break to cruise. In a classy booth toward the front of the show, Avery bumps into Getman, the producer he cajoled for an invite. "We're expecting ten thousand people," Getman says. For this show, Getman spent $55,000 on advertising. "I've sold something already," Avery says, hoping to impress Getman. "A statue similar to this one, but much smaller." He points to a nearly full-size marble figure of a woman. "For how much?" Getman asks. "Five hundred," Avery says, crestfallen. Afterward, he says he was caught off guard. He ruminates on why Getman even asked about the price, how Getman will interpret that.

Avery is anxious that Getman will look for an excuse to un-invite him. "He's judging, believe me," Avery says. This becomes evident the next day, Saturday, as Getman strolls the floor preshow. At Avery's booth, without speaking a word, Getman picks up a standing lamp and moves it. "That's four inches over the line," he says. The line is some invisible boundary, as there's a good thirty feet between Avery's booth—the last in a row—and the outer wall of the conventional hall, where the security guard is playing an energetic game of air basketball. "The fire marshal could walk through the hall," Avery explains later, but it seems to me that with all the space surrounding Avery's booth, Getman's gesture is not about eliminating a fire hazard.

We return to finish the setup. Avery is worried that his inventory is weak for this elite show. "I keep getting cherry-picked," he says. "I'm walking into this big huge fat show with dregs." He can't hang on to his best objects for a show, not if a collector is calling. A dealer has to seize the moment; there's no guarantee of another offer. Besides that, as an object is exposed at more shows, value seems to leech out, that elusive "freshness" factor—the piece gets stale. People wonder why it hasn't sold. The more nobody wants it, the more nobody wants it—the opposite of irrational exuberance at an auction. Value in antiques is more subjective and fluid than in cars or cameras or clothes, things with fixed or at least comparable values and quantifiable manufacturing costs. Selling an antique, often a sui generis object, can require a tricky and artful blend of factors—timing, perception, salesmanship, context, credibility—not to mention the imperceptible factors that motivate buyers—emotion, impulse, wealth.

I ask Avery if he brought the sailboat weathervane, the one he'd snuck into his house. I thought it might be a perfect high-end item for this show. "I didn't want to bring the ship because I don't know what it's worth," he says. "I could guess at $1,500 and I might be in the ballpark, but that could also be a real fuckup." (Later, he sells the ship through an auction for $3,800.) He wasn't sure what to bring, both because this is a new show, and because the antiques market is down. "I was afraid to bring just Americana. I mixed it up, brought some decorative items."

During setup, it seems almost physically impossible for Avery to stop taking things out of boxes. I keep saying, "Now it's cluttery." That's the magic word, the dreaded word that Getman used to damn Avery's booth and nearly exclude him. When we're done setting up around 4:00 P.M., we step back and review the booth. Avery has achieved a look that can be called "organized clutter." With about a quarter less stuff than usual, it's crowded, but nothing is piled atop anything else. Black tablecloths lend an air of elegance.

After setup, Avery and I walk around the arena for another two hours. In the middle of the hall, Avery says of a "living room" booth, "That's the type of look Getman wants. The total value in that booth is $6,000. In my booth, I have $30,000 worth of antiques." The dealers, he says, have "very typical" stuff. "I could replace everything in that booth to-morrow." In front of another red-carpet booth, he says, "This guy could order four more tables like that if he sells one. And Getman wants this guy and not me." Near another booth where the dealers are finishing their setup, Avery comments sotto voce about a child's chair priced at $650, "I wouldn't give you $10 for that fucking chair. It's a Mexican piece of shit." About another booth: "This guy is an auctioneer. This is all the stuff he's stolen out of houses." An Imari bowl like one Avery recently sold for $250 is priced at $600, and we see a hetchel priced at $175. "That's a $50 thing," he says.

But there are plenty of booths offering great objects. At a large booth by the main entrance, a posh, spacious, beautifully arranged room-booth,

Avery shows me a spoon rack mounted on the wall, price tag $48,000. The rack is two feet tall, a foot wide, crudely carved of dark wood, with slots for spoons. "Chip carved, compass-rose designed," the label reads. "They used a compass to make the design," Avery tells me, which explains how each carved, geometrically shaped rose petal is uniform. "I had one of these, but mine was more rudimentary," he says. "This thing belongs in a museum."

ON SATURDAY, we arrive two hours before the show opens. Amazingly, Avery has brought more boxes and he starts to layer things. I feel an acute wave of anxiety. "It's beginning to get cluttery again," I warn. He removes some things, stores them under tables, repositions items, trades places. At five in the morning, the shirt that Linda had ironed for him—one of two dress shirts he owns—didn't fit, so she ironed the other one, a plain royal blue, which he wears tucked into khakis. He's wearing the new Florsheim shoes, polished and shiny, but his feet are killing him from the cement floor. He's brought a small area rug for underfoot, took it right out of his kitchen.

The pianist, who looks to be in his eighties, opens the show with a number from *The Sound of Music*, "These are a few of my favorite things," apposite to the occasion. The gate is strong, but it takes a while for the crowd to mill toward the back. There is no stampede, or frenzied competition like at Brimfield. The crowd is well-to-do and older, carrying bright yellow handled bags, which I think is a good sign; they are spending money, filling up the bags. But Roger, the dealer across the way, who has cases and cases of jewelry, says, "Look inside one of those bags. There's nothing in there but magazines." Turns out there was a huge line at the entrance for the free bags, which people filled with free glossy home decorating magazines.

Avery sells a leaded glass pitcher for $250, which suddenly clears a space for something else. Nature abhors a vacuum; so does Curt Avery. He sells three gorgeous Wedgwood platters in mint condition—giant plates for a suckling pig or twenty-five-pound turkey—for $1,200. Avery's friends Lee and Barbara stop to say hello. Lee, who's in his mid-sixties but still boyish looking, has been in the business since he was twenty-one. He's never done anything else. He chides Avery, says his booth is still "too busy." Avery counters that he's selling well. "But you had to beg to get in," Lee says. Lee and Barbara work shows like Brimfield, but their booth here is sparse and roomlike. I ask Barbara if her profits dropped when she switched to a cleaner look. "No," she says, "because the people could see the stuff." She admits it was nerve-wracking to make the transition. Avery's booth looks good, she says, things are going in the right direction, a set of large silver serving spoons neatly aligned. "This makes it easier to look at," she says.

I might not have believed her if I hadn't read Paco Underhill's *Why We Buy: The Science of Shopping*. Underhill demonstrated that minor but strategic changes increased sales—placing products at eye level, repositioning displays, asking clerks to greet customers. In a well-known study at a fast-food restaurant in the mid-1990s, Underhill found that instructing cashiers to ask customers if they wanted to "supersize" their drinks succeeded 47 percent of the time. Antiques are not fast food, but these principles could apply. Here, the sparser look doesn't seem to be hurting Avery. He sells a red painted chest to a former curator of Plimoth Plantation, a huge stoneware jug, and a set of "golf-ball" crystal, eight large goblets, eight small, and six cognacs, in clear glass with a huge dimpled green-glass ball on the stem.

IN THE BOREDOM of the slow afternoon, I venture over to the antiquarian book show. In the booth of a dealer from Vermont, I'm thrilled to see a first edition of Allen Ginsberg's *Howl*, alongside a postcard from Walt Whitman, written in graceful fountain pen cursive, dated November 27, 1888, addressed from 328 Mickle St., Camden, New Jersey, the only house Whitman owned, purchased partly with royalties from *Leaves of Grass*. In the postcard, Whitman thanks someone for the "plump sweet birds which arrived last night. I have had half of one for my breakfast today."

I wander through the textile show, which has the cloying perfume aroma of a boudoir. Racks of dresses for tiny corseted waistlines, furs, beaded purses, fans, paisley shawls, hats. I look for a hat with an entire stuffed bird on it, a Victorian custom that nearly caused the extinction of some species. (At a single 1902 London auction, the 1,608 packages of heron feathers sold for hat frills required the slaughter of 192,960 birds.) A single hat could be mounted with four or five birds, wired with springs for lifelike movement, flowers, fruit, even a mouse. Eventually, the wanton destruction of birds in the name of chic millinery sparked a protest, and eventually the birth of the Audubon Society. I see no hats with stuffed birds, but there are many with enormous fluffy ostrich feathers. An entire industry—ostrich farming—rose and fell with the hat fad.

BEFORE THE SHOW OPENED on Sunday, the final day, Avery rose at 5:00 A.M. and drove two hours to a bottle show in New Hampshire, bought a piece of stoneware and a piece of redware, and drove back to Boston. Perhaps because of this detour, he forgot to bring his dress shirt, and so has on just an undershirt. His remedy is to wear his jacket zippered up to the collar. It's a little beat-up, but better than his T-shirt. On Sunday, the crowd is leisurely, "like the mall," Avery says.

Three dealers stand in the aisle chatting. Avery says, "This show is very retaily." Most of the sales are to collectors, or people decorating their homes. The dealer-to-dealer wholesale trade is meager. One dealer replies, "I had a retail sale . . . once." This man is not a dealer, per se. He doesn't set up at shows; he's a picker. He buys things at shows or in antique stores, and drives them around in his truck, stopping at dealers' houses. "I usually sell it before I get home," the picker says. "Sometimes it takes three stops." A strange occupation, I think, transporting things from one location to another, a sort of reorganization of objects, filing them in their rightful places.

"I'm selling things for a lot less than I used to," the picker says.

Avery agrees. "Hooked rugs that used to sell for $350, I'm now getting $250. I'm not buying another hooked rug unless there's a bunny on it. That's all people are buying now."

The third dealer adds, "These people have million-dollar houses, but you know what you see in the driveway? Bob's Discount Furniture truck."

"There's very little antiquarian interest now," the picker says. "It's just the look."

Avery says, "I don't know what the hell I'm doing in this business."

Avery seems to be at a crossroads. He's not in the top tier of dealers (although he sells to that upper echelon). "There are the Kenos," he says, "then another level, and then me." In the socioeconomic strata of the antiques world, he's probably upper middle class, or perhaps lower upper class. It takes capital to make the leap to the highest rank. Even to buy the merchandise for the top-tier shows would take tens of thousands. Besides that, you need an invitation. Sometimes Avery dreams about the freedom to roam. He'd work the East Coast circuit hard, Maine to Florida, shoot over to the famous Nashville show (where in the past, dealers set up right in hotel rooms), Illinois and Indiana, then back to New England, a life on the road. At other times, he says, "I don't want to be doing this in ten years." Flying solo is difficult. "If you don't have two people," Avery says—like the many couples who work together, gay or straight, parent and child, business partners, retirees—"you can't be competitive at a certain level, especially if you have young children." It's not like Avery can hire help (with the exception of flunkies, like me, to unpack); the learning curve is too steep and long. Linda is busy raising two kids, and working full time in an office job, which provides a steady paycheck and the family's health insurance.

But Avery is buying and selling high-quality antiques to a growing roster of serious collectors and top dealers. He gave his friend Glen a redware jar to sell at the prestigious American Antiques Show in New York City, part of Americana Week. (A $1,000 ticket to the preview party bought you "cocktails at a fabulous Tribeca loft carved out of a Civil War–era building.") Avery found the redware piece at Brimfield. "Everyone was out shopping, scouring and scouring," he says. "I always manage to get back to my booth ten seconds before the gates open, so I was walking back real fast and I saw this jar labeled 'French redware, $45.' It was out there for an hour and nobody bought it." I asked Avery how he could tell the jar was American and not French. "The weight, the feel, and this weird bow around the top, like pinched clay." He says that Gary Stradling, the *Antiques Roadshow* appraiser, bought a jar by the same Vermont maker, only signed, for nearly $20,000. At the American Antiques Show, a museum curator saw Avery's piece in Glen's booth and bought it for $8,000. I asked Avery if he regretted not making the contact himself with the museum buyer at the fancy New York City show. He shook his head. "Not at all." He has no desire to be the front man, mingling with wealthy clients. "I'd rather be the man behind the curtain," he says. "I don't know if I have the aspirations to be Leigh Keno. I just want to be happy."

IN THE END, the Boston Antiques Weekend was anticlimactic for Avery, and for several other dealers in the lower-rent district. He did well enough—five grand—though he earns this at Brimfield and Wilmington, where setup costs are cheaper. Some of Avery's neighbors did not fare nearly as well. One couple sold only one item for $300. In another booth, the dealer sold nothing. The dealers up the aisle, a "living room" booth with large furniture, including a swing-out side desk that Avery had shown me, took in $6,000, but they were in the expensive real estate. Avery's next-door neighbor—another dealer trying to up her game—says she broke even.

Avery is invited to the Boston Antiques Weekend the following year, so he's cleared this hurdle, proven himself (and his objects) worthy. But then the economy free-falls and the next show is canceled because of the recession. "If the economy is bad, it hits the antiques field ten-fold," Avery says. Even the top dealers were not exempt from the sluggishness. At the New York Armory show in 2009, dealers reported that prices were down as much as 30 percent.

Crowds were "thinner" and dealers sold "on tight margins," the *Maine Antique Digest* reported. "There were a lot of sighs" among these elite dealers. "I'm scrambling," Avery says. "Everybody is." According to the National Auctioneers Association, auction revenue for "antiques and collectibles" dropped by 9.3 percent in 2008. The James D. Julia auction house in Maine ran full-page ads announcing "The James D. Julia, Inc. Stimulus Plan"—zero percent commissions, cash advances, finder's fees, and free pickup. Pook & Pook auctioneers of Pennsylvania advertised their "TARP" program—"Troubled Antiques Relief Program." Pook & Pook paid $100 toward hotel costs, offered free catalogs (usually $40), and sponsored a night of "free food and drinks" for anyone who spent $1,000 at their mid-January auction.

In 2009, Avery worked harder than ever, setting up at forty shows. His May Brimfield routine turned into a grueling circuit. Instead of selling at two shows all week, he set up at four. Monday he sold at a flea market just over the town line that piggybacked on Brimfield. On Tuesday, he was up at 5:00 A.M. to "pick" the fields before setting up at the Acres North show at 10:00 A.M. He packed up his booth that night, and on Wednesday, he shopped three shows. On Thursday, he hopped over to May's field to sell all day before packing up and moving across the road that night to set up for the J&J show on Friday and Saturday. When I see him on Sunday right after this blitz, he has a glazed expression, his hair is sticking out like a mad scientist's. "It beat on me pretty good," he says of the circuit. "I don't think I can continue. This business is hard on the family and relationships." Most families barbecue or picnic at the beach on summer weekends, but Avery is always away at shows.

On his first day of "rest" after Brimfield, at 6:00 A.M., Avery drove three hours one way to check out a desk-on-frame that was possibly real, possibly eighteenth century, only to find it had been cut and reshaped. On the second day, he had a tooth pulled. The economic situation worsened over the year. At the July 2009 Brimfield week, Avery earned a "hard, hard $1,800," he says, a record low. "I swear, that show took *life* out of me."

THE GENERAL RULE for antiques in a down economy, according to a Sotheby's specialist in decorative arts, is that cheap objects and great objects sell, but the middle-of-the-road stuff suffers. This middle ground is Avery's territory. "Out of good, better, or best," he says, "there's no market for 'better.' I have a tea table with cookie-cut corner ends. One slightly older than mine, with a better form—an oval top and button feet—maybe an eight or nine on a scale of one to ten, sold for $19,000. I can't get $800 for mine because it's a five or a six," he says. "Even if you find something great, it's hard to sell it for what it's worth, unless it's super great."

Even before the recession, the antiques trade had been declining. "The antique business is going downhill," Avery says. "Shows are slowly disappearing, dealers are disappearing. There are openings at the highest-level shows. There should be a hundred dealers waiting to spend $10,000 to set up at these New York City shows. Shops are disappearing, too." Market consultant Paco Underhill wrote, "Retailers must accept the fact that there are no new customers—the population isn't booming." This "fact" is manifest in the antiques trade. "You don't see younger people coming into the field," Avery says. "The next generation of buyers is not there." He continues. "People know less and less about antiques. A 1770s Chippendale mirror used to sell for $300. Now you get $75. The carnival glass that is suddenly worth more than the Chippendale chair. The Pez container. No matter how much I know, it is not going to help if the customers don't know." The antiques world, Avery says, "needs a shot in the arm."

In 2009, the Antiques Trade Steering Committee launched a campaign to boost the antiques trade, with ads that read: WANTED! NEW COLLECTORS—EVERY COLLECTOR ADD A COLLECTOR–IT'S SO EASY! The ads exhort dealers to "ask two of your good customers to interest someone and mentor them in antiques collecting." They beseech collectors to "interest and mentor one or more of your friends or children in antiques." Even the New York Armory show in 2009 held for the first time a "Young Collector's Night." (There was no age range for "young," but the $175 door charge was not targeted at the average ten-year-old stamp collector.)

Hollie Davis and Andrew Richmond, two "thirty-somethings" who sell and collect antiques, write a column in the *Maine Antique Digest* called "The Young Collector," and a blog. Their tagline: "We're not old, but our stuff is!" They published a quasi-manifesto in 2010, the "Top Ten Reasons" why young people should buy antiques, among them: "There are enough ten-year-old futons on Craigslist"—translated as "antiques retain value," and "George Washington did not sit in your La-Z-Boy"— antiques have historical importance. My favorite reason: "There's no such thing as a McBlanket Chest"—antiques are unique. The list is an earnest "call to collect" for their generation.

Another reason on Davis's and Richmond's top ten list is that antiques are "100 percent post-consumer content" and "the most environmentally responsible choice for home decorating." In the documentary *Objectified*, designer Karim Rashid said, "If the shelf life of a high-tech object is less than eleven months . . . my laptop should be made out of cardboard." Antiques don't enter the waste stream, or not as quickly, and in some cases, the opposite: they are pulled from the trash. *Antiques & Fine Art* magazine created an ad campaign: "Go Green, Buy Antiques," with an image of a Windsor chair. The ad asks readers to "spread the word" with a free window decal. It's an odd concept—highboys and six-board chests as tools against global warming—but the campaign has merit. According to Ellen Ruppel Shell in *Cheap: The High Cost of Discount Culture*, there's a good chance that the table you buy from IKEA, cheaply assembled in China, is manufactured from illegally harvested wood. (IKEA, the world's third largest consumer of wood, has been called "the least sustainable retailer on the planet.") IKEA—the Walmart of the hipster demographic—has "stoked a 'cut and consume' cycle that is destroying the world's forests at a rate unprecedented in human history," Shell writes. Go Green. Buy Antiques.

IT'S NOT JUST YOUNG people or environmentalists who might help to revive (or not) the antiques trade, but women. "The major social change playing itself out during our time has to do with the lives of women," Paco Underhill contends. "Retail must pay attention to how women wish to live, what they want and need, or it will be left behind."

Avery has scanned women's and home decorating magazines, a different kind of homework from eighteenth-century estate inventories or museum bulletins. "God help you connecting with these people," he says. "They don't know why they should pay $500 for a cupboard. They opt for the *Country Living* look for $78. That is what is killing this business. IKEA and the Christmas Tree Shops." Avery swears he's going to sell what people want, decorative accessories, "lady slayers." "Mark my words," he says. "I'll have a whole new look. The new me."

Marketing professor Dr. Peter Bloch has studied "the look," as Avery calls it. Bloch measured consumers' desire for visually pleasing objects, and found that today there is "an emphasis on product design unmatched since the art deco era of the 1930s. . . . Vegetable peelers, wireless phones, car-washing buckets and lawn tractors" are designed "with attention to the aesthetic value of their appearance." Cultural critic Virginia Postrel wrote that "aesthetics is not a luxury, but a universal human desire." Walmart, she gushes, has "made aesthetic goods available and affordable to many more people." Even at the low end of the economic continuum, though, people deserve beauty *and* quality.

Ellen Ruppel Shell observes in *Cheap* that IKEA has convinced millions of people that "mass-manufactured furniture . . . is not only affordable and stylish but *soulful*." IKEA's round wooden boxes in the Shaker style have little to do with the Shaker spirit of craftsmanship. Craftsmanship is "dwelling on a task for a long time and going deeply into it, because you want to get it right," wrote philosopher Matthew Crawford, in *Shop Class as Soulcraft*. People who repair vintage motorcycles—"mechanic-antiquarians," Crawford calls them—depend on a "collective historical memory." Stephanie Zacharek, in her review of *Cheap*, wrote, "If we want to stop valuing—and buying—craftsmanship, the very idea of making something with care and expertise is destined to die, and something of us as human beings will die along with it." The metaphor of mortality resonates with Avery. "The fakers, the forgers, and the sellers of cheap reproductions have finally put the nails in the coffin."

People seem to want the old and the unique, objects with flaws and idiosyncrasies, values inherent to antiques, but they can get those qualities more cheaply than they can by buying real antiques. The latest technology can make things appear old or vintage, with the quirky flaws inherent to manual or outdated processes. "Hipstamatic," an iPhone application, will make photos appear to be taken with a cheap old plastic camera, resulting in images with "beguiling imperfections" and "washed-out colors," writes Rob Walker, author of *Buying In: The Secret Dialogue Between What We Buy and Who We Are.* There is software that mimics the static and blips of vinyl records, and fonts that create the whorls and tremors of old-fashioned cursive. We are nostalgic for the imperfect, the individual, but we want convenience.

In the recession, and in a cultural climate where more and more people are satisfied with cheap, mass-manufactured ersatz antique-*looking* things, to stay in the antiques business, Avery says, "you have to have a wicked passion for it." Avery is wistful about the world of antiques. "It's like a great machine. Sand gets in the gears, and grime, and slowly it just grinds to a halt." Lovers of antiques are, perhaps, becoming an endangered species, as rare as the objects they cherish.

"We're going to have to adjust," Avery says. "Some of this stuff is never coming around. That's a wake-up call. You have to change or you'll be the loon in the corner with sixty pewter plates and nobody knows what they are." I've witnessed this shift in just six years. Shopping with Avery at a Cape Cod flea market in summer 2010, we see a one-quart butter churn that is just like the one he bought years ago at the Rotary Club flea market, my first show with him. He picks up the butter churn, which is priced at $75, half its former value. "Nobody wants these anymore," he says, and places it back on the dealer's table. The butter churn, that flawed invention, sits unwanted all day.

The antiques trade is changing. "You can sell $20 purple bottles and you can sell a killer Shaker box," Avery says, but the middle market is soft. "Leaving the middle behind is hard, to train yourself not to raise your hand when you see the $50 thing that you can sell for $300." To stay in the business, he says, "You have to reinvent yourself."

"How will you reinvent yourself?" I ask.

"I keep thinking about it," he says. "Once I get out from under my giant ball of wax"—his backlog of inventory, the vexing crowded house problem—"I'll concentrate on picking better items. It's like fishing for rare fish. You get no bites for days, then the fifth day, it was all worthwhile."

Recently Avery spotted one of those "rare fish" in an antique shop: a seventeenth-century Bible box for $1,000. "The paint was faded, but the rest of the box was intact," he says. Somewhere along the line, people thought these boxes were used to safeguard Bibles, but Avery believes they held valuables. "Why would they have huge metal locks and hasps? Bibles were not that valuable and did not need to be locked up." Within a month, he sold the box for $9,500. If Avery can catch these "rare fish" just ten times a year, he'll make a decent living, and maybe even clear out his house.

In spite of the gloom about the antiques trade during the recession, Avery is still "cautiously optimistic" about the future. "Antiques are a commodity," he says. "People would invest if they knew how. I can't help but think that as time goes by the more money and the more people there are, the more good antiques will increase in value." I mention the unprecedented transfer of wealth taking place as the baby boomers inherit an estimated $8 trillion from their affluent post–World War II parents. "I just hope they are not looking for Batman lunch boxes," he says. "They are going to have all this wealth and no taste. I'm scared of when that happens. They will be buying reproduction furniture and Batman lunch boxes. It's happening right now."

He's right, it's happening now. In February 2010, a copy of Detective Comics No. 27, the first appearance of "The Bat-Man" in 1939, sold for a record $1,075,500. Just two months later, in April 2010, Action Comics No. 1, the debut of Superman, "the Man of Steel," beat Batman when it sold for $1.5 million. Will Spider-Man defeat Batman and Superman? What about Antiques Man? Stay tuned.

CHAPTER 20

Captain Antiques

As a kid in the 1960s, my brother Patrick would fasten a towel around his neck with a clunky cloth-diaper pin, and jump from chair to couch—Superman or Superboy, some sort of caped crusader. Now, my six-year-old nephew, Donny, does the same, only as Spider-Man. His costume shames my brother's bath towel. In full Spider-Man regalia, Donny wears red from head to toe, with a mask, cape, and web-shooting gloves.

"We all did that," says Austin, a thirty-two-year-old Superman collector I met at the Indianapolis Comic Book Show. Austin's love of Superman started with Underoos—"Underwear that's fun to wear!" the slogan goes. "My mom and dad got me all the Underoos," he says. "I've liked Superman since I was a little kid." His collection was jump-started when his friends bought him Superman Burger King glasses as a graduation gift. "Now I just have a ton of things." Austin still buys the new Superman comics every week. "I used to volunteer on Wednesdays in a comic store," he says. New comics are released weekly on Wednesdays. For fans, comic book dealer Shawn Hilton says, "Wednesdays are like going to church."

IF COMIC BOOK COLLECTING is a religion, Superman is God. Vince Zurzolo, cofounder of ComicConnect, the online outfit that sold the

$1.5 million Superman comic, said that in terms of quantity, Spider-Man is their biggest seller, but in terms of value, "Superman dwarfs them all." Spider-Man, who's done phenomenally well at the box office, has not fetched the sky-high prices in comic book form commanded by Superman. The record for a Spider-Man comic is $227,000 for the debut issue, Amazing Fantasy No. 15, sold through ComicLink.com in 2007. Perhaps Spider-Man sells for less because he's a younger superhero, born in 1962 when Marvel Comics writer Stan Lee thought "somebody crawling on walls could be interesting." Lee considered a fly and a mosquito before he hit on Spider-Man.

In 1938, the original Superman debut issue cost 10 cents, and some 130,000 of them sold, but only about 100 remain today. It's a rare, if "young," antique. Today's collectors, Zurzolo says, "don't want a Van Gogh or a Picasso. They want a collectible that means something to them." Objects from our pasts have a particular magic—they connect us to earlier versions of ourselves. Yale psychology professor Paul Bloom calls this an "endowment effect"—even if we've possessed something only for minutes, that object becomes more valuable to us simply because of that brief contact. Amazing Fantasy No. 15, the debut of Spider-Man, is Zurzolo's favorite because it affects him today as it did when he was a boy. "The first time I read Amazing Fantasy No. 15," he says, "I'll never forget reading, 'With great power comes great responsibility.' I got a tingly feeling down my spine then, and still do now. To help your fellow human." For comic book collectors, the passion begins in childhood. "I used to look at the pictures in my brothers' comics before I could read," Zurzolo says. "As I got older I scrounged around for change in the couch and bought comics at the local luncheonette. I loved Spider-Man, and team-ups, which were two superheroes. Spider-Man has been my favorite throughout my life."

By one account, "typical" comic book readers are males from age eight to forty-five, with 67 percent older than eighteen. Shawn Hilton, who owns Comics Cubed in Kokomo, Indiana, says, "My demographic is from about sixteen to forty-five. That really is the range." Stergios Botzakis wrote in the *Journal of Adolescent & Adult Literacy* in 2009, "When people think of comic-book readers, they typically get a vision of a stunted person who lives in his parents' basement and spends countless hours arguing the minutiae of his particular popular culture interest." One of Botzakis's interviewees, "Roger," recalled that in the 1980s, his comic habit "was coming between me and French kissing." Writer and comic book collector William Bradley admitted that as a kid, his favorite character was the Flash, "because he was good-looking and athletic and generally all these things I thought I wasn't."

Before I can ask Vince Zurzolo about the comic geek stereotype, he volunteers, "I played sports in school. I wasn't just sitting around reading comics. I dated girls." I laugh. "I've had sex with a lot of women. Please put that in the book," he jokes. The "nerdy" stereotype, he says, "has been dispelled over the years." In France, comic book readers get more respect; they tend to be better educated and have a higher socioeconomic status than their countrymen. Charles de Gaulle and François Mitterrand both enjoyed comics, like *Tintin*. In Japan, comics, or manga, are read by 90 percent to 95 percent of all literate consumers, and in Mexico, comics have nearly 90 percent market penetration among the literate population. In the 1940s, comic books were in 90 percent of American households, but by the early 1990s this figure had slipped to 50 percent. Sales in North America plummeted between 1997 and 2000 from nine million to four million per month—the great comic book crash.

"There was a time in the early 1990s— shortly after the first *Batman* movie came out—when the public became aware that these old comic books sold for tens of thousands of dollars," Bradley explains. "Publishers relaunched their most popular characters so they could sell, say, Spider-Man No.1 again. They would publish four or six versions—different covers, or with different bound-in trading cards—believing that hard-core collectors would have to have every single one. The result was the 'speculator boom.' People were buying all of these comic books thinking they'd sell them in thirty years to pay for their early retirements. Not too long after that was the bust—people wound up with these worthless, way overproduced comic books, and Marvel Comics almost went out of business." For comic book collectors, Bradley believes, the crash was much more significant than the $1.5 million Superman sale. "There was real concern that an entire industry or American pop art form could be dying."

The comic book industry has perked up since the crash. In 2001, Stephen A. Geppi, owner of Diamond Comic Distributors, the world's largest distributor of English language comic books, began "Free Comic Book Day," and handed out millions of issues worldwide. Sales were spurred also by "the nostalgia trend" following the attack on the World Trade Center on September 11, 2001, according to a Marvel Comics spokesman. Superman, of course, could have turned back time and prevented the attack, or at least leaped tall buildings to save the trapped people.

ASIDE FROM NOSTALGIA, comic books have become desirable as a commodity. Zurzolo started selling comic books at sixteen. "My friend and I put an ad in the *Comic Buyer's Guide* in the 1980s. Our company was called VM for Vincent and Mark comics." After college, Zurzolo faced a choice. "I could either work in the corporate world, or I could work from my basement in my underwear, on the phone buying collections." After college, Zurzolo began peddling comics on the sidewalks of Manhattan—"I had two card tables and eight boxes"—then worked his way up to conventions. In 1985, he opened a showroom, Metropolis Comics and Collectibles. "We have 150,000 vintage comic books for sale, the largest inventory of vintage comics in the world. That dwarfs the closest competitor three-fold," he says. (Mile High Comics in Denver claims to be "America's Largest Comics Dealer," with over five million comics in stock, though not all "vintage." Founder Charles Rozanski started selling comics from his parents' basement at thirteen, lugged 10,000 comic books into his dorm room in the early 1970s, and now has five stores, an online venue, fifty employees, and annual sales of over $5 million.)

Since 2005, Zurzolo has hosted a weekly talk show, *Comic Zone Radio*, and in 2007, he and Stephen Fishler founded ComicConnect.com. "I started out selling on the sidewalks of Broadway, now I have a showroom on Broadway," he says. "It's been a fun ride." Zurzolo attributes his success to respect for the genre. "Comic books are one of the true great American art forms. You can point all the way back to cave drawings, those were the first comics. But an actual comic book with pages stapled and a cover—that's a uniquely American art form. Every culture has its superheroes. The ancient Greeks had their gods. These are our myths. 'Truth, justice, and the American way'—that pretty much says it all."

Bradley concurs. "Those early superheroes were concerned with stuff most Americans could relate to—Superman beating up corrupt mill owners, Batman beating up organized crime figures, Wonder Woman bringing milk to starving orphans. And then they served as propaganda during World War II with Batman fighting the villainous Japanese criminal Dr. Daka in his first movie serial—'Dr. Daka, you're as yellow as your skin!'—and Superman advising his readers to buy war bonds and 'slap a Jap.'" Superhero comic books adapt to the times, Bradley says. "There's a great Captain America storyline where the villain is revealed to be Richard Nixon, back to get his revenge against the American people." As a collector, Bradley sees his role as a cultural archivist of sorts. Comics, he says, "keep me tethered to a past I can recognize. We're never going to lose the Beatles or *Casablanca*. But Speedball, the 1980s Marvel Comics hero whose power was—I kid you not—the ability to bounce around a lot, really fast? Yeah, he's pretty much gone. Nobody really cares, and probably no one should care, but this kind of stuff matters to me."

In much the same way that a six-board blanket chest signifies a particular moment in history—the beginnings of a nation in the seventeenth century—Superman reflects a national self-image, our hopes and fears during the twentieth century. "Superman is the most well-known fictional character in the world, outside of maybe Mickey Mouse," Zurzolo says. "I love Batman, don't get me wrong, but Superman ushered in the age of the superhero." It might be difficult to prove Zurzolo's claim, but in 2003, when VH1 ranked the top two hundred pop icons, in a weird conflation of the fictional with flesh-and-blood, Superman ranked second behind Oprah Winfrey, but ahead of Elvis Presley. Spider-Man and

Batman made the list, too. A different pop culture ranking in 2010 put Homer Simpson on top, which might say something about our cultural aspirations now, or our notion of "heroic."

IN SPITE OF the 1990s slump in the comic book industry, vintage comics have remained strong. "The track record of comic books over the last seventy years is fantastic," Zurzolo says. "When the economy is bad, people are terrified of the stock market and the banks pay nothing, so they buy tangible assets. Sales were consistent through the dot-com bust, and now through this recession." Maybe it's not coincidental that superheroes are popular now as pundits predict the decline of America's global power. Over the last decade, vintage superhero comics doubled and tripled in value. The Superman debut issue, the "Holy Grail" for collectors, sold for $200,000 in 2000, leaped to $485,000 in 2005, and skyrocketed to $1.5 million in 2010. The debut issue of "The Bat-Man" sold in 2000 for $175,000, flew to $410,000 in 2005, and broke the million-dollar mark in 2010. Amazing Fantasy No. 15, Spider-Man's arrival, sold for $86,000 in 2003, jumped to $122,000 in 2004, and then hit $227,000 in 2007.

Heritage Auctions, which only began selling comics online in 2001, averaged $18 million in sales annually by 2006. Heritage holds the record for the largest comic book auction, a total of $5.2 million in 2002. And in 2003, Heritage sold the collection of actor Nicolas Cage, who faced financial difficulties. Cage's 420 comic books sold for a total of $1.7 million, including $126,500 for All Star Comics No. 3, the introduction of the Justice Society of America. The sale, which jolted the market, was called by *Forbes* "the biggest payday in American nerdhood since Bill Gates went public."

In 2007, Kevin Hassett, an American Enterprise Institute fellow, adviser to George W. Bush's and John McCain's presidential campaigns, and comic book collector, claimed that comic books outperformed other collectibles—and even stocks—in long-term financial value. Hassett analyzed data from price guides to calculate return on investment over time, and found that superhero comic books generated an average 26 percent rate of return. For example, a Superman No. 1 returned a 23 percent investment since its inception in 1938 to 2007 (and that was before the banner year of 2010). The average annual return for coins, stamps, art, and rare books were "all in the low single digits." The superheroes of investments, Hassett concluded, were comic books, "an object of intense nostalgia" among baby boomers who now have money.

While the "super-best" comic books might be bulletproof investments, the bulk of the trade fluctuates in ways similar to the antiques market. "The comic collectible market will always go up and down," Shawn Hilton says. "You'll have something super hot this week, like a *Chew* No. 1 book I'm selling for $60, and then a year from now, something else. Books that sold for a couple hundred bucks you can now find in a twenty-five-cent box." I ask Hilton why *Chew* No. 1, which cost $2.99 when it came out in 2009, would appreciate so steeply in a year. "It flew under the radar," he says. "They didn't make a ton of copies, and at first nobody got excited about it. It's such a weird idea." In *Chew*, Tony Chu is a "cibopathic" cop; he receives knowledge from the food he eats about its origin. (The Latin *cibo* means "to feed.") By tasting corpses of murder victims, he receives psychic impressions that are clues to solve the crime. "When it came out, everyone thought it was pretty cool," Hilton says, "so now people are looking for it." Another sought-after series is *The Walking Dead*, a zombie book. "Zombies are super huge right now," Hilton says. "Zombies are beating up robots and vampires. Maybe not vampires, but I can still hope."

AS WITH NEARLY EVERY category of antique or collectible, there are phonies. "Restoration has been part of the comic book business," Zurzolo says. "Years ago people did it innocently, trying to make the comic books look nicer with felt-tip markers, but people have been ripped off." Restoration, Hilton says, "is a horrible, horrible word. You have to be careful. I've been in this business for twenty years, but with a million-dollar book, I'm still calling in two buddies. I might be a little starstruck—like I want this book so badly. I'm going to bring in the biggest guns I can find and nitpick." While Hilton doesn't think the problem is dire, there are "experts" who can restore a sun-bleached book to full color. "Even if they are up-front about restoration, there's still a little stigma. If you are not telling people about it, that's a big problem."

Unlike the antiques world, comic book collectors have a near fool-proof way to guard against fraud. Founded in 2000, Certified Guaranty Company (CGC) rates the condition and quality of comic books, from 0.5 for tattered to 10 for pristine. (The $1.5 million Superman had an 8.5 rating.) In a temperature- and humidity-controlled room, rubber-gloved CGC employees inspect comic books for restoration, assign each a grade, and then seal them in hard plastic cases with a "tamper-evident" label—"slabbing" in comic industry lexicon. Restored comics get a pur-ple seal, like the proverbial scarlet letter, the "the kiss of death" for value, collectors say.

CGC receives over 100,000 comic books annually for grading—about 19 percent of which are Spider-Man comics, Zurzolo tells me. Sanction-ing by CGC is not cheap. The least expensive examination is $23 for a book valued up to $150, with a forty-day turnaround. A five-day express service for a book valued up to $3,500 costs $85. For the highest-value books and the most expedient service, CGC takes 2.5 percent of the fair market value, with a cap of $1,500. There are qualms about slabbing. "Let's say the comic has been CGC'd and it's in that sealed package— you are supposed to never open that again," Hilton says. "Well, if it's a million-dollar book, I'm not buying that without opening it up. Imagine buying an antique and it's somehow hermetically sealed."

THE ANNUAL COMIC CONFERENCE in San Diego, run by Comic-Con International, is the largest in the country with over 100,000 at-tendees, including A-list celebrities—in 2010 Angelina Jolie, Sylvester Stallone, David Duchovny, Jeff Bridges, Bruce Willis, Helen Mirren, who seemed out of place but starred in the comic-book-based film *Red*, and the grand pooh-bah, William Shatner, who dropped in by helicopter. Outside of this star-studded event, you can find comic conventions across the country any weekend of the year. In the Midwest in October alone, there were nine shows: Champaign/Urbana, Green Bay, Rockford, Chicago, Omaha, Kansas City, Indianapolis, St. Louis, and Peoria.

In a generic, carpeted meeting room of the Ramada Inn just off I-70 in Indianapolis in August 2010, I wander through my first-ever comic book convention. The show manager, Andy Holzman, a dealer and collector himself, expected four to five hundred people. "This is a small show," he says, unlike the Chicago show, which is "gigantic, like ten thousand people a day for three or four days." At this show, he laughs, and says, "Nobody is dressed as Superman." For the $3 door fee, I'm handed a goody bag with comic book swag—a ninety-eight-page special edition of Marvel's "Heroes Return" from October 1997, originally priced at $3.99, and a cello-wrapped set of *Star Trek Voyager*, Season One—Series Two cards. (Random draw: "Time and Again—Episode 104: Captain's Log. Supplemental. The ship has been struck by a shock wave from a Class-M planet in a red dwarf system we're passing through.")

The windowless room is a bit dreary, but sunlight fades the value from comic books. The attendants here are about 90 percent male, but there's one woman in her sixties, a few wives of dealers, a couple women in their twenties, and a teenage girl whose father is a dealer. Contrary to my expectations, I see just two or three children. I ask Hilton if he was worried that kids weren't reading comics. "They're getting into it later," he says. "The subject matter now is much more adult. It's keeping up with society."

The show starts at 9:30 A.M., though the opening is sluggish. The dealer-to-dealer trade, like at the flea market, has already happened. "The dealers spend more money before the show begins," Hilton says. "Like, this dealer here is from Kentucky, so he's brought up stuff that maybe he can't sell there, and he's willing to dump it. But I'm like, 'Yeah, Bobby Knight is super hot.' We trade products." As with flea markets and antique shows, dealers flock to fresh merchandise. "If dealers see someone brand new, they'll all hit that table," Hilton says. "I've seen people buy out a guy's entire table, take it across the aisle, reprice it and sell it. Forty-dollar profit, ten feet away."

Most of the booths here have tables laden with comic-book-sized boxes, filled with Mylar-encased issues. Higher-ticket comics are show-cased on newsstands. Some booths have toys and vintage DVDs of sixties television shows. The oldest thing in the convention hall appears to be from the 1930s, though much of the merchandise is younger than I am. I was born in 1960, so if I were a superhero—and if I were in better condition—I might sell as "vintage" for thousands.

The promoter, Andy Holzman, looks too young to have a twenty-eight-year-old daughter and twin twenty-four-year-old sons. He has curly black hair, and wears a black dress shirt with a cartoon motif. His background is art therapy, and he works as a counselor. "Comics have always been part of my life," he says. He recalls lying in bed at age seven, with chicken pox, copying drawings from comic books. When Holzman was ten, his father died. "I comforted myself with comics and drawing," he says. Comic books are "all about remembering, connecting to your childhood."

For William Bradley, comic books like *The Flash* inspired his obsession with time travel. As a boy he dreamed of zooming to the future. Now, comic books jog his memory—a sort of time travel back to childhood. "I sometimes wish I could go back and just experience parts of the past again," he says. "Not that I'd want to live in the past, but to visit?" I experience this time warp when in one booth I spot a box of Wacky Pack-ages. These stickers, which were sold by Topps Chewing Gum Company from the 1960s through the 1990s, spoofed actual products in *Mad Mag-azine* fashion—"Crust" instead of "Crest" toothpaste, or "Satan Wrap" instead of "Saran Wrap." Seeing the Wacky Packages, I'm flooded with a Proustian rush of memory—the sense I had as a ten-year-old that the stickers were cool and somehow pleasurably subversive. Until this mo-ment, I'd completely forgotten these Wacky Packages existed. This glimpse of my past doesn't summon a whole episode from my life, but I can see how objects can be impregnated with memories. Later, I'm as-tonished to learn that even though Wacky Packages were produced in enormous quantities—fourteen million just in series #14 from 1975—an early "Good and Empty" sold for over $1,000 on eBay. I'm even more

surprised that Pulitzer Prize–winning artist Art Spiegelman, author of
Maus, was "one of the godfathers of the Wackys." The dealer here is
selling a Wacky Package from 1979 for $35. "I'm starting to get a de-
mand for them," he tells me.

IN THE FIRST BOOTH in the hall, Eric, a forlorn-looking young black
man, tells me he deals comic books on the side, though lately, he says,
"Times are tough." Eric sells at about ten shows a year. "There's not as
many shows as there used to be in this area," he says. I ask if he sells
comics for fun or profit, and he says, "The profit part is getting kind of
sad. People just don't have money." It seems telling that in Eric's booth
you can buy the Marvel comic issue in which Spider-Woman first
appeared, April 1978, for just $5. "To Know Her Is to Fear Her," the
cover warns.

One of the largest booths at the show has thirty feet of tables covered
with boxes of comic books, racks inside the booth, and a shelf with action
figure parts in baggies. One grouping for $20, marked "Blade Series V,"
contains a three-inch plastic sword, like a thick toothpick, a teeny gun,
and a nickel-sized boomerang. Vintage comics range from $5 to $25, but
a box in the back holds high-end issues, like Amazing Spiderman No. 36:
Spidey as you like him! In College! In Trouble! In Action! Action! Action! The
original cover price in 1966 was 12 cents, but now it's $250.

When he's not busy helping customers, the ponytailed dealer, Mark,
a high school wrestling coach, reshuffles the contents of his boxes, like a
librarian reshelving books to make space or close a gap. When I ask him
whether the recent spate of seven-figure prices has affected the trade, he
says, "Sales are actually down at the shows lately." The million-and-a-
half Superman was "an anomaly," he says. "That's a very high-grade
book, but as far as regular collectibles that most people buy, it's stagnant
or even less than it has been." The record price did have an effect—it
inflated expectations. "Unfortunately, because of that Superman comic
book, people think that what they have is valuable. They check the guide
for Action No. 1 and it might say thousands of dollars, but in the condi-

tion they have it in, it might be worth just a few hundred. You have to tell them, 'I'm sorry.'"

Holzman, who's been organizing this show for twenty-three years, says, "The really high end—the $1.5 million Superman—is doing well, and the low end—the 25-cent comics—are doing well, but the middle ground is not selling," a refrain familiar to the antiques trade. He thinks the comic trade is following the culture at large. "Well, the middle class is being forced out, right? In some ways, the middle class is disappearing." Lately, Hollywood has boosted the comic book industry. "With Spider-Man movies, it's gotten a little better," Holzman says. "I started this show in 1987, and the high point was like 1996 or 1997." As many as 1,200 people attended his shows then. "Then it dipped. The early 2000s was pretty down. It's come up the last year or two."

I ask Hilton, one of the few full-time dealers here, if he's optimistic about the future of the business. "Yeah," he says, but adds, "It's changing. If you are not willing to change as the comic world changes, you aren't going to do well. I'm willing to sell the variant covers," limited editions made for the collectors' market. "Some guys might snub those, but as long as it's in good taste, I'm all for it." Nowadays, you can download comics to your iPad. "There's Marvel online," a collector named Nich, who works in the tech industry, tells me. "Some of the books you'd never find, like the couple-hundred-dollar books, you can download for 99 cents. They retouch up the art on older books, brighten it up with Photoshop." Hilton doesn't think this technology will hurt collectibles. "People still want that comic book they can hold in their hand. The whole point of antiques and collectibles is ownership, possessing something. You can't own an electronic thing—it's a little pixel on the screen. It's almost like having an imaginary friend instead of a real friend."

At first, I find myself strangely attracted to the vintage comics, but after three hours I grow tired of the homogenous superhero images: the females with melon breasts, tiny, anatomically impossible waistlines, and what can only be called "flowing tresses." Male superheroes are stereotypes, too, though not as sexualized (there's no analog beneath Captain Marvel's Spandex for the female characters' fetishized grapefruit breasts).

In current issues, Spider-Man should be called Steroid-Man for his grotesque musculature; his bicep looks like an artichoke in Lycra. Wonder Woman and the Cheetah, a villainess with spotted skin, are more provocative than the illustrated model on a 1954 *Playboy* on sale in one booth; the *Playboy* cover resembles the stylized cartoon covers of *The New Yorker*. The dealer, John, a retired elementary school teacher, has several 1950s *Playboy*s priced at $150 each. He still owns every issue of *Playboy* since 1979 when he began reading them, he tells me. "*Playboy* collectors know the magazines inside out." No doubt. Marilyn Monroe was the first *Playboy* model in the inaugural issue in 1953, he says, which also included Sir Arthur Conan Doyle's story "Introducing Sherlock Holmes." Even in very poor condition, the Monroe issue has sold for over $2,000. One signed by Joe DiMaggio sold for $40,250 at Sotheby's in 1999.

CURT AVERY HAS SEEN how nostalgia for the past—the near past, as opposed to the distant past of the Pilgrim century—has affected the antiques trade. "This show in western Massachusetts used to be a good antiques show, but people aren't looking for antiques," he says. "There was a guy there with a horrible booth. His booth looked like Woolworth's from 1963—floor-to-ceiling G.I. Joes and Barbies. He ruined the look of the show. His booth took the antique shows down three notches."

If I hadn't cut the hair on my Barbie dolls, perhaps today I could sell them and buy a new car—or a really good antique. In 2003, a Ponytail No. 1 Barbie from 1959, wearing a strapless, zebra-stripe bathing suit, with crimson polished fingernails, gold hoop earrings, and a weird sideways glance fixed in her heavily lined eyes—as if a rogue Ken doll were stalking her—sold for $25,527. In 1959, Mattel sold 250,000 of these dolls. Everything from my childhood, it seems, is now collectible, which might argue for the wisdom of hoarding. But even if I saved all my milk money from school, I still couldn't afford my childhood lunch box. In 2007, a mint 1954 Superman lunch box sold for $13,300. Superheroes are the most revered categories of lunch boxes—Superman, Batman,

Green Hornet, Wonder Woman—but even a 1962 Dudley Do-Right fetched $2,000.

In the mid-1990s, my niece brought a rotary phone to third grade for show and tell; my sister had saved it from our childhood home. Few things make you more conscious of your fading youth than objects from your own life becoming "antique," quaint and collectible. A vintage Apple-1 computer from 1981—*my sophomore year in college*—sold in 2003 for $22,000. In 1976, Steve Wozniak and Steve Jobs hand-built about two hundred Apple-1s in Jobs's parents' garage. (That model originally sold for $666.66, a price that freaked out Christian fundamentalists.) In 2009, an Apple-1 with its original packaging, invoice, ads, manuals, and a letter signed by Jobs explaining how to hook up the keyboard and monitor had a starting bid of $50,000.

My friend Mark, a systems architect, recalls his precalculator days in college thirty years ago, when slide rule users fell into two distinct camps, the Picketts versus the K&E users (Keuffel & Esser), like the chasm today between Mac and PC users. After dinner one night, Mark dug his slide rule out of the attic, pristine in its original leather case. I'm ashamed to admit that this was my first encounter with a slide rule. Since its invention in 1622, the slide rule served scientists, mathematicians, and engineers for over three centuries. As many as forty million slide rules were manufactured in the twentieth century alone. But in the 1970s, the calculator rendered the slide rule obsolete. The slide rule is today's version of a whale oil lamp. Now, collectible slide rules fetch thousands of dollars. Walter Shawlee, founder of the Slide Rule Universe, earns over $100,000 annually selling and restoring slide rules.

Rotary phones, computers, slide rules—the very notion of "antique" is creeping closer to the present moment. Perhaps in an attempt to slow time, an aging American population clutches at the objects of our childhoods.

TODD AND AMBER JORDAN, who sell vintage toys, are young enough to *be* my children. They are unquestionably the youngest dealers at the

Indianapolis Comic Conference. I have a sense of being left behind when I visit their booth. Their business, Kokomo Toys & Collectibles, specializes in toys from the 1970s on. Amber, a pretty, petite woman with blond hair and blue eyes, is wearing a My Little Pony T-shirt. Her husband, Todd, looks twenty-one, but they both grew up in the 1980s. Todd launched their business by selling his own childhood toys, and then buying the toys of other people his age.

"When we were kids in the 1980s, I played with Rainbow Brite," Amber says. "That's what I loved, so that's what I collect." Rainbow Brite is a blond, ponytailed doll who rides a flying, rainbow-maned horse called Starlite. Hallmark created the character in 1983; an animated TV show followed in 1984. Rainbow Brite has seven "partners" named after the spectrum, like Red Butler, Patty O'Green, and Shy Violet, who foil enemies like "Murky Dismal" and other "forces of gloom." People born in 1980 turned thirty in 2010. "It's nostalgia," Todd says, that drives his customer base to collect. "That whole generation is starting to have money."

The Jordans sell at toy and comic conventions, through their Web site, and out of their one-thousand-square-foot garage-turned-showroom, but 90 percent of their sales are through eBay. "eBay is really not so great," Amber says. She mentions the fees, the hassles, but mostly, she says, "It's always better when the customer can pick something up and touch it. We like to talk to people. They come in and tell their stories."

A hot category in 1980s collectibles, Amber says, is My Little Pony, mass-produced in vinyl in 1983. "Those are expensive now," she says. On the Jordans' Web site, a 1984 vintage My Little Pony Mail Order Satin Lace costs $250. "I've seen some foreign ones that have never been opened priced in the thousands," Todd says. "The old toys are a lot better than the new stuff. The new stuff is kind of junky. Classic toys are better quality."

It's all relative, I suppose. Antiques dealers like Curt Avery and Jimmy Desjardins would consider 1980s "classic" toys to be "junky." But perhaps compared with the products sold in the 2000s, the 1980s junk *was* less junky. "Collectibles are fine," Avery says, "but they are just highly overvalued. Most of them are mega-mass-produced stuff." My Little Pony,

Hasbro's Web site reads, "continues to be a worldwide favorite with nearly 130 licensees" who in 2010 will "bring My Little Pony branded products to the global marketplace." When I see the "mega-mass-produced" plastic My Little Pony toys for sale, I can't help feel dispirited about Curt Avery's handmade, tail-less, sawdust-stuffed pony, with real glass eyes, threadbare and worse for its two hundred years of wear, sitting unwanted at show after show.

One "classic" toy is G.I. Joe. The Jordans have the largest selection of G.I. Joes in the Midwest. "We have about two hundred thousand G.I. Joe parts," Todd says. "It's crazy." G.I. Joe—the grandfather of action figures, icon of American masculinity—debuted as "America's Moveable Fighting Man" in 1963, the same year that the Gulf of Tonkin incident escalated the war in Vietnam. Within one year, Hasbro's sales of G.I. Joe reached $36.5 million, but by 1968 they plummeted as the Vietnam War became less palatable to Americans.

The size of the G.I. Joe doll seems to correspond with its popularity. The first G.I. Joe was 11.5 inches tall, but when sales dropped during the Vietnam War, and with high oil prices in 1976 inflating the cost of plastics, the doll shrank to 8 inches. G.I. Joe disappeared altogether in 1978, but came back in 1982 when *Star Wars* repopularized action figures, though Joe was diminished—just 3.75 inches tall. In the 1990s, Joe experienced a growth spurt, from 4.5 inches to 6 inches, and since the late 1990s he's stood nearly a foot tall. Along with his former height, G.I. Joe has regained respect. In 2004, he was inducted into the National Toy Hall of Fame (along with forty-four other toys, like Barbie, Easy-Bake Oven, Monopoly, and Slinky). A first-issue 1964 G.I. Joe—with battle-scarred face, dog tags, an M-1 rifle, flamethrowers, and a bayonet—is displayed in the Smithsonian. And G.I. Joe has earned his keep. Just the outfit from a 1967 G.I. Joe Fighter Pilot—without the doll—sold for $6,362 at an auction in 2004.

I ask the Jordans if they think they are at the forefront of collecting. "I think so," Amber says. But Todd adds, "Recently there's been such hard economic times. A lot of dealers are getting out, liquidating their inventories." If it's any indication of the trend in collectibles, the Chicago

Toy Show, held at the Kane County Fairgrounds for thirty-seven years, with seven hundred vendors, is twice the size of the antiques and flea market there, Todd tells me. "It's gargantuan," he says. "It takes us five hours to go through it." Todd and Amber "pick" these shows the way Curt Avery picks Brimfield. "I'm going to go around here in a little bit," Amber says, of the Indianapolis show. "We're like *American Pickers*, but we call ourselves the Toy Hunters. We drive all over the place, Phoenix, Boston." The Jordans are actively buying in the deflated market. "Hopefully when the market picks back up, it'll work out," Todd says. Whether it does or not, Amber adds, "We love it."

IN ONE OF THOSE bizarre stories where real life imitates fiction, a Superman comic book rescued a family from disaster. In summer 2010, the family (who wishes to remain anonymous) was packing boxes to move out of their soon-to-be-foreclosed home. The couple had remortgaged the house to finance a business, which then failed in the recession. In the basement, they stumbled upon some comic books, including Action Comics No. 1, the debut of Superman. Recognizing that it might be valuable, they contacted ComicConnect. After being certified and rated (5.0 for "Very Good"), the comic book was appraised at $250,000. (This same issue, with a rating of 6.0, sold in March 2009 for $317,200.) Stephen Fishler, cofounder of ComicConnect, phoned the bank and halted the foreclosure. "Superman saved the day," Vince Zurzolo told ABC News. In September 2010, the family's Superman comic book sold for $436,000.

Meanwhile, back in the land of antiques, no deus ex machina has swooped in to rescue Curt Avery from a struggling antiques market. "It's a pyramid," he says. "There are very few people on top, but those people are dying and dropping off." He mentions Carla, a dealer who "knows nothing" about antiques. "She sells stuff that is listed in Kovels [a collectibles price guide] for $9, and she's asking $3. The object is in its infancy of even getting into a book. Before that, it wasn't even in anyone's mind. That's what people are buying."

U.S. Customs defines an "antique" as any artwork, furniture, or decorative object that is over one hundred years old. Antiques purists place the threshold before 1830, prior to the Industrial Revolution. But as Avery says, age seems to matter less and less. In 2009, the venerable New York Winter Antiques Show at the Armory raised the cutoff year for the date of "antiques" to 1969, allowing for "modern" and "contemporary" objects and works of art. They are redefining the notion of what an *antique* is. "The future is all about collectors mixing early and later pieces," Leigh Keno told a trade journal. The Pilgrim-century artifacts—Avery's specialty, the things he loves—obsolete as objects, may now become obsolete as antiques.

In this unpredictable and changing market, Avery's obsessive, workaholic, hyperbolic strategy of overloading his booth is saving the day for him. "At the last three shows I was the talk of the town," he says in summer 2010. At a better show in New Hampshire, with a $20 gate fee— where the producer had chided, "Bring the best, leave the rest! You bring too much stuff, Curt"—the "fifteen-special-item" dealers bombed, Avery says. "They didn't sell their few pieces." He covered his bases by straddling the low end with $20 bottles and the high end with $2,000 stoneware. "I did well by sheer attrition," he says. "I was the first person in, the last person out." Avery's success is not glorious, though, or easy. It's his "workman's attitude," he says, that is helping him survive. "I just did a big show and did well," he says. "I'd been up since three A.M. for that show, so the last thing I wanted to do was more work." The next day, he "slept in" until 7:00 A.M., but then he was back out on the hunt.

An interviewer once asked Bob Harras, former editor-in-chief of Marvel Comics in the 1990s, what super power he'd most like to have. Harras wanted the ability to stretch, "because I'm basically a lazy person and would like to be able to get my coffee without leaving my desk." Curt Avery—Captain Antiques!—has no secret to success, no super power— just the power of his knowledge (his antique laser vision), the power of his passion, and, as he says, "the power of showing up." After his "talk of the town" success in New Hampshire, the next place he shows up is my doorstep.

Life with Principle

Curt Avery sits at my kitchen table one August morning before we drive to Union, Maine, for the largest outdoor antique show in the state. As I set the table, I say proudly, "You'll be eating with antique silver!" I'd pored through boxes of utensils at flea markets with a magnifying glass. Avery says gently, "These aren't silver." He tells me that silver has a "925" stamp (or less if the silver content is lower) or a "sterling" mark. (My mistake was thinking that any mark meant the piece was silver; my forks and spoons were all silver plate.) I'm a little embarrassed by my pronouncement, but then he asks, "But what is this you are serving cinnamon rolls on?"

"That's my dollar, fake flow-blue plate," I reply.

"No, it's your late-eighteenth-century China export Imari, worth about $100."

In spite of what Avery has tried to teach me over the years, I get it wrong all the time. After breakfast, he walks through my house, sees a large bowl that I bought for ten bucks, now holding potatoes, which he says is a "nice piece of ironstone," worth about $90. Then I show him my "Sandwich glass" candlesticks with a cracked handle. He studies them for a minute in the sunlight and says, "These aren't real Sandwich glass. If they were, a single one would be worth thousands." He does a double-take to make sure. "But they are excellent reproductions. They are a twentieth-century copy by Duncan-Miller of a very early Sandwich glass pair." The "crack" in the handle is a production flaw.

I hand him a Wedgwood tile I bought at a flea market for $20. "What do you think of this?" I ask. He admires it briefly, but he's too quiet.

"How much is it worth?" I ask.

"About thirty bucks."

Next, I show him my Sandwich glass curtain tie-backs; I'd admired a pair he had in his booth once, priced at $300. Mine aren't as ornate, and I didn't know if they were real, but I liked them for $38. He says they are real, and while not fancy, worth about $80. Real Sandwich glass is rough on the edges, he says, and the metal fittings are housed in the glass. With fakes, the hardware is screwed onto the back. I ask about my hooked rugs, which I purchased at a junk shop years ago. Avery says they are machine-loomed, so only worth the $50 I paid, but the oriental rug I bought at a yard sale for $35 and thought too ragged to be valuable "looks good," he says. I should have it appraised, and repair the edges.

After breakfast, Avery walks into the woods behind my house, and spots an old dump. He kicks at the ground, then picks up a small blue bottle and hands it to me. "Here's a dollar," he says. The world around me is filled with treasure. If only I could recognize it.

THIS IS MY FOURTH time setting up with Avery at Union—it's become a tradition as the show is just an hour from my house. He arrived the night before, straight from "New Hampshire Week," a series of quality shows: Manchester Pickers Market, the Nan Gurley Americana Celebration, Mid-Week in Manchester, and the annual New Hampshire Antiques Dealers Association Show, a fifty-year tradition. "These shows are so friggin' awesome," he says. "The Pickers Market is filled with guys with killer shit and tons of money, a *Who's Who* of antiques." This is Avery's idea of heaven, "the stuff dreams are made of," he says. "I'm like a kid in a candy store." Avery bought a tavern table for $150 and sold it a few hours later for $500. The guy he bought it from called it a "porch table," because "it came off a porch." Avery earned $10,000 selling at the

Americana show in 2010, excellent in the recession. "I just had the right stuff," he says. "I bought two things for $80 and sold them for $3,200." Union is a solid antique show, but it's a step down from the New Hampshire shows. Avery has an idea for hopping from high-end shows to "second tier" shows. "I'm going to buy two trailers, one for knuckleheads, and one for collectors."

The drive to Union takes us along cow pastures and kettle ponds, tree limbs arching cathedral-like over hilly lanes. Avery reminisces about the euphoric highs he's had in his peripatetic life, meandering on country roads. "I ate at this old inn once after a show," he says. "It was very nostalgic, as if I were in a WABAC Machine. 'Today, Sherman, we're going back to 1969.' While I was there, a couple danced to Patsy Cline on the jukebox." The Union fairgrounds has this old-time flavor as it typically hosts county fairs with tractor pulls and cow-pie slinging contests. There's a horse track, and sawdust-floored stables that now house dozens of dealers. The bathrooms are new this year, an improvement over the dank three-stall unit they replaced, in which an old woman in a thin cotton dress and orthopedic shoes sat in a chair holding a plastic container for tips. In the new lavatories, a young woman and her husband are in charge; their handwritten sign reads, "We pay for all soap and towels. Tips appreciated."

I stake out a spot at the edge of the dealers' parking area and set up my tent. I have learned the creature comforts that make the difference between halfway decent sleep and insufferable torture: an eye mask, ear plugs, bug spray, a real pillow, and enough padding so my hip bones don't ache. In Avery's truck, I spot a box of Quaker Breakfast Cookies—he eats on the fly, like an astronaut. The field is huge with over 350 dealers, who are, as usual, partly setting up, partly shopping. Joan Christianson is next to Avery, and down the row is Eighteenth-Century Dave, a fiftyish ex-hippy with a swirl of reddish hair. Dave gets his nickname because he "proselytizes" everything in his booth as "from the eighteenth century," Avery says, though he has little faith in Dave's assessments. "At one show, he came back with a 1700s child's chair. My first reaction was, *that can't be right*. It's just an impossible thing to find. They only exist in museums, but that's the second one I've seen in six months. That means something is wrong. They're coming in from England, or someone is making them. I want nothing to do with them." Eighteenth-Century Dave sets his chair across the lane from his booth and watches people as if this were a sociological experiment. He has a theory on theft at antique shows: "Watch out for a bus of old lady tourists. One in three is a thief." Another dealer chimes in, "It's always a babe, a beautiful woman. Finally it occurred to me—stupid! What's she doing talking to an old guy like me?"

Avery and I set up the tent, then stroll the grounds, dipping in and out of booths. "There's a nice rug," I say, an image of a house with lollipop trees. "Actually, it's not," he says. "Too Hansel and Gretel-ish. The fiber is not right either." I feel chastened. We see a very old, twenty-four-slot cane stand on sale for $450, which Avery examines closely. "People spend thousands on canes," he says. "This is very esoteric." The piece is out of Hazelton, Pennsylvania, the dealer says. "We don't see them up here in New England," Avery says. The dealer says he was an auctioneer for thirty-five years. "Real stuff is getting harder and harder to buy," he says. (I once asked Avery if antiques will run out, "like overfishing in the Gulf of Maine." He said, "Not if you have knowledge, and you're willing to go clamming and scalloping.") At the next booth, Avery says, "If you ever see these hyacinth vases with a funnel foot, those are the ones you want." He gives me twenty tips a show, but I never remember both the item and the specific detail about it. If I see a hyacinth vase in the future, I might recognize it, but forget what subspecies of vase is most valuable and how much I should pay.

In one of the cow stable booths, I unearth a small area rug.

"What do you think? It's sixty-five," I say.

"I like it," he says. I feel vindicated after my previous rug comment. "Are you going to buy it?" he asks.

"If you can make some money, then you take it." I don't want to take bread and butter off his table.

He buys the rug and hands it to me. "Here. For helping me."

I thank him, say he doesn't have to do that, and he says it's the least he can do, I say he's helping me with the book more than I'm helping him, and we dance that little two-step. "Show it to Tildy this weekend," he says, his rug-dealer friend.

We return to the booth to unpack. I see the birdcage lamps I saw in Wareham (the "heat stress" show). How many shows will these lamps see before someone loves them for $250? I wonder about other objects. I ask Avery about the small ivory cup he bought for $1,000 at Brimfield a couple years ago. "It's tucked away. I'm waiting for the right moment to do something with it." I ask about the portrait of the woman from the York show. He hasn't put her out again, but he's not worried. "Great things are always great," he says. "I don't want to overexpose her. I love her so much, I'll take her home and live with her for a while."

ON SATURDAY, the weather is near-perfect, high sixties, dry and sunny, a few puffball clouds floating in a robin's-egg-blue sky. It's almost a pleasure being outside to finish the setup. *Almost.* There has been record rainfall in Maine, and so on this first lovely sunny weekend, the crowd comes out, the wealthy "summer" people with coastal "cottages." Early buyers are lined up for an eight o'clock entry, two hours before the general public. As ten o'clock approaches, cars pour onto the field and are shunted to the parking area. The crowd slowly thickens and people pass in and out of the booth.

A woman examines a quilt. "That's nineteenth-century chintz," Avery says, then under his breath to me, "so stop handling it like it's a moving pad." Chintz is so delicate, it's a wonder the quilt survived. "Chintz" comes from the Hindi word *chint*, meaning variegated, but printed cotton cloth like this was also known as calico, from the original term, Calicut cloth, made in Calcutta. Avery's price for the chintz quilt is $495, but he'll let it go for $350. Another dealer tells him it was wise to sell the chintz rather than hold out for a higher price; every show wears the fragile fabric, reducing its value.

Avery says to a customer looking over a small stand, "That's very fresh. Attic fresh. It doesn't get much fresher." A fresh antique, an oxymoron. Two women who run a fancy shop rush into Avery's booth. One says,

"We made a beeline for this booth. We got stuck in traffic and we're an hour late!" They praise Avery to people who wander in. "He's a great dealer," one of the women says. In the afternoon, the weather turns erratic. Every once in a while a cloud squeezes a burst of rain over a small area, like personalized weather, your very own two-minute shower. It gets breezy, but not dangerously so. Then a brief thunderstorm erupts, followed by a double rainbow, which seems auspicious. During the slow periods, Avery examines a small redware pot he found on the field. "That bottom is hard to deny," he says. "This is a study piece. It shows age, but the bottom has no wear at all." He'll ask some of his friends to look at it throughout the day. "Nobody gets it," he says. "I bought it for nothing because I liked the shape." The pot looks unworn, but Avery dates it by the whitish spots and minuscule divots in the surface, which he sees with his loupe. He thinks it might be an American potter's attempt to replicate a Chinese Qianlong pot in a glaze called "sang de boeuf," or oxblood.

Avery's retail sales, predictably, are for decorative items. An older couple negotiates hard for $725 on a pair of samplers. As Avery wraps the samplers, I tell the woman to add 5 percent Maine sales tax to her check. Her husband balks, and then flat refuses to pay. I say, "You'll have to talk to Curt Avery," and so once again they begin to dicker, but now the husband isn't so polite. "Seven-twenty-five is the bottom line. We are not paying any more than that." He grows red in the face. Avery remains calm. "I have to pay sales tax," he says, $36.25. He doesn't have much profit margin in the samplers, especially with the deal he gave them, but the man refuses. The wife is embarrassed by her now belligerent husband. I'm appalled. This couple would never announce to the proprietor in one of the dozens of antique stores along Maine's touristy Route 1 that they were simply *not* going to pay the sales tax. Or any other store for that matter. It's a standoff for a minute until Avery says, "I'll split the sales tax with you." At first the man refuses, but he notices his wife's pained expression, and consents. The joy of buying the samplers—already priced below their retail value—is tarnished. This is part of the problem of "selling antiques in a cow pasture," as Avery says.

On the way to Union, Avery stopped for ten minutes at a roadside flea market and bought a piece of china for ten bucks, which now sells for $115. "Pays for gas," he says. Worth the stop. A woman picks up a redware plate. "That's a train wreck," he says, an odd sales pitch. It's a small sandwich-sized plate, beat up around the edges. "But it shows the humanity of it," the woman responds, though she passes on the plate. Two men admire Avery's Weller umbrella stand on sale for $1,400, the jade-green ceramic one I'd seen years before at Brimfield. "That's a sexy piece," one man says. They don't buy it, though. A young couple wanders into the booth. The man picks up a tiny pair of brass pliers, says, "Look, honey, what they used to pull your teeth."

"That's not what those were used for," I say, trying to be helpful. "They were used to form lead bullets in the Civil War." The implement has handles like pliers. You pour molten lead into a small spoon and close the cover until it hardens, one bullet at a time. The man is uninterested, though, since I made him look stupid in front of his girlfriend. I had come by this knowledge only moments earlier, when I heard Avery telling a customer. My aggressive approach is off-putting. Most of the time, I can't answer any customers' questions, so I'm overeager when I know something.

Avery has found the right balance, the right rhythm. A woman asks about two bottles, and he tells her that one is a Stiegel-type liquor bottle from the eighteenth century, for $225, and the other a cologne for $65. She asks to take them out of the case. Avery shows her a fold around the neck of the liquor bottle, says it was "double dipped" for strength. "It would have had a cork stopper," he says. She asks about its age and he invites her to step into the sunlight to see the crizzling. She buys the cologne bottle for her windowsill, and Avery instructs her to clean the inside with liquid soap, warm water, and fine sand, to swish with a gentle rolling motion. "Make sure there are no little rocks or grains in the sand," he says.

I've complimented Avery's sales style in the past, and he seemed surprised. He doesn't think he's good with people, but his passion shows. And his honesty. Often, the first thing he points out is a chip, or a repair, like an anti–sales pitch. His antipitch doesn't seem to spook customers; instead, they develop trust.

After another quick jaunt around the field, Avery comes back carrying a huge six-board chest. "I need another one of these like I need a hole in the head," he says. But it was only *fifty bucks*. "A study piece." When traffic is slow, he examines the six-board. The snipe hinges are original, as are the rose-head nails. He shows me the original eight nails used to build the box. He studies the leg cut-outs, a South Shore Massachusetts feature. Later, another dealer glances at the trunk and says, "First quarter of the eighteenth century," confirming Avery's suspicions. It's exciting to find this stalwart piece of furniture, essential to the eighteenth-century household, on this field three hundred years later. But as Avery has said before and says again today, "Nobody cares."

LATER, AVERY AND I take my rug over to Tildy. She's rejoicing because a large rug she'd hauled to four shows has just sold for $1,400. She unfurls my rug and exclaims, "How lovely!" She studies the back, points out the unusual border. "And that deer!" Oh, the little deer lying in a glade with a little black dot of an eye. "That makes the piece," she says, "and there are two of them!" I hadn't even *seen* the deer. The front of the rug is washed out, but the back is bold, revealing the extent of the fading on the front. She shows us the fine $\frac{1}{32}$-inch stitching, a tight, difficult stitch, and finally she announces that my $65 rug, which Avery actually paid for, is worth $400. She says I should mount it on an acid-free backing and frame it in nonglare glass. Now the rug presents a problem. I was planning on using it in my living room, but now that it's a $400 antique, a classic example of craftsmanship, I can't risk further damage. I try to give the rug back to Avery, but he insists I keep it. He is happy that the rug is worth more. I'm sure he knew that when he gave it to me.

I carry the rug back to my car, and gingerly roll it in plastic. Avery returns to the booth with an American stoneware grease lamp a dealer has loaned him for closer examination. The lamp is priced at $1,200. He pulls out his 16X loupe and sees the "right" wear on the high points of the base, and tiny nicks along the edges. He dates the piece from 1770 to 1830. "It's an obscure item," he says. "If you appreciate lighting, this is a rarity." An hour later, the dealer lets Avery have the piece for $750. I understand why Avery never has enough room in his truck. For every object he sells, he buys something else.

As the show closes, from Avery's spot near the loading area, we watch people carrying faux antique tables, reproductions, and "paintings of nothing," he says. "Here comes the girl with a repro canister with a fake tin lid." He's disappointed in these people; they've let him down with their lame purchases. Just down the aisle is a semitrailer full of repro-ductions, new-old apothecary jars, "primitive" cabinetry, "rusted" cast iron tables. Tons of crap imported from China. In an ad brazenly placed in *The Journal of Antiques and Collectibles*, the "Repro-Depot" boasts of importing two forty-foot containers per week of "cast iron, decorative French wire, urns, statues, china, porcelain, bronzes, lamps, sconces, leaded window panels, mirrors, pottery & more." The repro dealer at Union has the largest booth, running the entire length of the eighteen-wheeler he drove in on. We see a lot of people walking out with this repro stuff.

"The audience doesn't understand real antiques anymore," Avery says, but adds, "I'm not going to worry about it." There is—and probably always will be—a "die-hard" population who appreciate good antiques. "At the Wilmington show, this girl who bought a compote sent me a check right away with an article on Bible boxes," he says. "She still has the passion. There are people like that."

"You can't kill them," he says.

"Like vampires," I joke.

Avery has a catholic outlook; he wants *everyone* to love old things, to feel the joy he gets from antiques. This is a generous impulse, but he is also realistic. "People *want* to buy antiques, but they don't know what to buy and how much to pay. And they don't have time to care." But his optimism prevails. "If people could just learn about antiques, they would never buy anything new again, at least not some things. They have two

SUVs and a $495,000 home that they fill with junk from Pier 1. Why would you buy a $495,000 house and put $18 things in it? It makes no sense. They settle for the fake thing that has absolutely none of the charm and intrinsic value," he says. "You would be so much better off spending the money and buying the thing that's real. I have a cupboard like that in my bedroom. I love that thing. It's wonderful, it's so original. And every time I walk by it I get this warm, fuzzy feeling. You never get that feeling from a fake, pretend thing. It's like you are ripping yourself off."

Six years after my first foray into this world, I finally understand what Avery means. At a small antique show in Maine in 2010, I fell in love with a lamp. The price was $200, more money than I've ever paid for a home furnishing other than a bed. (My bathroom sink was salvaged from the dump, my couch a castoff I reupholstered.) I told myself if the lamp was still there at the end of the show, I was fated to buy it. Two hours later, there it was, and to my surprise, I still loved it. So I bought it. I didn't even ask for a deal. The piece was not something I suspected was underpriced or mislabeled; it was not some hidden gem. Two hundred dollars was the retail price—for me a major expenditure, but perhaps in proportion to the wealth that Jerry Lauren has and the $5 million he shelled out for the Indian weathervane.

The lamp is cast iron, Art Nouveau, with delicate hand-painted birds in flight over a bronze-colored mica shade. I've never seen one like it. As the self-anointed Queen of the Flea-Market Dollar Table, I was at first horrified I'd paid so much for a lamp. But when I see the lamp on my kitchen table, I have that feeling that Avery and other collectors and dealers have, a blush of warmth, pride, and even something that feels like—I'm slightly embarrassed to admit—affection. Since I bought the lamp, I've grown to love it more. If my house were on fire, I'd take the things I cherish most, family photos, drawings by my nieces and nephews, original paintings by my sister, Sally, an artist, and now the lamp. I'm convinced that I'll own the lamp until I die, after which I hope someone else will love it, too, and then pass it forward, this beautiful antique handmade thing that brings a glow to my kitchen, and my spirits.

———

WHILE THE ANTIQUES TRADE fell sharply during the recession, by 2010 its pulse shows signs of quickening. Brimfield saw the largest attendance in a decade, and in mid-2010, Ron Bourgeault of Northeast Auctions told *The Boston Globe*, "The auction market is definitely on the rise," with increased sales and higher prices. Everything is cyclical. People will tire of crap, throwaway objects, sad, shoddy things. The interest in substance and quality will return. The zeitgeist is shifting already. An online clearinghouse for handmade crafts, Etsy, founded in 2005, earned $1.7 million in sales monthly by 2008; these figures doubled in 2009. Its founder believes the desire for artisanal and handmade objects is a rebuttal to the Walmartization of consumer culture.

Marketing experts Andrew Benett and Ann O'Reilly, in *Consumed*, predict a new paradigm of "mindful" consumption, which may bode well for the antiques trade. They published survey results that show people want objects "of solid, good quality," that don't extract a high price in environmental destruction or exploitation of workers, and are aesthetically well designed—products that match their personal values. These "mindful" consumers seek interaction with local merchants and artisans, like life in the nineteenth century—the butcher, the baker, the candlestick maker. These desires echo the reasons people offered for visiting flea markets and antique shows in a study twenty years ago—to seek the imperfect, to escape the "sterile" mall environment, to join a social atmosphere, to appeal to their creative and adventurous spirits.

Companies will succeed, Benett and O'Reilly suggest, if they offer authenticity, provenance, and personal connection. They cite a restaurant chain that offers "classic" cocktails from historical eras—"each drink comes with information about its origins and the provenance of the ingredients." A distiller promotes the "archaeological back-story" and "historical timeline" of its whiskey to make drinkers feel "connected to something larger and more compelling than the here and now." This trend—a "heritage aesthetic"—crosses industries. "Origin myths, legacy stories, reverence for founding dates, forefathers and artifacts . . .

heritage has become hip," Brenner Thomas wrote in 2010 in *Women's Wear Daily*.

The conventional wisdom has been that Americans are allergic to history, but historians Roy Rosenzweig and David Thelen confounded that idea in their first-of-its-kind, landmark survey in 1994. They extrapolated that some 76 million Americans have a hobby or a collection related to the past. In *The Presence of the Past*, they reported that 57 percent of respondents visited a history museum or historic site in the previous year, and 53 percent had read a book about the past. More recently, David Glassberg, in *Sense of History: The Place of the Past in American Life*, wrote that "if Americans do not have a strong sense of history, they certainly spend a lot of their leisure time looking for one, in historical pursuits of one kind or another." He concluded that "popular interest in the past has never been greater."

Antiques make us *conscious* of history. Sometime between my fourth-grade field trip to Plimoth Plantation—mandatory class trip for every school kid from Massachusetts—and a tenth-grade history class with Mr. Green, a Barney Rubble–looking ex-marine with a flat affect, I lost all interest in the past. After hanging around Curt Avery's world, my appreciation for history has become vastly different from (or perhaps the same as) when I was a kid. The greatest reward of trailing Avery has been to rekindle my fascination with history.

ON SATURDAY NIGHT in Union, after closing the show, several dealers gather at Avery's booth: Joan Christianson, and Eighteenth-Century Dave, and Wild Willy, who began drinking beer at noon. In his late twenties, Wild Willy is the youngest antiques dealer I've met, with a long hippie ponytail. He's the last of a dying breed, "young, knowledgeable, enthusiastic," Avery tells me. "He loves the early stuff. The period furniture people are frightened to death when he shows up at an auction. His attitude is, if you want something, be serious. Take a good swing at it. Just whack it and get another beer." Lester is here, too, an older dealer who speechifies about the dangers to Maine's forests from the Asian long-horned beetle. Seems he was an arborist in a previous life. Most dealers were something else in a previous life.

Avery lights candles set in three-foot-tall, nineteenth-century ornamental lanterns. Having forgotten to bring paper plates and plasticware, we eat potato salad and smoked trout from nineteenth-century Japanese Imari plates, using antique three-tined forks. If we were really going to be authentic, we'd stab our odd-looking forks into a hunk of meat heaped on a wooden trencher, pinning the meat while we cut a piece and then eat straight from the knife. Forks, at one time, were a luxury. Early Americans ate with knives, or even a "sharp-pointed piece of cane." The first known fork in the colonies is from 1721, listed in the estate inventory of a wealthy Massachusetts man. The first recorded English silver fork, in 1623, had just two tines. A third tine was added sometime around 1690, but it took nearly another century to add that fourth tine; a four-tine fork is first recorded around 1780. The Tremont House in Boston, America's first grand hotel in 1829, was the first to offer its guests four-tined forks, which they called "divided spoons."

Knowing this history, I can no longer disregard a fork. Instead, I wonder why it took *a hundred years* to add that fourth tine, why it took centuries to create this simple but perfect eating utensil (and four tines *is* perfect; five would be superfluous). In the fork I can read a story of human ingenuity, of trial and error. Once a luxury, now a table standard, the fork is a tool as basic and primitive as a wheel, but so ingenious that it's still used by astronauts at the International Space Station, a grand floating hotel 240 miles above the earth, visible to the naked eye but just a dot.

Here in rural Maine, we are far enough away from city lights so that the sky is inky black and dotted with pinprick stars. The moon is luminous and full, its silvery light casting shadows across the grass. The air is crisp, the night insects buzz and hum. Tired as I am from the long day, I feel radiantly alive. Each year at this time the earth passes through the Perseid meteor showers—I've seen three shoot across the sky already from my perch on a cooler—and with each blaze I get a frisson of time passing, of infinity, of our smallness on the planet, how we won't last. It's a grand finale to selling antiques all day, passing forward the things we've made with our hands, things that have survived two hundred or three hundred years and will live on, objects that hold the stories our great great grandchildren will hear.

ONCE, I ASKED CURT AVERY if, after nearly twenty years, he was still having fun selling antiques. "It seems like you are," I said. After a long pause, he replied, "Jeepers. It's a hard question because it's yes and no. Part of the reason I do this is because I love the stuff." He paused. "There are days when everything is for sale, and the next day you want to jump off a bridge, but I can't imagine getting out of it. I'm too obsessed with it, to be honest with you." Avery considered my question for another moment. "It's not about money," he said. "If I wanted money, I'd become a banker. And it's not the passion of the hit. It's the passion for the things, the love of the objects." Thoreau wrote in "Life Without Principle," "You must get your living by loving," a credo for the antiques dealer; its counterpart for the antiques buyer: "Do not hire a man who does your work for money, but him who does it for the love of it."

Avery turned fifty in 2010, a vintage model himself now, but still relatively young among antiques dealers. Over the years, he's transformed his hard work and study into steady success in a difficult trade. Knowledge *is* a super power. Avery doesn't look much different from six years ago—the wild hair is tamed and thinner, silvering at the temples. He still wears his signature baggy shorts and sneakers. His house is still too full for comfort, but he has a new truck, and as the odometer ticks the miles away he scours the countryside searching for that "super-great" thing, that "killer" object, the Holy Grail. His is, after all, a labor of love.

A Thousand Years

One day Curt Avery said to me, "This weird thing happened that might make an interesting ending to your book." At a small, sixty-dealer antique show in Swansea, Massachusetts, he spotted a clock-reel yarn winder. The show itself was a bust. "A thousand people came through and I sold $70 worth of stuff." He laughs. "It was not a knowledgeable crowd, but I was happy because I found the yarn winder." Yarn winders are like "sideways spinning wheels," he says. "They're colonial, but they're falling by the wayside, sadly." At the antique show, "this kid, Ralph, dragged one in. I must have walked by it four times before I stopped to look."

The clock-reel yarn winder was painted, with black lettering, circa 1840. "It was in such good condition it looked fake," Avery said, "but when I took it outside in the daylight, it looked right as rain." He bought the yarn winder for $90, and was going to stow it away for a high-end show, but then he had a revelation. "It didn't dawn on me for ten minutes, but then I thought, *this thing almost looks Shaker.*" Shaker pieces can be "very sleepy," he said. "At Brimfield, these three guys were talking over coffee, one of them was leaning on a cupboard. All of a sudden he looked at the cupboard and said, 'Hey, is this Shaker?' The guy ended up buying it and then making a shitload of money, like $28,000."

Ralph had bought the yarn winder for $40 from a woman who'd pulled it out of a dump. "Ralph's a smart guy," Avery said, "so I don't know how he missed this. He's smarter than I am, but he just missed it. Many know-ing eyes passed this by. But even when I bought it, I didn't know it was Shaker. I bought it for the fantastic paint." Avery is still learning Shaker, but he's had a couple Shaker objects before. "I bought a knife box for $250 and sold it for $900." He bid on a Shaker cobbler bench at an auc-tion once, but dropped out at $250 because the drawer was missing. The dealer who bought the bench eventually sold it for $2,800. "That's one more lesson."

"Shakers were a community started by this woman in the late 1700s," he told me. "She had four children and they all died. She had the worst luck ever. So she started this religion based on Christianity, but they were celibate. They were devout, like Quakers or Mennonites, a group of odd ducklings. They'd sober up the street bum and turn him into a cabinet maker." Shakers originated in Manchester, England, in 1747. The sect's official name is the United Society of Believers in Christ's Second Ap-pearing, but they were called "Shaking Quakers" for their wild fits of ecstasy. The founder, Ann Lee, was beaten for her religious beliefs, even by her own brother, and thrown in jail. In her cell, she had a vision. "I felt the power of God flow into my soul like a fountain of living water," she said.

The Shakers believed in racial and sexual equality and that God pos-sessed masculine and feminine traits, radical notions in the eighteenth century. To escape persecution, in 1774, Ann Lee and eight followers sailed from Liverpool to New York City. But in the colonies "Mother Ann" and her followers were accused of witchcraft, caned, cudgeled, whipped by angry mobs, and driven out of their dwellings—a lot of brou-haha for fewer than a dozen people. They finally settled on land near Albany, New York, but peace eluded them. Avowed pacifists, Shakers were jailed as suspected British spies during the American Revolution, and reviled for their stands against individual property ownership, slav-ery, and bearing arms. When they began to proselytize and their num-bers swelled, critics grew vociferous. In 1831, Nathaniel Hawthorne wrote that Shakers led a "good and comfortable life," but twenty years later he called them "hateful" and "disgusting," and wrote "the sooner the sect is extinct the better." In spite of their unpopular doctrines, and their commitment to forsaking "carnal gratifications of the flesh," by the mid-1800s the Shaker population grew to some five thousand followers in New York, New Hampshire, Maine, Massachusetts, Connecticut, Kentucky, Ohio, Indiana, Florida, and Georgia.

Suspecting his clock-reel yarn winder was Shaker, Avery called Willis Henry, whose auctions, a Shaker historian noted, are "cultural events" that set "the ultimate measure of Shaker worth." "Oprah Winfrey collects Shaker," Avery said. "It's great stuff. A three-inch-long oval box in yellow paint sold for $30,000 because it was Shaker. That's the power of that stuff." Winfrey set a record in 1990 at a Willis Henry auction for a single Shaker item—$220,000 for a pine counter. (She beat the previous record from 1989 held by Bill Cosby, who paid $200,000 for a Shaker cupboard.) Shaker is still strong. Even in the recession of 2009, a Shaker cherry dining table sold for $117,000.

I wonder what the Shakers—who eschewed excess—would have thought about their crafts being sold for record prices to the wealthiest people in the most materialistic culture. Collectors' desire for Shaker objects took hold in the 1920s when tables could be had for six bucks, a bureau for twenty-five. It was further kindled in 1935 when the Whitney Museum staged an exhibit of Shaker "handicrafts." Later in the twentieth century, when the Shakers were in decline, they abetted the trade by selling their "old time relics" that were "dear" to them—"regretfully," one member wrote in 1949. With their population severely dwindling, they had an "immediate need of money."

AVERY HAD BEEN SAVING Shaker objects for months for the annual Shaker auction, including an embroidery hoop, and a wooden bowl thirty-two inches in diameter, found in a barn "known to have been used by Shakers," he said. The bowl had a repaired crack. "Normally that's the kiss of death. People who collect Shaker are very anal and they want the stuff perfect," a standard in the spirit of the Shakers. "But the repair itself is very Shaker," he said. "They took a metal band and riveted it onto

the overlap, but then they filed down the corners. It's perfectly sym-
metrical." The Shakers' Millennial Laws were specific and exhaustive,
from detailed instructions for weaving wool hats, to a stricture against
adorning buildings. "Fancy articles of any kind, or articles which are su-
perfluously finished, trimmed or ornamented, are not suitable for Believers." As craftsmen, they were fastidious and ingenious. Shakers were
granted more than thirty patents, including one for a washing machine
that won a gold medal at the 1876 Centennial Exhibition in Philadelphia.

Avery met Willis Henry to show him the Shaker pieces. Henry wasn't
excited about the bowl or the embroidery hoop, but when he saw the
clock-reel yarn winder, "his eyes lit up," Avery said, even though the yarn
winder had a small repair. "He flipped out. He said, 'I love it. It's absolutely Shaker.'" Henry showed Avery the details that proved the yarn
winder was Shaker. "Tiny little planes and carved lamb's tongue on the
edges," Avery said. "It was beveled on every freaking detail, whether you
can see it or not." To the Shakers, craftsmanship was a form of worship.
"Put your hands to work and your hearts to God," Mother Ann said.
Shakers, wrote Adam Gopnik, "imbu[ed] the ordinary with a sense of the
numinous." The famous Shaker round boxes, he wrote, are fashioned
with an "underlying delirium . . . an obsessive overcharge to finish, the
sense of a will to perfection." Edward, Avery's mentor, showed him a
telltale clue that a box was Shaker—a "whoosh" when you open the box
because it's so well made, so airtight.

Avery's clock-reel yarn winder—which looked like a small windmill—
was an invention born of necessity. For the year of 1844, two sisters spun
"198 run of flax and 248 of worsted"—worsted is a type of yarn combed
into long strands. The same sisters in that year sewed "70 pairs linen
trousers and 26 pairs cloth trousers, 40 cotton gowns and 40 winter
gowns, 13 drab cloaks, and 24 bonnets, 68 caps, 24 hats for brethren, 3
great coats, 31 jackets, 9 frocks, 80 shirts." In *The Shaker Experience in
America*, Stephen Stein notes the work of the Church sisters, who in 1836
produced "696 runs of tow and linen yarn, 1,981 runs of worsted wool,
1,449 yards of cloth, 3,166 yards of woven tape, 150 pounds of worked
wool, 6 jackets, and 63 pairs of trousers." This prodigious output—and

its calculation—was possible with the Shakers' innovative tools, like the clock-reel yarn winder.

AVERY GAVE HENRY the $90 yarn winder for the auction to be held that autumn. "It's long money, but more money. That's always a smart way to do it," Avery said. Henry estimated the yarn winder would bring $1,000, maybe $1,500. "He was cagey about the price," Avery told me. "I hope he's being coy, that he doesn't want to inflate the hope." Henry featured Avery's clock-reel yarn winder on the postcard advertising his annual Shaker auction, a promising sign.

With six months before the auction, Avery tried to keep mum about the yarn winder. "I told no one," he said. But word got out, eventually back to Ralph. Then Avery ran into Ralph. "I said, 'Ralph, when I bought that thing I had no idea, I walked by it five times. It didn't dawn on me until later that it was Shaker.'" Ralph took it well. He told Avery that several high-end dealers had inspected the yarn winder. "Dealers who do these highly respected Americana shows passed this thing for $90," Avery said. "Just goes to show you how deceiving that stuff is."

Avery didn't attend the Willis Henry Shaker auction, so he learned over the phone that his $90 yarn winder sold for $6,500. "I have mixed emotions about the result," he said. "I don't know what it should have brought." The yarn winder was "extremely rare," so its potential could have been much higher. "I think Willis did all he could for it," Avery said, "but I wonder if in different times and with no repair, that thing could have been the hit of my life." The jackpot. The lottery ticket. Still, Avery was happy, even though the proceeds slipped almost immediately through his hands. Just after he received the check for the yarn winder, his family's beloved dog, Niko, fell ill with an intestinal blockage, underwent surgery, caught a superbug infection, and was in the hospital for a week. The veterinarian's bill was just under $7,000.

Shaker objects will probably always be desirable for their craftsmanship and simple, elegant designs, but also because there is a finite supply of Shaker crafts. The last four Shakers in the world live in Sabbathday

Lake, Maine, from its inception one of the smallest and poorest communities. Active for 228 years, the Sabbathday Lake community has dwindled to two men in their forties who joined in the mid-1980s, and two women, one in her seventies and an eighty-four-year-old woman who has lived there since she was orphaned at ten. The Sabbathday Lake Shakers receive about seventy inquiries a year, but they "rarely hear back" from prospective members. "Do all your work as though you had a thousand years to live, and as you would if you knew you must die tomorrow," Mother Ann said. The Shakers have nearly died out, but their "work"—attended to with religious devotion, cherished by collectors, preserved and passed forward in time by dealers like Curt Avery—may live a thousand years. Or longer.

ACKNOWLEDGMENTS

I am indebted to so many who helped make this book possible and who helped make possible the opportunity to write at all. I am forever grateful to "Curt Avery," without whose knowledge, patience, generosity, passion, and sense of humor there would be no story. Thanks to "Linda Avery" for her kindness and for allowing their story to be told, and to "Dylan" and "Kristina" Avery for their contributions. A heartfelt thanks to all of the dealers and collectors who generously shared their stories, passions, and opinions: "Tucker Small," "Joan Christianson," "Jimmy Desjardins," "Wesley Swanson," "Ken Hartwell," Rick Carney (though his story of ocean diving for antique bottles was not told here), William Jamieson, Vince Zurzolo, Shawn Hilton, Andy Holzman, William Bradley, Todd and Amber Jordan, and all the antique dealers, collectors, show promoters, and experts I met or spoke with who appear briefly but importantly throughout this book. I'm indebted to several people for expertise, background, and fact checking: Corinne and Russell Earnest explained differences between "fraktur" and "family records"; Kory Rogers, associate curator of the Shelburne Museum in Vermont, spoke with me about band boxes; Kristin Schwain, associate professor of American art and architecture at the University of Missouri, pointed me to excellent sources on material culture; Gene Orlando, curator of the Oujia board Web site, www.talkingboards.com, fact checked my text on Oujia boards; Jill Lukesh of J&J Promotions verified material about Brimfield; Mark Aukeman provided background on slide rules. I'm grateful to Marsha Bemko, executive producer, and Judy Matthews, senior publicist, of *Antiques Roadshow* for allowing me behind the scenes at a show taping, and thanks to Sharon Black at the University of Missouri for her insight into the show's appeal. Thanks to Jocelyn Bartkevicius, editor of *The Florida Review*, for publishing a longer version of "Roadshow Rage" in the winter 2008 issue.

Many organizations have provided financial support for this book and for my writing in general, for which I am most grateful: the University of Missouri Research Council and Research Board; the National Endowment for the Arts; The Maine Arts Commission; Money for Women/Barbara Deming Memorial Fund; Change, Inc.; Mary Roberts Rinehart Fund; Ludwig Vogelstein Foundation; the MacDowell Colony; the Ronald Goldfarb Family and the Virginia Center for the Creative Arts; St. Mary's College of Maryland Artist House and Voices Reading Series. Special thanks to the wondrous Jennifer Cognard-Black at St. Mary's for arranging residencies when I most needed them and for encouragement, support, and inspiration. Thanks to Dr. Joanna Buffington, who offered her lovely home on Cape Cod; to Holly Pye for "good luck writing" discounts on tax preparation; and Dr. Matthew Hanna and the Mid Coast Medical Group for reduced charges when I had no health insurance.

This book would not exist without the excellent work of my agent, Wendy Strothman, and her able assistant, Lauren McLeod. I'm wildly grateful to my editor, Eamon Dolan, for his faith in this project from its earliest incarnation; this is a far better book for his wise and gentle guidance. I'm grateful to the team at Penguin Press who brought this book into the world, in particular Emily Graff, Michael Burke, Sarah Hutson, Tracy Locke, and Stephanie Gilardi.

I've been so fortunate to have friends, teachers, and mentors who've provided spiritual, moral, and practical support since I began this midlife writing journey. At the University of Missouri, I'm grateful to my mentors Marly Swick and Trudy Lewis, to George Justice for sage advice, and to Steve Weinberg for unflagging friendship. I'm enormously grateful to my talented teachers at Ohio State University— Lee K. Abbott, Brenda Brueggemann, Stephanie Grant, Michelle Herman, Melanie Rae Thon, and especially Bill Roorbach, who taught me everything I know about writing creative nonfiction. I'm grateful to Mimi Schwartz for her insight in the early stages of this project, and long-standing friendship and support. Thanks to Sydney Lea, who has no doubt forgotten me but whose inspiration and benediction I will never forget. Many thanks to my inspiring and generous friend Ira Sukrungruang. Michael Steinberg has been a great friend and mentor since we met in a writing group in Lansing, Michigan. He introduced me to "creative nonfiction" and has led the way ever since; I'm truly grateful for his championing of my work.

I'm indebted to Nancy Sferra for steadfast friendship, for making me feel safe in the world, for teaching me to use power tools and kayak in the ocean. In an extraordinary act of kindness, she read more than nine hundred pages of messy notes and raw material and helped me find the story within for this book. I'm grateful to my dear friend E. J. Levy, for her fierce and tender heart, and brilliant writing that inspires me always. I thank my mother, Clarissa, and my father, Patrick, for providing resources when I was long past the age at which that was their charge, and for love, inspiration, and the wind at my back. The late Edward N. Maset gave me my first truck, my best jobs, and lessons in spackle and caulk. I owe everything to my beloved family—Sue, Steve, Stephanie, Joe, Natalie, Sally, Terry, Miles, Joanne, Matthew, Kevin, Sara, Patrick, Michelle, Barbie, Ken, Donny, Michael, Ann Marie, Samuel, Ben, and Colin—who have financed me, housed me, fed me, fixed my car, repaired my shack, who cheer me up and on and bring me great joy.

LIST OF PSEUDONYMS

(In order of mention in the book)

Curt Avery

Wesley Swanson

Linda Avery

Kristina Avery

Dennis (childhood friend)

Ken Hartwell

Chet (yellowware dealer)

Elgin Crittendon (Acres North)

Tucker Small

Sam (electrician with burl bowl)

Dylan Avery

Vinnie (R.I. auction)

Edward (mentor)

Jimmy Desjardins (eBay)

Jerry (shopping friend)

Alex (former musician)

Betsy (firkin)

Joan Christianson

Sydney (prison teacher)

Mitch (Hubley's)

Walt Johnson (Hubley's)

Glen (rooster weathervane)

Tildy (rug dealer)

Richard (snuff bottle)

Greg Tierney (York)

Marion (bus driver)

Lee Massey (yard sales)

Leon (glass dust)

Bert (fraktur)

"Joe" (Mary Blood Mellen)

Jane (butternut cabinet)

Al Whitmore (scout)

Barbara Massey (Boston)

Eighteenth-Century Dave (Union)

Wild Willy (Union)

Lester (Union)

Ralph (yarn winder)

NOTES

Prologue: Treasure Hunters: The Reality

2 *Alexandre Iacovleff. The painting:* "A 'Well-Hidden' Classic,"*Antiques Roadshow Insider,* Vol. 7, No. 4 (April 2007), p. 1. See also: "School Faces Dilemma on Valuable Art." NPR, February 7, 2007, http://www.npr.org/templates/story/story.php?storyId=7244113>; Amy De-Melia, "Art One in a Million," *The Sun Chronicle,* February 2, 2007.

Chapter One: Opium Bottles and Knuckleheads

7 *"suburban subversive":* John F. Sherry, "A Sociocultural Analysis of a Midwestern American Flea Market," *Journal of Consumer Research,* Vol. 17, No. 1 (June 1990), pp. 13–33.

7 *"libidinous":* Les Abrams, "Urban Marketplaces and Mobile Vendors: The Flea Market in the Metropolitan Economy. A Case Study of Two Flea Markets—Aqueduct and Roosevelt Raceway Flea Markets," Ph.D. dissertation, City University of New York, 2007, p. 4. See also: Sherry, "A Sociocultural Analysis of a Midwestern American Flea Market."

7 *marche aux puces:* Flea market history was derived from several sources, including: Robert E. Brown, *Brimfield: The Collector's Paradise* (Brimfield, MA: Brimfield Publications, 1996). See also: Sandy Price, *Exploring the Flea Markets of France* (New York: Three Rivers Press, 1999); Jerry Stokes, "A Flea Market by Any Other Name Is a Flea Market," Rupert Thomas and Eglé Salvy, *Antique & Flea Markets of London & Paris* (London: Thames & Hudson, 1999); "Napoleon Bonaparte & Paris," *France Monthly,* January 2005, www.francemonthly.com/n/0105/index.php; "The Code Napoleon (1804)," The History Guide, www.historyguide.org/intellect/code_nap.html.

8 *more [visitors] than the Eiffel Tower:* These estimates are from the Paris Tourism Research Department 2009 report, "Tourism in Paris" (which reports on 2008 statistics), accessed 2/18/2010, http: eu/parisinfo/com. See also these Paris tourism Web sites: www.parispuces.com and www.discoverfrance.net. Estimates for annual visitors to St.-Ouen flea market, which is open every weekend all year, range from 120,000 to 200,000 per weekend, from various sources; this amounts to 6.2 to 10.4 million visitors per year. In 2007, the Eiffel Tower had 6,797,409 visitors, slightly more than the lowest estimate of visitors to the flea market, but far fewer than the number of visitors by the highest estimate.

8 *Quimper plates:* Adela Meadows and Judy Penz Sheluk, "Quimper Pottery: A Brief History," *New England Antiques Journal,* archived article, undated, www.antiquesjournal.com/pages04/archives/quimper.html. See also: http://www.oldquimper.com.

10 *eighty million bottles for opium:* Hartgen Archeological Associates, "Then and Now: Arche-

ology at Fort Stanwix—Patent Medicine: Cure or Poison?," 2005, www.hartgen.com/ FOST/archeo_medicine.htm. This site has a photo of a Dr. McMunn's Elixir of Opium bottle. The photo caption notes that eighty million bottles for opium were produced in 1859 by the Folembray Glass Works of France. See also: Fort Stanwix National Monument, U.S. Department of the Interior, Rome, NY, www.nps.gov/fost/index.htm.

10 *Street's Infants' Quietness:* BLTC Research, United Kingdom, www.opioids.com. See also: Edward M. Brecher, *Licit and Illicit Drugs: The Consumer Union Report* (New York: Little, Brown, 1973), p. 2.

10 *de Quincey "panacea for all human woes":* Thomas de Quincey, *Confessions of an English Opium-Eater* (London: George Routledge & Sons, 1886). The First Edition (*London Magazine*) text p. 41. Penn State Electronic Classics Series Publication. <http://www.hn.psu.edu/faculty/ jmanus/dequincey.htm>.

10 *Bayer product called Heroin:* Martin Booth, *Opium: A History* (New York: Simon & Schuster, 1996), pp. 77–79. See also: BLTC Research United Kingdom, "Future Opioids," http://bltc .com; "The Plant of Joy," http://opiates.net, 1999; Jim Hogshire, *Opium for the Masses* (Port Townsend, WA: Loompanics Unlimited, 1994); Barbara Hodgson, *Opium: A Portrait of the Heavenly Demon* (Berkeley, CA: Greystone Publishing, 2004).

Chapter Two: One Man's Trash

14 *John Cheever's 1941 story "Publick House":* John Cheever, "Publick House," *Collected Stories and Other Writings* (New York: Library of America, 2009), pp. 880 and 885.

15 *"piggeries":* David Freeman Hawke, *Everyday Life in Early America* (New York: Harper Perennial, 1999), p. 77. See also: Jack Larkin, *The ReShaping of Everyday Life: 1790–1840* (New York: Harper Perennial, 1988), p. 158.

Chapter Three: Boot Camp

19 *as many as 250,000 visitors:* Figures for Brimfield attendance vary widely from source to source, from year to year, and between the May, July, and September shows. The 250,000 figure is from the Brimfield Show Homepage, www.brimfieldshow.com,. accessed 08/27/10. One veteran show promoter claimed that up to 500,000 people attended Brimfield. Quoted in: Jaclyn C. Stevenson, "Thrill of the Hunt," *Business West Magazine*, May 12, 2008, p. 59. Other articles and sources claim up to 150,000. I have used the figure in the middle of this range of estimates.

19–20 *Rose Bowl "the world's largest flea market":* Quoted in: Rick Sebak, *A Flea Market Documentary*, Rick Sebak, Producer/Narrator, Kevin Conrad, Editor, WQED Pittsburgh, 2001.

20 *First Monday Trade Days "the world's oldest and largest flea market":* Quoted in Sebak, *A Flea Market Documentary*.

20 *4,000 flea markets:* Kitty Werner, *The Official Directory to U.S. Flea Markets*, seventh edition (New York: House of Collectibles Publishing, 2000), p. 6. Note: Werner does not indicate her source for her figures on the number of flea markets.

20 *$10 billion in gross sales annually:* John F. Sherry, "Dealers and Dealing in a Periodic Market: Informal Retailing in Ethnographic Perspective," *Journal of Retailing*, Vol. 66, No. 2 (Summer 1990), pp. 174–201.

20 *annual sales exceeding $30 billion:* National Flea Market Association, http://www.fleamar kets.org, date stamp: 12/1/2004. Representatives listed on the NFMA Web site did not respond to my e-mail and phone messages for updated statistics. See also: Statistics attributed to NFMA quoted in Ariana Eunjung Cha, "Internet Auctions Bring a Big Shift to Once-Quirky Flea Markets," *Post-Newsweek* Business Information, Inc., August 1, 2005.

20 *the Rolling Stones:* A claim made by Lois Shelton, of Shelton Antique shows, in Robert L. Brown, *Brimfield: The Collector's Paradise* (Brimfield, MA: Brimfield Publications, 1996), p. 8.

20 *a couple got married:* According to Jill Lukesh, of J&J Promotions, in 2002, "a couple did

get married before the show opened and the bride spent part of the day shopping in her gown." E-mail from Jill Lukesh to me on July 9, 2010.

20 *Smithsonian sponsored a research expedition:* Charlene James-Duguid, "Brimfield Was My Inspiration," in Brown, *Brimfield: The Collector's Paradise,* pp. 36–37.

23 **fresh merchandise:** *Maine Antiques Digest,* February 2010, ad for J&J Show at Brimfield.

24 *"topsy-turvy doll":* Mildred Jailer-Chamberlain, "Two Hundred Years of Black Paper Dolls," *Antiques and Collecting Magazine,* February 2007, pp. 20–24. See also: "Our Little Ones: The Topsy-Turvy Doll," *Christian Observer,* March 30, 1910, p. 17.

25 *nutcrackers:* Barbara Keevil Parker, "Nut Crackin' Nutcrackers," *Antiques & Collecting Magazine,* December 2006, pp. 29–32.

25 *oldest toys known:* Lana Robinson, "Marble Mystique," *Antiques Roadshow Insider,* May 2007, p. 7. See also: John Windsor, "Keeping Your Marbles," *The Observer,* April 22, 2001; The American Marble and Toy Museum, www.akronmarbles.com; Paul Baumann, *Collecting Antique Marbles,* 4th ed. (Iola, WI: Krause Publications, 2004).

25 *Bert Cohen owns two 2,300-year-old Roman marbles:* Matthew Holm, "Marvelous Marbles," *Country Living,* Vol. 21, No. 5 (May 1998), p. 96.

26 *Charles "Buster" Rech:* Windsor, "Keeping Your Marbles." See also: Dan Ackman, "Now No One Plays for Keeps," *The Wall Street Journal,* June 25, 2009, p. D6.

26 *German-made Indian sold for $4,082:* "Marble Auction Internet Bidder Wins $341,975 Lot," *Antiques and the Arts Online,* December 18, 2001, http://antiquesandthearts.com/AWO-12-18-2001-12-29-29.

26 *For a penny, a kid could buy a fistful:* "A Brief History of the Birth of the Modern American Toy Industry in Akron, Ohio," American Toy Marble Museum, Akron, OH, www.americantoymarbles.com, accessed July 21, 2010.

26 *"crushed my heart":* Peter Eaton and John Fiske, "What's American About Early New England Furniture?," *New England Antiques Journal,* January 2007, p. 39. Peter Sawyer, a dealer from Exeter, New Hampshire, sold the c. 1760 fan-crested banister-back armchair with Spanish feet in original painted surface to Arthur Liverant, who was quoted in *Maine Antique Digest.*

26 *"Collecting is a way of linking past":* William Davies King, *Collections of Nothing* (Chicago: University of Chicago Press, 2008), p. 27.

26 *Jean-Paul Sartre:* Jean-Paul Sartre, *Being and Nothingness* (Paris: Gallimard, 1943), p. 755.

27 *"Buying is much more American":* Andy Warhol, *The Philosophy of Andy Warhol (From A to B and Back Again)* (New York: Harcourt Brace, 1975), p. 229.

30 *fingerprint on the canvas:* David Grann, "The Mark of a Masterpiece," *The New Yorker,* July 12 and 19, 2010, pp. 51–71. In this article, some experts claim that the fingerprint itself is a forgery.

31 *$50 million:* Brianna Bailey, "A $50 Million Find," *The Daily Pilot* (Newport Beach and Costa Mesa, CA), November 22, 2008. See also: www.artnewsblog.com/2008/10/5-jackson-pollock-painting-for-50.htm; Don Hewitt, executive producer, *Who the #$&% Is Jackson Pollock?,* 2007, DVD. This documentary provides an excellent overview of the case of the found Pollock.

31 *"Without knowledge you cannot make a living":* Charlene James-Duguid, "Brimfield Was My Inspiration," in Robert L. Brown, *Brimfield: The Collector's Paradise* (Brimfield, MA: Brimfield Publications, May 1996), pp. 36–37.

31 *Joshua Glenn and Rob Walker, hired people to write backstories:* "Significant Objects: A Doll with a Story," National Public Radio, December 20, 2009, interview by Selena Simmons-Duffin for host Guy Raz.

Chapter Four: An Antiques Dealer Is Made

37 *"Leigh and I had been selling items":* Leigh Keno and Leslie Keno, *Hidden Treasures: Searching for Masterpieces of American Furniture* (New York: Warner Books, 2000), p. 43.

37 *"first love":* Quoted in Thatcher Freund, *Objects of Desire: The Lives of Antiques and Those Who Pursue Them* (New York: Penguin, 1993), p. 206.

37 *a position he earned at age twenty-six:* Marsha Bemko, *Antiques Roadshow: Behind the Scenes (New York:* Simon and Schuster, 2009), p. 118.

37 *"our very souls":* Keno and Keno, *Hidden Treasures,* p. 255.

41 *"greatest decoy maker":* "Crowell Decoys Surpass $1.1 Million in Private Treaty Sale," *Antiques and the Arts Online,* September 25, 2007, http://antiquesandthearts.com/Antiques/Trade Talk/2007-09-24_09-08-44.html. See also: Nancy N. Johnston, "Decoys," *Antiques & Fine Art,* Fall 2009, http://antiquesandfineart.com/articles/article.cfm?request=842.

41 *sold for $1.1 million each:* "Crowell Decoys Surpass $1.1 Million in Private Treaty Sale"; Johnston, "Decoys."

42 *admits he's still learning:* Bemko, *Antiques Roadshow,* p. 117.

Chapter Five: That Good, Good Thing

43 *"the ephemerality of experience":* —Danet, Brenda and Tamar Katriel. "No Two Alike: Play and Aesthetics in Collecting." *Interpreting Objects and Collections.* Ed. Susan M. Pearce. Routledge: London. 1994. p. 223.

44 *ship skilled workers from England:* John Fiske, "Yours Sincerely," *Antiques Journal,* August 2009, p. 82. See also: Ellen K. Rothman, Mary Babson Fuhrer, and Liz Nelson, Massachusetts Foundation for the Humanities, "Mass Moments" Web site, "May 5, 1643: Winthrop Buys Passage for Ironworkers," www.massmoments.org.

47 *"a race of batmen":* Kory W. Rogers, "Bandbox Papers at the Shelburne Museum," *Antiques & Fine Art Magazine,* Summer 2006, pp. 137–141. See also: Richard A. Locke, "Great Astronomical Discoveries Lately Made By Sir John Herschel, L.L.D., F.R.S., & c.," *New York Daily Sun,* August 28, 1935; Bev Norwood, "Wallpapered Bandboxes: Small Treasures to Savor," *Northeast Antiques,* Vol. 13, No. 11, September 2007, pp. 1 and 16.

47 *"Vespertilio-homo":* Locke, "Great Astronomical Discoveries Lately Made By Sir John Herschel, L.L.D., F.R.S., & c."

47 *"proselytizing to the bat-men":* Telephone interview with Kory W. Rogers, curator of exhibits at the Shelburne Museum, Shelburne, Vermont, on September 29, 2006.

48 *record was set for a bandbox:* David Hewett, "The Celebrated Egan Collection," *Maine Antique Digest,* October 6, 2006, www.maineantiquedigest.com/articles_archive/articles/oct06/egan1006.htm. Photo caption text: "This wallpaper-covered pasteboard hatbox, 9" high with a 10" x 12" top, now holds the record for the highest auction price recorded . . . it went to a phone bidder at $26,680." Photo is box in blue paper decorated with objects like gloves, pens, and white dots.

49 *One collector even cashed in retirement:* Brook S. Mason, "Viva Americana," *Art & Antiques,* Vol. 27, Issue 9 (October 2004), p. 54.

51 *last passenger pigeon:* "Passenger Pigeon," Chipper Woods Bird Observatory, www.wbu.com/chipperwoods/photos/passpegeon.htm, accessed 03/23/2010.

52 *"If he wanted to be a great dealer":* Thatcher Freund, *Objects of Desire* (New York: Penguin, 1993), p. 226.

Chapter Six: Everything Rich and Strange

55 *Everything Rich and Strange:* I used several excellent books to assemble the history of collecting, including: Russell Belk, *Collecting in a Consumer Society* (London: Routledge, 1995); Philipp Blom, *To Have and to Hold: An Intimate History of Collectors and Collecting* (Woodstock and New York: Overlook Press, 2002); Robert E. Brown, *Brimfield: The Collector's Paradise* (Brimfield, MA: Brimfield Publications, 1996); Steven Calloway, *Obsessions: Collectors and Their Passions* (London: Mitchell Beazley, 2004); Joan Carroll Cruz, *Relics* (Huntington, IN: Our Sunday Visitor, Inc., 1984); Leah Dilworth, *Acts of Possession: Collecting in America* (Piscataway, NJ: Rutgers University Press, 2003); Patrick Mauries, *Cabinets of Curiosities* (London: Thames & Hudson, Ltd., 2002); Werner Muensterberger, *Collecting: An Unruly Passion* (Princeton, NJ: Princeton University Press, 1994); Susan M. Pearce, *Interpreting Objects and Collections* (London: Routledge, 1994); Stephen Jay Gould and Rosamond Wolff Purcell, *Finders, Keepers: Eight Collectors* (New York: W.W. Norton, 1992); Susan Stewart, *On Longing: Narratives of the Miniature, the Gigantic, the Souvenir, the Collection* (Durham, NC: Duke University Press, 1993); Mitch Tuchman, *Magnificent Obsessions* (San Francisco: Chronicle Books, 1994).

55 *one third of North Americans:* Brown, *Brimfield: The Collector's Paradise*, p. 78. Brown reports that a study found 62.5 percent of households surveyed have at least one collection, with an average of 2.6 collectors per household.

55 *a cache of "interesting" pebbles:* Belk, *Collecting in a Consumer Society*, p. 2.

55 *Archaeologists have found collections:* Pearce, *On Collecting: An Investigation into Collecting in the European Tradition*, pp. 57–66.

55 *"we found a great number":* Howard Carter, *The Tomb of Tut.ankh.Amen: The Annexe and Treasury* (London: Duckworth, 1933), p. 135.

56 *Persian tombs:* Randy O. Frost and Gail Steketee, *Stuff: Compulsive Hoarding and the Meaning of Things* (Boston: Houghton Mifflin, 2010), p. 51.

56 *ancient Greeks housed collections:* Pearce, *On Collecting: An Investigation into Collecting in the European Tradition*, p. 91.

56 *Individuals, families, and town councils:* Ibid., p. 94.

56 *"maniacal and violent":* Muensterberger, *Collecting: An Unruly Passion*, pp. 52–53. See also: Pearce, *On Collecting*, p. 93.

56 *pieces of saints, and holy objects:* Mauries, *Cabinets of Curiosities, p. 7.*

56 *Medici dynasty:* Eilean Hooper-Greenhill, *Museums and the Shaping of Knowledge* (London: Routledge, 1997), p. 29. Hooper-Greenhill quotes E. H. Gombrich, *Norm and Form: Studies in the Art of the Renaissance II* (Oxford: Phaidon Press, 1985). See also: Pearce, *On Collecting*, p. 104; Belk, *Collecting in a Consumer Society*, p. 28.

56 *narwhal tusk:* Calloway, *Obsessions: Collectors and Their Passions*, p. 20.

56 *Lorenzo the Magnificent and bezoars:* Cristina Acidin Luchinat, *Medici, Michelangelo, and the Art of Late Renaissance Florence* (New Haven, CT: Yale University Press, 2002), pp. 60–61.

57 *"dragons and mermaids":* Blom, *To Have and to Hold*, p. 91.

57 *King Philip II of Spain:* Ibid., p. 31.

57 *Rudolf's collection . . . siren from Odysseus's journey:* Ibid., pp. 40–42.

57 *"Anything that Is Strang":* Ibid., p. 54.

57 *Tradescant's Ark:* Belk, *Collecting in a Consumer Society*, p. 42.

58 *robe worn by the "King of Virginia.":* Pearce, *On Collecting: An Investigation into Collecting in the European Tradition*, p. 116.

58 *Peter the Great:* Blom, *To Have and to Hold*, p. 70 (Foma) and p. 73 (teeth). See also: Elif Batuman, "The Ice Renaissance," *The New Yorker*, May 29, 2006, p. 44.

58 *"two headed mutant foetuses and odd body parts":* Simon Richmond, et al., *Russia & Belarus*, 3rd ed. (Footscray, Victoria, Australia: Lonely Plant Publications, June 2003), p. 266.

58 *Charles Willson Peale:* Belk, *Collecting in a Consumer Society*, pp. 48–49. See also: Tuchman, *Magnificent Obsessions*, pp. 9–10.

59 *Celebrations of the country's centennial:* Thomas J. Schlereth, "Material Culture Studies in America, 1876–1976," *Material Culture Studies in America* (Lanham, MD: AltaMira Press, 1981), p. 12.

59 *"turning point in America's appreciation of the past":* Briann G. Greenfield, *Out of the Attic: Inventing Antiques in Twentieth-Century New England* (Amherst: University of Massachusetts Press, 2009), p. 19.

59 *reprinted eight times, and published in America in 1874:* Elizabeth Stillinger, *The Antiquers: The Lives and Careers, the Deals, the Finds, the Collections of the Men and Women Who Were*

Responsible for the Changing Taste in American Antiques, 1850–1930 (New York: Knopf, 1980), p. 45.

59 *"[D]istinguishing good from bad design"*: Charles L. Eastlake, *Hints on Household Taste in Furniture, Upholstery, and Other Details*, 2nd ed. (London: Longmans, Green & Co., 1869), pp. 6–8.

59 *"the invention of antiques as aesthetic objects"*: Greenfield, *Out of the Attic: Inventing Antiques in Twentieth-Century New England*, p. 4.

59 *the antiques "craze" of the 1920s and "antiqueering"*: Stillinger, *The Antiquers*, pp. xi, 1–16, 187.

59 *"antique departments"*: Greenfield, *Out of the Attic: Inventing Antiques in Twentieth-Century New England*, pp. 9–10.

59 **The Magazine Antiques:** Ibid., p. 30.

59 *Association of Antique Dealers:* Ibid., p. 218 n.26.

59 *"into a super-modern world"*: Homer Eaton Keyes, *"Antiques* Speaks for Itself," *Antiques: A Magazine for Collectors and Others Who Find Interest in Times Past & in the Articles of Daily Use & Adornment Devised by the Forefathers*, Vol. 1, No. 1 (January 1922), p. 7. Note: The original title of *The Magazine Antiques* is stated above.

59 **Fred Bishop Tuck:** Greenfield, *Out of the Attic: Inventing Antiques in Twentieth-Century New England*, p. 21.

59 *antique shops listed in a business directory:* Ibid., p. 58.

60 *J. Pierpont Morgan:* Belk, *Collecting in a Consumer Society*, p. 49.

60 *William Randolph Hearst:* Blom, *To Have and to Hold*, p. 134.

60 *raided the palaces and monasteries of Europe:* Belk, *Collecting in a Consumer Society*, p. 50.

60 *"everything is for sale"*: Charles Edward Jerningham and Lewis Bettany, *The Bargain Book* (New York: Frederick Warne & Co., 1911), p. 9.

60 *"denuding Europe of its treasures"*: Blom, *To Have and to Hold*, p. 128.

60 *Malcolm Forbes:* Malcolm Forbes, *More Than I Dreamed: A Lifetime of Collecting* (New York: Simon and Schuster, 1989), pp. 205–23. All Forbes quotes are from this memoir.

60 *Forbes collection sold for $20,069,990:* Lita Solis-Cohen, "History for Sale: The Forbes Sale," in *Maine Antique Digest: The Americana Chronicles*, ed. Lita Solis-Cohen (Philadelphia: Running Press, 2004), p. 391.

60 *"[I]t felt like a new frontier"*: Leigh Keno and Leslie Keno, *Hidden Treasures: Searching for Masterpieces of American Furniture* (New York: Warner Books, 2000), p. 39.

61 *"the decade of collecting"*: Marilynn R. Glasser, "A Recreation Experience Profile of Reported Attributes and Attitudes of Adults Who Collect Antique and Contemporary Collectibles," Ph.D. dissertation, New York University, 2000. In her dissertation, Glasser quotes Timothy Luke, former director of collectibles at Christie's.

61 *"that number exceeds 30,000"*: Harry L. Rinker, "Rinker on Collectibles," *Antiques & Collecting Magazine*, March 2007, p. 31.

61 *"is got to dream"*: Arthur Miller, *Death of a Salesman* (New York: Library of America, 2006), Requiem, p. 138.

Chapter Seven: Ovoid Nuts and Southern Belles

62 *"America's Best Antique Shows"*: "America's Best Antique Shows: Our Coast-to-Coast Guide," *Country Living*, Vol. 33, No. 5 (May 2010), p. 65.

62 *"the father of all Brimfield antique shows"*: Carol Sims, "Brimfield Closes the Season with Smiling Faces," *Antiques and the Arts Online*, September 24, 2002, http://antiquesandthearts .com/Antiques/TradeTalk/2002-09-24_12-05-51.html.

65 *perused the London* Times *obituaries:* Ralph Cassady, Jr., *Auctions and Auctioneering* (Berkeley: University of California Press, 1967), p. 99.

65 **Southern Living** *magazine:* All quotes in this section pertaining to the *Southern Living* catalog are from: *Southern Living at Home* Catalog, Spring 2005, Southern Living, Inc., P.O. Box 830951, Birmingham, AL 35283-0951.

68 *"burn bright till nine o'clock of the morning":* Gerald S. Graham, "The Migrations of the Nantucket Whale Fishery: An Episode in British Colonial Policy," *The New England Quarterly*, Vol. 8, No. 2 (June 1935), pp. 179–202.

69 *"I have tried to formulate a criterion":* Terence J. Nelson, "Review of Bernard Leach's Famous Work: *A Potter's Book*," 2003, www.tjnelson.com/apottersbook.htm, October 29, 2009.

69 *Christie's expert called them "marvelous":* Simon Freeman and Barrie Penrose, "The Stirred Pot: Or How the Art World Was Duped," *The Sunday Times* (London), October 2, 1983, Pp 5g.

69 *inmates were so enthusiastic:* Brian Learmount, *A History of the Auction* (London: Barnard & Learmount, 1985), p. 176.

69 *the age of the deceased:* Jack Larkin, *The Reshaping of Everyday Life: 1790–1840* (New York: Harper Perennial, 1988), p. 98.

Chapter Eight: All Sad Things Are Just Like This

71 *"never heard from again":* Ken Hall, "Ken's Korner: Rembrandt Etching Stolen from Gallery," *Antiques & Collecting*, September 2007, p. 40.

72 *priceless Chinese jewelry from the British Museum:* Pam Kent, "Museum Thefts, Again," *The New York Times*, November 27, 2004, p. 12.

72 *ranks fourth in worldwide criminal activities:* David S. Smith, "Art Crimes Investigator, Then and Now: Retired FBI Agent Robert K. Wittman," *Antiques and the Arts Online*, May 5, 2009.

72 *"falsifiers of all sorts":* Dante Alighieri, *The Divine Comedy*, Cantos XXIX and XXX (New York: Classic Books International, 2009; orig. published ca. 1308–1321), pp. 77–82.

72 *gilded them to look like solid gold:* Troy Lennon, "Cheats on Canvas in Brushes with the Law," *The Daily Telegraph* (Australia), August 9, 2006, p. 45.

72 *clothing to Odysseus:* Russell Belk, *Collecting in a Consumer Society* (London: Routledge, 1995), p. 23.

72 *Michelangelo painted a Ghirlandaio:* Laney Salisburyand Aly Sujo, *Provenance: How a Con Man and a Forger Rewrote the History of Modern Art* (New York: Penguin, 2009), p. 234.

72 *"Bogus Antiques":* Craig Clunas, *Superfluous Things* (Honolulu: University of Hawaii Press, 2004), p. 111.

73 *pope's certificate forged:* "A Great Disappointment," *The New York Times*, January 21, 1885. No byline.

73 *Meissen wares bore a mark:* "Meissen Porcelain," http://www.antique-marks.com/meissen .html, February 4, 2010.

73 *the tiara was too well preserved:* "Which Smile Is Mona Lisa's?", *Life Magazine*, September 26, 1955, p. 141.

73 *"monstrosities" that sold in high-end antique shops:* Harold Sack, *American Treasure Hunt: The Legacy of Israel Sack* (Boston: Little, Brown, 1986), pp. 28–29.

73 *"Brewster chair":* Henry Ford Museum and Greenfield Village, "April Fool 2000: The Brewster Chair and the Game of 'Fool the Experts,'" www.thehenryford.org. See also: Myrna Kaye, *Fake, Fraud, or Genuine?: Identifying Authentic American Antique Furniture* (Boston: Little, Brown, 1987), p. 6.

74 *object lessons:* Rita Reif, "Antiques: How to Avoid a Phony Powder Horn," *The New York Times*, April 10, 1988.

74 *glass lacked impurities:* Rita Reif, "Arts/Artifacts; Exposing Deceit and Error Under an Eagle X-Ray Eye," *The New York Times*, October 12, 1997.

74 *"forge ahead":* — Eric Hebborn, *The Art Forger's Handbook* (New York: Overlook Press, 1997), p. xvii.

74 *"stout, coffee, tea, chicory and liquorice":* Ibid., p. 18.

74 *"the forging of a signature":* Ibid., p. 187.

74 *both were pilloried:* Jack Larkin, *The Reshaping of Everyday Life: 1790–1840* (New York: Harper Perennial, 1988), p. 293.

74 *"mysterious death":* Sarah Jane Checkland, "Attack of the Clones; Forgery Is Now Endemic in the Art World," *The London Independent*, August 22, 2005, pp. 38–39.

74 *John Myatt created over 240 fake paintings:* Salisbury and Sujo, *Provenance*, p. 169.

75 *"Genuine Fakes":* Ibid., p. 303.

75 *The object is removed if it doesn't meet the show's standards:* Quoted on the Web site for the Winter Antiques Show ("Frequently Asked Questions"), www.winterantiquesshow.com, accessed 6/16/2010.

75 *ironed to look like highly prized silk:* Colin Haynes, *The Complete Collector's Guide to Fakes and Forgeries* (Greensboro, NC: Wallace-Homestead Book Co., 1988), pp. 53–54.

77 *"claim our reluctant admiration":* Mark Jones, "Why Fakes?," in *Interpreting Objects and Collections*, ed. Susan Pearce (London: Routledge, 1994), p. 97. See also: Wendy Steiner, "In London, a Catalogue of Fakes," *The New York Times*, April 29, 1990, Arts Section.

77 *"their sheer genius":* www.artfake.net, October 24, 2009.

78 *Windsor Castle in England in the early 1700s:* Joseph Aronson, *The Encyclopedia of Furniture* (New York: Crown, 1965), p. 461.

78 *set them in boats:* Ibid.

78 *Jacques Rigaud,* **Queens Theatre,** *Stowe Gardens, Buckinghamshire:* Wallace Nutting, *Windsor Chairs: An Illustrated Handbook* (New York: Dover Publications, 2001, reprint of orig. ed., Boston: Old America Company, 1917), p. ix.

78 *estate inventory of John Jones of Philadelphia:* Nancy Goyne Evans, *American Windsor Furniture: Specialized Forms* (Manchester, VT: Hudson Hills Press, 1997), p. 93. See also: Nancy Goyne Evans, *Windsor-Chair Making in America: From Craft Shop to Consumer* (Hanover, NH, and London: University Press of New England, 2006).

78 *exported over 6,000 Windsor chairs:* Dean A. Fales, *American Painted Furniture* (New York: Bonanza, 1986), p. 85.

78 *Ben Franklin in a Windsor chair:* J. Stogdell Stokes, "The American Windsor Chair," *Bulletin of the Pennsylvania Museum*, Vol. 21, No. 98 (December 1925), pp. 47–58.

78 *Jefferson penned parts of the Declaration of Independence:* Ibid. See also: Evans, *American Windsor Furniture: Specialized Forms*, p. 93.

78 *"equal to those made in Philadelphia":* Deborah Dependahl Waters, "Wares and Chairs: A Reappraisal of the Documents," *Winterthur Portfolio*, Vol. 13 (1979), pp. 161–73.

79 *"without molestation":* Quoted in Elizabeth Stillinger, *The Antiquers* (New York: Knopf, 1980), p. 23.

79 **Windsor chairs:** General background and history of Windsor chairs also from: Charles Santore, *The Windsor Style in America*, Volumes I and II (Philadelphia: Courage Books, 1997); Florence de Dampierre, *Chairs: A History* (New York: Abrams, 2006); Edwin Tunis, *Colonial Craftsmen and the Beginnings of American Industry* (Baltimore: Johns Hopkins University Press, 1965); Carol Prisant, "I Want to Buy a Windsor Chair," *House Beautiful*, Collecting Column, Oct./Nov. 2006, p. 60.

79 *"treacherously weak":* Nutting, *Windsor Chairs: An Illustrated Handbook*, p. 45.

79 *"multitude of sins":* Ibid., p. 41.

80 *"think they are infallible":* Kaye, *Fake, Fraud, or Genuine?*, pp. 4–5. See also: Harold Sack, *American Treasure Hunt: The Legacy of Israel Sack* (Boston: Little, Brown, 1986), p. 207; David Loughlin, *The Case of Major Fanshawe's Chairs* (New York: Universe Books, 1978), p. 19.

80 *"could not stop laughing":* "Prison Potter Convicted of Conspiracy," *The Times* (London), April 29, 1983, p. 3g. No byline.

80 *"Fakes can teach us many things":* Jones, "Why Fakes?," p. 92.

81 *"It is the responsibility of the prospective bidders to examine lots":* Language about auction houses' "conditions of sale" are from Web sites of: Northeast Auctions, www.northeast auctions.com/aboutus/conditions.php, 2/14/10; Skinner, Inc., "Auction Evaluations," www .skinnerinc.com/appraisals/form.asp, 2/14/10; and Sotheby's catalog for its "Fine and Rare

Wines, Spirits & Vintage Port" sale in London, Feb. 17, 2010, www.sothebys.com/app/live/pub/pubcatdetail.jsp?event_id=30120.

81 *"empathetic trance"*: Salisbury and Sujo, *Provenance*, p. 8.

82 *Armand LaMontagne spent two months:* Kaye, *Fakes, Fraud, or Genuine?*, p. 6.

83 *"never glued up of two parts"*: Nutting, *Windsor Chairs: An Illustrated Handbook*, p. 29.

83 *chestnut blight:* Leonard Alderman, "The American Chestnut," American Chestnut Foundation, www.chestnut.acf.org.

84 *paints:* There may not be books now, as Swanson says, but there were books in the period, for example: *The painter's and colourman's complete guide*, by P. F. Tingry, published in 1831; and *The Painter, Gilder, and Varnisher's Companion containing Rules and Regulations in Everything Relating to the Arts of Painting, Gilding, Varnishing and Glass-Staining*, by an anonymous author, published in 1850.

85 *"easy mark for a faker"*: Nutting, *Windsor Chairs: An Illustrated Handbook*, p. 161.

85 *"produce the best forms"*: Nutting is quoted in Rudy Parent, "Dr. Wallace Nutting," The Wallace Nutting Library, www.wallacenuttinglibrary.com, July 30, 2009.

85 *sold to J. P. Morgan, Jr.:* John Steele Gordon, "Inventing Antiques," *American Heritage Magazine*, Vol. 50, Issue 6 (October 1999), www.americanheritage.com/articles/magazine/ah/1999/6/199_6_16.

86 *"in plain capitals"*: Nutting is quoted in Parent, "Dr. Wallace Nutting."

86 *commode with a cabinet to hide the chamber pot:* Nancy Goyne Evans, *American Windsor Furniture: Specialized Forms* (Manchester, VT: Hudson Hills Press, 1997), pp. 94–95.

86 *"unpretentious charm" and "dignified"*: Nutting, *Windsor Chairs: An Illustrated Handbook*, pp. 5, 139.

86 *"why spoil the thrill?"*: Salisbury and Sujo, *Provenance*, p. 73.

88 *reflections would be "pleasant"*: Nutting, *Windsor Chairs: An Illustrated Handbook*, p. 5.

88 *displayed as real in Winterthur:* Kaye, *Fake, Fraud, or Genuine?*, p. 145.

89 *"There is nothing more puzzling in human nature"*: Nutting, *Windsor Chairs: An Illustrated Handbook*, p. 107.

89 *"treacherous territory"*: Kaye, *Fake, Fraud, or Genuine?*, p. 197.

Chapter Nine: Hot Potato

90 *"longest running auction"*: Not long after this auction, Hubley's closed its doors for good. Robert Cann, Sr., who'd run the house since 1943 after he married Elinor Hubley, turned ninety-one. He told a reporter at the final sale that he was "disconsolate" now that he was out of the business, and looking "for something to do." Frances McQueeney-Jones Mascolo, "Bidding Adieu, F.B. Hubley's Conducts Its Final Auction," *Antiques and the Arts Magazine*, June 24, 2008, http://antiquesandthearts.com/Antiques/AuctionWatch/2008-06-24.

92 *auction history:* Among other sources, I am indebted to these excellent texts for background on auctions: Russell W. Belk, *Collecting in a Consumer Society* (London: Routledge, 1995); Ralph Cassady, *Auctions and Auctioneering* (Berkeley: University of California Press, 1967); Brian W. Harvey and Franklin Meisel, *Auctions: Law and Practice* (London: Butterworths, 1985); Brian Learmount, *A History of the Auction* (London: Barnard & Learmount, 1985); Pamela Klaffke, *Spree: A Cultural History of Shopping* (Vancouver: Arsenal Pulp Press, 2003); Paul Klemperer, *Auctions: Theory and Practice* (Princeton, NJ: Princeton University Press, 2004); Vijay Krishna, *Auction Theory* (San Diego: Academic Press, 2002).

92 *"auctionarium" and "wink or a nod"*: Cassady, *Auctions and Auctioneering*, pp. 28, 108.

92 *shift to England:* Belk, *Collecting in a Consumer Society*, p. 36.

92 *"pubs," and coffeehouses:* Harvey and Meisel, *Auctions: Law and Practice*, p. 4.

92 *Sir Horace Walpole's art collection:* "Auction Houses: Christies," *Antiques Roadshow* Web site, www.pbs.org/wgbh/pages/roadshow/series/houses.html, accessed 11/18/2005. Auction information on the *Antiques Roadshow* Web site is provided by the auction houses.

92 *Madame du Barry:* Daniel Nissanoff, *Future Shop: How the New Auction Culture Will Revo-*

lutionize the Way We Buy, Sell, and Get the Things We Really Want (New York: Penguin Press, 2006), p. 48.

93 **"worthy poor":** Jack Larkin, *The Reshaping of Everyday Life: 1790–1840* (New York: Harper Perennial, 1988), p. 14. See also: James Midgley, Martin Tracy, and Michelle Livermore, *The Handbook of Social Policy* (Thousand Oaks, CA: Sage Publications, 1998), p. 85.

93 **Thomas Jefferson's "130 valuable negroes":** Quoted in Ben Wallace, *The Billionaire's Vinegar* (New York: Crown, 2008), p. 83.

93 **poster advertising an auction:** The quotes are from a poster reproduced in Learmount, *A History of the Auction*, p. 35.

93 **"the evils of auction":** Learmount, *A History of the Auction*, p. 91.

93 **Reasons Why the Present System of Auction Ought to Be Abolished:** *Ibid.*, p. 86.

93 **"every man has a right to be ruined in his own way":** Ibid., p. 89.

94 **"illiberality and meanness":** Ibid., p. 95.

94 **Sotheby's and Christie's suit:** Department of Justice Press Release, Wednesday, May 2, 2001, "Former Chairmen of Sotheby's and Christie's Auction Houses Indicted in International Price-Fixing Conspiracy," www.justice.gov/atr/public/press_releases/2001/8128.htm. See also: Ralph Blumenthal and Carol Vogel, "Ex-Chairman of Sotheby's Gets Jail Time," *The New York Times*, April 23, 2002.

94 **fined $256 million:** Anna Rohleder, "Who's Who in the Sotheby's Price-Fixing Trial," *Forbes Magazine*, November 14, 2001.

94 **Eldred's failed to accurately appraise the vase:** John Fiske, "In My Opinion," *New England Antiques Journal*, Vol. XXII, No. 3 (September 2003), p. 3.

95 **settled out of court:** Samuel Pennington, "Eldred Sued Over $1.55 Million Chinese Vase," *Maine Antique Digest*, August 2003, http://maineantiquedigest.com/articles_archive/articles/ eldr0802.htm. See also: "Strong Museum and Eldred's Settle Lawsuit over $1.55 Million Chinese Vase,"*Maine Antique Digest*, 2004, http://maineantiquedigest.com/articles_archive/ articles/jan04/stro0104.htm. Note: In a more recent, similar case, a woman named Jeanne Marchig brought suit against Christie's for "negligence" and "breach of warranty" for failing to properly assess and attribute a drawing they sold for $22,000 that was later identified as a Leonardo da Vinci and estimated to be worth up to $150 million. Since the finger-print evidence used to connect the drawing to da Vinci is in question, the case is compli-cated. David Grann, "The Mark of a Masterpiece," *The New Yorker*, July 12 and 19, 2010, pp. 51–71.

95 **"looking round to make sure that no one has noticed":** Learmount, *A History of the Auction*, p. 117.

95, 96 **"disguise their interests" and "the hat the higher":** Frances Larson, *An Infinity of Things: How Sir Henry Wellcome Collected the World* (Oxford: Oxford University Press, 2009), p. 81.

97 **"in the grain" of the fabric:** Deborah E. Kraak, "Ingrain Carpets," *The Magazine Antiques*, January 1996. See also: "Antique Ingrain Carpet Runner," *Victoriana: The Online Magazine*, www.victoriana.com/Carpet/ingrain-rug.html, accessed 10/01/2009.

99 **"chairman":** David Freeman Hawke, *Everyday Life in Early America* (New York: Harper Perennial, 1999), p. 56.

99 **Others sat on stools, chests, benches:** James Deetz, *In Small Things Forgotten: An Archaeology of Early American Life* (New York: Anchor, 1996), pp. 166–67.

99 **assessment of homes in the Chesapeake area:** Hawke, *Everyday Life in Early America*, pp. 55–56.

99 **doubled from about 1800 to the 1830s:** Larkin, *The Reshaping of Everyday Life: 1790–1840*, p. 139.

99 **voyeuse or voyelle:** Joseph Aronson, *The Encyclopedia of Furniture* (New York: Crown, 1965), p. 278 (photo of cockfight chair), and p. 139. NB: Edward Lucie-Smith, in *Furniture: A Con-cise History* (London: Thames and Hudson, 1979), notes that a "voyeuse" chair designed for men was "often miscalled in English a cock-fighting chair." He contends the chair was made for "spectators at a card-game" (p. 8). Florence de Dampierre notes on p. 183 of *Chairs: A*

History, that the "voyelle" chairs were used for card games but "also used by spectators at cock fights."

99 *"Gossip chairs":* Anne Gilbert, "The Antique Detective," *Antiques & Collecting Magazine,* December 2006, p. 43.

99 *fumeuse:* Dampierre, *Chairs: A History,* p. 340.

99 *"easie chairs":* Ibid., pp. 167–68.

99 *used by invalids or the elderly:* Ibid., pp. 167, 193–94. See also: Brock Jobe and Myrna Kaye, *New England Furniture: The Colonial Era* (New York: Houghton Mifflin, 1984), p. 366; Myrna Kaye, *There's a Bed in the Piano: The Inside Story of an American Home* (Boston: Little, Brown, 1998), pp. 63–66.

101 *"bee box":* Jack Hope, "In Search of a Bee Tree," *Natural History,* Vol. 107, No. 9, November 1998, p. 26.

102 *sales by "mineing":* Ralph Cassady, Jr., *Auctions and Auctioneering* (Berkeley: University of California Press, 1967), p. 32.

102 *"cunninger" than the rest:* Quoted in: Learmount, p. 26.

106 *"asymmetrical information":* Klemperer, *Auctions: Theory and Practice,* p. 15. See also: Lawrence M. Ausubel and Paul Milgrom, "The Lovely but Lonely Vickrey Auction," published at www.stanford.edu, accessed 10/22/09.

107 *British government "third generation" bandwidth:* "UK Mobile Phone Auction Nets Billions," BBC News, Thursday, April 27, 2005, http://news.bbc.co.uk/1/hi/business/727831 .stm.

107 *"reversal of the anchoring effect":* Adam D. Galinsky, Gillian Ku, and Keith Murnigham, "Starting Low but Ending High: A Reversal of the Anchoring Effect in Auctions," *Journal of Personality and Social Psychology,* Vol. 90, No. 6 (2006), pp. 975–86.

109 *Longwy:* "Longwy," Pottery Studio, www.studiopottery.com/cgi-bin/mp.cgi?item=27. See also: Jack R. Wiedabach, "Dip into History," www.soic.com/StainedFinger_sample_pages. pdf; "Invitation to the Longwy Country," http://www.infotourisme.net/tourist-route/ meurthe-et-moselle/discover-the-meurthe-et-mos, accessed 10/01/09; "Longwy," InfoFaience, www.infofaience.com/en/longwy_histoire.htm, accessed 10/01/09; William Percival Jervis, *Encyclopedia of Ceramics* (New York: Canal Street, 1902).

Chapter Ten: Tea for Two

112 *weathervane peak in 2006:* Lita Solis-Cohen, "Monumental Indian Weathervane Sells for Record $5,840,000," *Maine Antique Digest,* January 2007, www.maineantiquedigest.com/ articles_archive/articles/jan07/sothebysweathervane. See also: Dick Kagan, "Vane Glory," *Art & Antiques,* January 2007, p. 37.

112 *Jerry Lauren buys weathervane for $5,840,000:* David S. Smith, "Wind & Whimsy: Weathervanes and Whirligigs from Twin Cities' Collections," *Antiques and the Arts Online,* January 16, 2008, www.antiquesandthearts.com/2008-01-16_08-29-32.html&page=1. See also: "What's Hot," *Art & Antiques,* Vol. 29, Issue 12 (December 2006), p. 40; *Antiques and the Arts Online,* October 10, 2006.

112 *"a love affair":* Nancy N. Johnston, "The Art of It: The Stellar Folk Art Collection of Jerry and Susan Lauren," *Antiques & Fine Art,* http://antiquesandfineart.com/articles.cfm?request =852. Article not dated, but after 2007.

114 *Samuel Lancaster Gerry:* John J. Henderson, "Samuel Lancaster Gerry (1813–1891)," White Mountain Art and Artists, http://whitemountainart.com/Biographies/bio_slg.htm. Revision 2009-08-10. See also: Lawrence J. Cantor & Company, Important 19th, Early 20th Century American & European Paintings, http://www.fineoldart.com, "Samuel Lancaster Gerry (American 1813–1891).

115 *suspected British spies:* "Faneuil Hall," The Freedom Trail Foundation, Boston, MA, http:// www.thefreedomtrail.org, accessed 6/23/10. See also: http://www.american-architecture .info/USA/USA-Boston.

115 *"cured and fixed":* Myrna Kaye, *Yankee Weathervanes* (New York: E. P. Dutton, 1975), p. 12.

115 *steal "Black Hawk":* "Police Investigate Theft of Weather Vane," *USA Today*, August 14, 2006, http://www.usatoday.com/weather/news/2006-08-14-weathervane-theft_x.htm.

115 *"Figure":* Vermont Morgan Horse Association, "Justin Morgan Had a Horse," 2006, http://vtmorganhorse.org.

116 *"one of the most important pieces of vernacular folk art sculpture":* Stephanie M. Mangino, "Winchester Weather Vane up for Sotheby's Auction," Associated Press State & Local Wire, January 16, 2009.

116 *"Old Uncle Jake" weathervane failed to sell:* Virginia Bohlin, "Heft Meets Thrift at the Auctions," *Boston Globe*, February 1, 2009, Metro, p. H14. See also: "'Old Jake' Stays in Winchester," *Maine Antique Digest*, Vol. XXXVII, No. 8 (August 2009), p. 12; Eve M. Kahn, "Tracking the Progress of Some Special Items Over the Past Year," *The New York Times*, December 18, 2009, Section C, Column O, Antiques, p. 33.

117 *backs of hooked, yarn-sewn, and shirred rugs:* Joel Kopp and Kate Kopp, *American Hooked and Sewn Rugs: Folk Art Underfoot* (Albuquerque: University of New Mexico Press, 1995), pp. 132–33.

117 *"as complex and as rich as the passage of time itself":* Jack Kerouac, *On the Road* (New York: Penguin, 1997), pp. 107–8.

118 *like a burlap grain sack:* Jane Viator, "Folk Art Underfoot," *Antiques Roadshow Insider*, February 2007, pp. 9–10.

118 *Eleanor Blackstone rug:* Kopp and Kopp, *American Hooked and Sewn Rugs: Folk Art Underfoot*, p. 72.

119 **Theoremetrical System of Painting:** Bev Norwood, "Focus on Folk Art: Theorems: When Decorative Art Become Enduring Folk Art," *Antiques Journal*, April 2007, p. 49. See also: Bev Norwood, "Theorems: When Decorative Art Becomes Enduring Folk Art," *Northeast Antiques*, Vol. 13, No. 7 (May 2007), pp. 1, 16.

119 *enamel snuff bottle sold for a world-record price:* "A Million-Dollar Snuff Bottle," *Maine Antique Digest*, July 2010, p. 10-A.

120 *"snakes and ladders" painted game board:* From Skinner, Inc., Web site, dated 10/02/2009, www.skinnerinc.com/press/company-background.php.

122 *blind socket:* Nancy Goyne Evans, *Windsor-Chair Making in America: From Craft Shop to Consumer* (Hanover, NH, and London: University of New England Press, 2005), p. 122.

123 *"Mammy" and "Sambo" images, "Darkie" toothpaste:* George Alexander, "Collecting Our History," *Black Enterprise*, February 2000, p. 261.

123 *James P. Hicks collection:* "In Search of African American: One Collector's Experience—The James Hicks Collection," http://hoover.archives.gov/exhibits/africanamerican/introduction/hicks.html, accessed: 08/10/10.

123 *50,000 collectors of black Americana:* Ronald Roach, "Auctioning Off Yesterday—Protest Against the Sale of African American Historical Artifacts and Documents," Diverse Education, July 12, 2007, www.diverseeducation.com/cache/print.php?articleID=8392, accessed: 8/9/10. NB: Roach quotes *USA Today* as the source for this statistic.

123 **Roots** *(130 million people watched):* Associated Press, "'Roots' Producer David Wolper Dies at 82," August 11, 2010, National Public Radio Web site, www.npr.org/templates/story/story.php?storyId=129132755.

123 *celebrity collectors Spike Lee, Oprah Winfrey, Branford Marsalis, Whoopi Goldberg, Bill Cosby:* Syl Turner, "Collecting a Troubling Past: Black Americana," *Southeastern Antiquing and Collecting Magazine*, archived article, no date, http://www.go-star.com/antiquing/black_americana.htm, accessed: 08/10/2010. See also: Dennis Gaffney, "Tips of the Trade: African Americana," *Antiques Roadshow* Web site, www.pbs.org/wgbh/roadshow/tips/african americana.html, posted: July 17, 2000.

123 *scholars "lag behind collectors":* Elvin Montgomery, "Recognizing Value in African American Heritage Objects," *The Journal of African American History*, Vol. 89, No. 2 (Spring 2004), p. 177.

123 *Hicks first took offense:* Quoted in: "In Search of African America: One Collector's Experience—The James Hicks Collection." <http://hoover.archives.gov/exhibits/african american/introduction/hicks.html> Accessed: August 8, 2010.

124 *Mayme Agnew Clayton collection, and her son Avery Clayton's quote:* Jennifer Steinhauer, "Black History Trove, A Life's Work, Seeks Museum," *The New York Times*, December 14, 2006, Arts Section, www.nytimes.com/2006/12/14/arts/14clay/html.

124 *"Sally come up" sheet music:* Library of Congress, African American sheet music, 1860–1920, http://memory.loc/gov/cgi-bin/query/D?aasm:2:/temp/~ammem_1IXW.

124 *Philip J. Merrill . . . "no history book can":* Quoted in Gaffney, "Tips of the Trade: African Americana."

124 *Lynching photographs:* Turner, "Collecting a Troubling Past: Black Americana."

124 *Merrill said, "a picture of a boy . . .":* Quoted in Gaffney, "Tips of the Trade: African Americana."

125 *hooked rug by Dr. George Washington Carver:* Price listed at www.broadstreetantiquemall .com/blackhistorystore on August 10, 2010.

125 *Chicago Art Institute purchase Frederick Douglass daguerreotype:* Colin Westerbeck, "Chicago Art Institute Pays $185,000 for Douglass Portrait," *Ebony*, February 1997, p. 34.

125 *David Patterson and Tavis Smiley protest Christie's:* Roach, "Auctioning Off Yesterday—Protest Against the Sale of African American Historical Artifacts and Documents."

125 *profit about $25,500 per year:* Calculations from www.measuringworth.com for the year 1840 compared with 2009. Exact figures are: $2.00 in 1840 has the purchasing power of $51.20 in 2009; ten cents in 1840 has the purchasing power of $2.56 in 2009.

125 *"L.M. says this handle will crack":* On *Antiques Roadshow* in 2001, a woman brought in a Dave the Slave pot, which she bought at an estate auction in 1995 for $60. Dated June 28, 1854, signed by Dave, with this note: "L.M. says this handle will crack." Valued at $6,000. Pete Prunkl, "The Potter Poet," *Antiques Roadshow Insider*, March 1, 2006.

126 *dairywoman's signature:* Jack Larkin, *The Reshaping of Everyday Life: 1790–1840* (New York: Harper Perennial, 1988), p. 28.

126 *"a pot to piss in":* Ibid., p. 161.

126 *"Treat me nice and keep me clean":* Quoted in James Deetz, *In Small Things Forgotten: An Archaeology of Early American Life* (New York: Anchor, 1996), p. 85.

127 *average New England household had fewer than three candles:* Larkin, *The Reshaping of Everyday Life: 1790–1840*, pp. 41, 136.

128 *Fore River Shipyard in Quincy:* Anthony F. Sarcone and Lawrence S. Rines, "A History of Shipbuilding at Fore River," Fore River Shipyard, www.forerivershipyard.com/historylong .php, accessed: July 23, 2010.

129 *Barry and Nansi Nelson:* Stuart Lavietes, "Barry Nelson, Broadway and Film Actor, Dies at 86," *The New York Times*, April 14, 2007. See also: David Hewett, "Missed Property Tax Payment Results in $1 Million Loss for Collector Nansi Nelson," *Maine Antique Digest*, 2008; "Hundreds of Antiques Reported Stolen from Kingston, N.Y. Residence," *Antiques and the Arts Online*, November 27, 2007.

131 *Asa Peabody Blunt:* *Maine Antique Digest*, November 2006, p. 48G, advertisement for Crocker Farms, Inc.

131 *world record for New England stoneware:* Ad from Crocker Farm, Inc., Summer 2009, "To Be Sold, October 31, in York, PA . . ." NB: The record for the highest price paid at a stoneware *specialty* auction was broken in March 2009 at a Crocker Farm, Inc., auction, when Leigh Keno bought for $103,500 (which includes the 15 percent buyer's premium) a signed, dated 1817 Boynton water cooler. From Tom Hoepf, "Crocker Farm Reaps Record Price for Stoneware Auction," *The Antique Trader*, April 9, 2009, www.antiquetrader.com/article/ Crocker_Farm__reaps. The record price for stoneware at *any* (not a specialty) auction was set in 1991 by Sotheby Parke Bernet in New York City: $148,500 for a heart-shaped inkwell made by William Crolius, dated 1773. Karl H. Pass, "Recently Discovered Boynton Stoneware Cooler Highlights Spring Ceramic Sale," *Maine Antique Digest*, June 2009.

132 *introduced into England around 1650:* Jane Polley, ed., *Stories Behind Everyday Things* (New York: Reader's Digest Assoc., 1980), p. 353.

132 *imports had risen to eleven million pounds:* S.W., "On the Tea Table," 2000, The Georgian Index, http://www.georgianindex.net/Tea/ttable.html, accessed 6/23/10.

132 *"the affairs of their families":* "A Social History of the Nation's Favorite Drink," U.K. Tea Council, www.tea.co.uk/page.php?id=09, October 9, 2009. See also: Sarah Fayen, "Tea Table, Coffee Table," *Antiques & Fine Art Magazine*, Spring 2007, pp. 143–47.

132 *"The Negro's Complaint":* Ronald W. Fuchs II, "Peace, Plenty, and Independence: Selections from a Collection of English Ceramics Made for the American Market, 1770–1820," *Antiques & Fine Art Magazine*, October/November 2006, pp. 210–13.

132 *"table" spoons:* Myrna Kaye, *There's a Bed in the Piano: The Inside Story of the American Home* (Boston: Little, Brown, 1998), pp. 197–208 (tea tables) and p. 198 (tea spoons).

132 *tea "geer":* Brock Jobe and Myrna Kaye, *New England Furniture: The Colonial Era* (Boston: Houghton Mifflin, 1984), p. 112.

132 *today's value might be around $2,000:* It is difficult to make a direct translation of 1763 Rhode Island currency (first backed by land, but later based on future taxes) to 2010 dollars, for many reasons, the first being that each colony had its own coins and paper money with different and shifting values. The best historical currency converter I've found (www.measuringworth.com) begins in 1774, over a decade after the year Goddard bought the tea table, which translated $90 in 1774 to $2,470 in 2009, the last year for which they provide information. I've rounded this figure down because Rhode Island currency may have been less valuable, and the sale was ten years earlier than this translation. The $2,000 is at best a "ballpark" figure. The Continental Congress did not adopt the dollar as a unit of national currency until 1785, and there were marked periods when various currencies—wampum, British currencies, and other foreign units, the currency of each colony, as well as bills of credit or exchange (like today's checks), and goods that were traded—experienced deflation, or shifts in value. An example: "A Spanish piece of eight . . . on the eve of the [American] revolution would have been treated as 6 s. [shillings] in New England, as 8 s. in New York, as 7 s. 6 d. in Philadelphia, and as 32 s. 6 d. in Charleston." One estimate of cash per capita in 1774 in the "middle colonies" was £1.8 pound sterling, the British currency, which was much more valuable than currency from the colonies, perhaps ten times as much. But by this standard, the chair would have been very expensive, and affordable only to a vastly wealthy man like Nicholas Brown. Roy Michener, "Money in the American Colonies," *Economic History Encyclopedia*, ed. Robert Whaples, June 8, 2003, Economic History Services, http://eh.net/encyclopedia/article/michener.american.colonies.money.

132 *through Sotheby's for $8,416,000:* Sotheby's Auction catalog, https://www.sothebys.com/app/live/lot/LotDetail.jsp?lot_ie=4CW2R, "Property of the Goddard Family," Sale N08055, Session 1: Sat., January 22, 2005.

132 *first million-dollar auction sale of tea table:* Myrna Kaye, *Fake, Fraud, or Genuine?: Identifying Authentic American Antique Furniture* (Boston: Little, Brown, 1991), p. 181.

Chapter Eleven: Crowded House

138 *adds more halls and galleries:* The history of Catherine the Great's acquisitions and the Hermitage Museum is detailed at the museum's Web site, www.hermitagemuseum.org.

138 *"so wretched an abode":* Quoted in Werner Muensterberger, *Collecting: An Unruly Passion* (Princeton, NJ: Princeton University Press, 1994), p. 75. See also: Robert E. Brown, *Brimfield: The Collector's Paradise* (Brimfield, MA: Brimfield Publications, 1996), p. 83.

138 *"trails hacked into a bookman's jungle":* Nicholas Basbanes, *A Gentle Madness: Bibliophiles, Bibliomanes, and the Eternal Passion for Books* (New York: Holt Paperbacks, 1999), p. 22.

138 *"But still there was not enough space":* Frances Larson, *An Infinity of Things: How Sir Henry Wellcome Collected the World* (Oxford: Oxford University Press, 2009), p. 247.

138 *the only "normal" rooms:* Associated Press, "22 Years After Death, Warhol's Junk Lends Insight," August 19, 2009.

138 *Guillermo del Toro bought a second house:* Guillermo del Toro, transcripts from interview with Guy Raz, National Public Radio, June 13, 2009, "Director Guillermo del Toro Is a Novelist, Too."

138 *storage unit rentals increased by 90 percent:* Randy O. Frost and Gail Steketee, *Stuff: Compulsive Hoarding and the Meaning of Things* (Boston and New York: Houghton Mifflin, 2010), p. 263. NB: Frost and Steketee cite statistics from a *New York Times* article.

139 *"I wish my house were less cluttered":* Andrew Benett and Ann O'Reilly, *Consumed: Rethinking Business in the Era of Mindful Spending* (New York: Palgrave MacMillan, 2010), p. 189.

139 *cluttered Walton's home:* Thatcher Freund, *Objects of Desire: The Lives of Antiques and Those Who Pursue Them* (New York: Penguin, 1993), p. 162.

139 *John Sisto looted documents:* "Arrivederci: Recovered Italian Artifacts Headed Home," *Antiques Journal*, August 2009, p. 14.

139 *"you could barely move in the house":* Dave Itzkoff, "Thousands of Artworks are Deemed Stolen," *The New York Times*, June 10, 2009, p. 2, Section C. See also: "Son 'Relieved' to Tell Cops of Dad's Stolen Artifacts," National Public Radio Interview, *All Things Considered*, July 8, 2009.

139 *"oppressive to others":* William Davies King, *Collections of Nothing* (Chicago: University of Chicago Press, 2008), p. 6.

139 *Warhol, the icon of material culture:* Andy Warhol, *The Philosophy of Andy Warhol: From A to B and Back Again* (New York: Harcourt, Brace, 1975), pp. 195–96.

144 *"the fault of the house and not what's in it":* Elizabeth Stillinger, *The Antiquers* (New York: Knopf, 1980), p. 87.

Chapter Twelve: Two Heads Are Better Than One

145 *early as age three:* Russell W. Belk, "Collecting: From Whence It Began," in Robert E. Brown, *Brimfield: A Collector's Paradise* (Brimfield, MA: Brimfield Publications, 1996), p. 78, quoting C. F. Burk, "The Collecting Instinct," *Pedagogical Seminar*, Volume 7 (1900), pp. 179–207.7.

145 *"discovered with more pleasure":* Saint Augustine, *On Christian Doctrine*, quoted in Archibald M. Young, "Some Aspects of St. Augustine's Literary Aesthetics," *Harvard Theological Review*, Vol. 62, No. 3 (July 1969), p. 294.

146 *JFK collected scrimshaw carvings:* Leigh Keno and Leslie Keno, "Field Notes," *Find! Magazine*, Fall 2004, p. 95.

146 *Saddam Hussein was a collector:* Ken Hall, "Ken's Korner: News and Views from the World of Antiquing and Collecting," *Journal of Antiques and Collectibles*, July 2003, p. 10.

146 *Augusto Pinochet collected Napoleana:* Jon Lee Anderson, comments from Nieman Conference on Narrative Journalism panel, March 21, 2009, Boston, MA. Anderson discussed his interview with Pinochet.

146 *Napoleon's penis:* Judith Pasco, "Collect-Me-Nots," *The New York Times*, May 17, 2007, p. A-27.

146 *Green Car Burning 1:* "Christie's Sets Auction Record for Andy Warhol at $71.7 Million," *Art Knowledge News*, May 19, 2007, www.artknowledgenews.com/Andy_Warhol.html.

146 *certain "quality of mind":* Malcolm Forbes, *More Than I Dreamed: A Lifetime of Collecting* (New York: Simon and Schuster, 1989), p. 206.

146 *Steve Jenne:* Michael Michelsen, "A Passionate Collector: Steve Jenne," *Antiques & Collecting Magazine*, August 2007, p. 24.

146 *"contagious magic":* Paul Bloom, *How Pleasure Works: The New Science of Why We Like What We Like* (New York: W.W. Norton & Co., 2010), pp. 101–5. NB: This book contains an excellent discussion of the theory of "contagious magic."

146 *"I've never missed a cutting":* Joshua Glenn and Carol Hayes, *Taking Things Seriously: 75 Objects with Unexpected Significance* (New York: Princeton Architectural Press, 2007). A photo of Amy Kubes's fingernails and this quote appear on p. 92.

147 *"I'll spare you the clams, crabmeat, mussels . . .":* William Davies King, *Collections of Nothing* (Chicago: University of Chicago Press, 2008), p. 6.

147 *"All collectors are anal-erotics":* Ruth Formanek, "Why They Collect: Collectors Reveal Their Motivations," *Interpreting Objects and Collections*, ed. Susan M. Pearce (London: Routledge, 1994), pp. 327–35.

147 *surrogate for sexual desire:* Ibid.

147 *a sense of "nothingness":* Werner Muensterberger, *Collecting: An Unruly Passion* (Princeton, NJ: Princeton University Press, 1994), p. 44. Muensterberger quotes an unnamed collector he has interviewed who collects as a "hedge against nothingness."

147 *compensate for their inability to bear children:* Russell Belk, *Collecting in a Consumer Society* (London: Routledge, 1995), p. 97.

147 *"directs his surplus libido":* Quoted in Lynn Gamwell, "A Collector Analyzes Collecting: Sigmund Freud on the Passion to Possess," in Stephen Barker, ed., *Excavations and Their Objects: Freud's Collection of Antiquity* (New York: SUNY Press, 1995), pp. 1–12. See also: Belk, *Collecting in a Consumer Society*, p. 37; Brown, *Brimfield*, p. 74.

147 *Freud greeted his beloved statuary:* Barker, *Excavations and Their Objects: Freud's Collection of Antiquity*, pp. 6–7.

147 *Baboon of Thoth statue:* Ibid. See also: Juliet Flower MacCannell, "Signs of the Fathers: Freud's Collection of Antiquities," in Barker, *Excavations and Their Objects: Freud's Collection of Antiquity*, p. 45.

147 *Viagra ad:* "Pfizer Mocks Antiques Collecting," *Maine Antique Digest*, February 2010, p. 11-A.

147 *"ward off undercurrents of doubt":* Muensterberger, *Collecting: An Unruly Passion*, p. 31.

147 *"a wound we feel so deeply":* King, *Collections of Nothing*, p. 7.

148 *"Collecting fills a hole":* Simon Garfield, *The Error World: An Affair with Stamps* (New York: Houghton Mifflin, 2009), p. 2.

148 *"psychological security":* Belk, *Collecting in a Consumer Society*, p. 90.

148 *"a need for psychoanalysis":* Frances Larson, *An Infinity of Things: How Sir Henry Wellcome Collected the World* (New York: Oxford University Press, 2009), p. 5.

148 *"love sickness":* Susan Orlean, *The Orchid Thief* (New York: Ballantine Books, 1998), p. 53.

148 *Caius Verres:* Muensterberger, *Collecting: An Unruly Passion*, pp. 52–53. See also: Susan M. Pearce, *On Collecting: An Investigation into Collecting in the European Tradition* (London: Routledge, 1999), p. 93 (Cicero quoted in Pearce).

148 *Ralph Ellis:* Nicholas Basbanes, *A Gentle Madness: Bibliophiles, Bibliomanes, and the Eternal Passion for Books* (New York: Holt, 1999), p. 21.

148 *Asperger's:* Philipp Blom, *To Have and to Hold: An Intimate History of Collectors and Collecting* (Woodstock and New York: Overlook Press, 2002), p. 170.

148 *"[T]he serial killer":* Sara Knox, "The Serial Killer as Collector," *Acts of Possession*, ed. Leah Dilworth (Piscataway, NJ: Rutgers University Press, 2003), pp. 286–302. Quote from p. 299.

148 *"the collector is interested in quality":* Brenda Danet and Tamar Katriel, "No Two Alike: Play and Aesthetics in Collecting," *Interpreting Objects and Collections*, ed. Susan M. Pearce (London: Routledge, 1994), pp. 224–25.

148 *"improve concentration and reduce isolation":* Daniel B. Smith, "Can You Live with the Voices in Your Head?," *New York Times Magazine*, March 25, 2007.

148 *"defend against depression and loneliness":* Paul H. Ackerman, "On Collecting—A Psychoanalytic View," *Maine Antique Digest*, May 1990, p. 23A-9. Quoted in: Brown, *Brimfield*, p. 83.

148–49 *"I love it dearly":* Malcolm Forbes, *More Than I Dreamed: A Lifetime of Collecting* (New York: Simon and Schuster, 1989), pp. 205–23. ("I love it dearly" on p. 217.)

149 *True collectors "persevere"*: Garfield, *The Error World: An Affair with Stamps*, p. 66.

149 *"the homemade universe"*: Susan Stewart, *On Longing* (Durham, NC: Duke University Press, 1993), p. 162.

149 *"may act as sacred priests"*: Belk, *Collecting in a Consumer Society*, p. 94.

149 *the Association for All Collectors*: www.collectors.org.

149 *6,082 member clubs*: The Association of Collecting Clubs, http://collectingclubs.com.

150 *"supporting barbed wire collectors"*: http://collectingclubs.com, accessed: 10/16/2009.

150 *five hundred patented types of barbed wire*: "A Brief History of Barbed Wire," The Devil's Rope Barbed Wire Museum, www.barbwiremuseum.com/barbedwirehistory.htm.

150 *"defy the threat of mortality"*: Deyan Sudjic, *The Language of Things: Understanding the World of Desirable Objects* (New York: Norton, 2009), p. 23.

150 *antiques "lengthened my life"*: Quoted in Elizabeth Stillinger, *The Antiquers* (New York: Knopf, 1980), p. 87.

150 *"He never thought he would die"*: Larson, *An Infinity of Things*, p. 4.

150 *ads in trade magazines*: Ad text from Jamieson's ad in *Antiques & The Arts Weekly*, November 3, 2006. NB: William Jamieson's ads have run for years in several trade magazines, including every monthly issue of *Maine Antique Digest*. The latest, as of this writing, in the March 2011 issue of *MAD*, is on p. 34A. In the last few years, the text has changed somewhat, but the images in reverse-white print remain: skull, mermaid, and gorgon-like creature.

151 *"I love the macabre, weird stuff"*: Most of Jamieson's quotes are from my telephone interview with him on Saturday, December 9, 2006. Other quotes from published interviews and articles are sourced.

151 *A shrunken human head costs $15,000 to $20,000*: Ginger Strand, *Inventing Niagara: Beauty, Power, and Lies* (New York: Simon and Schuster, 2008), p. 82. NB: Strand interviewed Jamieson, who purchased the contents of Canada's oldest museum, the Niagara Museum, for a chapter of her book.

151 *Nicolas Cage's shrunken heads*: Brian McIver, "Nic's Gilded Cage," *The Mirror* (London), December 1, 2009, pp. 26–27.

152 *Andy Warhol and Ernest Hemingway*: Ripley's Believe It or Not! Museum, Times Square, New York. Web site: www.ripleysnewyork.com.

153 *"the strangest thing I saw is man"*: From brochure for Ripley's Odditorium, Times Square. New York.

154 *"preparing to take his first head" and "you couldn't get laid"*: Rita Zekas, "Collector's Skulls Are the Real Deal," *The Toronto Star*, April 8, 2006, p. M04.

154 *hunter-gatherer ancestors*: Belk, *Collecting in a Consumer Society*, pp. 78–79. Belk discusses Pavol's and Humphrey's belief in the "instinct" to collect.

154 *"one locates the prey"*: Formanek, "Why They Collect: Collector's Reveal Their Motivations," pp. 327–35.

154 *hamsters in laboratory studies*: Steven W. Anderson, Hanna Damasio, and Antonio R. Damasio, "A Neural Basis for Collecting Behaviour in Humans," *Brain: A Journal of Neurology*, Vol. 128, No. 1 (2005), pp. 201–12.

154 *rational part organizing the collecting impulse*: Ibid. See also: Jonathan Beard, "Chronic Collectors," *Scientific American Mind*, Vol. 16, No. 1 (2005), p. 8; Julio Rocha do Amaral, M.D., and Jorge Martins de Oliveria, M.D., Ph.D., "Limbic System: The Center of Emotions," The Healing Center On-line, www.healing-arts.org/n-r-limbic.htm.

154 *our intellect plays second fiddle*: William B. Irving, *On Desire: Why We Want What We Want* (New York: Oxford University Press, 2006), p. 283.

154–55 *The collector's dilemma*: Ibid., p. 286.

155 *"The most important object"*: Blom, *To Have and to Hold*, p. 157.

155 *"we've had enough"*: Martin Lindstrom, *Buyology: The Truth and Lies About Why We Buy* (New York: Doubleday, 2008), p. 63.

155 *"we want, well, stuff"*: Ibid., p. 199.

Chapter Thirteen: Stump the Dealer

156 *$50 million annually:* Jaclyn C. Stevenson, "The Thrill of the Hunt," *Business West Magazine*, May 12, 2008, p. 59.

157 *William Crolius heart-shaped inkwell:* Karl H. Pass, "Recently Discovered Boynton Stoneware Cooler Highlights Spring Ceramics Sale," *Maine Antique Digest*, June 2009, www.maineantiquedigest.com/stories/index.html?id=1267.

159 *"nuking" bottles:* Reggie Lynch, "Presentation: Fake Bottle Colors," *Raleigh Bottle Club Newsletter*, Raleigh, NC, Bottle Club, April 2002, www.antiquebottles.com/raleigh.

159 *"ultraviolently [sic] tampered":* Elaine Henderson, "This Color Purple—An Unnatural Disaster," *The Antique Trader*, July 1994, www.eapglass.com/purple.htm, accessed 11/14/2010.

160 *family registers and fraktur:* Corinne and Russell Earnest, "Fraktur: Folk Art & Family," *Antiques and the Arts Online*, http://antiquesandthearts.com/archive/frak.htm, June 28, 2009. See also: Corinne and Russell Earnest, *Fraktur: Folk Art & Family* (Atglen, PA: Schiffer Publishing, Ltd., 1999). NB: I am indebted to the Earnests for their excellent and beautifully photographed book on fraktur, which was the source of much of the background on fraktur. Fraktur are quite varied, and have a long history, to which my brief summary does not do justice. Thanks to the Earnests for answering my questions about fraktur, particularly sorting out the difference between fraktur and family registers.

160 *Ausfullers traveled from farm to farm:* Earnest, *Fraktur: Folk Art & Family*. See also: Jennifer L. Mass, Catherine R. Matsen, and Janice H. Carlson, "Materials of the Pennsylvania German Fraktur Artist," *Antiques*, September 2005, pp. 128–35.

160 *about $2.40 today:* The value of 10 cents in 1790 has the equivalent purchasing power of $2.42 in 2009, according to a currency conversion Web site: www.measuringworth.com, accessed 08/09/2010.

160 *Daniel Otto "dog-faced alligator" and 1801 Geistweite fraktur sales:* Lita Solis-Cohen, "Fraktur Heads Strong Sale," *Maine Antique Digest*, 2002 (late April or early May issue). Record price for Geistweite, paid by David Wheatcroft in 2004. Lita Solis-Cohen, "The Farm Sale of All Time: The Koch Sale," *Maine Antique Digest: The Americana Chronicles* (Philadelphia: Running Press, 2004), p. 347.

161 *survey of seventeen thousand kids:* "Games," *Consumer Reports*, Vol. 59, No. 12 (December 1994), p. 764. No byline.

161 *divining board history and "Oriole Talking Board":* Robert Murch, "The Oujia Board: History," www.williamfuld.com, 2007.

161 *The* Kennebec Journal: Untitled article, *Kennebec Journal*, October 2, 1903, posted on www.williamfuld.com.

162 *"wandering almost nude in the streets":* "Crazed Through 'Ouija': Neglected by Her Lover She Seeks Comfort of a Fortune-Telling Device," *Boston Daily Globe*, November 21, 1891. No byline. Posted on www.williamfuld.com. I am indebted to the following Web sites, sources, and researchers for the background on the Ouija board: Eugene Orlando, Museum of Talking Boards, http://museumoftalkingboards.com, copyright 1996–2010. NB: I am grateful to Eugene Orlando, who reviewed this Ouija board text for factual accuracy. The history and background of the Ouija board is much more complex than I have conveyed here, but Orlando's Web site gives a comprehensive history and overview of the "talking board" phenomenon. Additional sources include: James P. Johnson, "Ouija," *American Heritage*, Vol. 34, Issue 2 (February/March 1983), p. 247, www.americanheritage.com/articles/magazine/ah/1983/2/1983_2_24; Robert Murch, owner of the Web site www.williamfuld.com.

164 *"the latest triumph of chemical science":* "Antique Fire Grenade Bottles," www.antiquebottles.com/firegrenade, accessed: 12/26/09.

166 Manchester Harbor: "Skinner Sets New $5.5 Million World Record for Fitz Hugh Lane," www.skinnerinc.com/resources/highlights/fitz-hugh-lane-world-record-php.

168 shunga: International Netsuke Society, http://netsuke.org.

Chapter Fourteen: Shop Victoriously

171 *"institutionalization of the flea market":* Richard Satran, "Plucking Jewels from the Embers," *Chain Store Executive Magazine,* Vol. 59, No. 1 (January 1993), pp. 55–56. NB: Confirmed by Howard Davidowitz via e-mail to me, July 9, 2009, Davidowitz & Associates, New York.

171 *world's wealthiest thirty-two-year-old:* Connie Bruck, "Millions for Millions," *The New Yorker,* October 30, 2006, pp. 62–73.

171 *fastest-growing company in history:* Meg Whitman, CEO, eBay, Inc., in David Faber, Producer, *The eBay Effect: Inside a Worldwide Obesssion,* CNBC Production, 2005.

171 *one quarter of all online sales:* "Ebay's Sales Shrink 16% Year Over Year in the First Quarter," *InternetRetailer.com, Daily News,* Wednesday, April 22, 2009.

171 *"ninth most populous:"* Meg Whitman, in Faber, *The eBay Effect: Inside a Worldwide Obsession.*

171 *chunks of debris:* Christine Frey and P. J. Huffstutter, "Ebay Cancels Auctions of Attack-Related Items," *Los Angeles Times,* September 12, 2001, http://articles.latimes.com/2001/sep/12/news/mn-44919.

171 *military rations:* Ken Hall, "Ken's Korner," *Antiques and Collecting Magazine,* Vol. 111, No. 3 (May 2006), p. 17. See also: Government Accountability Office report, Gregory D. Kutz, Managing Director, Forensic Audits and Special Investigations, "Investigation: Military Meals, Ready-to-Eat Sold on eBay," February 13, 2006, Report No. GAO-06-410R.

171 *three grams of plutonium:* Ivan Gale, "The Web's Black Market (Ebay Works Closely with the FBI)," *The Industry Standard,* Vol. 3, No. 46 (December 2000), p. 32.

171 *tickets to a death row execution:* Ibid.

171–72 *breast milk:* Faber, *The eBay Effect.*

172 *a human kidney:* Kirsten Hawkins, "Top 10 Strangest eBay Items Ever Sold," www.hotlib.com/articles/show.php?t=Top_10_Strangest_eBay_Items_Ever, date stamp: 11/21/2005. Viewed on www.auctionseller411.com.

172 *William Shatner's kidney stone:* Ken Hall, "Ken's Korner," *Antiques and Collecting Magazine,* April 2006, p. 19.

172 *a prom date:* Faber, *The eBay Effect.*

172 *"Young Man's Virginity":* "Ebay's Idiot Auctions," *Wired,* April 2005, pp. 25–27. No byline.

172 *man put his wife up for sale:* Ken Hall, "Ken's Korner," *Antiques and Collecting Magazine,* Vol. 112, No. 5 (July 2007), p. 16.

172 *Israeli couple tried to sell advertising space:* "Absolut Exodus," *Harper's Magazine,* November 2005, p. 21. No byline.

172 *Massachusetts man sold his soul:* "Ebay's Idiot Auctions."

172 *"more than two-hundred million people":* Bruck, "Millions for Millions," p. 68.

173 *auction fraud:* "2007 Internet Crime Center Annual Report," Internet Crime Complaint Center, Federal Bureau of Investigation and National White Collar Crime Center, www.ic3.gov.

173 *in 2006, it logged 30,837:* Federal Trade Commission Annual Reports, 2007, 2008. Section Two: Consumer Protection Mission, 2007, p. 24, and 2008, p. 34. See also: Bureau of Justice Assistance 2008 Internet Crime Report. NB: eBay works with the FBI, the State Department, the Bureau of Alcohol, Tobacco and Firearms, the U.S. Fish and Wildlife Service, the Treasury, and the Postal Service to identify fakes and illegal items, and to halt sales of fraudulent merchandise.

173 *"tomb raiders":* "Ebay Saves Historic Treasures by Selling Fakes," *Techweb,* May 5, 2009.

173 *signed by Ted Williams:* Margaret Mannix, "Sure It's a Great Deal. But Is It Real?," *U.S. News & World Report,* Vol. 129, No. 23 (December 11, 2000), p. 58.

173 *fake "Tiffany" jewelry:* Katie Hafner, "Seeing Fakes, Angry Traders Confront eBay," *The New York Times,* January 29, 2006, Technology section, www.nytimes.com/2006/01/29/technology/29ebay.html. See also: Ken Hall, "Ken's Korner: Tiffany, eBay Square off in a Nasty Lawsuit," *Antiques & Collecting,* January 2008, p. 16.

173 *Louis Vuitton and Christian Dior sued eBay:* Ken Hall, "Ken's Korner," *Antiques & Collecting*, December 2006, p. 14.

173 *"we don't have any expertise":* Hafner, "Seeing Fakes, Angry Traders Confront eBay."

173 *$61 million in damages to Moët Hennessy Louis Vuitton:* Catherine Holahan, "Ebay Claims Victory in the Tiffany Lawsuit," *BusinessWeek*, July 14, 2008, http://blogs.businessweek.com /mt/mt-tb.cgi/11004.1361914388. See also: *Antiques and the Arts Online*, "Tiffany Loses Case Over Counterfeits on Ebay," July 15, 2008, http://antiquesandthearts.com/Antiques/ TradeTalk/2008-07-15; Daniel Nissanoff, *Future Shop: How the Auction Culture Will Revolutionize the Way We Buy, Sell, and Get the Things We Really Want* (New York: The Penguin Press, 2006), p. 168.

174 *100,000 contacts in North America:* Faber, *The eBay Effect*.

175 *133,000,000 items . . . a pair of shoes sold every three seconds:* eBay 2008 Annual Report, www .shareholder.com/visitors/dynamicdoc/document.cfm?docmentid=2493&co.

175 *Fetchbid.com, Oktshun.com, or Branica.com:* George Gardner, "Misspelled eBay Auction Search Engine Launches," www.tech.blorge, July 16, 2007.

176 *one of over 500,000 nationwide:* Katie Deatsch, "Transforming eBay," *Internet Retailer*, February 2009, www.internetretailer.com/printArticle.asp?id=29241, accessed December 17, 2009.

177 *Great Road Pottery and Cain pottery:* "Check List of Potters Along the Great Road in Virginia and Tennessee, 1776–1880," Blue Ridge Institute and Museum, www.blueridge institute.org. No byline. See also: J. Roderick Moore, Director, Blue Ridge Institute, "Earthenware Potters Along the Great Road in Virginia and Tennessee"; Angela Wampler, "Early Regional Pottery: Q&A with John Case," *A! Magazine for the Arts*, Vol. 17, No. 7 (June 30, 2009), www.artsmagazine.info, accessed July 2010; John Case, "Early Regional Pottery: Local History," *A! Magazine for the Arts*, Vol. 16, No. 8 (September 2009).

177 *Knoxville auction:* "Highlights from the May 16th, 2009 Antiques and Art Auction in Knoxville," Case Auctions, Knoxville, TN, www.caseantiques.com.

178 *"shadowing":* Ken Steiglitz, *Snipers, Shills, & Sharks: eBay and Human Behavior* (Princeton, NJ: Princeton University Press, 2007), p. 42.

181 *Cleopatra recommended hair-growing potion:* Karyn Siegel-Maier, "Hair Supply—Hair Loss Prevention," *Better Nutrition*, Vol. 62, No. 11 (November 2000), p. 52.

181 *"A Treatise on Bear's Grease":* Library of Congress image. http://openlibrary.org/b/ OL13460465M/treatise-on-bear%27s-grease, Library of Congress, Eighteenth Century— reel 9929, no. 06. Pagination: [8], 71 [1] plate.

181 *Jackie Kennedy bought an antique Sandwich glass:* Harold Sack, *American Treasure Hunt: The Legacy of Israel Sack* (Boston: Little, Brown, 1986), pp. 196–97.

Chapter Fifteen: Gold Is Where You Find It

183 *"based on trial and touch":* Paco Underhill, *Why We Buy: The Science of Shopping* (New York: Simon & Schuster, 1999), p. 218.

183 *customers "never tried them":* Ibid., p. 218.

183 *"never seriously challenge real live stores":* Ibid., p. 158.

185 *more than five hundred dealers:* www.nhantiquealley.com, December 27, 2009.

185 *"Halloween girl" doorstop:* Jane Viator, "Decorative Arts," *Antiques Roadshow Insider*, December 2006, p. 9.

188 *Darwin married his first cousin, Emma Wedgwood:* "Name This Famous Person," *The Journal of Antiques and Collectibles*, Vol. X, No. 6 (August 2009), p. 45.

188 *"pure white" glaze:* Brian Dolan, *Wedgwood: The First Tycoon* (New York: Viking, 2004), p. 72.

188 *"Liverpool" pottery:* Sources on Wedgwood and Liverpool pottery include: Dolan, *Wedgwood: The First Tycoon*; Marilyn Gould, "England & America: The Liverpool Connection," *Antiques and the Arts Weekly*, November 3, 2006, pp. S-12–13; Miriam Kramer, "The Patronage of George III and Queen Charlotte," *The Magazine Antiques*, August 2004.

188 *"The Negroes Complaint" and "Am I Not a Man and a Brother"*: Ronald W. Fuchs II, "Peace, Plenty, and Independence: Selections from a Collection of English Ceramics Made for the American Market, 1770–1820," *Antiques and Fine Art*, October/November 2006, pp. 210–13.

Chapter Sixteen: Roadshow Rage

190 *more viewers than* **60 Minutes**: As Marsha Bemko, executive producer, explained to me: "The number of viewers we use is an average weekly audience, a weekly cumulative average. We don't sell advertising per show or time slot, so we are not concerned with the number of eyeballs on us on one night, like regular television. A weekly average is fine. We are capturing people at different times since the various PBS stations may air the show during different times."

191 *WGBH, picked it up:* The origin of the series was a 1979 BBC documentary about a London auction house doing a tour of the West Country in England. WGBH in Boston, a PBS station, licensed the British show. There is a Canadian version, named *Canadian Antiques Roadshow*, which debuted in 2005, and a Dutch version in the Netherlands under the name *Tussen Kunst & Kitsch* ("Between Art and Kitsch"). See also: Debbie Cleveland, "*Antiques Roadshow* Premiers 10th Season on Monday Night," *Framingham Online News*, January 8, 2006, www.fra mingham.com/news/general_interest/antiques_roadshow_premiers_10th; Marsha Bemko, *Antiques Roadshow: Behind the Scenes* (New York: Simon and Schuster, 2009), pp. 10–12.

191 *Richmond, Virginia, a woman fainted:* Kimberly Lankford, "Behind the Scenes at *Antiques Roadshow*," *Kiplinger's Personal Finance*, Vol. 53, Issue 2 (February 1999), p. 100.

191 *"How will we know it's us without our past?"*: John Steinbeck, *The Grapes of Wrath* (New York: Penguin, 1939; edition with notes by Robert DeMott, 2006), p. 88.

193 *seventy to eighty experts:* At each new location, *Roadshow* producers look at the "retail community" for suitable appraisers, and glean names from auction houses in the cities they visit. "We work with a trustworthy group of appraisers," Marsha Bemko, the show's executive producer, told me. In the show's first season, antique ordnance expert Russell Pritchard III and a cohort, George Juno, staged two phony appraisals. The show "terminated" its association with the pair. Russell Pritchard, Jr., was at one time the director of Philadelphia's Civil War Library. He was "duped" by his own son, Russell Pritchard III, who was found guilty of stealing more than $1 million worth of Civil War artifacts, as well as staging the phony appraisals on *Antiques Roadshow*. However, the father was found guilty of fraud also when he helped his son cheat a distant relative out of the value of a Confederate uniform (by undervaluing and underpaying for the uniform, or promising it would go into a museum collection, but selling it for much higher value and keeping the profits). Joseph Slobodzian, "Antiques Experts Charged with Fraud," *Philadelphia Inquirer*, March 16, 2001; "Bryn Mawr Dealer Charged Again," *Philadelphia Inquirer*, May 18, 2001; "Civil War Expert Sentenced to Halfway House," *Philadelphia Inquirer*, May 25, 2002; "Antiques Trader Sentenced for $1 Million Fraud."

195 *marble top:* People send in photos and histories of furniture ahead of time, and a few are selected to be featured on the show. Thus people are generally not lugging enormous heavy furniture through the streets of downtown Philadelphia only to be told it is worthless, though that doesn't prevent some people from hoping and hauling. *Antiques Roadshow* pays a bonded shipper to deliver the preselected items to the set at the Convention Center, if the owners live within fifty miles of the show site.

195 *less than a one-half of 1 percent chance:* *Antiques Roadshow* estimates a "less than 2 percent" chance, based on "approximately 6,000 people," though they give away "a total of 3,800 pairs of tickets." While not all the ticket holders will bring two items for appraisal, some might bring more than two. At 7,600 tickets times two items (15,200), and only 50 items selected, the chance of appearing with your object on *ARS* might be as low as 0.32894 percent, or less than one half of one percent. Thus, the range of probability is between .3 and *ARS*'s stated "2 percent." Bemko, *Antiques Roadshow: Behind the Scenes*, pp. 6, 71.

196 *valued at $500,000 "on a good day"*: Ibid., p. 9. See also: Dennis Gaffney, "A Hand-woven Treasure," www.pbs.org/wgbh/pages/roadshow/series/highlights/2002/Tucson/tucson_foll ow1.html.

197 *"this elusive trophy"*: Bemko, *Antiques Roadshow: Behind the Scenes*, p. 88. See also: Claudia Parsons, "First $1 Million Find for U.S. Antiques Roadshow," *Yahoo!News*, http://news .yahoo.com/s/nm/20090630/od_uk_nm/oukoe_uk_usa_antiques.

198 *"soft-core porn for antique fetishists"*: Rob Sheffield, "Television," *Rolling Stone*, No. 808, March 18, 1999, p. 73. See also: Joshua Shenk, "The Things We Carry: Seeking Appraisal at *Antiques Roadshow*," *Harper's*, Vol. 302, Issue 1813 (January 2001). Shenk borrows the term "value porn" from sociologist Andras Szanto.

199 *"the price tag is everything"*: Alain de Botton, "If It's Old, Flog It, Fast," *New Statesman & Society*, Vol. 9, Issue 387 (January 26, 1996), p. 33.

Chapter Seventeen: Wilmington, aka the John Malkovich Show

202 *Barbra Streisand at Wilmington:* Jeanne Schinto, "Greater Boston Antiques Festival: Barbra Goes Shopping," *Maine Antique Digest*, February 2007, Section E.

203 *"became believers after the show"*: Quoted in ibid.

203 *"even when it's down, is big"*: Jeanne Schinto, "Boston Welcomes Its New Antique Shows," *Maine Antique Digest*, June 2007, p. 13-C.

208 *"Do you display in a room setting booth?"*: New England Antique Shows Web site: www .neantiqueshows.com/new%20site/contractrequest.htm, December 28, 2009.

208 *"Tabletop dealers will be at the back"*: Schinto, "Greater Boston Antiques Festival: Barbra Goes Shopping."

209 *"South Jersey house, generally Wistarburgh"*: Wistarburgh is spelled three different ways in literature (Wistarburgh, Wistarberg, or Wistarburg). Wistarburgh, the spelling I have used, is from an original map of the property made public in 2007 by Gayle Wistar, a direct descendant of Caspar. This information is from Dale Murschell, *Wistarburgh: Window Tiles, Bottles, and More* (Self-published, 2007), pp. 5, 117.

209 *"Noted for their Strength and Warranted for 7 years"*: Quoted in Edwin Tunis, *Colonial Craftsmen and the Beginnings of American Industry* (Baltimore: Johns Hopkins University Press, 1965), p. 137.

209 *Wistarburgh mug, with nearly a three-inch crack, sold for $55,000:* "Auction Prices Realized," *Maine Antique Digest*, August 2010, p. 3D. No byline. [p. 146 Digital Edition].

210 *"vision of this world-class show"*: Quoted in Schinto, "Boston Welcomes Its New Antique Shows."

Chapter Eighteen: Living the Pilgrim-Century Life

211 *"limits to the charms of the New England six-board"*: Robert Hughes, "Claw Daddy," *The New York Times*, May 29, 2005, p. 50, Section 6, Column 1.

211 *Wallace Nutting six-board quotes:* Wallace Nutting, *Furniture of the Pilgrim Century (of American Origin, 1620–1720)* (Boston: Old America Co., 1924), p. 55.

212 *one linen napkin:* Laurel Thatcher Ulrich, *The Age of Homespun: Objects and Stories in the Creation of an American Myth* (New York: Alfred A. Knopf, 2001), p. 112.

212 *Blanket chests were used for:* Brock Jobe and Myrna Kaye, *New England Furniture: The Colonial Era* (Boston: Houghton Mifflin, 1984), pp. 3, 113.

214 *fireplace lintel in a house Knowlton built:* Gerald C. Mingin, and John B. Vander Sande, "Attributing a Vernacular Six-Board Chest," *The Magazine Antiques*, Vol. 171, No. 5, May 2007, pp. 135–37.

219 *forged by Mordecai Lincoln:* Scituate Historical Society, Cudworth House, www.scituate historicalsociety.org/sites_cudworth_html.

220 *early nail making:* Edwin Tunis, *Colonial Craftsmen and the Beginnings of American Industry*

(Baltimore: Johns Hopkins University Press, 1965), pp. 58–59. See also: Myrna Kaye, *Fake, Fraud, or Genuine: Identifying Authentic American Antique Furniture* (Boston: Little, Brown, 1991), pp. 76–77.

221 *Connecticut heart and star-flower carved six-board:* "Monahan Collection Puts Hearts Under the Hammer at Northeast," *Antiques and the Arts Weekly*, August 7, 2001, http://antiques andthearts.com/wrappersstory.asp?file=2001-08-07.

221 *decorated "possibly Virginia" blanket chest:* "On the Lookout," *Antiques Roadshow Insider*, Vol. 7, No. 6 (June 2007), p. 1.

Chapter Nineteen: Red Carpet Affair

223 *"most prestigious and profitable" antiques event:* Quoted on the Web site for the Winter Antiques Show ("Frequently Asked Questions"), www.winterantiquesshow.com, accessed 6/16/2010.

223 *Philly show's "preview party":* Prices quoted are for the 2010 Preview Gala Reception listed on the Philadelphia Antiques Show Web site, www.philaantiques.com/store/.

223–24 *"A world-class event for a world-class city":* Quoted in Jeanne Schinto, "Boston Welcomes Its New Antiques Show," *Maine Antique Digest*, June 2007, p. 12-C.

224 *"the projects":* After this show, the producer, Marvin Getman, fielded "complaints galore" about the limited carpet, so the following year he carpeted the entire show. "I listen to my dealers," he said. Quoted in Schinto, "Boston Welcomes Its New Antiques Show," p. 13-C.

224 *231 dealers total:* Ibid., p. 12-C.

225 *Getman spent $55,000 on advertising:* Ibid.

228 *"supersize" their drinks:* Paco Underhill, *Why We Buy: The Science of Shopping* (New York: Simon & Schuster, 1999), p. 235.

228 *"I have had half of one for my breakfast today":* The Whitman postcard was displayed in the booth of a dealer named John Waite from Ascutney, Vermont.

229 *the birth of the Audubon Society:* Jennifer Price, "Hats Off to Audubon," *Audubon Magazine*, December 2004, http://audubonmagazine.org/features0412/hats.html. See also: Joanne Haug, "Wings, Breasts & Birds," Victoriana.com, http://www.victoriana.com/Victorian -Hats/birdhats.htm, December 23, 2009.

230 *"cocktails at a fabulous Tribeca loft":* From the Web site for the American Antiques Show, January 21–24, 2010, www.theamericanantiquesshow.org/gala-benefit-preview.

231 *canceled because of the recession:* Jeanne Schinto, "Second Annual Boston Antiques Weekend: When Times Are Tough, the Tough Get Getman," *Maine Antique Digest*, July 2008.

231 *prices were down as much as 30 percent:* Lita Solis-Cohen, "The Winter Antiques Show: The Show Must Go On," *Maine Antiques Digest*, April 2009.

231–32 *"antiques and collectibles" dropped by 9.3 percent:* National Auctioneers Association, "Auction Industry Holds Strong in 2008 with $268.5 Billion in Sales," report prepared by the National Auctioneer Association with support from the National Auctioneers Foundation, www.auctioneers.org. This is the latest data from this organization, as of July 19, 2010. NB: It is telling that while art, antiques, and collectible auction sales dropped in 2008, a sign of the weak economy, sales for residential real estate, agricultural land, machinery and equipment, and commercial real estate increased, another sign of a weak economy, especially residential real estate auctions.

232 *James D. Julia, Inc., Stimulus Plan:* James D. Julia, Inc., full-page advertisement in *Maine Antique Digest*, January 2010, p. 27E.

232 *Pook & Pook "TARP":* "Pook Institutes TARP," no byline, *Maine Antique Digest*, January 2010, p. 11-A.

233 *Sotheby's specialist in decorative arts:* The antiques "maxim" of the best and worst selling was attributed to William W. Stahl, Jr., of Sotheby's in Thatcher Freund, *Objects of Desire: The Lives of Antiques and Those Who Pursue Them* (New York: Penguin, 1993), p. 29.

233 *"the population isn't booming":* Underhill, *Why We Buy*, p. 201.

233 *Every Collector Add a Collector:* Ad placed in *Maine Antique Digest*, May 2009, p. 21-B. Contact info for ad: everycollector@snet.net, 978-464-2476. These ads ran throughout 2008 and through at least August 2010 when I stopped my research.

233 *"interest and mentor one or more of your friends":* Ad in *Maine Antique Digest*, March 2010, p. 42-B. Contact info for ad: everycollector@snet.net, 978-464-2476. "Wanted! New Collectors."

234 *"We're not old, but our stuff is!":* Hollie Davis and Andrew Richmond, "Top Ten Reasons Young People Should Buy Antiques," *Maine Antique Digest*, August 2010, p. 26-D. The blog URL is: http://youngantiquescollectors.blogspot.com.

234 *"the most environmentally responsible choice":* Ibid.

234 *"my laptop should be made out of cardboard":* Quoted in *Objectified: A Documentary Film*, produced by Gary Hustwit, Swiss Dots Ltd., 2009.

234 *"Go Green, Buy Antiques":* *Antiques and Fine Art Magazine* advertisement, Summer 2009.

234 *"the least sustainable retailer":* Quoted in Ellen Ruppel Shell, *Cheap: The High Cost of Discount Culture* (New York: The Penguin Press, 2009), p. 139.

234 *"stoked a 'cut and consume' cycle":* Ibid., p. 130.

234 *"will be left behind":* Underhill, *Why We Buy*, p. 240.

235 *Dr. Peter Bloch study:* "Sensory Shopping," *Illuminations*, University of Missouri, Columbia, MO, Spring 2005, pp. 7–8. See also: Peter H. Bloch, Frederic Brunel, and Todd J. Arnold, "Individual Differences in the Centrality of Visual Product Aesthetics: Concept and Measurement," *Journal of Consumer Research*, Vol. 29, No. 4 (March 2003), pp. 551–56.

235 *"aesthetics is not a luxury":* Quoted in Lee Eisenberg, *Shoptimism: Why the American Consumer Will Keep on Buying No Matter What* (New York: Free Press, 2009), p. 235.

235 *"aesthetic goods available and affordable":* Virginia Postrel, *The Substance of Style* (New York: Harper Perennial, 2003), p. 42.

235 *"stylish but* soulful*":* Shell, *Cheap*, p. 135.

235 *Shaker spirit of craftsmanship:* Stephen Bowe and Peter Richmond, *Selling Shaker: The Commodification of Shaker Design in the Twentieth Century* (Liverpool: Liverpool University Press, 2007), pp. 198, 293.

235 *"dwelling on a task for a long time":* Matthew B. Crawford, *Shop Class as Soulcraft: An Inquiry into the Value of Work* (New York: Penguin, 2009), p. 20.

235 *"collective historical memory":* Ibid., p. 25.

235 *"something of us as human beings will die":* Stephanie Zacharek, "Ikea Is as Bad as Wal-Mart," *Salon Magazine*, Salon.com, July 12, 2009.

236 *"washed-out colors":* Rob Walker, "Consumed: Brilliant Mistakes," *The New York Times Magazine*, July 25, 2009, p. 19.

237 *$8 trillion:* Underhill, *Why We Buy*, pp. 129–30. See also: Harry Rinker, "It's About Time Someone Recognized the Purchasing Power of Us Old Farts," *Unravel the Gavel*, Vol. 17, No. 10 (November 17–December 14, 2006), pp. 12A–13A.

237 *"The Bat-Man":* Ralph and Terry Kovel, "Batman Whips Superman," www.kovels.com, March 3, 2010. See also: Heritage Auctions, www.ha.com, Auction #7017, February 24, 2010, Lot # 91126. In April 2010, Superman Action Comic No. 1 sold through www.Comic Connect.com for $1.5 million, a battle of the superhero comic books. Reported in Kovels, April 7, 2010, www.kovels.com/issues/newsflash/1_189/news.

Chapter Twenty: Captain Antiques

239 *The record for a Spider-Man comic:* The price for the $227,000 Amazing Fantasy No. 15 is from Comic Link www.comiclink.com/text/2007-10AuctionSalesSample.htm. Accessed 9/10/2010. Verified by e-mail, 9/11/2010 from Josh Nathanson, founder of Comic Link.

239 *"somebody crawling on walls could be interesting":* Quoted in Mark Lacter, "Stan Lee, Marvel Comics," *Inc.*, Vol. 31, No. 9 (November 2009), p. 96.

239 *"They want a collectible that means something to them":* Quoted in Katie Scott, "Superman Auction Smashes Comic Book Records," *Wired*.Co.Uk., March 31, 2010, www.wired.co.uk/news/archive/2010-03/31/superman-auction-smashes-comic-book. See also: Jack Markowitz, "Collectible Comic Book Prices Soar in Super Sale," *Pittsburgh Tribune-Review*, Sunday, April 4, 2010.

239 *"endowment effect":* Paul Bloom, *How Pleasure Works: The New Science of Why We Like What We Like* (New York: W.W. Norton, 2010), p. 99.

239 *'With great power':* As the origin story goes, Peter Parker, an outcast teased at school, gains spiderlike powers after being bitten by a radioactive spider at a science exhibit. At first, he uses his powers for financial gain, wrestling Crusher Hogan for $100. One day, Spider-Man witnesses a crime, but fails to help a cop apprehend the crook. Later, Peter learns that his beloved uncle was murdered by the same crook that, as Spider-Man, he hadn't bothered to stop. Remorseful, Peter-slash-Spider-Man realizes, "With great power there must also come—great responsibility!"

239 *males from age eight to forty-five:* Alessandra Bianchi, "Comic Attitudes," *Inc.*, April 1993, p. 108.

240 *"a vision of a stunted person":* Stergios Botzakis, "Adult Fans of Comic Books: What They Get Out of Reading," *Journal of Adolescent & Adult Literacy*, Vol. 53, No. 1 (September 2009), p. 50.

240 *"was coming between me and French kissing":* "Roger" is quoted in ibid.

240 *comic book reading in international markets:* Milton Mayfield, Jacqueline Mayfield, and Alain D. Genestre, "Strategic Insights from the International Comic Book Industry: A Comparison of France, Italy, Japan, Mexico and the U.S.A.," *American Business Review*, Vol. 19, No. 2 (June 2001), pp. 82–93.

240 *this figure had slipped to 50 percent:* Alessandra Bianchi, "Comic Attitudes," *Inc.*, April 1993, p. 108.

241 *"Free Comic Book Day":* Peter Shawn Taylor, "Wanted: Comic Relief," *Canadian Business*, Vol. 79, No. 9 (April 24–May 7, 2006), p. 13.

241 *"the nostalgia trend":* Anonymous Author, "Comic Book Classics Recharge Film Industry," *DSN Retailing Today*, Vol. 41, No. 14 (July 29, 2002), p. S15. The connection between comic book sales and the 9/11 attacks was made by a Marvel Comics spokesperson in this article.

241 *over five million comics in stock:* From Web site for Mile High Comics, www.milehighcomics.com, accessed 8/16/2010.

241 *fifty employees, and annual sales of over $5 million:* Sales figures from Anonymous Author, "Funny Business," *People Magazine*, Vol. 50, No. 11 (September 28, 1998), p. 86.

242 *VH1 ranked the top two hundred pop icons:* Daniel P. Finney, "Nothing Funny About Comics: Fans of the Spandex-Clad Brethren Take Their Collecting As Seriously As Their Pleasure," *St. Louis Post-Dispatch*, July 31, 2003, p. F1.

243 *Homer Simpson on top:* Jen Chaney, "Revising the List of 100 Greatest Pop Culture Characters," *The Washington Post*, June 1, 2010, http://voices.washingtonpost.com/celebritology/2010/06/revising_the_list_of_100_great.htm, accessed 09/07/2010.

243 *Sale of vintage superhero comics in the 2000s:* Sources for comic book prices in the 2000s: www.comiclink.com/text/2007-10AuctionSalesSample.htm; "Industry News" for 1/24/2004 on http:scoop.diamondgalleries.com, accessed 09/10/2010. The Spider-Man comics were all rated 9.4, and the other record-setting sale prices for superhero comics were for the highest grade books.

243 *Heritage Auctions:* Rachel Emma Silverman, "True Mystery: Who Sold Famous Batch of Vintage Comics?," *Wall Street Journal* (Eastern Edition), August 5, 2006, p. A-1.

243 *"the biggest payday in American nerdhood":* Stephane Fitch, *Forbes*, Vol. 171, No. 2 (January 20, 2003), p. 43.

243 *comic books outperformed other collectibles:* Kevin Hassett, "Comics Rule!," *The American* March/April 2007, www.american.com/archive/2007/march-april-magazine-contents/comics-rule/article. NB: Hassett's analysis seems flawed in at least one way. For example, he analyzed coin values over twenty-one years, from 1970 to 1991, which excludes the 1990s boom years. But he analyzed comic books over seventy years, from 1937 to 2006, which was before the economic crash in 2008. His information was derived from price guides, a flawed source at best, as noted by Jimmy Desjardins, and Hassett focused on superhero comics, which might skew the statistics. Hassett did not respond to my contact for a further explanation of his analysis.

245 *"kiss of death":* Conor Dougherty, "Collecting: Bang! Pow! Cash! As Comic Prices Soar, Disputes Flare; Avoiding the Purple Label of Death," *The Wall Street Journal,* September 23, 2005, Weekend Journal.

245 *fair market value, with a cap of $1,500:* Rates and terms for Comics Guaranty Company cited here are from CGC Web site: www.cgccomics.com/services/services_and_fees.asp, accessed 9/4/10.

245 *William Shatner, who dropped in by helicopter:* "Celebrities at Comic-Con 2010," KSWB Television, http://www.fox5sandiego.com/news/comiccon/kswb-pg-cc-celebs-2010,0,1714274, accessed 09/05/2010. See also: David Ward, "Mass Appeal Key to Comic Book Pickup," *PR Week,* Vol. 10, No. 48 (December 10, 2007), p. 13.

246 *In the Midwest in October nine shows:* Comic book conventions across the country are listed at www.epguides.com/comics/schedule.shtml.

248 *"one of the godfathers of the Wackys":* Background on Wacky Packages is from a nonprofit Web site: www.wackypackages.org, accessed 9/5/10.

250 *the Monroe issue has sold for over $2,000:* Price estimate from eBay listing: "Playboy No.1 Marilyn Monroe 1953 Original Cover Complete." Seller: misjif. http://cgi.ebay.com/ws/eBayISAPI.dll?ViewItem&item=310239760535&si=C%2B%2FK4, accessed 9/4/10. See also: www.Americanmemorabilia.com. On this site on September 4, 2010, a 1953 Marilyn Monroe *Playboy* was being auctioned, highest bid at that time: $2,827, accessed, 9/4/10.

250 *signed by Joe DiMaggio:* Auction price from Sotheby's Web site: www.sothebys.com. Sale date: Thursday, September 30, 1999, in New York. Lot No. NY7354—1688. http://browse.sothebys.com/?sla=1&slaform=1&q=MarilynMonroeplayboy.

250 *Mattel sold 250,000:* Sharon Verbeten, "Golden Years," *Antiques Roadshow Insider,* Vol. 7, No. 6 (June 2007), pp. 11–12.

250 *1954 Superman lunch box:* Sharon Verbeten, "Carry-Out Collectible," *Antiques Roadshow Insider,* Vol. 7, No. 2 (February 2007), pp. 1, 14.

251 *sold for $666.66:* Leander Kahney, "For Sale: A Piece of Mac History," *Wired,* February 19, 2003, www.wired.com/print/gadgets/mac/news/2003/02/57721.

251 *had a starting bid of $50,000:* "Original Apple-1 Is up for Sale on eBay for $50,000!" Posted on www.edibleapple.com on Friday, November 20, 2009. Accessed 9/6/10.

251 *forty million slide rules:* The Oughtred Society Web site www.oughtred.org/history.shtml, accessed 9/6/10.

251 *the calculator rendered the slide rule obsolete:* Michele Alice, "Collector's Corner: Slide Rules," AuctionBytes.com, June 5, 2005, www.auctionbytes.com/cab/abu/y205/m06/abu0144/s06.

251 *Walter Shawlee:* Ian Austen, "Slide Rules Tap Into Nostalgia of the Pocket Protector Crowd," *The New York Times,* June 17, 1999, Section G, Page 4, Column 5. See also: Tam Pui-Wing Tam, "Calculating Collector: Fans of Slide Rule Count on Mr. Shawlee," *The Wall Street Journal,* February 18, 2003, Section A, Page 1, Column 4.

252 *My Little Pony, mass-produced in vinyl in 1983:* Debra L. Birge, Web site: http://mylittleponyworld.com, accessed 9/4/10. Note: Birge is the author of *The World of My Little Pony,* First Edition (2007) and Second Edition (2010), Atglen, PA: Schiffer Publishing.

253 *"My Little Pony branded products":* Web site for Hasbro: http://www.hasbro.com/corporate/media/press-releases/MY-LITTLE-PONY.cfm, accessed 9/4/10.

253 *G.I. Joe—the grandfather of action figures:* Michele Alice, "Collector's Corner: GI Joe," *AuctionBytes.com,* December 5, 2004, accessed 9/3/10.

253 *National Toy Hall of Fame:* From National Toy Hall of Fame Web site: www.museumofplay
.org/nthof/inductees.php, accessed 9/6/10.

253 *sold for $6,362:* Alice, "Collector's Corner: GI Joe."

254 *This same issue, with a rating of 6.0, sold in March:* Price for the 6.0 Action Comics No.1 is
from www.comicconnect.com. Auction ended: 7:10 P.M. EDT, 03/13/2009. Accessed 9/6/10.

254 *"Superman saved the day":* Quoted in Ray Sanchez, "Superman Comic Saves Family Home
from Foreclosure," ABC News Internet Ventures, http://abcnews.go.com/print?id=11306
997, accessed 9/5/10.

254 *family's Superman comic book sold:* Final auction price listed on www.comicconnect.com.
NB: Auction ended Monday, September 20, 2010, at 8:32 P.M. EDT with a final auction
price of $436,000. The auction listing described the book as "The Superman comic that
will save a family's home."

255 *U.S. Customs defines an "antique":* Jeff McLaughlin, "What Is an Antique?" *The Boston
Globe*, May 7, 1995, p. 81.

255 *allowing for "modern" and "contemporary" objects:* Lita Solis-Cohen, "The Winter Antiques
Show: The Show Must Go On," *Maine Antique Digest*, April 2009.

255 *"The future is all about collectors mixing":* Quoted in ibid.

255 *"get my coffee without leaving my desk":* Quoted in Marc Shapiro, "Serious Business: Captain
Marvel," *Marvel's Heroes Return Special* (New York: Wizard Press, October 1997), p. 6.

Chapter Twenty-one: Life with Principle

260 *Calicut cloth:* The process of making chintz fabric was laborious. First, the fabric was "sized"
or stiffened with milk or plant extracts. Then the textile worker drew patterns on the fabric
using iron oxide mixed with sugar or fruit juice, which turned black when exposed to the
tannic acid from the sizing. The fabric was dyed in reddish madder root or chay root. The
tanning agent was removed with cow dung, and then sections of the fabric were covered
with beeswax or resin and dyed again in indigo. Hot water melted the wax, and then those
spots were painted yellow using turmeric or saffron or pomegranate peel. M. E. Riley, "An
Introduction to 18th Century Printed Textiles," 2003, www.marariley.net. See also: Mark
McCauley, Home and Garden TV, "15 Things You Didn't Know about Fabric," www.hgtv
.com/ghtv/cda/article_?A15.

264 *"Repro-Depot":* Ad copy is from a quarter-page ad in *The Journal of Antiques and Collectibles*,
April 2007, p. 73.

266 *Brimfield saw the largest attendance:* www.thebostonchannel.com/chronicle/23234138/de-
tail.html, WCVB—Channel 5, April 26, 2010, story on Brimfield and interview with Bob Wyss.

266 *"The auction market is definitely on the rise":* Quoted in Virginia Bohlin, "Auctioneers Sense
Spring in the Air," *Boston Sunday Globe*, April 25, 2010, p. G11.

266 *Etsy earned $1.7 million:* 2008 sales figures for Etsy found in Rob Walker, *Buying In: The
Secret Dialogue Between What We Buy and Who We Are* (New York: Random House, 2008),
pp. 230–48.

266 *these figures doubled in 2009:* Andrew Benett and Ann O'Reilly, *Consumed: Rethinking Business in the Era of Mindful Spending* (New York: Palgrave MacMillan, 2010), p. 133.

266 *"of solid, good quality":* Ibid., p. 119.

266 *in a study twenty years ago:* For consumers' attitudes about flea markets, see: John F. Sherry,
"A Sociocultural Analysis of a Midwestern American Flea Market," *Journal of Consumer
Research*, Vol. 17, No. 1 (June 1990), pp. 13–33. See also: John Sherry, "Dealers and Dealing in a Periodic Market: Informal Retailing in Ethnographic Perspective," *Journal of Retailing*, Vol. 66, No. 2 (Summer 1990), pp. 174–91.

266 *offer authenticity, provenance, and personal connection:* Benett and O'Reilly, *Consumed*, p. 130.

266 *"connected to something larger":* Ibid., p. 132.

267 *"heritage has become hip":* Brenner Thomas, *Women's Wear Daily*, Vol. 199, No. 102 (May
13, 2010), p. 1.

267 *76 million Americans have a hobby or a collection:* Roy Rosenzweig and David Thelen, *The Presence of the Past: Popular Uses of History in American Life* (New York: Columbia University Press, 1998), p. 34.

267 *53 percent had read a book about the past: Ibid.,* p. 234, Table 1.

267 *"popular interest in the past has never been greater":* David Glassberg, *Sense of History: The Place of the Past in American Life* (Amherst: University of Massachusetts Press, 2001), p. 6.

268 *then eat it straight from the knife:* Francesco Mosto, "The History of Taste in a Single Object," *House Beautiful,* April 2006, pp. 84–89.

268 *"sharp-pointed piece of cane":* Jack Larkin, *The Reshaping of Everyday Life, 1790–1840* (New York: Harper Perennial, 1988), pp. 132, 181.

268 *had just two tines:* Ivor Noel Hume, *A Guide to Artifacts of Colonial America* (Philadelphia: University of Pennsylvania Press, 1969), p. 180.

268 *third tine was added sometime around 1690:* David Freeman Hawke, *Everyday Life in Early America* (New York: Harper and Row, 1988), p. 52c (photo caption).

268 *a four-tine fork is first recorded around 1780: Ibid.,* photo and text appearing just after page 52 (no page number on photo pages).

268 *"divided spoons":* Jane Polley, ed., *Stories Behind Everyday Things* (New York: Reader's Digest Association, 1980), pp. 176, 203–4. See also: Daniel E. Sutherland, *The Expansion of Everyday Life, 1860–1876* (Fayetteville: University of Arkansas Press, 2000), p. 77.

269 *"You must get your living by loving":* Henry David Thoreau, "Life Without Principle," quoted in *Atlantic Monthly,* Vol. 12, Issue 71 (1863), pp. 484–95. See also: Henry David Thoreau, *Collected Essays and Poems* (New York: Library of America, 2001), "Life Without Principle," p. 352.

269 *"Do not hire a man who does your work for money":* Thoreau, *Collected Essays and Poems,* "Life Without Principle," p. 351.

Coda: A Thousand Years

271 *beaten for her religious beliefs:* June Sprigg, "Foreword," in Nardi Reeder Campion, *Mother Ann Lee: Morning Star of the Shakers* (Hanover, NH: University Press of New England, 1990), p. xii.

271 *"I felt the power of God":* Frederick William Evans, *Ann Lee (founder of the Shakers), A Biography, with Memoirs of William Lee, James Whittaker, J. Hocknell, J. Meacham, and Lucy Wright; Also a Compendium of the Origin, History, Principles, Rules and Regulations, Government, and Doctrines of the United Society of Believers in Christ's Second Appearing* (London: J. Burns, Progressive Library, 1858), p. 23.

271 *"good and comfortable life":* Quoted in Stephen J. Stein, *The Shaker Experience in America* (New Haven, CT: Yale University Press, 1992), p. 217.

271–72 *"the sooner the sect is extinct the better": Ibid.,* pp. 218–19.

272 *"the ultimate measure of Shaker worth": Ibid.,* p. 405.

272 *record from 1989 held by Bill Cosby: Ibid.,* pp. 405–6.

272 *cherry dining table sold for $117,000:* Jeanne Schinto, "Shaker Devotees Keep the Faith," *Maine Antique Digest,* January 2010, pp. 36B–39B.

272 *exhibit of Shaker "handicrafts":* Stephen Bowe and Peter Richmond, *Selling Shaker: The Commodification of Shaker Design in the Twentieth Century* (Liverpool: Liverpool University Press, 2007), p. 29.

272 *"immediate need of money":* Stein, *The Shaker Experience in America,* pp. 395, 399.

273 *stricture against adorning buildings: Ibid.,* p. 46.

273 *"not suitable for Believers":* Quoted in Edward Deming Andrews, *The People Called Shakers: A Search for the Perfect Society* (Toronto: General Publishing Company, Ltd., 1963), p. 282. Andrews has included in his book the entire text of the Shaker's *Millennial Laws,* Revised 1854. This quote is from Section IV: "Concerning Superfluities not Owned."

273 *more than thirty patents:* "Books About Antiques: *The Shakers, an Entrepreneurial Sect,*" *Antiques Magazine*, August 2007, p. 40. No byline.

273 *gold medal at the 1876 Centennial Exhibition:* Christian Goodwillie, "The Shakers and the Invention of the Circular Saw: A Circular Argument," *Inspired Innovations: A Celebration of Shaker Ingenuity*, ed. M. Stephen Miller (Hanover, NH: University Press of New England, 2010), p. 194.

273 *"Put your hands to work":* Campion, *Mother Ann Lee: Morning Star of the Shakers*, p. 43.

273 *"a will to perfection":* Adam Gopnik, "Shining Tree of Life: What the Shakers Did," *The New Yorker*, February 13 and 20, 2006, pp. 162–68.

273 *"3 great coats, 31 jackets, 9 frocks, 80 shirts":* Edward L. Purcell, *The Shakers* (New York: Crescent Books, 1992), p. 73.

273 *"6 jackets, and 63 pairs of trousers":* Stein, *The Shaker Experience in America*, p. 140.

275 *"rarely hear back":* Stacey Chase, "The Last Ones Standing," *The Boston Globe*, July 23, 2006. See also: "History of the United Society of Shakers at Sabbathday Lake, Maine," www .Maineshakers.com/history.html.

275 *"if you knew you must die tomorrow":* Purcell, *The Shakers*, p. 11. See also: Stein, *The Shaker Experience in America*, p. 27.

BIBLIOGRAPHY

Books

Alighieri, Dante. *The Divine Comedy*. (Originally published circa 1308–1321). New York: Classic Books International, 2009.

Andrews, Edward Deming. *The People Called Shakers: A Search for the Perfect Society*. Toronto: General Publishing Company, Ltd., 1963.

Appadurai, Arjun. *The Social Life of Things: Commodities in Cultural Perspective*. Cambridge, UK: Cambridge University Press, 1986.

Aronson, Joseph. *The Encyclopedia of Furniture*. New York: Crown, 1965.

Barker, Stephen. *Excavations and Their Objects: Freud's Collection of Antiquity*. New York: Suny Press, 1996.

Basbanes, Nicholas. *A Gentle Madness: Bibliophiles, Bibliomanes, and the Eternal Passion for Books*. New York: Holt Paperbacks, 1999.

Bauman, Paul. *Collecting Antique Marbles, 4th ed*. Iola, WI: Krause Publications, 2004.

Belk, Russell W. *Collecting in a Consumer Society*. London: Routledge, 1995.

Bemko, Marsha. *Antiques Roadshow: Behind the Scenes*. New York: Simon & Schuster, 2009.

Benett, Andrew, and Ann O'reilly. *Consumed: Rethinking Business in the Era of Mindful Spending*. New York: Palgrave Macmillan, 2010.

Block, Robert. *Marbles*. Atglen, PA: Schiffer Publishing, 2002.

Blom, Philipp. *To Have and to Hold: An Intimate History of Collectors and Collecting*. Woodstock and New York: Overlook Press, 2002.

Bloom, Paul. *How Pleasure Works: The New Science of Why We Like What We Like*. New York: W. W. Norton & Co., 2010.

Booth, Martin. *Opium: A History*. New York: Simon & Schuster, 1996.

Bourdieu, Pierre. *Distinction: A Social Critique of the Judgment of Taste*. Cambridge, MA: Harvard University Press, 1984.

Bowe, Stephen, and Peter Richmond. *Selling Shaker: The Commodification of Shaker Design in the Twentieth Century*. Liverpool: Liverpool University Press, 2007.

Bradford, William. *Of Plymouth Plantation, 1620–1647*. New York: The Modern Library, 1981.

Brecher, Edward M. *Licit And Illicit Drugs: The Consumer Union Report*. Boston: Little, Brown, 1973.

Brown, Robert E. *Brimfield: The Collector's Paradise*. Brimfield, MA: Brimfield Publications, 1996.

Calloway, Steven. *Obsessions: Collectors and Their Passions*. London: Mitchell Beazley, 2004.

Campion, Nardi Reeder. *Mother Ann Lee: Morning Star of the Shakers*. Hanover, NH: University Press of New England, 1990.

Cardinal, Roger. *Cultures of Collecting*. London: Reaktion Books, 2004.

Carter, Howard. *The Tomb of Tut.Ankh.Amen: The Annexe and Treasury*. London: Duckworth, 1933.

Cassady, Ralph Jr. *Auctions and Auctioneering*. Berkeley: University of California Press, 1967.

Cheever, John. *Collected Stories and Other Writings*. New York: Library of America, 2009.

Chervenka, Mark. *Antique Trader Guide to Fakes and Reproductions*. Iola, WI: Krause Publications, 2007.

Clunas, Craig. *Superfluous Things*. Honolulu: University of Hawaii Press, 2004.

Cohen, Adam. *The Perfect Store: Inside eBay*. Boston: Little, Brown, 2002.

Collector Books. *Garage Sale & Flea Market Annual*. Paducah, KY: Schroeder Publishing, 2007.

Cossons, Malcolm, Editor in Chief. *Sotheby's Preview*. July 2003. London: Sotheby's, Inc., July 2003.

Crawford, Matthew B. *Shop Class as Soulcraft: An Inquiry into the Value of Work*. New York: Penguin, 2009.

Cruz, Joan Carroll. *Relics*. Huntington, IN: Our Sunday Visitor, Inc., 1984.

Cullity, Brian. *A Cubberd, Four Joyne Stools & Other Smalle Thinges: The Material Culture of Plymouth Colony*. Sandwich, MA: Heritage Plantation of Sandwich, Loan Exhibition, May 8–October 23, 1994.

Davis, Lance Edwin, Robert E. Gallman, and Karin Gleiter. *In Pursuit of Leviathan*. Chicago: University of Chicago Press, 1997.

De Dampierre, Florence. *Chairs: A History*. New York: Abrams, 2006.

Deetz, James. *In Small Things Forgotten: An Archaeology of Early American Life*. New York: Anchor, 1996.

De Quincey, Thomas. *Confessions of an English Opium Eater*. Middlesex, UK: Penguin, 1971.

Dilworth, Leah. *Acts of Possession: Collecting in America*. Piscataway, NJ: Rutgers University Press, 2003.

Dolan, Brian. *Wedgwood: The First Tycoon*. New York: Viking, 2004.

Earnest, Corinne and Russell. *Fraktur: Folk Art and Family*. Atglen, PA: Schiffer Publishing, 1999.

Eastlake, Charles L. *Hints on Household Taste in Furniture, Upholstery and Other Details*. New York: Dover, 1969. Reprint of Fourth Edition, London: Longmans, Green & Company, 1869.

Eisenberg, Lee. *Shoptimism: Why the American Consumer Will Keep on Buying No Matter What*. New York: Free Press, 2009.

Evans, Frederick William. *Ann Lee (Founder of the Shakers), A Biography, with Memoirs of William Lee, James Whittaker, J. Hocknell, J. Meacham, And Lucy Wright; Also a Compendium of the Origin, History, Principles, Rules and Regulations, Government, and Doctrines of the United Society of Believers in Christ's Second Appearing*. London: J. Burns, Progressive Library, 1858.

Evans, Nancy Goyne. *American Windsor Furniture: Specialized Forms*. Manchester, VT: Hudson Hills Press, 1997.

———. *Windsor-Chair Making in America: From Craft Shop to Consumer*. Hanover, NH, and London: University Press of New England, 2006.

Fales, Dean A. *American Painted Furniture: 1660–1880*. New York: Bonanza Books, 1986.

Farquhar, Michael. *A Treasury of Deception*. New York: Penguin, 2005.

Forbes, Malcolm. *More Than I Dreamed: A Lifetime of Collecting*. New York: Simon & Schuster, 1989.

Fortuna, Michael. *Brimfield: A Novel*. Cohasset, MA: Hothouse Press. 2000.

Freund, Thatcher. *Objects of Desire: The Lives of Antiques and Those Who Pursue Them*. New York: Penguin, 1993.

Frost, Randy O., and Gail Steketee. *Stuff: Compulsive Hoarding and the Meaning of Things*. Boston and New York: Houghton Mifflin, 2010.

Garfield, Simon. *The Error World: An Affair with Stamps*. New York: Houghton Mifflin, 2009.

Gelfman Karp, Marilynn. *In Flagrante Collecto: (Caught in the Act of Collecting)*. New York: Abrams, 2006.

Gillham, Leslie, ed. *Miller's Affordable Antiques Price Guide 2003*. Kent, UK: Miller's Publications, 2003.

Glassberg, David. *Sense of History: The Place of the Past in American Life*. Amherst: University of Massachusetts Press, 2001.

Glenn, Joshua, and Carol Hayes. *Taking Things Seriously: 75 Objects with Unexpected Significance*. New York: Princeton Architectural Press, 2007.

Gosling, Sam. *Snoop: What Your Stuff Says About You*. New York: Basic Books, 2008.

Gould, Stephen Jay, and Rosamond Wolff Purcell. *Finders, Keepers: Eight Collectors*. New York: W. W. Norton, 1992.

Green, Harvey. *The Uncertainty of Everyday Life, 1915–1945*. Fayetteville, AR: University of Arkansas Press, 2000.

Greenfield, Briann G. *Out of the Attic: Inventing Antiques in Twentieth-Century New England*. Amherst: University of Massachusetts Press, 2009.

Harvey, Brian W., and Franklin Meisel. *Auctions: Law and Practice*. London: Butterworths, 1985.

Hawke, David Freeman. *Everyday Life in Early America*. New York: Harper Perennial, 1999.

Haynes, Colin. *The Complete Collector's Guide to Fakes and Forgeries*. Greensboro, NC: Wallace-Homestead Book Co., 1988.

Hebborn, Eric. *The Art Forger's Handbook*. New York: Overlook Press, 1997.

Hodgson, Barbara. *Trading in Memories: Travels Through a Scavenger's Favorite Places*. Vancouver, BC, Canada: Greystone, 2007.

Hooper-Greenhill, Eilean. *Museums and the Shaping of Knowledge*. London: Routledge, 1992.

Hume, Ivor Noël. *A Guide to Artifacts of Colonial America*. Philadelphia: University of Pennsylvania Press, 1969.

Hunt, Stoker. *Ouija: The Most Dangerous Game*. New York: Harper & Row, 1985.

Huxford, Bob. *Garage Sale and Flea Market Annual*. Paducah, KY: Collector Books 2004.

Irving, William B. *On Desire: Why We Want What We Want*. New York: Oxford University Press, 2006.

Jerningham, Charles Edward, and Lewis Bettany. *The Bargain Book*. New York: Frederick Warne & Co., 1911.

Jervis, William Percival. *Encyclopedia of Ceramics*. New York: Canal Street, 1902.

Jobe, Brock, and Myrna Kaye. *New England Furniture: The Colonial Era*. Boston: Houghton Mifflin, 1984.

Kaye, Myrna. *Fake, Fraud, or Genuine: Identifying Authentic American Antique Furniture*. Boston: Little, Brown, 1987.

———. *There's a Bed in the Piano: The Inside Story of the American Home*. Boston: Little, Brown, 1998.

———. *Yankee Weathervanes*. New York: E. P. Dutton, 1975.

Keno, Leigh, and Leslie Keno. *Hidden Treasures: Searching for Masterpieces of American Furniture*. New York: Warner Books, 2000.

Kerouac, Jack. *On the Road*. New York: Penguin, 1997.

Kettell, Russell Hawkes. *The Pine Furniture of Early New England*. New York: Dover Publications, 1929.

King, William Davies. *Collections of Nothing*. Chicago: University of Chicago Press, 2008.

Klaehn, Jeffery. *Inside the World of Comic Books*. New York: Black Rose Books, 2007.

Klaffke, Pamela. *Spree: A Cultural History of Shopping*. Vancouver, BC, Canada: Arsenal Pulp Press, 2003.

Klemperer, Paul. *Auctions: Theory and Practice*. Princeton, NJ: Princeton University Press, 2004.

Kopp, Joel, and Kate Kopp. *American Hooked and Sewn Rugs: Folk Art Underfoot*. Albuquerque, NM: University of New Mexico Press, 1995.

Kovel, Ralph, and Terry Kovel. *Kovel's New Dictionary of Marks: Pottery and Porcelain 1850 to the Present*. New York: Crown, 1986.

Krishna, Vijay. *Auction Theory*. San Diego: Academic Press, 2002.

Lafarge, Albert. *U.S. Flea Market Directory*. New York: St. Martin's, 2000.

Larcom, Lucy. *A New England Girlhood*. Boston: Northeastern University Press, 1986.

Larkin, Jack. *The Reshaping of Everyday Life: 1790–1840*. New York: Harper Perennial, 1988.

Larson, Frances. *An Infinity of Things: How Sir Henry Wellcome Collected the World*. Oxford, UK: Oxford University Press, 2009.

Leach, Bernard. *A Potter's Book*. London: Faber & Faber, 1988.

Learmount, Brian. *A History of the Auction*. London: Barnard & Learmount, 1985.

Leslie, Naton. *That Might Be Useful: Exploring American's Secondhand Culture*. Guilford, CT: Lyons Press, 2005.

Lindstrom, Martin. *Buyology: Truth and Lies About Why We Buy*. New York: Doubleday, 2008.

Little, Nina Fletcher. *Little by Little: Six Decades of Collecting American Decorative Arts*. Boston: Society for the Preservation of New England Antiquities, 1998.

———. *Neat & Tidy: Boxes and Their Contents Used in Early American Households*. Boston: Society for the Preservation of New England Antiquities, 2001.

Loughlin, David. *The Case of Major Fanshawe's Chairs*. New York: Universe Books, 1978.

Lubar, Steven, and W. David Kingery. *History from Things: Essays on Material Culture*. Washington, D.C.: Smithsonian Institution Press, 1993.

Luchinat, Cristina Acidin. *Medici, Michelangelo, and the Art of Late Renaissance Florence*. New Haven, CT: Yale University Press, 2002.

Lucie-Smith, Edward. *Furniture: A Concise History*. London: Thames & Hudson, 1979.

McConnell, Kevin. *Redware: America's Folk Art Pottery*. Atglen, PA: Schiffer Publishing, 1988.

McCree, Cree. *Flea Market America: The Complete Guide to Flea-Enterprise*. Santa Fe, NM: Ocean Tree Books, 1983, 2003.

McCutcheon, Marc. *The Writer's Guide to Everyday Life in the 1800s*. Cincinnati, OH: Writer's Digest Books, 1993.

Mallalieu, Huon. *The Illustrated History of Antiques*. London: Quantum Books, 2003.

Martin, Laura C. *Tea: The Drink That Changed the World*. North Clarendon, VT: Tuttle Publishing, 2007.

Mauries, Patrick. *Cabinets of Curiosities*. London: Thames & Hudson, 2002.

Merrill, Althea. *Shaker Girl*. South Portland, ME; Pilot Press. 1987.

Midgley, James, Martin Tracy, and Michelle Livermore. *The Handbook of Social Policy*. Thousand Oaks, CA: Sage Publications, 1998.

Miller, Arthur. *Death of a Salesman* [1949]. In *Collected Plays*. New York: Library of America, 2006.

Miller, M. Stephen. *Inspired Innovations: A Celebration of Shaker Ingenuity*. Hanover, NH: University Press of New England, 2010.

Muensterberger, Werner. *Collecting: An Unruly Passion*. Princeton, NJ: Princeton University Press, 1994.

Murschell, Dale. *Wistarburgh Window Tiles, Bottles, and More*. Springfield, WV: self-published, 2009.

Nissanoff, Daniel. *Future Shop: How the Auction Culture Will Revolutionize the Way We Buy, Sell, and Get the Things We Really Want*. New York: Penguin, 2006.

Norman, Donald A. *The Design of Everyday Things*. New York: Basic Books, 1998.

———. *Emotional Design: Why We Love (or Hate) Everyday Things*. New York: Basic Books, 2004.

Nutting, Wallace. *Furniture of the Pilgrim Century (of American Origin) 1620–1720*. Boston: Old America Co., 1924.

———. *Windsor Chairs: An Illustrated Handbook*. New York: Dover Publications, 2001. Reprint of original edition, Boston: Old America Company, 1917.

Orlean, Susan. *The Orchid Thief: A True Story of Beauty and Obsession*. New York: Ballantine Books, 1998.

Pearce, Susan M. *Interpreting Objects and Collections*. London: Routledge, 1994.

———. *On Collecting: An Investigation into Collecting in the European Tradition*. London: Routledge, 1999.

Pepys, Samuel. *Diary of Samuel Pepys*. Richard Le Gallienne, ed. New York: Dover Publications,, 2004.

Philbrick, Nathaniel. *Mayflower*. New York: Penguin, 2006.

Piña, Leslie. *Furniture in History*. New York: Prentice Hall, 2003.

Polley, Jane, ed. *Stories Behind Everyday Things*. New York: Reader's Digest Inc., 1980.

Postrel, Virginia. *The Substance of Style: How the Rise of Aesthetic Value Is Remaking Commerce, Culture, & Consciousness*. New York: Harper Perennial, 2003.

Price, Sandy. *Exploring the Flea Markets of France*. New York: Three Rivers Press, 1999.

Prisant, Carol. *Antiques Roadshow Primer*. New York: Workman Publishing, 1999.

Prown, Jules David, and Kenneth Haltman. *American Artifacts: Essays in Material Culture*. East Lansing, MI: Michigan State University Press, 2000.

Purcell, Edward L. *The Shakers*. New York: Crescent Books, 1992.

Richmond, Simon, et al. *Russia & Belarus*. Footscray, Victoria, Australia: Lonely Planet Publications, 2003.

Rosenzweig, Roy, and David Thelen. *The Presence of the Past: Popular Uses of History in American Life*. New York: Columbia University Press, 1998.

Sack, Albert. *Fine Points of Furniture: Early American*. New York: Crown, 1950.

Sack, Harold, and Max Wilk. *American Treasure Hunt*. Boston: Little, Brown, 1986.

St. George, Robert Blair. *The Wrought Covenant: Source Material for the Study of Craftsmen and Community in Southeastern New England, 1620–1700*. Brockton, MA: Brockton Art Center–Fuller Memorial, 1979.

Salisbury, Laney, and Aly Sujo. *Provenance*. New York: Penguin, 2009.

Santore, Charles. *The Windsor Style in America*. Volumes I and II. Philadelphia: Courage Books, 1997.

Sartre, Jean-Paul. *Being and Nothingness*. Paris: Gallimard, 1943.

Schlereth, Thomas J. *Material Culture Studies in America*. Lanham, MD: Altamira Press, 1999.

———. *Victorian America: Transformations in Everyday Life*. New York: Longman, 1997.

Schroy, Ellen T. *Warman's American Furniture*. Iola, WI: Krause Publications, 2000.

Scott, Kenneth. *Counterfeiting in Colonial America*. Philadelphia: University of Pennsylvania Press, 1957.

Sennett, Richard. *The Craftsman*. New Haven, CT: Yale University Press, 2008.

Shell, Ellen Ruppel. *Cheap: The High Cost of Discount Culture*. New York: Penguin Press, 2009.

Smith, Kenneth L. *Estate Inventories: How to Use Them*. Morgantown, PA: Masthof Press, 2000.

Smith, Mary Ann. *Gustav Stickley, The Craftsman*. New York: Dover Publications, 1993.

Snider, J. H., and Terra Ziporyn. *Future Shop: How New Technologies Will Change the Way We Shop and What We Buy*. Bloomington, IN: Iuniverse, 2008.

Solis-Cohen, Lita. *Maine Antique Digest: The Americana Chronicles*. Philadelphia: Running Press, 2004.

Solomon, Robert C. *Love: Emotion, Myth, & Metaphor*. Amherst, NY: Prometheus, 1990.

Spielman, Patrick, and Adolph Vandertie. *Hobo and Tramp Art Carving: An Authentic American Folk Tradition*. New York: Sterling Publishing Co., 1995.

Steiglitz, Ken. *Snipers, Shills, & Sharks: eBay and Human Behavior*. Princeton, NJ: Princeton University Press, 2007.

Stein, Stephen J. *The Shaker Experience in America*. New Haven, CT: Yale University Press,1992.

Steinbeck, John. *The Grapes of Wrath [1939]*. Reprint, New York: Penguin, 2006.

Stewart, Susan. *On Longing: Narratives of the Miniature, the Gigantic, the Souvenir, the Collection*. Durham, NC: Duke University Press, 1993.

Stillinger, Elizabeth. *The Antiquers: The Lives and Careers, the Deals, the Finds, the Collections of the Men and Women Who Were Responsible for the Changing Taste in American Antiques, 1850–1930*. New York: Knopf, 1980.

Stradling, J. Garrison, and Diana Stradling, eds. *The Art of the Potter*. New York: Main Street/Universe Books, 1977.

Strand, Ginger. *Inventing Niagara: Beauty, Power, and Lies*. New York: Simon & Schuster, 2008.

Sudjic, Deyan. *The Language of Things: Understanding the World of Desirable Objects*. New York: W. W. Norton, 2009.

Sutherland, Daniel E. *The Expansion of Everyday Life, 1860–1876*. Fayetteville, AK: University of Arkansas Press, 2000.

Thomas, Rupert, and Eglé Salvy. *Antique & Flea Markets of London & Paris*. London: Thames & Hudson, 1999.

Thoreau, Henry David. *Collected Essays and Poems*. Selected by Elizabeth Hall Witherell. New York: Library of America, 2001.

———. *The Journal: 1837–1861*. Introduction by John R. Stilgoe. New York: New York Review Books, 2009.

Tracy, Lisa. *Objects of Our Affection*. New York: Bantam, 2010.

Tuchman, Mitch. *Magnificent Obsessions*. San Francisco: Chronicle Books, 1994.

Tunis, Edwin. *Colonial Craftsmen and the Beginnings of American Industry*. Baltimore, MD: Johns Hopkins University Press, 1965.

Turkle, Sherry. *Evocative Objects: Things We Think With*. Cambridge, MA: MIT Press, 2007.

Ulrich, Laurel Thatcher. *The Age of Homespun: Objects and Stories in the Creation of an American Myth*. New York: Knopf, 2001.

Underhill, Paco. *Why We Buy: The Science of Shopping*. New York: Simon & Schuster, 1999.

Walker, Rob. *Buying In: The Secret Dialogue Between What We Buy and Who We Are*. New York: Random House, 2008.

Wallace, Ben. *The Billionaire's Vinegar*. New York: Crown, 2008.

Warhol, Andy. *The Philosophy of Andy Warhol: From A to B and Back Again*. New York: Harcourt, Brace & Co., 1975.

Webb, Dennis. *Greenberg's Guide to Marbles*, 2nd ed. Waukesha, WI: Kalmbach Publishing Company, 1994.

Werner, Kitty. *The Official Directory to U.S. Flea Markets*. New York: House of Collectibles Publishing, 1994 and 2000.

Wyss, Bob. *Brimfield Rush: The Thrill of Collecting and the Hunt for the Big Score*. Beverly, MA: Commonwealth Editions, 2005.

Zubrod, Sheila, and David Stern. *Flea: The Definitive Guide to Hunting, Gathering, and Flaunting Superior Vintage Wares*. New York: Harper Perennial, 1997.

Magazines and Journals

Antiques and the Arts Magazine
Antiques & Collecting Magazine
Antiques & Fine Art
Antiques Roadshow Insider
Art & Antiques
The Journal of Antiques and Collectibles
Journal of the History of Collecting
The Magazine Antiques
Maine Antique Digest
New England Antiques Journal
A Simple Life: Antiques, Early Homes, History, Museums
Unravel the Gavel

Television/Film

Faber, David. "*The eBay Effect: Inside a Worldwide Obsession*." CNBC-TV Production, 2005. Air date: October, 8, 2007.

Hewitt, Don, executive producer. *Who the #$&% Is Jackson Pollock?* DVD, 2007.

Hustwit, Gary. *Objectified: A Documentary Film*. Swiss Dots Ltd., 2009.

Sebak, Rick, producer/narrator. *A Flea Market Documentary*. Kevin Conrad, editor. Copyright 2001 WQED, Pittsburgh. DVD.

INDEX